Disabling Globalization

Disabling Globalization

Places of Power in
Post-Apartheid South Africa

GILLIAN HART

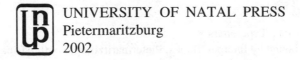

UNIVERSITY OF NATAL PRESS
Pietermaritzburg
2002

Published in South Africa by
University of Natal Press
Private Bag X01
Scottsville 3209
South Africa
E-mail: books@nu.ac.za
www.unpress.co.za

Published in the United States of America by
University of California Press, Berkeley and Los Angeles, California

ISBN 1-86914-015-X

Editor: Sally Hines
Cover designer: Sumayya Essack, Dizzy Blue Design
Cover painting: '1964 Evictions' by Trevor Makhoba 2001

Typeset by Alpha Typesetters cc
Printed and bound by Interpak Books, Pietermaritzburg, South Africa

Dedicated to the memory of Govan Mbeki

Contents

List of Maps   viii
List of Abbreviations   ix

Introduction   1
Chapter 1:   Re-Placing Power in Post-Apartheid South Africa   16

PART I: FORGING PLACES
Chapter 2:   'The Land of our Comfort': Regional Contours of
             Agrarian Transformation   59
Chapter 3:   Losing Ground and Making Space: Dispossession and
             Township Formation   96
Chapter 4:   Manufacturing Connections: Labor, Township, and
             Industrial Politics   127

PART II: TRANSNATIONAL TRAJECTORIES
Chapter 5:   Taiwanese Networks in Newcastle: The Production of
             Knitwear and of Difference   165
Chapter 6:   The China Connection: Agrarian Questions in an Era
             of Globalization   198

PART III: POST-APARTHEID POSSIBILITIES
Chapter 7:   Accumulating Tensions: Remaking the Local State   235
Chapter 8:   Enabling Alternatives: Re-Envisioning the Future   290

Postscript and Acknowledgements   314
Appendix   323
Notes   328
Select Bibliography   350
Index   373

Maps

Map 1   Industrial decentralization areas in the 1980s   3
Map 2   Area of study in South Africa   61
Map 3   Area of study in KwaZulu-Natal   62
Map 4   New local government demarcations, 2000   279

Abbreviations

AAC	All-Africa Convention
AFRA	Association for Rural Advancement
ANC	African National Congress
BAD	Bantu Affairs Department
BIC	Bantu Investment Corporation
CBD	central business district
CDE	Centre for Development and Enterprise
COSATU	Congress of South African Trade Unions
DA	Democratic Alliance
DAB	Drakensberg Administration Board
DBSA	Development Bank of Southern Africa
DDA	Department of Development Administration
DLA	Department of Land Affairs
EDC	Economic Development Corporation
FCI	Federated Chamber of Industries
FDI	foreign direct investment
FOSATU	Federation of South African Trade Unions
GEAR	Growth, Employment and Redistribution
ICU	Industrial and Commercial Workers' Union
IDC	Industrial Development Corporation
IDP	Industrial Development Point
IEC	Independent Electoral Commission
IFP	Inkatha Freedom Party
JCRR	Joint Commission of Rural Reconstruction
JMC	Joint Management Centre
JSB	Joint Services Board
KFC	KwaZulu Finance Corporation
KLA	KwaZulu Legislative Assembly
KMI	KwaZulu Marketing Initiative
KMT	Kuomintang

LDO	Land Development Objectives
LED	Local Economic Development
LRA	Labour Relations Act
LRAD	Land Reform for Agricultural Development
MAWU	Metal and Allied Workers Union
MEC	Minerals-Energy Complex
MERG	Macro-Economic Research Group
MK	Umkhonto we Siswe
MLA	member of the Legislative Assembly
MP	member of parliament
NAD	Native Affairs Department
NEUM	Non-European Unity Movement
NGO	non-governmental organization
NIC	Natal Indian Congress
NNLA	Northern Natal Landowners Association
NNC	Natal Native Congress
NUMSA	National Union of Metal Workers of South Africa
NUTW	National Union of Textile Workers
OECD	Organization for Economic Cooperation and Development
PAC	Pan African Congress
RDAC	Regional Development Advisory Committee
RDP	Reconstruction and Development Programme
RIDP	Regional Industrial Development Programme
RSC	Regional Services Council
SACP	South African Communist Party
SACTU	South African Congress of Trade Unions
SACTWU	South African Clothing and Textile Workers Union
SADT	South African Development Trust
SAMWU	South African Municipal Workers Union
SANNC	South African Native National Congress
SLAG	Settlement and Land Acquisition Grant
SOE	state-owned enterprise
SPP	Surplus People's Project
SST	The State and Social Transformation
TINA	There is no alternative
TLC	Transitional Local Council
TOB	Transkei Organised Bodies
TTT	Trans Tugela Transport

TVE	Township and Village Enterprise
UDF	United Democratic Front
VFS	Vumela Facilitation Services
WHAM	winning hearts and minds

Introduction

To articulate the past historically does not mean to recognize it
'the way it really was' . . . It means to seize hold of a memory as
it flashes up at a moment of danger. (Benjamin 1969: 255)

SOON AFTER THE local government elections in 1996, a group of
newly elected African National Congress (ANC) councilors and
community leaders in Ladysmith-Ezakheni called me to account for myself
and my research. They wanted to know who I was, what I was doing, who
was sponsoring and funding my research, and how, if at all, they could use
it. The meeting began early on a bitterly cold morning in July, and lasted
until evening. It took place in the tiny front room of a house belonging to
one of the councilors in the sprawling, dusty township of Ezakheni, with
about a dozen of us crowded around a highly polished dining table that took
up most of the space. From my seat at the table I could see hanging on the
wall a picture of the owner of the house as a young man taken 40 years
earlier, before his arrest and incarceration on Robben Island. In 1994 he had
been central in negotiating a peace accord that ended a spate of terrible
violence in Ezakheni, and township residents had pressed him to stand in
the local elections. 'I am an old tree,' he declared at the start of the meeting.
'Now they have planted a new tree.'

This was, for all of us, a kaleidoscopic moment when everything shifted
to form new patterns. For the local councilors this moment of assuming
formal power was one of fulfillment of long years of struggle and enormous
promise for the future, as well as a moment of profound danger; of being
thrust into an arena of power strewn with the detritus of the apartheid past,
and sharply circumscribed by the negotiated settlement. It also coincided
with the ANC national government's announcement of a package of
conservative neoliberal economic policies. Many South Africans closely
allied with the ANC were shocked and dismayed not only by this apparent
retreat from redistributive social change, but also the arbitrary manner in

1

which key officials handed it down as a *fait accompli*. For me this was a moment of profound repositioning, a moment when my relationships to different groups in my research sites and in South Africa more generally were reconfigured, along with my understandings of who I was, what I was doing there, and why it mattered.

Participants in the meeting questioned me at some length about my history and my political and institutional location; about how my research was funded; about the information I had been collecting over the past two years; and about its relevance to their concerns. In response I sought to explain how, in the course of this research, I was re-engaging with my native South Africa after years of studying and teaching in the US and doing research on agrarian change in Asia.

On returning to South Africa in 1990 after an absence of nearly 20 years, I was drawn to places like Ladysmith-Ezakheni because they embodied key features of the geographies of racial capitalism: historical and contemporary processes of dispossession; industrial decentralization; and direct connections with East Asia. Starting in the 1960s, millions of black South Africans were ripped from the land in rural 'white' South Africa, and packed into huge relocation townships like Ezakheni on patches of land defined as part of purportedly self-governing 'bantustans.' Many such townships were situated in predominantly rural areas within 15–20 km of former white towns like Ladysmith. In the early 1980s, the apartheid state deployed massive subsidies – reputedly the most generous in the world – to entice South African and foreign industrialists to locate in these out-of-the-way places. More than 40 'industrial decentralization points' mushroomed all over the country, either in or adjacent to relocation townships (Map 1).

At precisely that moment, large numbers of small-scale industrialists came under enormous pressure to leave Taiwan, driven out by rising wages, rents, and escalating exchange rates – conditions created by the stunning pace of their own industrial investment and export drive. During the 1980s well over 300 Taiwanese factory owners moved to these racialized spaces in the South African countryside, bringing with them not only equipment and labor-intensive production techniques that were rapidly becoming obsolete in Taiwan, but also a set of labor practices that proved socially explosive. Ironically, the flow of foreign investment into industries within (or adjacent to) bantustan borders coincided with the increasing isolation of South Africa through sanctions, divestment, and the severing of diplomatic

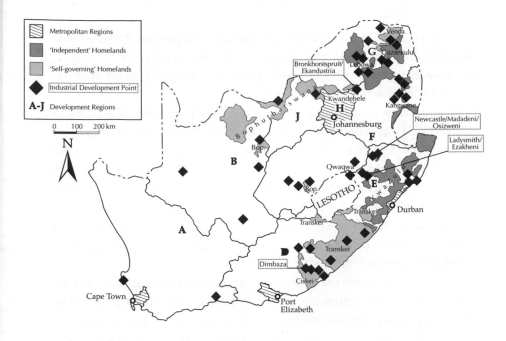

Map 1   Industrial decentralization areas in the 1980s.

links. Pickles and Woods (1989) explain how it was partly their shared status as international pariahs that drew South Africa and Taiwan together during the 1980s. These diplomatic ties helped pave the way for Taiwanese to become by far the largest group of foreign investors in bantustan industrial estates like that on the outskirts of Ezakheni.

My study started out in 1994 as a critique of how development experts, corporate interests, and state functionaries were deploying 'models from elsewhere' – particularly East Asia – to define and delimit possibilities in post-apartheid South Africa. Political liberalization had coincided with a moment of intense market triumphalism, and powerful political pressures were gathering force from within and beyond to press South Africa to conform to free market neoliberal orthodoxy. East and Southeast Asian 'miracles' featured prominently in these early post-apartheid discourses of development. Both foreign experts and those within South Africa promoting a neoliberal agenda eagerly invoked the (then) Asian 'miracles' to tout the advantages of export-oriented, market-led economic growth. They portrayed South Africa as a 'developing country' that had managed to evade structural adjustment and retain protectionist policies, but must now liberate its markets along with its newly enfranchised citizenry.

Taiwanese investment in South Africa was my initial point of entry, precisely because it had formed a key transnational connection during the relative isolation of the 1980s. In place of abstracted models of East Asian 'miracles,' I set out to trace how a small but significant group of transnational capitalists had taken hold in former white towns and adjacent relocation townships, and how they and their relationships within and beyond such places were changing in the post-apartheid dispensation. These radically globalized sites offered extraordinary vantage points from which to understand how key remnants of apartheid spatial engineering and racial capitalism – including transnational connections – were being refashioned in the post-apartheid era.

My decision to pursue research in these places crystallized in April 1993, when I came across a press report of how white local government officials in small, conservative, mainly Afrikaans-speaking towns adjacent to relocation townships were bypassing the national government and attempting to lure more Taiwanese into their fiscal nets. Entitled 'China's New Territories in Southern Africa,' the article went on to describe 'a new wave of Far Eastern business invasion into Southern Africa' spearheaded by local officials in Bronkhorstspruit, one such town about 60 km east of Pretoria (Map 1). 'I really love the Chinese,' a senior official was reported as saying: 'They are absorbed into our cultural and social life, and the people of Bronkhorstspruit have great confidence in them' (*Africa South & East* April 1993: 14).

This eager embrace of Taiwanese stood in sharp contrast to more mainstream views. On first returning to South Africa in 1990, I had been struck by the intensity with which both the left and the liberal right in South Africa regarded Taiwanese investment as a distasteful episode in recent economic history. For the labor movement and others on the left, Taiwanese industrialists represented predators intent on undercutting organized labor and worker protection, who had broken sanctions and taken advantage of repressive conditions and cheap labor in the former bantustans and border areas. Diplomatic links between the apartheid state and Taiwan added insult to injury. For large-scale corporate capital, Taiwanese industrialists represented unfair competitors whose presence in South Africa epitomized obnoxious industrial decentralization policies. Such sentiments found expression in South African popular culture, including for example theatrical productions such as *A Nativity* and *Jozi, Jozi*, in which Taiwanese were portrayed as figures of absurdity. South Africans of widely different political persuasions invoked metaphors such as 'The Great Chinese Take-Away' and the 'Seagull Syndrome' to depict Taiwanese as hungry predators who swoop in, gobble up state subsidies, and swoop off again. At a moment when discourses of non-racialism and the romanticism of the 'Rainbow Nation' were ascendant, Taiwanese stood out as the embodiment of otherness.

In addition to contesting 'models from elsewhere' and engaging some of the complexities of difference, I was drawn into this research by debates over South Africa's future cast in terms of 'the city' versus 'the country-side.' What concerned me were both the dichotomized terms of these debates, and the social and political forces – or lack thereof – that under-pinned them. Articulated most forcefully by the Urban Foundation, a corporate think-tank, the metropolitan vision represented a corporatist coalition between large-scale capital and elements of organized labor from which large segments of South African society were excluded. The claim here was that South Africa's future was metropolitan, and that resources should be concentrated in the large urban centers. Critics of this urban bias argued instead for a rural and agricultural strategy, and for creating peasants or small farmers wherever land became available through the market. Ironically, the small farmer vision was spearheaded in the early 1990s by a group from within the World Bank, and cast in predictably technocratic terms. This initiative in turn reflected the lack of an organized coalition from within rural society, as well as the urban-based liberation movement's historic neglect of agrarian questions.

Notably missing from these debates were any questions about the future of densely populated relocation townships – neither rural nor urban – where millions of black South Africans had some sort of home base. For metropolitan and peasant proponents alike such places simply represented unpleasant relics of apartheid spatial engineering, destined soon to disap-pear. Their logic was that the artificial conditions that had created these places no longer existed. In 1991, the De Klerk government had indeed slashed industrial decentralization subsidies, under pressure from both large-scale corporate capital and organized labor. Industry would 'bleed away' from these godforsaken places, many argued, and residents of relocation townships would pack their bags and move to the cities. Such easy presumptions seemed to me dangerously misleading. Many of these 'interstitial spaces' inherited from the past not only represented nodes of ongoing connection with sites in East Asia. They had also come to constitute major elements of the relations between the city and the countryside, and their transformation was likely to shape the post-apartheid transition more generally.

Shortly after the national election in 1994 I commenced research on two such sites in the province of KwaZulu-Natal – Ladysmith-Ezakheni, and the former white town of Newcastle along with the adjacent relocation townships of Madadeni and Osizweni (Map 1). The process through which I came to work in these places was quite fortuitous, but it yielded a remarkably felicitous design for comparative research. Both Ladysmith and Newcastle originated as British military outposts in colonial Natal in the mid-nineteenth century. Both are situated on major transport routes between Johannesburg and Durban. Both are surrounded by what were African freehold farms from which landowners and tenants were forcibly removed between the early 1960s and the mid-1980s, as well as by white-owned farms from which huge numbers of black workers have been (and continue to be) evicted, further enlarging the townships. Ladysmith-Ezakheni is somewhat smaller than Newcastle-Madadeni, but the structure of racialized spaces inherited from the apartheid era is remarkably similar. White local government officials in Newcastle were in fact the first in the country to launch a global strategy in the mid-1980s. By 1994 some 1,500 to 2,000 Taiwanese immigrants had settled in Newcastle, acquired significant chunks of real estate, and established over 60 factories that drew on African women workers from the townships. The Taiwanese presence in Ladysmith-Ezakheni was smaller, but still significant.

During the first phase of research, which spanned the second half of 1994 and June–July of 1995, I focused on histories of Taiwanese investment in the two places, and how it was changing in the context of sharply reduced subsidies and the new political dispensation. In addition to interviewing Taiwanese and South African industrialists and spending as much time as possible in their factories, I spoke at length with white local government officials in both places about their transnational strategies and their relationships with Taiwanese settlers. In this very early stage of local government restructuring, apartheid municipal structures and bantustan local authorities were still intact. Despite much jostling for position in so-called 'pre-interim' local government structures, it was clear that majority rule would fundamentally transform the local state as white towns and black townships administered as separate entities under apartheid became united under single local authorities. In other words, the white male bureaucrats who had launched transnational strategies were on the brink of having to cede a large chunk of local state power to a new black majority leadership from the adjacent townships which, until recently, they had defined simply as labor pools to be marketed abroad. Their anxiety at the time was palpable.

The meeting in early July 1996, when newly elected Ezakheni councilors and community leaders called me to account, represented a dramatic turning point in my research practices and political positionings, as well as in larger configurations of political and economic power. Local elections in KwaZulu-Natal at the end of June 1996 coincided precisely with the ANC national government's formal embrace of a package of conservative neoliberal economic policies known as GEAR – an acronym for Growth, Employment, and Redistribution. With the advent of GEAR, even some of the most fervid foes of the apartheid regime formally conceded to the 'natural' (if not supernatural) power of global markets and to the claim that, because of globalization, 'there is no alternative' (TINA) to orthodox neoliberalism. GEAR sits uneasily astride the emancipatory promises of the liberation struggle, as well as the material hopes, aspirations, and rights of the large majority of South Africans. Strong opposition from the Congress of South African Trade Unions (COSATU) and the South African Communist Party (SACP) has met with sharp rebuke, and invocations of 'globalization' have become a means to contain dissent, and to legitimize a retreat from promises of redistributive social change.

The coincidence of neoliberal orthodoxy in the form of GEAR with the reconstitution of the local state in mid-1996 was also deeply significant. As in many other parts of the world, fiscal austerity and the nation state's pulling back from direct welfare provision has been accompanied by a wide array of functions and responsibilities being devolved to what has come to be dubbed 'developmental local government.' In the name of both democracy and efficiency, local councilors and bureaucrats have been called upon to confront massive redistributive pressures with minimal resources. Simultaneously they have been assigned major responsibility for securing the conditions of accumulation under the aegis of 'local economic development.' The local state, in short, has become a key site of contradictions in the neoliberal post-apartheid order.

When I met with Ezakheni councilors in mid-1996, we were all keenly aware of the profound importance of the newly constituted local state, as well as the enormity of the task confronting the new leadership. Yet at the time it would have been difficult – if not impossible – to foresee how central the local state would become. What did start to emerge, though, were strong indications that processes of local state formation were taking shape very differently in Ladysmith-Ezakheni and Newcastle-Madadeni. For example, a particularly animated conversation turned around how one of the most controversial Taiwanese industrialists in Newcastle had joined the Zulu nationalist Inkatha Freedom Party (IFP) in the hopes of becoming mayor. As a consequence, he effectively handed the local government election to the ANC in what was widely regarded as an IFP stronghold. The tenuous hold of the ANC in Newcastle-Madadeni contrasted sharply with the resounding victory in Ladysmith-Ezakheni – a victory that had just prompted the resignations of six senior white municipal bureaucrats.

Early in my research I had been struck by how differently the initial stages of local government restructuring were playing out in the two places. While deeply interested in these divergent conditions and dynamics, I had not delved into them systematically. By 1996 the question of why Ladysmith and Newcastle were so different had become key concerns of ANC councilors, labor organizers and other activists in both places, and the direction in which they wanted our conversations to move. I returned to Ladysmith and Newcastle every year, and each time political dynamics in the two places seemed to diverge more sharply. Ladysmith-Ezakheni was the site of substantive local democracy with high levels of political mobilization and organization, while in Newcastle-Madadeni local political dynamics became increasingly disorganized and chaotic.

Over the years our conversations multiplied and came to resemble lively seminars, cross-cut by intense debates and interwoven with personal histories. They also contrasted sharply with the extractive interviews with industrialists and white local government officials that marked the first phase of my research in 1994 and 1995 – although material from these interviews often provided illuminating counterpoints. Particularly in Ladysmith I was often invited (or just pulled into) a wide array of local government meetings and events, and in both places the people I met in 1996 drew me into much wider networks of connection and arenas of interaction both in the townships and the former white towns. In the course of co-constructing local histories, I came to see myself less as a researcher than a participant in a collective process of meaning-making. Through all of this, I was profoundly aware of how our efforts to remake the future depend crucially on how we remember – and forget – the past, and of how it has taken a huge dose of official amnesia to render the neoliberal project palatable. By reconstructing dimensions of local histories and translocal connections, we were disrupting elements of this amnesia.

Histories of place are never just a straightforward accounting of 'the facts.' Like the life histories with which they are closely intertwined, they are always multiple, contested, deeply politicized, produced in specific contexts, and made to serve the needs of the present. Yet this is precisely the point: our reconstructions and comparisons of local histories and translocal connections were animated by the political imperatives of a very particular – and particularly crucial – political moment. The question of why the ANC and organized labor were so much stronger in Ladysmith than in Newcastle was the starting point, but the political stakes went far deeper than explaining electoral patterns. They took shape as we delved into how forced removals were more deeply contested in areas around Ladysmith than in comparable areas of Newcastle; into how these differentiated patterns of resistance to removals carried over into township politics and different patterns of connection to the liberation movement; into the complex linkages between township struggles and the labor movement; into the differing relations between different groups of capitalists and the local state, their diverse connections with regional, national, and transnational arenas of state power and capital accumulation; and how interconnected local struggles in turn reshaped these connections and relationships. We also caught glimpses of how people's understandings of themselves as political subjects and actors had taken shape in different ways in the two places through overlapping struggles in multiple arenas; how race and gender played out quite differently in the context of struggles over wages and working conditions; and how Zulu ethnic nationalism assumed startlingly different forms.

What emerged, in short, was a growing appreciation of contingency, openness, and possibilities – of how local worlds, and ways of understanding and acting in these worlds, had been made in quite different ways out of superficially similar conditions. There were moments of real excitement, when it felt as though we were unearthing what one scholar has called 'the sedimented forms of a power that has blurred the traces of its own contingency' (Laclau 1996: 103). Yet the spatio-temporal depth and breadth of these sedimentations also became painfully apparent. So too did the limits and constraints imposed by globally integrated capitalisms, their historically specific forms in South Africa, the proliferating discourses of globalization, and the multi-layered configurations of power through which post-apartheid neoliberalism made its problematic appearance on the ruins of the past. In short, multi-leveled constraints and limits loomed large and pessimistic, at times threatening to dwarf local contingencies and the sort of optimism they engendered.

Part of my task in this book is to trace the multi-layered arenas, and the key practices and plays of power and meaning, that have produced these different trajectories of social change. I will also trace the translocal connections through which these two globalized sites, and the political subjects who have made them, have themselves been made in strikingly different ways. Divergent dynamics in the two places vividly reveal how racial, ethnic, and gender differences can assume diverse forms, and are partly constitutive of class processes. At the same time, they bring into sharp focus how some of the most intense contradictions and tensions of the neoliberal post-apartheid order are playing out on the terrain of the local state.

Interlocking histories of dispossession and industrialization in this part of KwaZulu-Natal stand in sharp contrast to comparable rural industrial regions in Taiwan and Mainland China. These interconnections not only highlight how variable productions of racial, ethnic, and gendered forms of difference feed into economic life as active structuring forces. They also shed new light on *both* East Asia and South Africa, underscoring how sharply divergent histories of agrarian transformation have shaped the conditions of reproduction of labor, and of global competition.

Small-scale Taiwanese industrialists are a direct product of redistributive land reforms in the late 1940s and early 1950s that broke the power of the landlord class, transformed agrarian relations, and helped to create the conditions for rapid rural industrialization. The same is true of Mainland China, where spectacular industrial growth since the mid-1980s has taken place largely in villages and small towns. In short, redistribution of land and other resources – driven originally by Mao Tse-tung's mobilization of the Chinese peasantry in the first half of the twentieth century – underpinned the massive mobilization of low-wage labor in Taiwan and China, operating in effect as a social wage. By the same token, they represent what appear as distinctively 'non-Western' trajectories of industrial accumulation *without* dispossession of peasant-workers from the land – trajectories that have, since the 1970s, fundamentally defined the conditions of global competition.

When Taiwanese industrialists moved to places like Newcastle and Ladysmith, they encountered a workforce recently dispossessed from the land, and thrust into commodified forms of livelihood. These contrasts with East Asia compel attention to the *ongoing* significance of histories of racialized dispossession in South Africa. They enable us to see such dispossession not just as a 'natural' precursor of capitalist accumulation, or an event that can be consigned to some distant, pre-capitalist past. Through East Asian lenses, dispossession springs to life as an ongoing process that continues to define the conditions of existence for huge numbers of black South Africans. In short, East Asian histories of agrarian transformation render their South African counterparts peculiar, as well as profoundly significant in the present.

They also bring the politics of the agrarian question in South Africa into sharp focus. In the liberation movement and South African society more generally, invocations of the 'land question' – in particular, how the forces of colonialism and apartheid robbed black South Africans of 87 percent of their land and packed them into reserves or bantustans in the remaining 13 percent – continue to carry tremendous symbolic and moral force. Yet in practice, the mainly urban-based liberation movement has – with a few key exceptions – paid comparatively little attention to agrarian issues or to linking rural with urban struggles. In the post-apartheid era, this historic neglect of agrarian questions is nowhere more evident than in the painfully slow pace of land reform, the meager resources devoted to land redistribution and, particularly since 1999, the ANC's abandonment of a broadly redistributive agenda in favor of a strategy – narrowly defined in terms of agriculture – to create a black commercial farming class. Not surprisingly, these moves have elicited sharp critique from non-governmental organizations (NGOs) and others who are calling for land reform as part of a broader livelihoods strategy addressed to the escalating levels of poverty and inequality that are defining features of the neoliberal post-apartheid order.

East Asian post-war histories of land redistribution could certainly be used to support such appeals to policy makers. Far more importantly, though, East Asian-South African connections suggest how the powerful moral force of the 'land question' – a force that derives from histories and memories of racialized dispossession – might be harnessed and redefined to support the formation of broadly based political alliances to press for social and economic justice.

Growing out of these connections, a central argument of this book is the need to dis-articulate or delink the land question from agriculture and from individual restitution claims, and to re-articulate or reframe it in terms of the erosion of social security, and the moral and material imperative for a social wage. In the context of post-apartheid South Africa, this move extends the definition of the social wage beyond employment-based entitlements or even conventional social policy to insist on basic social security grounded in citizenship rights. By strengthening and extending claims for redistributive justice, this redefinition could also be used as a means for linking struggles in multiple arenas, as well as across the rural-urban divide.

A closely related argument is that any such strategy must be firmly located on the terrain of the local state, engaging with historically and geographically specific configurations of social forces, but also extending out from there to connect with forces at play in regional, national, and transnational arenas. Part of the reason, as my work in Ladysmith-Ezakheni and Newcastle-Madadeni shows very clearly, is that local political dynamics assume sharply divergent forms, even in places that are structurally very similar. More generally, the so-called 'developmental local state' has become a key locus of contradictions of the post-apartheid order, helping to expose the vulnerable underbelly of neoliberal capitalism. At the same time, the contrasting political dynamics in Ladysmith and Newcastle underscore the importance of a highly organized and mobilized civil society in defining (and in part becoming) the state, and pointing the way towards alternatives.

These concrete, intertwined historical geographies also speak to broader questions of 'globalization.' The title of this book conveys the premise that globalization – *both* in the sense of intensified processes of spatial interconnection associated with capitalist restructuring, *and* of the discourses through which knowledge is produced – is deeply infused with the exercise of power. It also seeks to convey how discourses of globalization play a key role in defining and delimiting the terrain of practical action and the formation of political identities, thereby actively shaping the very processes they purport to describe. Most importantly, it lays out the central question of the book: what is it that renders these discourses so disabling, and what might be entailed in more politically enabling understandings?

The discursive power of globalization is nowhere more evident than in what I call the 'impact model' that underpins neoliberal agendas in South Africa and elsewhere. Typically framed in terms of the impact of 'the global' on 'the local,' these discourses conjure up inexorable market and technological forces that take shape in the core of the global economy and radiate out from there. A number of other binaries map onto the global/local dichotomy. In addition to active/passive and dynamic/static, these include economics/culture, general/specific, abstract/concrete and, very importantly, dichotomous understandings of time and space, in which time is accorded active primacy, while space appears as a passive container. This conflation of 'the global' with dynamic, technological-economic forces restlessly roving the globe defines its inexorable – and inexorably masculine – character. By the same token, 'the local' appears as a passive, implicitly feminine recipient of global forces whose only option is to appear as alluring as possible. This counterposition and gendering of time and space are thus key components of discourses that naturalize neoliberalism. Dualisms of the impact model are pervasive, and underpin a number of more critical formulations of economic globalization. In addition, as we shall see in Chapter 1, portrayals of cultural globalization often share the same disabling elements as their economistic counterparts.

The larger contribution of this book is to suggest the political and analytical advantages of rethinking globalization in terms of the multiple, divergent, but interconnected *trajectories* of socio-spatial change taking shape in the context of intensified global integration. The Oxford Dictionary offers two definitions of a trajectory: 'the path described by a flying projectile,' and 'an object moving under the action of given forces.' I am emphatically not conjuring up flying projectiles moving inexorably towards a target or endpoint. My meaning is closer to the second definition, although I intend to invoke neither pre-given objects nor predetermined forces. Instead I use the term 'trajectories' to convey the ongoing processes through which sets of power-laden practices in the multiple, interconnected arenas of everyday life at different spatial scales constantly rework places and identities.

Since my understandings of multiple trajectories grew so directly from practical engagements with comparative questions along two intersecting axes – Ladysmith-Newcastle and East Asia-South Africa – I would also like to clarify my comparative method. I am definitely *not* using comparison to argue for uniqueness and endless difference. Yet neither am I claiming that key differences represent locally specific instances or variants of a more general or universal phenomenon. Rather, I am using what I call a relational concept of comparison that refuses to measure 'cases' against a universal yardstick. Instead of taking as given pre-existing objects, events, places, and identities, I start with the question of how they are formed in relation to one another and to a larger whole. In this conception, particularities or specificities arise through *interrelations* between objects, events, places, and identities; and it is through clarifying how these relations are produced and changed in practice that close study of a particular part can illuminate the whole.

A third, closely related point is that Ladysmith and Newcastle do *not* represent case studies of the impact of globalization. The concept of multiple trajectories and the method of relational comparison are grounded in an understanding of place not as a bounded unit, but as always formed through relations and connections with dynamics at play in other places, and in wider regional, national, and transnational arenas. These understandings of space, place, and power decisively reject questions cast in terms of the impact of 'the global' on 'the local.' Indeed, one of my ambitions is to wreak such destruction on 'impact models' that those who read this book will never again allow the term 'impact of globalization' to pass unquestioned.

In foregrounding the concept of multiple trajectories of socio-spatial change, I am *not* simply making the claim that capitalism takes different 'path dependent' forms in different places, and fails to converge on a single, 'fully developed' model. Nor am I endorsing culturalist notions of 'alternative modernities' which hold that 'modernity always unfolds within a specific cultural or civilizational context and that different starting points for the transition to modernity lead to different outcomes' (Gaonkar 2001: 15). Instead, I want to advance an understanding of multiple trajectories as spatially interconnected sets of practices – with their associated discourses and power relations – that actively *produce* and drive the processes we call 'globalization.' By insisting that we understand the multiplicity of historical geographies not simply as the *effects* of global flows and processes but as *constitutive* of them, the concept of multiple trajectories and the method of relational comparison fundamentally disrupt impact models and open the way for more politically enabling understandings and critical practices.

Critical engagement with the impact model and other economistic discourses of globalization does not imply that we can wish away the real and powerful effects of these discourses in bolstering the structures of the global economy, and the limits they impose. Nor does it imply buying into accounts of cultural globalization that uncritically celebrate mobility and hybridity, or into related post-Marxist notions of radical democracy that insist on radical contingency and openness. By refusing to recognize historically determined limits and structures, such accounts veer towards a form of voluntarism. The political and practical importance of the concept of multiple trajectories and the method of relational comparison is that they provide a means for steering a course between economism ('only one thing is possible') and voluntarism ('anything is possible') so as to illuminate what Jessop (1982) has called structural constraints and conjunctural possibilities.

I offer this book, then, as a concrete example of how close attention to a specific set of practices, places, and connections, can be used both to shed light on how broader processes are constituted in practice, and to suggest terrains of practical action.

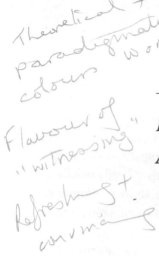

Theoretical ↑
paradigmatic
colours worn proudly

Flavour of
"witnessing"

Refreshing +
convincing

CHAPTER 1

Re-Placing Power in Post-Apartheid South Africa

THE PIVOTAL MEETING described in the Introduction when newly elected councilors in Ezakheni called me to account for my research not only transformed my research practices; it also forced me to confront and rework my understandings of how deeply politics, theory, and method are connected with one another. My purpose in this chapter is to make explicit the theoretical underpinnings of the broad arguments laid out in the Introduction, to spell out the political stakes, and to clarify how I am drawing on detailed historical and ethnographic studies to make broader claims and generalizations.

My task, in short, is to show how the framework of multiple trajectories and the method of relational comparison build on three closely related sets of concepts and claims. First is a non-reductionist understanding of class grounded in situated, material practices in the multiple arenas of everyday life – an understanding that attends as well to the production of gender, ethnic, and racial differences as active and interactive forces shaping diverse trajectories of socio-spatial change. This understanding owes a great deal to the Italian revolutionary and theorist Antonio Gramsci, who extended Marxist theory to encompass questions of politics and culture. Second, I draw directly on concepts of space and place as actively produced through everyday practices and, conversely, of social processes as spatially constituted. Third, I both build on and contribute to critiques of core-centric accounts of global capitalism, and insist on attention to multiple, interconnected, capitalist modernities that are not simply reactive to forces emanating from 'the West' but actively constitute broader global processes. Growing out of the relational comparisons of South Africa and East Asia, my contributions emphasize the ongoing significance of historically spe-

16

cific forms of agrarian transformation in shaping ongoing dynamics of accumulation and the possibilities for political action. I will also spell out more explicitly how in-depth historical and ethnographic studies grounded in particular places, but closely attentive to wider connections, can contribute both to the production of fresh understandings, and to illuminating terrains of practical action.

These concerns assume particular significance and urgency in South Africa in light of a profound irony of the post-apartheid moment: that political liberation and emancipatory promises coincided with the ascendance of market triumphalism on a global scale, defining the terrain on which the newly elected democratic state came to embrace neoliberalism. Accordingly, before going any further we must plunge into debates over how and why neoliberal forces came to dominate the post-apartheid order.

Post-Apartheid Paradoxes: Embracing Neoliberalism

> The transition reveals a paradox few foresaw: that a historic breakthrough can be achieved on the basis of accommodations, and set in motion reconfigurations which actually arrest the transformation process in a stunted form. (Marais 1998: 21)

When the ANC swept to electoral victory in 1994, its vision for the new South Africa was articulated in the Reconstruction and Development Programme (RDP), 'an integrated, coherent socio-economic policy framework' that would carry forward the national democratic revolution. Initial impetus for the RDP came from COSATU in consultation with other popular organizations. Propelled by concern that the transition from apartheid was being channeled into a narrowly political process focused on formal rather than substantive democracy, key figures within COSATU proposed a 'reconstruction accord' in 1993 that laid out a program of economic as well as political rights to overcome the legacy of apartheid. The ANC then participated in revising, diluting, and expanding the original document to produce its policy framework. What came to be called the RDP base document, a 146-page book published and widely distributed shortly before the national election in April 1994, made a series of pledges to meet 'basic needs' in a 'people-driven' manner that would set in motion a mutually reinforcing dynamic of redistribution and economic growth (African National Congress 1994). The bright primary colors of the RDP cover echoed those of the new flag, and both proclaimed the unproblematic melding of diverse social forces into an inclusive national citizenship. While the flag remains a cheerful – albeit somewhat tattered – symbol of the 'rainbow nation,' the conflicting forces that the RDP sought to paper over literally tore it apart.

That the RDP was under pressure became clearly evident in September 1994 with the publication of the RDP White Paper which, according to its preface, incorporated submissions from 'different offices of government, parastatal agencies, multiparty forums, development institutions, organizations of civil society, business organizations, and individuals.' The RDP White Paper claimed to set out a strategy for the new Government of National Unity to implement the RDP. In practice, critics quickly pointed out, in the process of accommodating a wider constituency of interests the White Paper fundamentally redefined key redistributive principles laid out in the Base Document, and replaced its Keynesian thrust with neoliberal trickle-down: ' "fiscal discipline" translates into "fiscal conservatism," since the White Paper commits the government at national, provincial, and local levels to reduce expenditures, finance the RDP primarily from restructuring the budgets, maintain or reduce levels of direct taxes, consolidate business confidence, enhance the environment for private sector expansion, and liberalise the economy' (Adelzadeh and Padayachee 1994: 4–5). In an incisive article written shortly before his death, Harold Wolpe (1995) pointed to profound tensions inherent in the RDP: 'Firstly, while the RDP operates on a deeply contested terrain, in crucial respects it eradicates sources of contradiction and probably contestation and conflict by asserting harmony; secondly, on this basis it constructs a consensual model of society which is the premise for the accomplishment of the goals of the RDP; and thirdly, on the basis of this premise it also conceptualises the state as the unproblematic instrument of RDP' (Wolpe 1995: 91).

The unveiling of GEAR in June 1996 marked the collapse of the consensual model. In contrast to the jagged consultative process that gave rise to the RDP, GEAR was the product of a team of technical experts whose claim to legitimacy lay in an econometric modeling exercise. The central premise of GEAR was that an orthodox neoliberal package – tight fiscal austerity, monetary discipline, wage restraints, reducing corporate taxes, trade liberalization, and phasing out exchange controls – would lure private investment (both domestic and foreign), unleash rapid growth, tighten labor markets, and drive up wages. In presenting GEAR as a *fait accompli*, ANC Finance Minister Trevor Manuel made clear that it was non-negotiable. Since then, criticisms of GEAR from within the alliance have met with sharp rebuke. If the RDP was a 'contested terrain' (Wolpe 1995), GEAR has become a veritable battleground on which profound tensions have taken shape within the ANC, as well as between the ANC and its alliance partners, COSATU and the SACP. More than a macro-economic strategy, it represented a shift in the balance of power within the ruling bloc.

The official ANC effort to legitimate GEAR is contained in an extraordinary – and extraordinarily tortuous – discussion document entitled 'The State and Social Transformation' (SST) circulated within the ANC in late 1996, and published in *The African Communist* (no. 146) in 1997. 'Globalization' figures prominently: 'The economic globalization and the effect of technological progress on a world scale imposes a certain surrender of a nation state's control over many areas,' the ANC document explained, including 'currency and fiscal policies, environmental control and global warming, the effect of the new international division of production and labor and the illegal narcotics trade' (African National Congress 1997: 60). The authors of SST also deploy the logic of globalization to issue stern warnings against an 'infantile and subjective approach to socio-economic development' by the working class and popular forces.[1] Invoking the 'scientific approach of the democratic movement,' the document goes on to assert that 'the task of educating the working class on the need to correctly balance the short term material gain with the longer objective to build sustainable economic growth and a secure democracy, is not the task to be left to the progressive trade union movement alone' (African National Congress 1997: 52). Yet, as Blade Nzimande and Jeremy Cronin of the SACP note in their incisive response published in the same issue of *The African Communist*, while the document exhorts labor not to be 'economistic' it hardly prescribes to capitalists at all: 'No expectations, no pressures are placed on "capital"' (1997: 68).

In a prescient article published in 1989, Mike Morris and Vishnu Padayachee warned of the likelihood of a '50 percent solution' – an argument Morris spelled out more fully in 1991 in terms that describe GEAR with uncanny precision:

> The growth model that is currently dominant within capital, as well as the National and Democratic parties, is one that we have termed the '50 per cent solution.' The basic terms of this model are political settlement and growth rather than that of redistribution. It specifically eschews radical state intervention to redistribute social and economic resources on a non-economic basis, and puts its reliance

instead solely on the operations of the free market. According to this growth model, a political settlement will result in a rapid inflow of foreign investment, and, if coupled with minimal state intervention and radical free-marketeerism, the consequent effect will be high rates of growth. Redistribution will follow as a trickle-down effect of accelerated growth so that, in the long run, if we let the rich get richer the poor will get richer also, which is why it can best be summed up as 'redistribution through growth.'

The social effects of this model will be to accelerate the tendencies already taking place in the occupational division of labor and economically incorporate those blacks at the upper end of the class ladder. These are the black bourgeoisie primarily based in commerce, the professional and managerial middle class, the small traders, the new skilled, clerical and supervisory black working class, and finally, although to a lesser extent, the better-paid strata of the semi-skilled black working class. The rest of the black population living on the periphery of the mass consumption economy are thus to be left to fend for themselves.

This would go hand in hand with a political strategy that resolves the national question with the maximum accommodation to demands for majority rule but with minimum accommodation to demands for major restructuring of the economic and social fabric of the society. The thrust of this strategy would be to establish hegemonic consent by politically appealing to the material interests of those classes amongst the black population who are to become the greatest beneficiaries of the '50 per cent solution.' Those on the other side of the divide would be symbolically accommodated but their material needs would not be systematically catered for. (Morris 1991: 57)

What appears to be emerging is something much closer to a 30 percent solution. A report entitled 'Winners and Losers: South Africa's Changing Income Distribution in the 1990s' (Whiteford and Van Seventer 1999) estimated that, while racial inequalities persist – white per capita income was almost nine times higher than Africans' in 1996 – the black share of income rose from 29.9 percent to 35.7 percent between 1991 and 1996. Yet almost all of this increase was concentrated in the top 10 percent of black households, while the poorest 40 percent of black households suffered a fall in income of around 21 percent. All indications are that these tendencies accelerated after 1996, with massive increases in unemployment, declining private sector investment, and strict fiscal austerity. Why GEAR has fallen so far short of its framers' extravagant claims and projections is the focus of heated debate.[2] What is painfully clear is the intense and persistent material deprivation of the large majority of black South Africans in the face of stark – albeit somewhat deracialized – concentrations of wealth and privilege.

The most immediate question is why a party with such a strong constituency in the working class and dispossessed majority could apparently shift so swiftly to a position that conflicts fundamentally with the hopes and rights of the majority of South Africans. The predictable answer, eagerly promoted by the *Financial Mail* and other business interests is that, under their tutelage, the ANC saw the light – that 'there is no alternative' (TINA) to the neoliberal Washington consensus. A less triumphal rendition of essentially the same argument is that the new state was simply unable to resist the forces of globalization, that the room to maneuver was (and is) minimal and that, however distasteful, there is in fact no alternative to biting the neoliberal bullet. The combined power of international financial agencies, foreign investors, and the domestic business community figure prominently in these explanations.[3] A third position accuses the ANC of selling out to white capital and a rapidly rising black bourgeoisie, and maintains that the time has come either to form a militant working class party, or to mobilize civil society against the state.[4]

A fourth set of arguments (to which this study is a contribution) recognizes the limits imposed by globally integrated capitalisms, the negotiated settlement, and the heavily concentrated corporate structure of South African capital. It does, however, challenge the sort of top-down narratives that deny any room to maneuver. This interpretation views the process that culminated in GEAR as driven neither by the inexorable forces of globalization nor by a simple sell-out, but by complex power struggles within and beyond the ANC and its alliance partners. In the course of these struggles, both critiques of neoliberalism and other possibilities were sidelined. A closely related set of arguments claims that possibilities for change will be shaped in crucial ways by the constitution of social forces within civil society, while warning that a strategy that counterposes (progressive) civil society to the (rapacious) state is likely to be misleading and self-defeating.

This fourth interpretation of how GEAR emerged triumphant rests on several key propositions about the character of the transition, spelled out succinctly by Hein Marais (1998). First, the basis for the transition lay in a historic deadlock between the ruling bloc and the liberation movement in the late 1980s, rather than in the unalloyed victory of the latter. What propelled the ruling bloc into negotiations with the ANC was the grinding down of the economy, and the recognition that the South African capitalist system had to be 'modernized' and 'normalized' – a move that required abandoning the exclusionary political framework of apartheid, and reconstituting the dominant alliance of social, political, and economic forces to include the ANC and its capacity to manufacture consent. Hence, Marais argues, the fundamental importance of 1994 was not simply the end of apartheid, but the dissolution of the old ruling bloc. The ANC's ascent to power did not simply fill the resultant vacuum; rather, it intensified the struggle over which set of forces would come to constitute the new ruling bloc.

While in exile, the liberation movement scored stunning successes both in international diplomacy and internal cohesion. It was not, however, prepared for the ruling bloc's gamble that the defence of capitalism required abandoning the exclusionary framework of racial capitalism embodied in apartheid. For much of its history in exile, the liberation movement saw the apartheid state as the center of oppression, and focused on a single, cataclysmic event – the seizure of state power. A widespread presumption underpinning this vanguardist strategy was that wresting control of the state (the national democratic revolution) would automatically pave the way for a second-stage socialist revolution.[5] This two-stage theory of revolution, focused in the first stage on destroying apartheid as a state form of racial oppression, pushed questions of class and economic inequality to the margins (along with gender), and enabled the movement to contain its own internal differentiation. It also meant that, at the time of its unbanning, the ANC's conceptions of how the national democratic revolution would project into the economic sphere, intersect with already-existing capitalism, and address extreme material inequalities were extremely vague: it had virtually no economic policy. It was precisely this vacuum into which the union movement stepped in 1993 with proposals for a reconstruction accord centered around redistribution that metamorphosed into the RDP. Concerns within the alliance over post-apartheid economic policy also led to the formation of the Macro-Economic Research Group (MERG) in late 1992.[6]

Central to understanding the ANC government's embrace of neoliberalism is that 'the settlement constituted and inaugurated not a rupture but a highly ambivalent series of reconfigurations that extended far beyond formal political agreements' (Marais 1998: 251). Key business interests, along with the Bretton Woods institutions and foreign governments, quickly heeded the *Financial Mail*'s injunction to 'patiently and systematically educate blacks into the economic realities of the world.' How these 'realities' were to be defined was hotly contested, particularly in the earlier phases of what came to be called 'the great economic debate'

(Kentridge 1993). In the course of this battle some definitions prevailed through a process far more complex than the unilateral exercise of white corporate power, or the top-down imposition of 'correct thinking' by the World Bank and IMF. On the contrary, as Fine and Padayachee (2000: 5) point out, 'South Africa is in the remarkable situation of having adopted and persisted with the policies of the Washington consensus when it was under no obligation to do so and, most ironically, after its nostrums had already been rejected by its most ardent exponents.'

An early indication of the growing power of conservative forces within the alliance was how key figures in the ANC's Department of Economic Policy garnered the power to discredit and sideline neo-Keynesian proposals for linking redistribution and growth set forth by MERG in 1993. One element, no doubt, was that segments of the rapidly expanding black bourgeoisie favored elements of the neoliberal strategy, although this seems a more plausible explanation of ongoing support rather than the shift in the early to mid-1990s.[7] It is also possible that certain strategically placed groups within the newly reconstituted state perceived advantages in a more open strategy that ensured access to transnational sources of expertise as a means of bypassing the old civil service.[8]

Particularly notable is the speed with which a number of former socialists acceded to neoliberalism, arguing either that 'there is no alternative' or invoking the imperatives for developing the forces of production. Padayachee (1998) offers a trenchant summation of shifts in the position of (mainly white male) intellectuals from pursuit of socialist alternatives in the first part of the 1980s, through a variety of social democratic and corporatist positions in the early 1990s, to neoliberalism. These shifts, he suggests, are primarily a reflection of changing configurations of power and legitimacy of key political patrons with whom (originally left) intellectuals aligned themselves. In the 1980s such power and legitimacy rested with the socialist-oriented workers' movement. In the early 1990s power shifted to the multi-class, nationalist-oriented ANC; and after 1994 it shifted out of the party and into the formal apparatus of the state.

The discursive strategies through which neoliberalism was made to appear natural are important. Patrick Bond (2000a) provides a vivid description of how key corporate interests deployed 'scenario planning' to define and delimit the policy terrain. In an account that is both funny and horrifying, Bond documents how corporate leaders worked with academics to produce metaphors that ranged from the fairly pedestrian (high and low roads), to the truly bizarre. Invoking avian images, corporate and academic sponsors of the *Mont Fleur* scenarios, for example, presented senior ANC officials with comic book depictions of neoliberal Flamingos, representing 'good government and macro-economic constraint' that 'take-off slowly, fly high, and fly together,' surpassing Icarus (the 'macro-economic populist' who rises rapidly and crashes in flames).[9] Those with any sort of socialist ambitions fell into the category of Lame Duck and Ostriches.

'Models from elsewhere' – particularly East Asia – also figured prominently. Prior to the Asian economic crisis that erupted in the second half of 1997, proponents of neoliberalism eagerly deployed East and Southeast Asian 'miracles' as incontrovertible evidence of the superiority of markets over state intervention. Generic 'Asian economies' appeared as lean, feline predators, unleashed by open market policies, prowling the global economy in search of market opportunities. The South African economy, in contrast, was portrayed as an ailing, deformed monster of apartheid state interventionism that had grown up inside protectionist barriers, and must be transformed through exposure to the icy winds of global competition. Interventionist moves on the part of the ANC government would simply nurture the monster's deformities, and render it more vulnerable to Asian tigers.

Following the financial meltdown in some regions of East and Southeast Asia, the language of 'miracles' and 'tigers' gave way with lightning speed to racialized idioms of contagion: the focus now was on the diseases emanating from Asia. The new imaginary of Asia as the source of economic disease and disorder proclaimed neoliberal policies to be the prophylactic protecting the South African economy from Asian viruses. This was also an opportunity for South African financial institutions to proclaim their cleanliness, honesty, and probity. At the same time, 'the Asian crisis' provided a large and capacious portmanteau explanation for the evident failure of GEAR to accomplish anything even vaguely approximating its stated goals of growth, employment, and redistribution. Things would have been far worse, South Africans were solemnly informed, if we had not had GEAR in place. Notably missing was any reference to Taiwan (which had refused to open its economy to short-term capital), or Malaysia (which imposed tight capital controls shortly after the crisis erupted). That the 'Asian crisis' provoked intense disputes about orthodox structural adjustment and further undermined the neoliberal Washington consensus had virtually no effect in South Africa. By that point, the political forces behind the home-grown neoliberal agenda were firmly in place.

Even at the height of the market miracle portrayal of East and Southeast Asian economies, the standard counter-narrative – namely that their rapid industrialization was in fact the product of direct and active state intervention – never really took hold in South Africa. Particularly for those in the labor movement, histories of labor repression no doubt rendered claims about Asian 'developmental states' deeply suspect, if not actively distasteful.[10] That the analytical and political purchase of neo-Weberian narratives of developmental states has been so limited in South Africa may also reflect the particular meanings and political heft attached to 'state' and 'market' in the race-class debates that raged through the 1970s and part of the 1980s.

The significance of market-state dichotomies extends beyond these intellectual debates, deeply politicized though they were. That neoliberalism could take hold so quickly in post-apartheid South Africa derives in part, I suggest, from how a dichotomous set of meanings could be articulated or connected with one another in a way that appealed powerfully to 'common sense':

Apartheid	Post-apartheid
State	Market
Repression	Freedom
Racial Fordism	Non-racial post-Fordism
Rigidity	Flexibility

These articulations are not confined to the conscription of former left intellectuals and political activists to the neoliberal project. In an incisive analysis of advertizing in post-apartheid South Africa, Eve Bertelsen (1998) shows how many advertisements aimed at black consumers have appropriated idioms of struggle, detached them from the socialist imaginaries of the 1980s, and used them to redefine democracy as individual freedom – especially freedom to consume. Bertelsen's study serves as an important reminder of the depth and complexity of market triumphalism in post-apartheid South Africa, of its infusion into the capillaries of everyday life and desire. At the same time, it underscores a bitter irony: that huge numbers of South Africans are excluded not only from the world of BMWs, cyberspace, and cell phones, but also some of the most basic means of material existence.

The question, then, is what are the possibilities for greater social and economic justice emerging from this particular configuration of social, political, and economic forces? In seeking to address this question, I want to start with the work of Antonio Gramsci, the Italian revolutionary and intellectual, whose writings in an Italian fascist prison in the late 1920s and early 1930s suggest particularly compelling ways of thinking about questions of social change in the face of a reversal of a revolutionary moment.

Theorizing After Apartheid: Political Stakes

In his prison notebooks, Gramsci offered an analysis of the ideology of free market capitalism that reverberates with conditions in post-apartheid South Africa.[11] *Laissez-faire* (or neoliberalism), Gramsci argued, is a form of state regulation, introduced and maintained by legislative and coercive means:

> It is a deliberate policy, conscious of its own ends, and not the spontaneous, automatic expression of economic facts. Consequently, *laissez-faire* liberalism is a political programme, designed to change – so far as it is victorious – a State's leading personnel . . . What is at stake [in *laissez-faire* liberalism] is a rotation in governmental office of the ruling-class parties, not the foundation and organisation of a new political society, and even less of a new type of civil society. (Gramsci 1971: 160)

At the core of Gramsci's analysis is a conception of the state that encompasses both political society (i.e. government or the juridical-administrative system) and civil society: 'The State is the entire complex of practical and theoretical activities through which the ruling class not only justifies and maintains its dominance, but manages to win the active consent over those whom it rules' (Gramsci 1971: 244). For Gramsci, civil society is not the sphere of freedom, but of hegemony. Hegemony in this sense does *not* refer to ideological domination, manipulation, or indoctrination. Rather, it is most usefully understood as a contested political *process*: 'A class is hegemonic not so much to the extent that it is able to impose a uniform conception of the world on the rest of society, but to the extent that it can articulate different visions of the world in such a way that their potential antagonism is neutralized' (Laclau 1977: 161). Understood in this way, hegemony is inherently fragile, and must be constantly renewed, recreated, defended, and modified. While by definition dominant, it is never total or exclusive: 'At any time, forms of alternative or directly oppositional politics and culture exist as significant elements' (Williams 1977: 113).

In *The Hard Road to Renewal* (1988), an insightful analysis of the rise of Thatcherism in Britain, Stuart Hall suggests that Gramsci's contemporary relevance stems from his efforts to come to grips with the humiliating defeat of the militant North Italian industrial workers' movement in the 1920s. Following his active engagement in helping to form anti-bureaucratic workers' councils during the dramatic period of the *biennio rosso* (the 'red years' of 1919–20) when profound change seemed possible, Gramsci confronted the intense reversal of a revolutionary moment. The parallels with contemporary neoliberal triumphalism – in South Africa even more than in Thatcherite Britain – are vivid. And yet, Hall warns, 'We can't pluck up this "Sardinian" from his specific and unique political formation, beam him down at the end of the twentieth century [or, for that matter, the beginning of the twenty-first], and ask him to solve our problems for us; especially since the whole thrust of his thinking was to refuse this easy transfer of generalisations from one conjuncture, nation or epoch to another' (Hall 1988: 161). The central lesson of Gramsci's *Prison Notebooks*, Hall suggests, is precisely the importance of attending, with all the 'pessimism of the intellect' at your command, to the specificity of a historical (and, one should add, geographical) conjuncture – namely, how diverse forces come together in particular ways to create a new political terrain.

In this era of rampant neoliberalism, Gramsci's relevance also derives from his insistent critique of economistic forms of understanding. Rejecting economism emphatically does *not* mean neglecting the powerful role of economic forces and relations, but rather recognizing that economic practices and struggles over material resources and labor are always and inseparably bound up with culturally constructed meanings, definitions, and identities, and with the exercise of power, all as part of historical processes. Part of what is so problematic about economism, Raymond Williams (1977) has pointed out in his exposition of some of Gramsci's ideas, is that it rests on a notion of abstract determinism – in other words on the isolation of supposedly pre-given, autonomous, 'objective' categories that are then seen as controlling. Such abstract economic determinism, Williams suggested – well before the heyday of discourses of economic globalization – derives from 'the historical experience of large-scale capitalist economy, in which many more people than Marxists concluded that control of the process was beyond them, that it was at least in practice external to their wills and desires, and that it had therefore to be seen as governed by its own "laws"' (Williams 1977: 86). There is a radical difference between this sort of abstract determinism, and historical determination – understood in the dual senses of the setting of limits as well as the exertion of pressures:[12]

> 'Society' is . . . never only the 'dead husk' which limits social and individual fulfillment. It is always also a constitutive process with very powerful pressures which are both expressed in political, economic, and cultural formations, and to take the full weight of 'constitutive', are internalized and become 'individual wills.' Determination of this whole kind – a complex and interrelated process of limits and pressures – is in the whole social process itself and nowhere else: not in an abstracted 'mode of production' nor in an abstracted 'psychology.' (Williams 1977: 87)

In other words, while material conditions and economic power relations define broad conditions of existence, they do not in any unilateral and automatic fashion guarantee the specific forms of ongoing material/cultural struggles or the formation of political identities. Emphasizing Marxism as a theory of praxis, Gramsci and his followers thus opened the way for understanding politics as *process*, encompassing not only formal electoral politics but also pervading the multiple arenas of everyday life. Political interests and identities do not follow automatically from the positioning of a class (or sections of a class) in the structure of socio-economic relations; rather, they must be actively constructed. An organic (or historically effective) ideology '*articulates* into a configuration different subjects, different identities, different projects, different aspirations; it does not reflect, it constructs a "unity" out of difference' (Hall 1988: 166; emphasis added). Thus, for example, Thatcherism encompassed a plurality of discourses – not only about the economy, but also the family, gender, national identity, race, crime, human nature, and so forth – that resonated with, or summoned up one another.

The concept of articulation that Hall is using encompasses both senses of the term – namely the joining together of different elements and enunciation, or the production of meaning through language. In this combined sense, articulation refers not just to a structural *effect*. The idea, rather, is that the 'unities' constructed through practices and processes of articulation are almost always contradictory, and must be continually renovated, renewed, and re-enacted. It is also important to emphasize that this conception of articulation is grounded in situated practices, with their associated discourses and power relations. Conceived in this way, articula-

tion offers a means for understanding how hegemonic discursive formations operate – for example, Hall's analysis of Thatcherism. But articulation
in this combined sense is also a way of thinking about possibilities for the
constitution of oppositional movements – how they must always operate on
the terrain of 'common sense' using material and symbolic resources given
from the past. '[T]he theory of articulation asks how an ideology discovers
its subject rather than how the subject thinks the necessary and inevitable
thoughts which belong to it; it enables us to think how an ideology
empowers people, enabling them to begin to make some sense or intelligibility of their historical situation, without reducing those forms of
intelligibility to their socio-economic or class location or social position'
(Hall 1996a: 142).[13]

In considering the contemporary salience of this particular concept of
articulation in South Africa, it is useful I think to trace a brief (and
necessarily partial) genealogy of the term in relation to South African
debates. Articulation in the structural Marxist sense of the joining together
of modes of production is, of course, deeply familiar to South African(ists)
through the work of Harold Wolpe (1972, 1975).[14] In his seminal
contribution to the 'race versus class' debate that raged through the 1970s
and into the 1980s, Wolpe used the concept to refute liberal (and indeed
orthodox Marxist) portrayals of the racial order in South Africa as an
irrational hangover of Afrikanerdom that would melt away with the further
development of capitalist market relations. Instead, Wolpe proposed that
capitalism in South Africa had latched on to subsistence agriculture in the
reserves, which provided a subsidy in the form of cheap labor power. In
other words, South African capitalism had developed in part through
articulation – or joining with – the pre-existing non-capitalist mode of
production; and the mode of political domination and legitimating practices
had, as a consequence, assumed distinctively racial and ethnic forms. By
the middle of the century, Wolpe argued, the capacity of the reserves to
sustain subsistence production had collapsed. Apartheid represented a new
racial capitalist order, with a panoply of repressive legislation and practices
directed towards regulating and reconfiguring the conditions of reproduction of labor. Thus apartheid was not simply an extension of the earlier
system of segregation, as some radical critics had argued. Instead, he
maintained, racial ideology in South Africa – and the political practices in
which it was reflected – sustained and reproduced capitalist relations of
production, although in complex, reciprocal (but asymmetrical) relation-

ships with changing social and economic conditions. Wolpe's intervention
sparked wide-ranging critiques, from which have emerged some extremely
important contributions to South African historiography.[15] Yet for all its
problems it represented by far the most substantive and significant
contribution to the race-class debate because it grappled so directly with the
problems of reductionism.

From a broad theoretical and political perspective – one that extended
well beyond South African race-class debates – the most significant response to Wolpe was Stuart Hall's 'Race, Articulation, and Societies
Structured in Dominance' published in 1980.[16] Engaging initially with the
South African race-class debate, Hall acknowledged Wolpe's deployment
of the concept of articulation – in particular, the advance it represented on
liberal and neo-Weberian formulations of racially structured social formations. At the same time, he drew on an extended neo-Gramscian conception
of articulation to argue that forms of racism cannot be read off economic
structures: 'One must start . . . from the concrete historical "work" which
racism accomplishes under specific historical conditions – as a set of
economic, political and ideological *practices* of a specific kind, *concretely
articulated with other practices in a social formation*' (Hall 1980: 338;
emphasis added). Thus, Hall went on to note, racialized practices are not
necessary to the concrete functioning of all capitalisms. Nor does it make
sense to extrapolate a common, universal structure to race and racism: there
is no 'racism in general.' Instead, it needs to be shown *how* race comes to be
inserted historically, and the relations and practices that have tended to
erode and transform – or to preserve – these distinctions through time, not
simply as residues or holdovers, but as active structuring principles of the
present organization of society and the forms of class relations:

> Race is thus, also, the modality in which class is 'lived,' the medium through which
> class relations are experienced, the form in which it is appropriated and 'fought
> through.' This has consequences for the whole class, not specifically for its
> 'racially defined' segment. It has consequences in terms of the internal fractioning
> and division within the working class which, among other ways, are articulated in
> part through race. This is no mere racist conspiracy from above. For racism is also
> one of the dominant means of ideological representation through which the white
> fractions of the class come to 'live' their relations to other fractions, and through
> them to capital itself. (Hall 1980: 341)

A serious lacuna in Hall's analysis is gender – a point to which we return
later.[17] Yet what Hall accomplished was to lay the foundations for non-

reductionist understandings of race, ethnicity, and other dimensions of difference firmly situated in material practices and inextricably linked with class processes, in particular historical and geographical conjunctures.[18] He did so by acknowledging what he calls the 'materialist premise' that forms the core of any Marxist analysis – namely that the analysis of politics and ideology must be grounded in their material conditions of existence. At the same time, he insisted that the forms of these relations cannot be deduced from abstract logics, but must be made historically specific; and that this, in turn, requires attention to race-class (and other) articulations forged through situated practices in the multiple arenas of daily life.

It is important to distinguish between Hall's formulation and what has become perhaps the single most influential critique of class reductionism and essentialism – namely, Laclau and Mouffe's *Hegemony and Socialist Strategy* (1985).[19] For Laclau and Mouffe, the basic obstacle in the left's capacity for analysis and action has been what they call *classism* – namely, 'the idea that the working class represents the privileged agent in which the fundamental impulse of social change resides – without perceiving that the very orientation of the working class depends upon a political balance of forces and the radicalization of a plurality of democratic struggles which are decided in good part outside the class itself' (Laclau and Mouffe 1985: 177). Although often portrayed as the avatars of postmodern politics, Laclau and Mouffe subscribe neither to postmodernist notions of fragmentation, nor to particularistic politics. On the contrary, they hold on to nominally Gramscian ideas of hegemony and articulation – although in a deeply modified form which, they claim, goes beyond Gramsci in its anti-essentialism. Their avowedly post-Marxist ideas of radical democracy underpin widespread notions of 'post-development' and they have also become quite influential in some circles in South Africa.[20]

It is precisely in their claims that they extend the concept of hegemonic articulations 'far beyond Gramsci' (1985: 3) that Laclau and Mouffe in fact fall far short. The fundamental problem is their failure to distinguish historical from abstract determinism, and their rejection of determinism *tout court* in *Hegemony and Socialist Strategy* on the grounds that it perpetuates economism. Yet, ironically, they fall back on a structural analysis of language that is every bit as rigid as the structural Marxism of which they are so critical.[21] Their abandonment of a concept of historical determination produces a deeply impoverished concept of articulation – one that abstracts from the historically and geographically specific processes, material conditions, and forms of power that set the conditions for articulatory practices. This disabling move lies at the heart of their incapacity to engage with questions of capitalism.[22] It also effectively cedes the terrain of 'the economic' and 'globalization' to neoliberal – or narrowly teleological – understandings. Rather than a retreat from class, as Pred and Watts (1992: 198) so eloquently put it, there is 'a desperate need to retheorize where class has gone to, and to rethink, and reassert it in nonessentialist ways.'

Ironically, it was Ernesto Laclau who first suggested that the concept of articulation be extended along Gramscian lines to encompass both joining together and enunciation, as a way of illuminating historically diverse processes and practices of hegemony. Indeed, Stuart Hall's illuminations of race-class articulations build directly on Laclau's (1977) brilliant analysis of populism, which argued that signifiers like 'freedom,' 'equality,' and 'the people,' have no fixed, intrinsic meaning or class belonging. Rather, Laclau showed how they can be reconvened as elements within very different discourses, positioning the popular classes in relation to the power bloc in quite different ways.

Viewed from this perspective, the post-apartheid state coalition has not only constructed a populist unity, articulating 'the people' into a political subject, as Laclau would put it, with – not against – the power bloc; it has also accomplished this apparent unity in the face of escalating material inequality and poverty, and economic policies that are patently unpopular with a large segment of its support base. In the mid-1990s discourses of non-racial national unity were ascendant, exemplified in the language of the 'rainbow nation,' and the towering moral authority of Nelson Mandela. Since the late 1990s the picture has become far more complex, as the power bloc led by Thabo Mbeki has shifted images from rainbows to the African Renaissance, positioning the ANC at the forefront of battles against racism. These and other discourses not only resonate with everyday experiences of racism by large numbers of black South Africans; they have also called forth overtly racist responses from the white liberal opposition that validate charges against them, and consolidate anew the ANC's populist unity. Through all of this, the power bloc centered around Thabo Mbeki consistently invokes 'globalization' to circumvent any questioning of neoliberal nostrums and policies, or of their alignment with capital. At the same time, Mbeki's pro-African, anti-poverty stance in international forums reinscribes national strategies to align 'the people' with the power bloc.

Shot through with contradictions, this apparent populist unity co-exists with powerful currents of discontent and critique from within the alliance; from segments of the NGO community; and, most importantly, from the interstices of everyday life where large numbers of South Africans navigate between the emancipatory promises of official discourses and the glamour of the mass consumption economy on the one hand, and harsh material deprivation on the other. The political challenge, as Marais (1998: 250) has suggested, is not just to revive the national democratic forces that fought for the overthrow of apartheid, but to *reconfigure* a broadly based popular movement on the basis of an explicitly transformative perspective. This is not a matter of pitting civil society (or some segment of it) against the state, but rather of a Gramscian recognition that

> state and civil society are interconnected, each defining the other through a complex of relations and constantly shifting engagements. Depending on the situation, elements of the one transmute into the other. A popular movement, therefore, is positioned neither outside nor inside the state or civil society. In the course of its activities it traverses two strategic fields. (Marais 1998: 250)

What is needed, in other words, is a flexible political strategy that recognizes multiple, interconnected arenas of material and cultural struggle; that presses on contradictions and slippages to open new spaces and understandings; that operates simultaneously on multiple fronts; and that searches for connections and alliances.

Spatializing Power: Multiple Trajectories of Socio-Spatial Change

My goal in this book is to contribute to precisely such a strategy of broadly based mobilization. The concept of multiple trajectories of socio-spatial change is the vehicle through which I try to convey a series of more concrete insights and arguments, and drive home their political stakes. Fashioned from Gramscian understandings, it also incorporates conceptions of space, place, identity, and power derived from Henri Lefebvre, as well as certain strands of feminist thinking.

In *The Production of Space* ([1974] 1991), Lefebvre launched a powerful critique of taken-for-granted notions of space and time that have come to dominate Western philosophy, in which space appears as a passive backdrop or container, and time as an active, dynamic force. He proposed not only that (social) space is a (social) product, but also that the space thus produced 'serves as a tool of thought and of action; that in addition to being a means of production it is also a means of control, and hence of domination, of power; yet that, as such, it escapes in part from those who would make use of it' (Lefebvre 1991: 26). He was also deeply critical of theorists (including Althusser, Foucault, Derrida, and Chomsky) who invoke spatial metaphors in abstraction from social practice.[23] As Smith and Katz (1993: 75) observe in their lucid exposition, 'spatial metaphors are problematic in so far as they presume that space is not.' The problem lies not with spatial metaphors *per se*, but rather with the very specific conception of space – namely *absolute* space – upon which such metaphors rely in order to ground social meaning. Despite its apparent abstract neutrality, absolute space is politically charged. It is precisely this absolutist conception of space as pre-existing emptiness divisible into discrete pieces that is both a product and a medium of capitalist domination.[24]

Lefebvre insisted on a relational understanding of space as actively produced through everyday practices that are simultaneously material and metaphorical, and on the inseparability of space and time. Lefebvre's point was not simply that space and society interact; nor was he making a claim that spatial patterns 'reflect' social structures or processes. As Neil Smith (1991: 77) points out, 'the spatial' and 'the social' can only interact or reflect each other if they are defined as separate in the first place – a definition that invokes a concept of space as an empty container separate from and prior to social processes. Instead, 'the production of space' implies that social practice and space are internally related in the sense that each entails the other. The production of space also implies the production of meanings, concepts, and consciousness about space (or space-time) that are inseparably linked to its physical production through situated practices.

In her potent critique of Laclau's (1990) deployment of spatial metaphor, Massey (1992, 1994) builds on Lefebvre to argue for a relational conception of space-time that attends explicitly to questions of politics. She asserts the importance of transcending dichotomous representations and counterpositions of time and space as separate entities, drawing an analogy with physics to argue for a four-dimensional conception of space/time:

> In classical physics both space and time exist in their own right, as do objects. Space is a passive arena, the setting for objects and their interaction. Objects, in turn, exist prior to their interactions and affect one another through force-fields. The observer, similarly, is detached from the observed world. In modern physics, on the other hand, the identity of things is constituted through interactions . . . It is

not that the interrelationships between objects occur in space and time; it is these relationships themselves which *create/define* space and time. (Massey 1994: 261, 263)

The point is not to collapse the spatial and the temporal, but to recognize them as mutually constitutive.

This relational conception of space-time as actively produced through multi-layered, situated practices that are simultaneously material, symbolic, and mediated through power relations enables us to think concretely of spatiality (or space-time) as 'constructed out of the multiplicity of social relations across all spatial scales, from the global reach of finance and telecommunications, through the geography of tentacles of national political power, to the social relations within the town, the settlement, the household, and the workplace' (Massey 1994: 3). It is, Doreen Massey goes on to note, a way of thinking in terms of the ever-shifting geometry of social/power relations, and it forces into view the real multiplicities of space-time. If spatiality is conceived in terms of space-time and formed through social relations and interactions at all scales, then place can be seen not as a bounded enclosure, but rather as 'a subset of the interactions which constitute [social] space, a local articulation within a wider whole' (Massey 1994: 4). Places are always formed through relations with wider arenas and other places; boundaries are always socially constructed and contested; and the specificity of a place – however defined – arises from the particularity of interrelations with what lies beyond it, that intersect or come into conjuncture in particular ways.[25]

Since the early 1990s, conceptions of the social production of social space derived from Lefebvre have come to figure prominently not only in the work of many geographers, but also growing numbers of anthropologists and sociologists.[26] Yet different authors have pushed the idea of the production of space in some sharply divergent directions, both analytically and politically. Thus, for example, David Harvey (1996, 2000)[27] and Neil Smith (1991, 1997) draw partly on Lefebvre to call for a more rigorous understanding of uneven capitalist development in which the concept of a nested hierarchy of spatial scales is central: 'Processes do not operate *in* but *actively construct* space and time and in so doing define distinctive scales for their development' (Harvey 1996: 53). At the same time, Harvey has taken Lefebvre to task for his insistence that 'the production of space must remain as an endlessly open possibility' (Harvey 2000: 183), and his refusal to confront the closure inherent in the materialization of space.

Other scholars, in contrast, reproach Lefebvre for 'sticking to a rigidly teleological evolution' (Keith and Pile 1993: 25), and propose selectively combining Lefebvre's ideas with those of Laclau and Mouffe (1985) and Laclau (1990) precisely to *avoid* the violence of closure and the pitfalls of historicism. Despite her devastating critique of Laclau in the early 1990s, Doreen Massey has recently taken ideas of the production of space in a similarly post-Marxist, radical democratic direction, asserting a concept of spatiality as the source of what Laclau calls 'dislocation,' and a precondition for a politics predicated on radical contingency and openness.[28] In short, far from constituting a single authoritative voice, Lefebvre's ideas have generated vibrant, ongoing debates around questions of space, power, identity, and difference, and what these mean for politics and the possibilities for social change.

My concept of multiple trajectories of socio-spatial change derives from the imperative of steering a course between economism and voluntarism. Recognizing that room to maneuver is always present but never unconstrained, it suggests a way of grappling with the question of limits and possibilities. The key analytical stakes turn around the crucial distinction, outlined earlier, between an economistic notion of 'determination' in the sense of abstract laws subject to predictable and inexorable development, and determination in the sense of historically and geographically defined processes of the setting of limits, as well as the exertion of pressures. Grounded in understandings of situated social practice as simultaneously material and meaningful, a relational conception of spatiality extends and enriches how we think about historical-geographical determination and the closely related conception of articulation in its extended sense.

The idea of multiple trajectories of socio-spatial change is also closely attentive to questions of gender, understood – following Joan Scott – as the knowledge that establishes meanings for bodily differences:[29]

> These meanings vary across cultures, social groups, and time since nothing about the body, including women's reproductive organs, determines univocally how social divisions will be shaped. We cannot see sexual difference except as a function of our knowledge about the body, and that knowledge is not 'pure,' cannot be isolated from its implication in a broad range of discursive contexts. Sexual difference is not, then, the originary cause from which social organization ultimately can be derived. It is instead a variable social organization that must itself be explained. (Scott 1988: 2)

Part of what is so useful about Scott's formulation is that it emphatically refuses to relegate gender and sexuality to the family or household.[30] Instead, it enables us to see how the meanings of masculinity and femininity are invoked and contested as part of the exercise of power in multiple arenas – including not only the workplace and the community, but also in domains like war and 'high politics' that seemingly have little directly to do with relations between women and men. Thus, Scott argues, feminist history becomes not just the recounting of great deeds performed by women, but 'the exposure of the silent and hidden operations of gender that are nonetheless present and defining forces in the organization of most societies' (Scott 1988: 27). Yet, as Vron Ware (1996) has pointed out, Scott's analysis would have been far more powerful had she attended explicitly to race and ethnicity as similarly defining forces; and indeed Hazel Carby (1982), Pratibha Parmar (1982), and others insisted some time ago on the deep entanglements of race and ethnicity with gender and sexuality, as have others more recently.[31]

In the chapters that follow, I will show how racial, ethnic, and gendered forms of difference are produced in relation to one another and to class processes through situated material practices and the exercise of power in multiple, interconnected arenas across different spatial scales. These historically and geographically specific articulations of difference actively shape and inflect diverse trajectories of socio-spatial change – they are, in other words, key constitutive forces. Multi-layered processes of production of difference are crucial both in illuminating structural constraints and conjunctural possibilities, and in pointing the way towards a politics of alliance.

The constitutive character of difference is closely connected with another element of the framework of multiple trajectories: a decisive rejection of accounts of capitalism and modernity as originating in 'the West' and radiating out from there to 'backward regions.' These core-centric notions pervade many contemporary narratives of globalization, and are part of what is so disabling about the 'impact model' that I dismantle later in this chapter. So-called 'non-Western' historical geographies, cultural formations, and forms of accumulation need to be understood not simply as the *effects* of accelerating global flows and connections, but as actively formative of them.

Some interesting suggestions about what might be entailed in reconfiguring core-centric understandings of global capitalism come from

The Production of Space, where Lefebvre (1991: 323–325) drew attention to a key lacuna in Marx's thought – the part played by land and nature, as concept and reality.[32] Fernando Coronil (1997) pursues Lefebvre's arguments further to suggest that the inclusion of land and nature (and of the agents associated with it) not only displaces the capital-labor relation from what he calls the 'ossified centrality' it has been made to occupy in Marxist theory. It also helps to displace core-centric accounts of global capitalism:

> Together with land, the capital/labor relation may be viewed within a wider process of commodification, the specific form and effects of which must be demonstrated concretely in each instance. In light of this more comprehensive view of capitalism, it would be difficult to reduce its development to a dialectic of capital and labor originating in the advanced centers and expanding to the backward periphery . . . By including the worldwide agents involved in the making of capitalism, this perspective makes it possible to envisage a global, non-Eurocentric conception of its development. (Coronil 1997: 61–62)

In extending this argument, I want to insist on the continuing salience of agrarian questions to grasping not only the multiplicity of capitalist and post-socialist trajectories in the contemporary world, but also their *interconnectedness* and the ongoing processes that define their constitutive character. These latter considerations are vital in distinguishing an understanding cast in terms of multiple trajectories from institutionalist notions of 'path dependency' that are prominent in work on industrial restructuring.[33] In different yet related ways, Michael Watts and I have argued that the so-called 'third world' literature on agrarian transformations has moved well beyond related work on industrial change in advancing a processual understanding that attends to power, culture, and material practices – including, very importantly, gender – while remaining grounded in classical political economy debates that grappled with the multiplicity of agrarian transitions (Watts 1996; Hart 1998a).[34] It was Kautsky in particular, Watts (1996) points out, who recognized both the inherently political character of these multiple transformations, as well as their transnational connections (see also Bernstein 1996a).

In a forceful statement of the continuing importance of agrarian questions – and, conversely, the fallacies of presuming that these questions are somehow 'resolved' once capitalism in agriculture has 'matured' – Watts and Goodman (1997: 6) maintain that 'agrarian questions are constantly renewed by the contradictory and uneven development of capitalism itself.' The ongoing salience of historically and geographically specific – but globally connected – agrarian questions turns not only around the changing conditions and spatially extended chains of food production and distribution, but also the ways in which agrarian institutions, social relations, and cultural practices carry over into the constitution of industrial districts. The diverse East Asian and South African trajectories of rural industrialization traced in this book are prime examples of the latter, as is fascinating research in India by Sharad Chari (1997).

My research illuminates another key dimension of how specific histories of agrarian transformation continue to play a vitally important role in shaping what appear as distinctively 'non-Western' trajectories of accumulation, and defining the conditions of global competition. The East Asian material illustrates not only how spectacular industrialization has taken place without dispossession from the land (although with state extraction from agriculture), but also how access to land and other resources has operated in effect as a social wage. These trajectories stand in sharp contrast to histories of racialized dispossession in South Africa.

These divergent trajectories allow us to extend Lefebvre's insights about the limits of focusing on capital-labor relations, and engage critically with what in the Marxist lexicon is known as 'primitive accumulation' (a term which, as we shall see in Chapter 6, is a mis-translation of the meaning Marx meant to convey). Orthodox understandings of primitive accumulation presume both that expropriation of direct producers from the land constitutes a key precondition for industrial accumulation, *and* that dispossession can be understood as a 'natural' event that can be consigned to the pre-capitalist past. East Asian-South African connections and divergences enable us to grasp specific historical geographies of so-called 'primitive accumulation' as *ongoing processes* as opposed to distant events, intimately linked with the reproduction of labor and the exercise of power in multiple arenas, from the household to the state. The simultaneously material and cultural practices of labor reproduction, in other words, continue to constitute key arenas of struggle, deeply entangled with the dynamics of accumulation, and actively shaping trajectories of socio-spatial change.

These insights not only illuminate the actively constitutive character of what appear as distinctively 'non-Western' trajectories of accumulation in defining the conditions of global competition. They also form the crux of how I put the concept of multiple trajectories and the method of relational comparison to use in post-apartheid South Africa: (1) they enable me to draw direct connections between histories of racialized dispossession and the crisis of the local state in the post-apartheid era, while also showing how locally specific intersections of township and labor politics have shaped the form and character of the local state in Ladysmith-Ezakheni and Newcastle-Madadeni; (2) they form an important element of my analytical argument about the fragility and contradictions of the neoliberal project in post-apartheid South Africa; and (3) they undergird my political argument about how re-articulations of the 'land question' in terms of a social wage might be used to connect struggles in different arenas.

At a more general level they also provide a means for illustrating concretely what it is about dominant discourses of globalization that renders them so disabling, and what might be entailed in more politically enabling understandings. Before engaging directly with these broader questions of globalization, I would like to spell out more fully the two key axes of multiple trajectories and relational comparisons, and foreshadow how I will bring them together.

Transnational Connections: The Contemporary Salience of Agrarian Questions

One of the apparent anachronisms of contemporary capitalism has been the dispersal of industry into villages and towns in predominantly rural regions. Rural industrialization appears almost oxymoronic. Yet some of the most spectacular instances of industrial accumulation in recent decades – including the so-called Third Italy, significant parts of the 'Taiwanese miracle,' and much of the stunningly rapid growth in China since the mid-1980s – all exemplify rural industrialization. So too, of course, do the industrial estates that sprang up in and adjacent to former bantustans in the 1980s.

Dispersed industrialization may be a defining feature of late capitalism, but the dynamics through which industrial capital in various guises encounters and intersects with agrarian conditions are enormously diverse. Sharply divergent trajectories of rural industrialization will become evident as we trace the differential emergence of industrial estates in Ladysmith-Ezakheni and Newcastle-Madadeni; follow one group of Taiwanese industrialists to northwestern KwaZulu-Natal and another to southern coastal regions of Mainland China; and go on from there to pay brief visits to towns and villages in Mainland China where rapidly growing industries are owned and operated by local governments.

The most obvious and widely held interpretations hold that the dispersal of labor-intensive industries has been driven by intensified competition, overaccumulation, and falling rates of profit.[35] Yet in itself this capital logic story is quite arid and limited, precisely because it abstracts from the diverse forms and dynamics that are tremendously illuminating.

First, tracing transnational connections across dispersed and differentiated sites enables us to see how the production of commodities is *inextricably* linked with the production of racial, gendered, and ethnic forms of difference, and how these dimensions of difference are produced in relation to one another as active, structuring forces. Diverse articulations of difference bring vividly to life how race, ethnicity, and gender are the modalities through which class is lived, the medium through which class relations are experienced, and the forms in which it is appropriated and fought through, to paraphrase Stuart Hall (1980). They also matter profoundly for broader questions of whether and how alliances are to be formed, and they compel a reconsideration of 'strategic class reductionism' (Harvey 1996) as well as radical democratic aspirations.

Second, relational comparisons shed light not only on how trajectories of agrarian transformation have shaped industrial dynamics, but also on the interconnections between production and the conditions of reproduction of labor power. Excursions from northwestern KwaZulu-Natal to sites of rural industrialization in East Asia turn the spotlight on how rapid industrial accumulation there took place *without* dispossession from the land; to the multi-layered politics and power struggles that shaped these trajectories, including peasant mobilization and its regional reverberations, as well as deeply gendered processes; and to historical formations of the social wage through redistributive reforms that effectively underwrote industrial accumulation. In short, I will show how trajectories of agrarian transformation in different regions of East Asia, shaped and inflected by multi-layered forms of struggle, have been crucial in defining the conditions of global competition.

From the perspective of South African debates, these comparative insights bring into focus how the legacy of dispossession from the land runs far deeper than the starkly racialized geographies of the agricultural sector. They also give another twist to Wolpe's (1972) argument about the collapse of subsistence agriculture in the reserves.[36] Accelerated dispossession and displacement of black South Africans from rural 'white' South Africa to densely populated bantustan townships during the apartheid era radically eroded the conditions of reproduction of labor power and the social wage, and pervades the fiscal crisis of the local state. In short, East Asian-South African connections bring to the forefront of attention the intertwining of land, labor, and the contradictory imperatives of the local state in the post-apartheid order – as well as the tensions among them ignited by neoliberal austerity.

This leads us to the politics of the agrarian question, or what Gramsci called 'the Southern question' in the context of his native Italy. Gaining the consent of the peasantry was essential, Gramsci argued, to a broad system of alliances that could cut across conventional class lines to unite diverse social forces. Accordingly, he underscored the importance of historically specific understandings of the complex relations between the city and the countryside, peasantry and proletariat, and the ways in which class formation and relations of dominance and dependence assumed regionally and culturally specific forms. Historically, the agrarian question has been a major lacuna in the South African liberation movement.[37] The 1940s to early 1960s was the last period of overt, widespread rural political agitation, in which efforts by Govan Mbeki and others to link rural and urban discontent received very little support from the urban-based leadership of the ANC and SACP (Bundy 1987).

The precarious politics of the agrarian question is clearly evident in the limited and halting character of post-apartheid agrarian reforms. Ironically, it was the World Bank that pushed the ANC to attend to agrarian reform in the early 1990s, invoking 'models from elsewhere' to assert the superior efficiency of small-scale family farms and insist on market-based reforms. The land reform program actually put in place after 1994 was considerably more modest than the original Bank proposals and, as we shall see in Chapter 6, has increasingly come to focus on the creation of a black capitalist farming class. There is, as Cherryl Walker (2000) has pointed out, a profound tension between morally charged narratives of dispossession that underpin individual restitution claims on the one hand, and the narrowly technocratic and radically underfunded land reform program on the other.

What I contribute to contemporary debates is to link the history of dispossession to the social wage and crisis of the local state. This move, in turn, opens the way for a new narrative – one that delinks dispossession from individual claims of restitution, redefines it in terms of erosion of social security, and enables broader redistributive claims. Also, it breaks the link between the land question and a narrowly sectoral definition of agriculture; and opens the way for organized labor and other social forces to engage with land and agrarian questions, and forge new alliances. This linking of dispossession and agrarian questions with reconfigurations of the local state coincides with new municipal demarcations, instituted in 2000, that have effectively dissolved rural-urban boundaries and opened the way for new politics.

This argument resonates in certain ways with that of Mamdani (1996), who maintains that one of the key limits of post-apartheid reforms in South Africa is that the alliance 'lacks a program for linking the urban and the rural on the basis of democratizing rural power' (Mamdani 1996: 297). Yet the dichotomized categories that Mamdani deploys – rural/urban, central-ized/decentralized despotism, and so forth – are limited because they suggest that politics can be read off structural conditions. They also obscure key dimensions of the agrarian question – namely, the dramatic dispossession that took place from the 1960s through forced removals and farm evictions, and the formation of huge townships with urban-like densities in rural areas.

In using links with rural industrial regions in East Asia to dramatize the contemporary salience and historically specific character of agrarian questions in South Africa, I am not simply reasserting South African exceptionalism in the sense that Mamdani uses the term. Mamdani's analysis of differences and commonalities between South Africa and the rest of Africa turns around a radical separation of economics and politics: 'It is only from an economistic perspective – one that highlights levels and industrialization and proletarianization – that South African exceptionalism makes sense' (Mamdani 1996: 27).[38] Accordingly, he goes on to argue, it takes a shift from the mode of production to the mode of rule to underline that which is African and unexceptional about the South African experi-ence. By situating South African agrarian transformations in relation to those in rural industrial regions of East Asia, I am working with a conception of political economy which insists that economic practices and processes are always socially and politically constituted, and refuses to separate accumulation and state formation. East Asian connections render South African dispossession peculiar and contestable, while also clarifying the historical erosion of the social wage and its intertwining with the contradictions inherent in the local state.

My use of East Asian connections to highlight the ongoing salience of historically specific trajectories of agrarian transformation is also distinctively different from neo-Weberian narratives of the East Asian 'developmental state.' It complements arguments set forth by Ben Fine and Zav Rustomjee (1996) who use South Korean industrialization partly as a foil to illuminate the specificities of South African industrial trajectories. They contend that the pattern of industrialization in South Africa associated with the development of what they call the Minerals-Energy Complex (MEC) is the product of historically and geographically specific configurations of class forces in relation to natural resources from which there emerged a highly concentrated corporate structure that fails to promote industrial diversification out of the MEC core-heavy industries. Relatively low levels of industrial investment and diversification have produced an over-bloated financial system, and corporate capacity to transfer funds abroad. Capital flight, in turn, exemplifies the singular failure of the macro political economy to mobilize domestically generated surpluses for domestic investment.

My own contribution illuminates the contradictory forces encapsulated within the local state in this era of neoliberal globalization, pointing in particular to the ongoing reverberations of histories and memories of racialized dispossession.

The 'Crisis' of the Local State

In the final decades of the twentieth century we witnessed the meteoric rise to prominence of the local state in many different regions of the world. This shifting of territorial state power to subnational scales of governance is clearly part and parcel of the post-1970s wave of global economic restructuring, neoliberal market reforms, and accelerated transnational capital flows.[39] The neoliberal impulses driving this process are powerfully evident in the World Bank's portrayals of local government as inherently more efficient than national government, and its touting of decentralized service delivery, local entrepreneurialism, public-private partnerships, and so forth, as part of many of the structural adjustment programs imposed in the 1980s.[40]

As the 1990s progressed, emphasis on decentralization primarily as a means of market deregulation and managerial efficiency gave way to a softening in official development discourse that Mohan and Stokke (2000) aptly term a revisionist neoliberalism. This shift, I suggest, is most usefully understood in terms of Karl Polanyi's (1944) contention that the unleashing of market forces wreaks havoc, and generates counter-tendencies and demands for social protection.[41] Institutional reforms, social development, and 'social capital' feature prominently in this more recent incarnation, along with a renewed emphasis on the local state as the key site not only of efficiency but also trust, social cohesion, and liberal democracy.[42] Presenting a kinder, gentler face than their orthodox neoliberal counterparts, revisionists invoke notions of accountability, transparency, and trust as prerequisites for local economic success and good governance.

Ironically, some of the fiercest critics of the development establishment – proponents of what has come to be termed 'post-development' – also promote 'the local' as the site of radical democracy and grassroots postmodernism.[43] Ideas derived from Laclau and Mouffe (1985) figure prominently in these efforts to define 'alternatives to development,' along with claims about the superiority of indigenous knowledge, the emergence from below of new social movements, and the imperatives for defence of place and local autonomy against the onslaught of global forces.

What unites the 'New Right' and the 'New Left,' several observers have pointed out, is an emphasis on civil society, typically understood as distinct from the state and the market.[44] Not only has this romanticized localism 'tended to essentialize the local as discrete places that host relatively homogeneous communities or, alternatively, constitute sites of grassroots mobilization and resistance' (Mohan and Stokke 2000: 264). In addition, these authors warn, 'local participation' can be used for different purposes by different stakeholders – including underplaying local inequalities and power relations, as well as national and transnational political and economic forces – thereby overtly or inadvertently cementing Eurocentric 'solutions' to development problems (Mohan and Stokke 2000: 264).

My contribution in this study is to posit a conjunctural analysis of the local state that flows directly from the concept of multiple trajectories and the method of relational comparison. Politically this analysis represents an effort to clarify the slippages, openings, and possibilities for emancipatory social change in this era of neoliberal capitalism, as well as the limits and constraints operating at different levels. Analytically it entails close attention to the differential constitution of political subjects through situated practices and their associated discourses and power relations in multiple, intersecting arenas of everyday life. In the specific context of South Africa, I will show how the local state has become a key terrain on which the contradictory imperatives of the neoliberal post-apartheid order are being constituted and fought out in everyday practice within and across key institutional arenas. At the same time, divergent locally specific forms are revealing of both limits and possibilities.

Tensions inherent in local state formation in South Africa are far from new. To appreciate the significance of post-apartheid reconfigurations – as well as historical continuities – it is useful to recall the invention of indirect rule in British colonial Natal in the 1840s.[45] Built on the remnants of indirect rule, Hendrik Verwoerd's bantustan strategy launched in the 1960s embodied precisely the sorts of claims about 'local authenticity,' autonomy, and indigeneity that figure so prominently in post-development discourses. Although Mahmood Mamdani's (1996) characterization of what he calls 'decentralized despotism' in the bantustans may be somewhat overdrawn, as I will argue later, it nevertheless serves as a signal warning against the sort of rampant romanticism often peddled by proponents of both revisionist neoliberalism and post-development.

Racialized processes of local state formation contributed directly to the demise of apartheid. In the early 1980s, under pressure from fiscal contraction as well as political opposition, the 'reformist' regime headed by P.W. Botha sought to devolve greater fiscal as well as administrative responsibility to so-called Black Local Authorities in urban townships. The townships literally exploded with rage, paving the way for what Seidman (1994) and others call social movement unionism that linked workplace and township struggles. In Chapters 3 and 4, I trace through in some detail how these struggles took shape in the Ladysmith and Newcastle townships. The local state, in short, became the Achilles heel of apartheid in its reformist guise.

In the post-apartheid era, the rise of what has come to be defined as 'developmental' local government – a term that central government officials have carefully avoided applying to themselves – encapsulates in a particularly intense form the opposing tendencies contained within contemporary decentralization moves more generally. Official narratives veer between stern neoliberal rhetorics of efficiency and fiscal discipline on the one hand, and invocations of local participation and democracy on the other. More concretely, a series of profound tensions pervade processes of local state formation. Local government restructuring since 1994 has entailed massive remapping, described in Chapter 7, through which areas defined as white and black under the Group Areas Act have become incorporated within single administrative entities.[46] In the face of determined efforts to preserve enclaves of privilege once exclusively white, although now more racially mixed, local authorities simultaneously confront intense pressure for redistributive social change to redress the staggering material inequalities between former white towns and black townships. Central government officials have also thrust on their local counterparts a series of additional responsibilities and functions on the grounds that local government is both more efficient and more democratic. Yet neoliberal austerity has meant that local governments have been starved of resources from the center, and made to rely heavily on their own restricted tax base. At the same time, local officials have been assigned the task of not only attracting capital, but also securing the conditions of capital accumulation – including a docile workforce – in the face of macro-economic contraction and a sharp decline of formal employment. Compounding these tensions are pressures to privatize municipal services and raise service charges and local taxes, all of which provoke outbursts of intense resentment.

Structural tensions define the broad terrain of local state formation in the post-apartheid order, but they do not in any simple or direct way determine the course of local politics. On the contrary, I will show how the contradictory imperatives condensed within the local state have been constituted, contested, and reworked in distinctively different ways in Ladysmith-Ezakheni and Newcastle-Madadeni. These sharply divergent trajectories of local state formation in two seemingly similar places show clearly how political subjectivities can neither be read off the structure of socio-economic relations nor deduced from hegemonic discourses. Instead they provide vivid illustrations of how places and identities are forged through practical engagements and the exercise of power in multiple, interconnected arenas both local and translocal. At the same time, these locally divergent articulations and trajectories emphatically do *not* signify radical openness and contingency. On the contrary, they help to illuminate multi-layered limits and constraints, as well as the ongoing processes through which such limits are reinforced or undermined.

This conjunctural analysis is also suggestive of how the fiscal and political crisis of the local state in the neoliberal post-apartheid order is intimately linked with histories, memories, and meanings of racialized dispossession, and the ways in which they have both shaped the conditions of reproduction of labor, and carried over into the constitution of the local state. These dimensions of dispossession are crucial to grasping the fragilities of neoliberal capitalism in post-apartheid South Africa, and to defining possible terrains of practical action.

This leads me to my third broad deployment of the concept of multiple trajectories: critical engagement with discourses of globalization. While primarily concerned with constructions of economic globalization that inform claims about the natural status of neoliberalism, I also point to how and why notions of cultural globalization are severely limited. Let me now specify the elements of these discourses that render them so disabling, and then go on to outline how the framework of multiple trajectories and the method of relational comparison reconfigure precisely these elements.

Disabling Globalization/Enabling Alternatives

> Globalization – even the term itself is hotly contested – is the modern or postmodern version of the proverbial elephant, described by its diverse observers in so many diverse ways. Yet one can still posit the existence of the elephant in the absence of a single, persuasive and dominant theory; nor are blinded questions the most unsatisfactory way to explore this kind of relational and multi-leveled phenomenon. (Jameson 1998: xi)

Later in the same volume Jameson calls attention to diverse – and often sharply divergent – portrayals of economic and cultural globalization in both celebratory and baleful terms, making an impassioned plea about the need to relate these diverse understandings to one another in a dialectical fashion so that a clearer picture of the elephant might emerge.

There are those, no doubt, for whom Godzilla on the rampage would be a more appropriate characterization of globalization than the gentle, intelligent, ponderous pachyderm. What is most fundamentally problematic about the elephant-groping metaphor, though, is its erasure of the profoundly political issues at stake in the multiple, competing claims about globalization. Who gets to define the elephant? In what circumstances? How does the locatedness of the observer define which body part is given prominence? And what (if any) are the effects of such exercises? In short, globalization is not only an enormously complex and varied set of simultaneously economic, cultural, and political processes. It is also, very importantly, a set of discourses through which knowledge is produced. Not only is the production of knowledge about globalization one of the most deeply politicized practices of meaning-making within and beyond academia. In addition and most importantly, some of the most influential discourses about economic and cultural globalization are profoundly disabling.

What is it about these discourses that renders them so disabling? There are, I suggest, three key elements that are, in varying degrees, shared by widely divergent representations of both economic and cultural globalization. First is a pervasive economism of either a neoliberal or an orthodox Marxist variety. Second, constructions of both economic and cultural globalization frequently deploy dichotomous understandings of time and space, in which time is accorded active primacy and space appears as a passive container. Third, and encompassing both of these, is the often implicit presumption that globalizing forces originate in 'the West' or 'the core,' and spread out from there to encompass more distant (or 'backward') regions of the world. These are, of course, precisely the elements that the framework of multiple trajectories sets out to reconfigure.

Discourses of economic globalization that underpin neoliberal agendas in South Africa and elsewhere typically invoke what I call an 'impact model' of globalization, framed in terms of the impact of 'the global' on 'the local.' This model conjures up images of active forces – defined primarily in terms of new information technology and/or markets – that take shape at the core of the global economy and radiate out from there. 'Placeless power' in the form of rapidly accelerating flows of information and capital ricochet around the world, bearing down upon and agglomerating in some 'powerless places' while bypassing others; hence the imperatives of conforming to orthodox neoliberalism. Claims about 'deterritorialization,' the disintegration of national borders, and the demise of the nation state often figure prominently in these discourses. Thus, for example, Kenichi Ohmae – one of the most influential proponents of globalization and the natural status of neoliberalism – speaks of how 'power over economic activity will inevitably migrate from the central governments of national states to the borderless network of countless individual market-based decisions' (Ohmae 1995: 9).

The global/local dichotomy, as we saw in the Introduction, maps onto a series of other dualisms: active/passive, dynamic/static, economics/culture; general/specific; abstract/concrete; and, very importantly, dichotomous conceptions of time and space, in which time appears as an active force, and space as a passive recipient or container. It is precisely this dualistic – and deeply gendered – portrayal of time and space of which Lefebvre (1991) is so critical.

Dualistic constructions akin to those of the impact model appear in modified form in a number of far more sophisticated and critical portrayals of economic globalization. One notable example is David Harvey's (1989) influential notion of globalization as 'time-space compression.'[47] In *The Condition of Postmodernity*, Harvey portrays time-space compression as capturing the essence of the history of capitalism – the annihilation of space by time, which intensified significantly with the transition from Fordism to flexible accumulation: 'We have been experiencing, these past two decades, an intense phase of time-space compression that has had a disorienting and disrupting impact upon political-economic practices, the balance of class power, as well as upon cultural and social life' (Harvey 1989: 284). Experiences of time-space compression form the link between political-economic and cultural processes, and define the condition of postmodernity. The political project for Harvey entails putting this condition into its historical context, so that it can be seen as arising out of the pressures of capital accumulation and the annihilation of space by time, and thus rendered accessible to historical materialist analysis and interpretation. In practice, however, numerous narratives of globalization deploy the notion of time-space compression as if it were an inexorable force of nature.[48]

Top-down globalization narratives are more explicit in Castells (1996), for whom the 'space of flows' comes to dominate the 'space of places' in the informational society. According to this similarly influential account, the network society is constructed around instantaneous flows of capital, information, technology, organizational interaction, images, sounds and symbols – a space of flows through which time is rendered timeless. The space of flows is comprised of (1) a circuit of electronic impulses that make up an encompassing global network (places do not disappear, but their logic and meaning becomes absorbed by the network); (2) nodes and hubs (in which the network links up with specific places that are functional to it); and (3) the spatial organization of dominant managerial elites. Thus 'dominant functions are organized in networks pertaining to a space of flows that links them up around the world, while fragmenting subordinate functions and people in the multiple space of places, made up of locales increasingly segregated and disconnected from each other' – and organized according to clock time (Castells 1996: 476). In short, rather than the domination of space by time, in Castells' schema space comes to organize time. What emerges, though, is a similarly dichotomous logic in which the space of flows/timeless time asserts structural dominance over the space of places/clock time.

One reaction has been to envisage 'the local' not as passive recipient but as the key site of resistance to global forces.[49] In this version, 'place' and 'the local' become equated with authenticity, ecological sensitivity, and the site of self-generating new social movements that represent alternatives to capitalism and 'development.' Yet, while revaluing 'the local' and 'the global,' proponents of this view effectively reinforce the dualisms of the impact model and endorse its top-down, core-centric narratives.

Accounts of 'cultural globalization' typically conjure up deterritorialization and a sort of transgressive transnationalism, while 'the local' represents stasis, incarceration, and subjection to the stifling, modernist clutches of the nation state. In practice there are remarkable parallels and convergences with economistic formulations. One influential example is Arjun Appadurai's formulation of globalization as a 'new imaginary' and his claim that the link between the imagination and social life is increasingly global and deterritorialized. Yet in fact Appadurai invokes technological change as the driving force responsible for the newly significant role of the imagination in the post-electronic world (Appadurai 1996: 5). In addition, his stress on deterritorialized flows and confident assertions that the nation state is on its last legs bear an eerie resemblance to Ohmae's corporate vision.

More generally, while deeply critical of Eurocentrism and the universalizing tendencies of economism, accounts of cultural globalization frequently (often implicitly) invoke markets and/or technology as the *deus ex machina* in ways not that different from the impact model. In an incisive critique of what he calls 'various discourses of "the post" ' Stuart Hall notes that 'what has resulted from the abandonment of deterministic economism has been, not alternative ways of thinking questions about economic relations and their effects, as the "conditions of existence" of other practices . . . but instead a gigantic and eloquent disavowal' (1996b: 258). Yet rather than just a disavowal of economic relations, I suggest, the abandonment of any understanding of determination has meant that a particularly crude and disabling form of economism tends to sneak in through the back door in accounts of cultural globalization.

Many proponents of cultural globalization also undermine their transgressive claims and aspirations by relying heavily on spatial metaphors. Kapur (1998: 192) offers a succinct account of pervasive spatial metaphors: 'A great deal of postcolonial cultural discourse overextrapolates on the idea of an "underlying world map" and treats it as some sort of semi-surreal terrain with interstitial spaces from which colonial/subaltern subjects work out sly strategies of complicity and subversion.' Jameson's influential account of the cultural logic of late capitalism invokes extravagant claims about the displacement of time and the spatialization of the temporal, and calls for a politics of cognitive mapping: 'In reality, nothing but a code word for "class consciousness" ' (Jameson 1991: 418). These and many other invocations of spatial metaphors exemplify precisely the problems to which Smith and Katz (1993) called attention – namely that, in order to ground social meaning, such metaphors rest on deeply problematic conceptions of space.

Relational conceptions of space-time and place outlined earlier make clear the dangers of reliance on spatial metaphors. In addition, they disrupt dualistic conceptions of 'the local' as passive recipient of – or transcended by – active, inexorable external forces, or as romanticized sites of resistance to 'the global.' They also sound strong warnings against imagining globalization simply or primarily in terms of deterritorialization, speed-up, and spaces of flows, and insist that such processes are the product of explicitly spatialized, power-laden practices at multiple levels, and must constantly be kept in tension with spatial reorganizations of social relations, and with the situated practices, and their associated discourses and power relations, through which such reorganizations (quite literally) take place.

The framework of multiple trajectories grapples explicitly with the economistic and core-centric elements of globalization models. It does so by combining these conceptions of spatiality with an historical – as opposed to an abstract – conception of determination, and with non-reductionist understandings of class. By insisting that we understand the multiplicity of historical geographies not simply as *effects* of global flows but as actively *constitutive* of them, it fundamentally disrupts impact models and opens the way for more politically enabling understandings. My central task in this book is to show concretely how these understandings help to steer a course between economism and voluntarism, illuminating possible terrains of practical action and the possibilities for alliances.

An Outline of the Book
The story I tell in this book unfolds in three parts, each comprising a tightly connected set of chapters. Part I (Forging Places) begins with a tour I took

through northwestern KwaZulu-Natal in 1994 that was formative in my decision to work in Ladysmith and Newcastle. Throughout this part of the book we move between the physical appearance of the regional landscape, and the locally differentiated, spatially-extended, and multi-layered practices, power-plays, and processes that have gone into its making.

Chapter 2 sketches the key contours of colonial power and agrarian transformation in the region from the mid-nineteenth to the mid-twentieth centuries that set the stage for dispossession in the apartheid era. In Chapter 3 we shift to a more finely grained focus on how dispossession played out in distinctive ways in the areas around Newcastle and Ladysmith and how, in turn, these processes played into divergent political dynamics in relocation townships. They encompass locally specific articulations of Zulu ethnic nationalism, as well as the distinctive (and distinctively gendered) character of oppositional youth movements in the two places, their differential connections with the liberation movement (both within South Africa and in exile), and how these struggles were reciprocally linked with locally specific forms of the resurgent labor movement and capital-labor relations.

Following these reverberations to other arenas, the action in Chapter 4 extends from the relocation townships to industrial landscapes and seats of local state power in the two towns. Here we will see how, since the late 1940s, white local government officials in Ladysmith and Newcastle competed fiercely with one another to lure industrial capitalists into their fiscal nets, drawing both on local resources and their connections into provincial and national offices of the state to assemble the bait. The volume and character of the catch shifted over time, swept into the region not only by changing waves of global capitalism but also the quantum of state-sponsored inducements for so-called border (and later bantustan) industries, as well as networks of connection into other sites. A particularly spectacular haul began in the mid-1980s, when more than 70 small-scale industrialists were drawn into Newcastle from Taiwan, bringing with them equipment that was rapidly becoming obsolete in Taiwan, as well as a clear set of understandings about what it meant to be a successful industrialist. By the early 1990s a significant group of them had established a satellite factory system, comprised of a series of small firms linked with one another – and with a large-scale Taiwanese yarn producer in Ladysmith – to manufacture cheap, brightly colored knitwear for the domestic market. On the surface, this network form of production appeared identical to that which drove the breakneck pace of decentralized industrialization in Taiwan. In practice, it proved socially explosive.

These conflicts form the point of departure for Part II (Transnational Trajectories). Chapter 5 locates Taiwanese industrialists in their own histories and their telling of these histories, and then traces the cultural politics of their engagements with white local government officials, black women workers, trade union officials and South African industrialists. Its purpose is to delve into how Taiwanese industrialists refashioned their everyday practices of accumulation when they moved to South Africa and how, in turn, their interactions were transformative of the conditions they encountered. What emerges is a vivid illustration of how the production of knitwear has simultaneously entailed the production of difference – in other words, race, ethnicity, and gender work in and through one another, and actively constitute class processes, the production of commodities, and the making of places.

Drawing mainly on the work of others, Chapter 6 charts additional comparative moves. First we follow a group of Taiwanese footwear producers to small towns in Fujian province in the southern coastal region of Mainland China – an expedition that further illustrates not only how the production of commodities simultaneously entails ongoing negotiations of meanings, definitions, and identities, but also their locally specific forms and dynamics. From there we move on to other regions of China where industries in small towns and villages are collectively owned and operated, and in at least some cases a large chunk of the surplus is retained and reinvested within local circuits.

These comparative moves not only illuminate the multi-layered power struggles that inflect divergent trajectories of rural industrialization. In addition, they pave the way for a broader argument about how the retention of peasant property – along with other state-sponsored subsidies securing the reproduction of the workforce – have been both underappreciated and central in defining the conditions of 'global competition' emanating from East Asia. Conversely they enable us to see how, when Taiwanese industrialists moved to South Africa, they unwittingly encountered a workforce stripped of subsistence guarantees and thrust into commodified forms of livelihood. More generally, histories of agrarian social property and power relations have played a central role in shaping locally and regionally specific trajectories of accumulation – and their legacies rever-berate in contemporary formations of the social wage. From the perspective of South African debates, these insights throw into sharp relief how the history of the agrarian question – along with its contemporary manifestation in limited and halting agrarian reforms – is intimately connected with the crisis of the local state in this era of neoliberal globalization.

Chapter 7 takes as its starting point this and other dimensions of the contradictory imperatives contained within the local state, and traces how they have been constituted and reworked in strikingly different ways in Ladysmith and Newcastle during the first phase of local government restructuring (1995–2000). The chapter ends with the 2000 local government elections based on a new system of demarcations that has, in effect, dissolved rural-urban boundaries – and brought us full-circle to confront the contemporary legacy of dispossession and displacement.

In Chapter 8 I return to the question of what it is about discourses of globalization that renders them so disabling, and what might be entailed in more politically enabling understandings. Mobilizing insights from the two intersecting axes of relational comparison – Ladysmith/Newcastle and South Africa/East Asia – I suggest how understandings cast in terms of multiple, interconnected trajectories of socio-spatial change can help to illuminate terrains of practical action, and point the way towards a politics of alliance.

Part I

Forging Places

CHAPTER 2

'The Land of our Comfort'
Regional Contours of Agrarian Transformation

If nations are, as Benedict Anderson has argued, 'imagined communities,' then countries are imagined geometries of landscape. South Africa, the country, is a geometry of conflict and accommodation, but above all it is a landscape ... Both White and Black people who call themselves Africans identify with the land, and claim it as their inalienable right. Both appeal to the blood that has been spilled on it, the dead that have been buried in it, the food that can be coaxed from it, and again and again, the beauty of it. The aesthetic beauty of the landscape is a political resource. (Thornton 1996: 153–154)

We have cherished our land with jealousy because of the presence of the ever running streams and innumerable springs with crystal clear waters ... Matiwane's Kop is the land of our comfort where we live creatively and peacefully. We cultivate all different kinds of vegetables that suit the climate. People who cannot find employment are able to make a living through land cultivation. (Memorandum prepared in 1980 by the people of Matiwane's Kop for presentation to the Minister of Co-operation and Development to protest their proposed removal.)

RATHER THAN ITS beauty, it is the blood spilled on it and the dead buried in it that define the landscape of northwestern KwaZulu-Natal in the imagination of most South Africans. Situated more or less in the center of the country, it is the site of a series of bloody conflicts over territory and control at key points during the nineteenth century and into the first decade of the twentieth. In promotional literature, regional and local authorities eagerly tout the 'Battlegrounds Route' as a major tourist attraction. Lacking much in the way of natural beauty, the region (or perhaps more accurately, those who run it) is trying to sell its history.

59

The Battlegrounds Route is also, quite literally, a battleground of meaning, on which the (re-)production of significant parts of South African history is at stake. In 1995, the Voortrekker Museum, supported by senior members of the National Party, proposed to build a 'medieval fortress with battlements, towers, and castellated gateways' (*Weekly Mail and Guardian*, February 2, 1995) to commemorate the Battle of Blood River at which Boer forces inflicted heavy losses on the Zulu army in 1838. The KwaZulu Monuments Council sharply opposed the plan, arguing that it would be politically dangerous for the Voortrekker Museum to go ahead with their plans without consulting other parties and ensuring that the process is 'people-driven.' The director of the Museum replied that in the new South Africa, the history of the Battle of Blood River would be viewed 'more objectively!'

Northwestern KwaZulu-Natal could also host a very different kind of historical tourism – one that traces out the history of forced removals and dispossession, which were particularly severe in this region. Maps 2 and 3 depict the patchwork of KwaZulu and Natal that defined the sub-region until April 1994. Between 1960 and 1991, according to the censuses, the population increased from 412,000 to over 1 million (Table 2.1). Yet during this period the number of people recorded as living in those pieces of the sub-region designated as Natal actually fell from 343,057 (83.3 percent of the total) to 293,726 (29.2 percent of the total), while KwaZulu's share of the sub-region's population rose from 68,852 (16.7 percent) to 716,490 (70.85 percent). Despite their spurious precision, these numbers testify to the intensity of removals in this area, the cruelty of which has been deeply etched into the landscape. Yet the landscape also bears traces of the limits of spatial engineering and capitalist expropriation, and the determined opposition to dispossession and displacement.

Instead of glossy pamphlets, prospective tourists would be handed a 572-page tome entitled *Forced Removals in South Africa: The SPP Reports, Vol. 4, Natal;* hereafter, I refer to it as SPP. Printed on yellowed sheets of coarse mimeograph paper in 1983, the Surplus People's Project (SPP) report represents an extraordinary research project launched in 1979 when a group of critical young academics and activists got together to document massive displacement and dispossession since the early 1960s.[1] In the Preface, the authors explain the genesis of the title in their initial presumption that people were being rendered surplus to the economy by the increasing capitalization of industry, agriculture, and mining. In the course

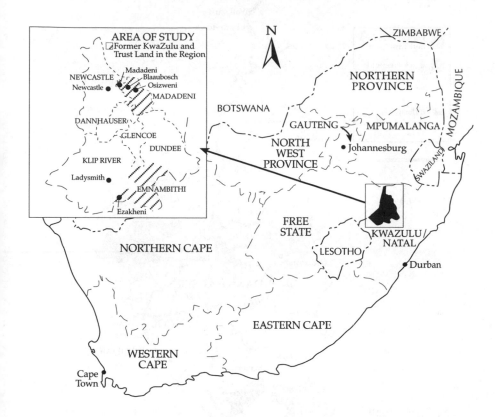

Map 2   Area of study in South Africa.

of their research, however, they came to see how some of the removals had 'a major political component to them' (SPP 1983: xv).

The 'removals tour' on which I was taken in October 1994 began in Matiwane's Kop, the 'land of our comfort' for which this chapter is named, 25 km north of Ladysmith. Matiwane's Kop is a long-established African freehold area whose residents managed to resist removal (Map 3). In the second half of the nineteenth century and the first decade of the twentieth century, Africans purchased large areas of land in this region from their colonial overlords. Through the first half of the twentieth century, African freehold farms in northwestern KwaZulu-Natal and elsewhere served as major catchment areas for huge numbers of people evicted from white-owned farms, as well as those evading the control of traditional authorities

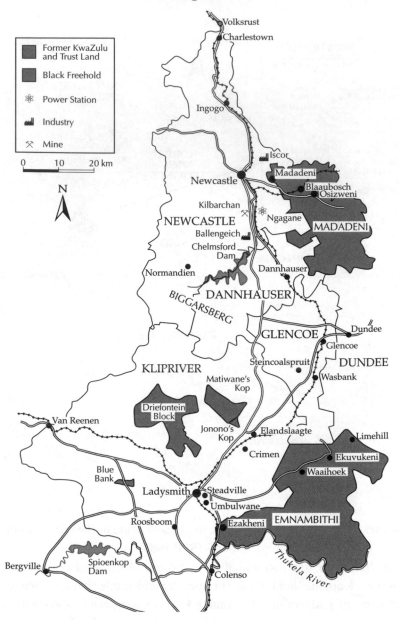

Map 3   Area of study in KwaZulu-Natal.

in the reserves. When functionaries of the apartheid state, operating in conjunction with white farmers, set out to eliminate '*die beswarting van die platteland*' (the blackening of the countryside) in the 1950s, they deployed the term 'black spot' to define freehold areas like Matiwane's Kop.

Table 2.1   Population distribution in northwestern KwaZulu-Natal, 1960–91.

	1960	1970	1980	1991
Natal districts				
Newcastle	47,673	45,342	55,690	53,584
Klip River (Ladysmith)	57,460	67,450	65,078	64,782
Other	237,924	257,163	256,081	175,360
Total northwestern Natal	**343,057**	**369,955**	**376,849**	**293,726**
	(83.3%)	*(68.3%)*	*(46.5%)*	*(29.1%)*
KwaZulu districts				
Madadeni	16,568	73,659	207,002	313,888
Emnambithi	33,897	67,579	155,863	205,639
Other	18,387	30,763	70,596	196,963
Total northwestern KwaZulu	**68,852**	**172,001**	**433,461**	**716,490**
	(16.7%)	*(31.7%)*	*(53.5%)*	*(70.9%)*
Total northwestern KwaZulu-Natal	**411,909**	**541,956**	**810,310**	**1,010,216**
	(100%)	*(100%)*	*(100%)*	*(100%)*

Source: Population Census Reports

Most of the people in Matiwane's Kop are poor by urban standards, and commute to Ladysmith and other places to earn a living. Yet the sense of community and historical attachment to the place so clearly conveyed in the memorandum protesting the proposed removal seem immediately evident to a visitor to Matiwane's Kop. The houses are substantial – some quite elegant wattle and daub structures – and widely scattered over a green landscape. On the Sunday afternoon in October 1994 when I visited, plots of land were plowed ready for planting, people sat around chatting under trees or on porches, and there was a lively soccer game underway. One's immediate impression was of a vibrant and viable community.

A survey conducted by the SPP in the early 1980s confirms these superficial impressions. At that time, the population of Matiwane's Kop was over 12,000 people living on 3,300 hectares of land. Although agricultural production formed a very small proportion of total income, the survey documented the many ways in which access to land contributed to livelihood and community. Despite generally low incomes, the diets of Matiwane's Kop residents were substantially better than those of people who had been removed to relocation settlements. Another interesting finding was that access to land meant that the orientation of workers was urban rather than rural – people living in Matiwane's Kop were able to avoid becoming agricultural workers on white-owned farms, despite their location in a white farming area. About 60 percent of the workers in the SPP sample had jobs in towns within the sub-region. Children in Matiwane's Kop attended local schools, including a high school completed in 1981 that was built and financed almost entirely by local community enterprise (SPP 1983: 453).

As soon as the structure was completed, officials appeared and painted numbers on the walls – the sign of impending removals. During the previous year, landowners were expropriated and their titles transferred to the state. The story of how Matiwane's Kop and surrounding freehold communities managed to resist dispossession occupies a prominent place in the history of removals. As the SPP (1983: 457) pointed out, Matiwane's Kop acquired a useful reputation of militancy; this and the adroit manner in which community opposition was mobilized encouraged other threatened communities in the area to take a stronger position. Documentary evidence testifies to this intransigence, including the following statement by the leadership of the Matiwane's Kop campaign published in the *Natal Witness* November 22, 1980:

> The Minister has promised that people will not be moved against their will. None of the people at Jonono's or Matiwane's Kop want to move. We intend to carry on as we always have done. They will have to bring guns to push us out or bury us here.

In a more recent recounting of local history, one of the authors of this statement described to me his simultaneous positioning in the chieftancy and in the union movement.

What might also not be immediately evident in a brief visit is the social differentiation within Matiwane's Kop between landowners and tenants, as well as between supporters of the ANC and IFP. Many present and former landowners in freehold areas – including many of those claiming restitution of land rights – are descendants of a highly educated and frequently quite prosperous agricultural and trading class that emerged in the second half of the nineteenth century. They also formed the backbone of the Natal Native Congress at the turn of the century, one of the precursors of the African National Congress. The political identifications and activities of this landowning class have been complex and varied including, as we shall see, the active role of leading representatives in the deployment of Zulu ethnic nationalism and the formation of the first Inkatha in the 1920s.

To leverage and facilitate removals, apartheid officials frequently played on conflicts of interest between landowners and tenants, particularly those related to rent payments. In nearby Jonono's Kop, for example, officials in Ladysmith tried to use a dispute between a particular landowner and his tenant to foment dissent within the community more generally; basically, they informed tenants that they no longer owed rent, since landowners had been expropriated (SPP 1983: 455). Partly through the intervention of leaders from Matiwane's Kop and local KwaZulu officials, the rift was avoided. In other freehold communities, agents of the apartheid state were quite successful in driving a rift between landlords and tenants, or in the exercise of naked force. More generally, local struggles over removals in the sub-region assumed widely different forms that continue to reverberate in contemporary local politics.

From Matiwane's Kop we traveled east to Limehill, where the brutality of forced removals was clearly evident more than 25 years after people were first moved there in 1968. Limehill is part of a block of land purchased by the South African Development Trust in the 1960s, and defined as part of KwaZulu for purposes of relocating people from 'black spots' and white-owned farms. White farmers in this region adamantly opposed the expansion of the reserves: 'Zululand is their territory, and it is no injustice to send them there,' declared the chairman of the Ladysmith Joint Bodies Association, which represented all the local farmers' associations plus the Ladysmith Town Council. In 1955, the same man admitted that land subsequently purchased by the Trust in the 1960s was 'arid and totally unsuitable for human settlement . . . ' (SPP 1983: 5).

He was right. Limehill in the mid-1990s was a vast, desolate, dusty-gray settlement, extending as far as the eye could see. Its situation within a rainshadow makes any sort of cultivation impossible, and the visual contrast with Matiwane's Kop was dramatic. Apart from a few odd shops, there was no evident source of livelihood. Limehill is in effect a distant township of Ladysmith, but with virtually none of the material and social resources of the freehold areas to the west. The road into Ladysmith was only paved in the early 1990s; until then, people moved back and forth over the 55 km separating them from the town on a rutted dirt road.

The road from Limehill to Ladysmith passes through Ekuvukeni, another resettlement township originally set up in 1972 when 20,000 people were moved from Crimen, Ruigtefontein, and Steincoalspruit – all 'black spots' near the tiny town of Wasbank. The first arrivals were provided with minute tin houses (known as fletcraft), bucket system toilets, and some water taps in the street. Although only 5 km down the road from Limehill, it was visually quite different. Limehill sprawled, but Ekuvukeni had the appearance of a classic, highly regulated township with boundaries sharply drawn by military access roads. Some of the houses were quite substantial, and there had clearly been far more investment in public facilities than in Limehill. Surrounded by hills that conveniently shield the blight of Limehill, Ekuvukeni was the kind of place where apartheid planners could take visitors.

Also in the vicinity of Ekuvukeni is Waaihoek, in the middle of a barren piece of veld off the main road, and reachable only on a rudimentary dirt track. Since the mid-1980s people had been moving into Waaihoek, mainly labor tenants displaced from farms in the Weenen district to the south. Labor tenancy is a crucial piece of the history of this region of KwaZulu-Natal, as are massive evictions from white-owned farms that continued well into the 1990s. In the mid-1990s, people were living in tiny regulation tin shacks packed one on top of the other, not much bigger than the toilets provided in site and service schemes. Apart from a small vegetable patch, there was no sign of anything green in Waaihoek when I visited there after the spring rains. It appeared a place of utter desolation. In a landscape of brutality, Waaihoek stood out as the most cruel of all. Local people called it *intshela* – the burnt bit left at the bottom of a pot of maize-meal porridge.[2]

From Waaihoek we drove southwest to Ezakheni, yet another resettlement township, but very closely linked to the formerly white town of Ladysmith, about 15 km away. Ezakheni is what a Bantu Affairs Department general circular issued in 1967 described as a 'self-contained Bantu town' or 'type a' settlement, explicitly designed 'to rehouse former municipal townships and provide accommodation for workers and their families in border industries' (SPP 1983: 59). In practice, many residents of the municipal township of Steadville and the adjacent settlement of Umbulwane managed to evade removal. Despite a few shops, a teachers' training college, a clinic, a post office, and offices for local government officials, Ezakheni in the mid-1990s was a huge, largely tree-less agglomeration of houses ranging from a few fairly substantial suburban villas belonging to local councilors, traders, and professionals, to a much larger array of small, township-style houses and shacks of various descriptions. The Ezakheni industrial estate, situated on the road to Ladysmith about 5 km from the residential area, was constructed in 1980 as one of the showpiece projects of the industrial decentralization thrust. As we drove quite quickly through Ezakheni, my tour hosts told of the intense violence that had wracked the township since the late 1980s and became particularly intense in the period leading up to the 1994 elections.

From Ezakheni we drove north, passing through coalfields that were for many years one of the main sources of economic activity in the region, although many are now defunct. Cutting across swaths of dry savannah interrupted by the soft green rolling hills of the Biggarsberg to the south of Glencoe and Dundee, the road forks off to a number of the famous battlegrounds. Before reaching Newcastle, it branches off 15–20 km to Madadeni and Osizweni – two relocation townships established in the 1960s – as well as to Blaaubosch, an old African freehold area that escaped removal by being situated in a designated part of the KwaZulu bantustan. Like Ezakheni, Madadeni was defined as a 'type a' settlement, and a recipient of relatively high subsidies from the KwaZulu government. Osizweni's endowments of official resources were clearly more limited. Yet they appeared similarly bleak and residential, despite the presence of an industrial estate in Madadeni (very much smaller than its counterpart in Ezakheni), as well as a large hospital and teachers' training college.[3] According to census statistics, the population of the Madadeni district (including Madadeni township, Osizweni, Blaaubosch, and surrounding areas of former KwaZulu) was 313,888 in 1991; that of the Emnambithi district (which includes Limehill, Ekuvukeni, Waaihoek, and Ezakheni) was 205,639 (Table 2.1). While Ladysmith-Ezakheni is smaller than Newcastle and its adjacent townships, a visitor would be struck by the similar racial geographies: in both places, the large black township complexes are separated from the former white towns by swaths of empty land stretching for 15–20 km – the so-called 'buffer zones' that apartheid spatial engineers delimited with military precision and, no doubt, intent.

From one perspective, the landscape traversed in the removals tour can be seen as a regional variant on a national theme of dispossession and displacement of huge numbers of black South Africans to densely packed areas defined as bantustans, many of them some distance from main urban centers. In a widely cited set of estimates, Simkins (1983) calculated that the percentage of the black South African population on white-owned farms declined from 31.3 in 1960 to 20.6 in 1980; those living in what were classified 'white' urban areas fell from 29.6 to 26.7 percent; and Africans living within the borders of bantustans grew from 4.2 million in 1960 (39 percent of all Africans) to over 11 million in 1980 (52.7 percent). Farm evictions continued apace during the 1980s. Between 1980 to 1985, according to Simkins' more recent estimates, some 1.6 million black South Africans disappeared from rural 'white' South Africa.[4]

Massive agglomerations of population within former bantustan borders, produced by farm evictions and removals from freehold land, defy conventional rural and urban categories. Simkins (1983) euphemistically called them 'closer settlements,' Murray (1988) used the term 'displaced urbanization' as well as 'rural slums,' Bradford (1987) called them 'rural ghettoes,' and Hindson (1987) coined the term 'quasi-urban' settlements to underscore the absence of an agrarian base. Alan Mabin (1989) makes the point that any labeling exercise obscures a wide array of conditions, some of which we touched upon in our quick tour through northwestern KwaZulu-Natal: 'They vary from places which are urban only in the negative sense that they are not primarily agricultural and have fairly high densities, to almost-urban areas with a modicum of services . . . and their geographical location varies from fairly close proximity to city centres . . . to hundreds of kilometres from the metropolitan cores' (Mabin 1989: 10; see also Soni and Maharaj 1991).

What united these diverse places during the apartheid era was their subjection to bantustan authorities – a mode of rule that Mahmood Mamdani (1996) terms 'decentralized despotism.' In a nutshell, Mamdani argues that the shift from segregation to apartheid following the National Party's electoral victory in 1948 entailed two simultaneous moves aimed at containing the escalation of urban protest: the reorganization of the apparatus of 'native control' in both the reserves and urban townships; and forced removals to shift the African population to rural areas and incorporate them into systems of customary rule. In the era of segregation, though mediated through chiefs and headmen, the administration of the reserves was centralized under the Native Affairs Department (NAD); in urban areas, white municipal authorities effectively regulated the entry, housing, and employment of Africans. Under apartheid, Hendrik Verwoerd's newly formed Bantu Affairs Department (BAD) took over the administration of townships from urban municipalities. At the same time, the Bantu Authorities Act of 1951 and Bantu Laws Amendment Act of 1952 removed the NAD from the reserves, while elaborating the system of tribal authorities and enhancing the powers of the chieftancy. Thus, Mamdani maintains, the architects of apartheid finally caught on to the secret of colonial control in the rest of Africa – indirect rule – the groundwork for which had been laid in British colonial Natal in the nineteenth century: 'From the native point of view, apartheid combined a decentralized despotism (indirect rule) in the rural reserves with a centralized despotism (direct rule) in urban areas' (Mamdani 1996: 101). Hence also the bifurcation of power along urban-rural lines, with an increasingly organized urban civil society taking shape on the one side, and a stagnant rural decentralized despotism, 'guarded over by the Native Authority' (Mamdani 1996: 61), retaining its hold on the other. The key challenge of the post-apartheid era, Mamdani argues, lies in linking the rural and the urban; and the central problem is that the pro-democracy movement 'lacks a program for linking the urban and the rural on the basis of democratizing rural power' (Mamdani 1996: 297).

In practice, I suggest, the processes through which millions of black South Africans were uprooted from the land in rural 'white' South Africa and brought under the sway of bantustan authorities was not just a matter of their incorporation into regimes of decentralized despotism. What's crucial, rather, are the complex, divergent local histories of contest, alliance, and acquiescence through which political subjects (and indeed citizens, *pace* Mamdani) have been constituted through experiences of – and struggles over – dispossession and displacement. The politics of dispossession have, in turn, played into the active processes of place-making through which relocation townships have taken shape in strikingly different ways. These processes, in turn, carry vitally important implications for social change. Rather than just variations on a theme of decentralized despotism, divergent local dynamics underscore how politics cannot be read off institutional structures.

They also point to the limits of surface appearances. A close reading of the SPP report might suggest clues as to how removals and resistance to them took shape in quite distinct ways in the areas around Ladysmith and Newcastle. Yet even the most assiduous and observant tourist would be unlikely to discern how contention over land and property rights has given rise to very different forms of township politics in Madadeni (Newcastle) and Ezakheni (Ladysmith); how these in turn have intersected with struggles in the workplace and in other institutional arenas both local and translocal; and how these multi-layered struggles continue to reverberate and shape contemporary dynamics. In short, former bantustan townships that appear on the surface as remarkably uniform products of apartheid spatial engineering and the imposition of decentralized despotism have, in practice, emerged as highly differentiated – and differentially contentious – sites of social interaction.

In the remainder of this chapter, I draw mainly on secondary sources to highlight (1) colonial processes of dispossession and land acquisition through which a large proportion of the rural African population came to be located *outside* the reserves in Natal, the incubator of indirect rule; (2) the regionally specific forms through which agrarian capitalism took hold in northwestern Natal in the first half of the twentieth century, the character of popular protest, and the regional dimensions of the national liberation movement's general neglect of the politics of the agrarian question; and (3) the central role of the disaffected African landowning class in the formation of Zulu ethnic nationalism in the 1920s and 1930s. These themes bear directly on regionally and locally specific dynamics of dispossession and displacement under apartheid.

Dispossession and Land Acquisition in Colonial Natal

> It is a myth that apartheid is the exclusive product of Afrikaner nationalism: its antecedents are to be found in Natal rather than in any of the other provinces. (Welsh 1971: 322)

In *The Roots of Segregation* (1971), David Welsh first called attention to the importance of the Shepstone system of land reservations and codifications of customary law in British colonial Natal in providing the template for twentieth-century segregation and apartheid, as well as indirect rule more generally. As Diplomatic Agent to the 'Native Tribes' of Natal, Theophilus Shepstone demarcated African 'locations' or reserves between 1848 and 1864, and placed a layer of British judicial and administrative machinery on top of pre-colonial African institutions (Etherington 1989: 172). Indirect rule found further expression in the Natal Code of Native Law first promulgated in 1878, and then elaborated and made legally binding in 1891.

Shula Marks warns against viewing the Shepstone system of land reservations and 'native law' as the unilateral exercise of colonial domination; it was a reflection rather, she argues, of the relative weakness of a colonial state seeking both to gain access to African labor and to control 'the still pulsating remains of powerful African kingdoms' (Marks 1986: 5).[5] Carolyn Hamilton (1998) carries this argument further, calling attention to how colonial discourse embodied in the Shepstone system was not just the imposition of 'invented traditions':

> In contrast to the charge that imperial agents 'sought, methodically, to "make history" for those who lacked it; to induct those people into an order of activities and values; to impart form to an Africa that was seen as formless; to reduce the chaos of savage life to the rational structures and techniques that, for the Europeans, were both the vehicle and the proof of their own civilization,' Shepstone adopted the history of the people whom he sought to dominate, molding his arguments to carefully selected aspects of its form and logic . . . So much form did he discern in the Zulu kingdom and in Zulu history that he sought to adapt it to his own purposes. (C. Hamilton 1998: 99)

Likewise, Thornton (1995) points to Shepstone's attempts at mutual incorporation as outright domination:

> Although formally designated a Native Agent, Shepstone understood his role in African terms, and was accepted by many Zulu as a chief in the indigenous idiom. In fact, each had captured aspects of the powers of the other's polity . . . Unable to establish unambiguous domination in any sphere, it was necessary to reify peoples and pursue strategies of alliance and accommodation with them and with the powers they were taken to possess. (Thornton 1995: 209)

Indirect rule emerged in the context of deep divisions within British colonial society in Natal about the form colonial exploitation and surplus extraction should take, and which fraction of capital would be the principal beneficiary. Many settlers sharply opposed the Shepstone system, which they saw as a threat to their capacity to mobilize African labor: 'The Shepstone system annoyed the colonists precisely because it inhibited the imposition of a work ethic, monogamy, a need for clothing, commodities, and civilization' (C. Hamilton 1998: 99). A commission of inquiry into the 'Past and Present State of Kafirs in the District of Natal' in 1852–53, on which landowning settlers were strongly represented, alleged that the size of the reserves enabled Africans 'to follow idle, wandering, and pastoral lives or habits, instead of settling down to fixed industrial pursuits' (cited by Welsh 1971: 34).[6] Representing the majority of colonists, Lieutenant-Governor Pine (1850–55) recommended that the 'enormous and unwieldy' reserves proposed by

Shepstone be divided into smaller ones, a form of individual tenure introduced, the power of the chiefs be broken down, and polygyny abolished. In her brilliant disquisition on how popular fiction of the time – specifically Rider Haggard's *King Solomon's Mines* – illuminates colonial discourse and the deployment of patriarchy, Anne McClintock (1995) observes that black women in Natal became the ground over which white men fought black men for control of land and labor:

> [C]olonial documents readily reveal that the assault on polygyny was an assault on African habits of labor that withheld from the resentful farmers the work of black men and women. The excess labor that a black man controlled through his wives was seen as a direct and deadly threat to the profits of the settlers. As Governor Pine complained, 'How can a Englishman with one pair of hands compete with a native with five to twenty slave wives?' (McClintock 1995: 254)

The Colonial Office backed the Shepstone system, which it saw as more likely to keep the peace than outright expropriation that might provoke rebellion among the indigenous population. For colonial administrators operating under imperatives of nineteenth-century economic liberalism, Shepstone's 'makeshift arrangement' was also very attractive from a fiscal point of view. In addition to reservations, the Shepstone system of 'Native administration' provided channels for revenue collection that were, from the viewpoint of the colonial exchequer, a resounding success. Taxes imposed on Africans – including a hut tax (in effect, a tax on polygyny), a variety of fees and levies, and high customs duties on commodities consumed mainly by Africans – formed the largest source of colonial revenue (Lambert 1995). While Africans suffered taxation without representation, as Etherington (1989: 175) has noted, white settlers enjoyed representation virtually without taxation.

By 1864, approximately 2.25 million acres in over 40 locations had been defined as reserves for African occupation (Brookes and Hurwitz 1957: 11). Significantly, there were no reserves established in the triangle of Natal between the Thukela and the Buffalo Rivers – the present day northwestern KwaZulu-Natal and a stronghold of stock farming. White stock farmers in northwestern Natal were particularly vociferous in their opposition to the Shepstone system, claiming that reserves were 'natural strongholds' from which Zulu armies 'could sweep the country in a single night and return with their plunder' (cited by Marks 1970: 16). Missionaries were accommodated through the establishment of Mission Reserves, whose lands they could allocate to Christian converts.[7] In 1864, the Mission Reserves totaled 144,192 acres. Over the next 90 years, the total area of the government reserves or ('locations') and Mission Reserves in Natal remained effectively unchanged (Table 2.2).[8]

By the early 1880s, according to Bundy (1988: 170), only about 40 percent of the African population of Natal, numbering approximately 374,000, was living in the reserves; 162,000 were renting land owned by white settlers and land speculation companies based in Britain, another 43,000 were renting Crown land, and a much smaller group were acquiring private property rights in land. More than 5 million of the 6 million acres owned by whites were in the hands of absentee proprietors, for whom rent extraction from African tenants was the chief source of revenue (Bundy 1988: 170).

Table 2.2   Area of locations and Mission Reserves in Natal, 1864–1953.

Year	Locations*		Mission Reserves	
	Number	*Acres*	*Number*	*Acres*
1864	**	2,262,066	**	144,192
1882	42	2,067,057	21	174,862
1905	42	2,192,568	17	127,211
1913	48	2,267,632	19	146,571
1953	48	2,267,632	19	146,571

Source: Brookes and Hurwitz (1957) Table 1, p. 11
Notes: * Excluding Zululand (see note 8); ** Not given

What emerges most dramatically from these figures is the dominance of a *rentier* economy closely linked, as Slater (1975) has shown, to British finance capital. Prominent among these colonial landowners was the Natal Land and Colonization Company, which brought together London financiers and speculators who had acquired land cheaply in the early 1840s following the collapse of the Voortrekker Republic of Natalia. Initially these and other colonial merchant-speculators pinned their hopes on white immigration, but by the 1850s concluded that 'the key to wealth lay in exploiting Natal's existing rural economy based on African producers rather than awaiting a transformation of the colonial sector, which showed little sign of coming about through the free play of market forces' (Slater 1975: 263). The colonial state defended the right of white absentee landlords to extract rent from African producers while, at the same time, supporting the embryonic capitalist agricultural sector – most notably, after 1860, by introducing indentured labor from India to work on sugar plantations (Richardson 1986). *Rentier* capital dominated the colonial economy of Natal through most of the second half of the nineteenth century, and it was only at the end of the century that the social and political balance of forces shifted decisively in favor of white capitalist agriculture – along with moves to close down African alternatives to working for white employers.

Both Bundy (1988) and Lambert (1995) document the substantial growth of African commercial crop production in nineteenth-century Natal. Money earned through supplying agricultural commodities to colonial markets enabled Africans to pay rents and taxes, and buy goods on which the high customs charges mentioned earlier were levied (Etherington 1989: 175). Yet the 'African peasantry' was highly differentiated, and the substantial growth of African commercial crop production in nineteenth-century Natal took place under a variety of conditions and compulsions:

> In colonial Natal . . . there were great differences between African cultivators who were labour tenants and those who paid rent; between westernized *kholwa* and the predominantly subsistence cultivators of the reserves. The term ['peasant'] remains useful . . . only if it is accepted that there was no single peasantry in Natal, but rather a number of different peasantries. Most were petty commodity producers, but their relationship to the colonial economy differed according to the terms under which they had access to land and resources. (Lambert 1995: 5)

For purposes of the present study, particular significance attaches to a small but prominent class of African landowners, who formed an important presence in the areas around Ladysmith and Newcastle. The African petty bourgeoisie in Natal originates from this group of early converts to Christianity (the *kholwa* or believers), whom Marks (1986: 45) terms 'the despised, the disparaged, and the disaffected, drawn to the mission stations by the prospects of land and security.' In the second half of the nineteenth century, Natal was one of the most heavily evangelized regions on earth (Etherington 1978). Prohibited by the Zulu aristocracy from operating in Zululand, missionaries focused their efforts on Natal where Shepstone provided them with fairly substantial reserves. The area around Ladysmith became a particularly important base of *kholwa* settlement. In 1867 a group of 30 to 40 men from the Edendale Wesleyan Mission outside Pietermaritzburg banded together in a syndicate to buy the Driefontein block north of Ladysmith, and subsequently some adjoining farms. They became the core of a much larger *kholwa* community in the district, many of them with strong connections to numerous missions in and around Ladysmith. Missionary activity was far more limited in Newcastle, where Africans' access to land appears to have been more difficult. By the end of the 1880s there were only about 10,000 *kholwa* in the Natal colony out of a total African population of some 350,000 (Morrell et al. 1996: 43); yet their economic and political influence was profound.

Many *kholwa* actively identified with mid-Victorian bourgeois liberalism and discourses of progress, distancing themselves from the African traditionalism and chiefly authority deployed through the Shepstone system. Their collaboration with the imperial order became starkly evident during the Anglo-Zulu War of 1879, when men from the Driefontein settlement outside Ladysmith fought on the British side. In addition to defining themselves as loyal subjects of Queen Victoria, large numbers of *kholwa* became actively engaged in accumulation. On the mission stations of Natal, Christianity went hand in hand with commerce and the promotion of private property. Along with education and Christian piety, missionaries encouraged and facilitated African acquisition of freehold land (Etherington 1989). Many *kholwa* responded with alacrity, purchasing land and entering colonial markets as agricultural producers, as well as traders, transport riders, and artisans. Many not only prospered, but also posed sharp competition to white farmers, particularly in maize production. White farmers' complaints about African competition were especially marked in the area around Ladysmith and Newcastle:

> When an 'Old Colonist' advised 'New Settlers' the book he edited contained notes on farming in different areas of the colony and several of these bore eloquent witness to what white colonists perceived as their own competitive weakness. The editor himself commented upon the low prices for grain, and the production of maize by Africans: 'their herds are so numerous, their own fields so prolific,' he complained, that they did not readily enter service. From Ladysmith came a long grumble by a farmer who explained why colonists there could not raise enough crops: he blamed foreign competition, inadequate transport facilities and the climate, but the district was one in which Africans on missions, on white-owned farms and on farms purchased by syndicates of peasants raised foodstuffs, and this was obviously an important factor. In Newcastle district, too, white colonists found that 'stock-breeding is more easy and more certain in its results than agriculture': and this in a district where many 'white' farms were entirely occupied by African crop producers. Moreover, explained Mr J. Scobie (who wrote the Newcastle section), 'Whereas the average produce of mealies per acre under white management is but five muids, the kafirs absolutely produce six muids to the acre!'(Bundy 1988: 178)

In Natal as a whole, Africans owned 12,357 acres of land in 1870 – a figure that had grown to nearly 400,000 acres by 1910 (Table 2.3). A significant proportion of this land was in northwestern Natal, where land was relatively cheap and there were no reserves. By 1890, for example, 40 percent of land in private African ownership in Natal was in the Klip River Division (Christopher 1969). Regulations promulgated in 1880 made it possible for the public to purchase Crown lands at low prices on extended credit (Lambert 1989: 378). In northern Natal, the only extensive Crown lands were in the vicinity of Newcastle. The colonial government actively encouraged Africans to tender, but some white farmers (presumably ranchers) strongly opposed African acquisition of Crown land: 'In the Newcastle division some thirty-two plots of Crown Land were bought by Africans, but (wrote the magistrate) "European farmers, especially the Dutch, are, as a rule, very much opposed to the Natives being allowed to acquire land in any form; and it is easy enough for Europeans to throw obstacles in the way of the natives" ' (cited by Bundy 1988: 182).

Table 2.3   African and church land ownership in Natal, 1870–1910.

Year	African	Church
1870	12,357	35,786
1880	62,012	66,629
1890	206,719	105,930
1900	395,113	129,992
1910	397,754	134,450

Source: SPP (1983) Table 2, p. 27

Through most of Natal, African agricultural producers found themselves in an increasingly embattled position as the predominantly *rentier* economy of the nineteenth century gave way to the development of white capitalist agriculture and intensified struggles over land and labor. The amount of land on white farms on which crops were reaped jumped from 23,387 hectares in 1882 to 46,787 in 1895 to 166,642 in 1909 (Lambert 1989: 383). White settlers more than doubled in numbers between 1891 and 1904 from 46,000 to 97,000 (Marks 1970: 6), with many of the new arrivals clamoring for land. Economic transformation was accompanied by a major shift in the locus and composition of political power when Britain granted the colony responsible government in 1893. Natal came under the rule of elected representatives of white colonists with an electoral system that favored rural areas, and control of the political economy shifted away from *rentier* interests who had a stake in the capacity of independent African production and into the hands of what Slater (1975: 276) describes as 'a burgeoning class of commercial farmers and its allies.' The new Natal parliament was openly hostile to African agricultural production, and moved quickly to stifle it and ensure a steady supply of labor (Guest 1989). In 1895 the taxes paid by tenants on Crown lands were doubled, and a number of new levies and fees imposed on Africans. The tax burden became even more onerous with the imposition of a poll tax in 1905 that ignited what came to be called the 'Bhambatha rebellion.'[9]

Major new restrictions on African land acquisition also appeared: between 1903 and 1905 individual purchases in Mission Reserves were prohibited, and the Lands Department was instructed to refuse bids for Crown lands from Africans. African agriculture was dealt a further blow by a series of devastating environmental disasters. Between 1897–98, virulent cattle disease destroyed over 80 percent of the herds owned by Africans and hence a huge proportion of their assets, since cattle represent a major store of wealth in Nguni society. Drought and pestilence also took their toll on white agriculture, but reserves of capital and access to credit enabled white farmers to deal with the crises in ways that were impossible for the majority of African producers. By the first decade of the twentieth century, many Africans were paying interest rates of 600–800 percent (Lambert 1989: 386), and conditions of labor tenancies had in general become far harsher. Crop devastation and cattle losses meant that negligible wages were often the only source of income for labor tenants; at the same time, the increased burden of taxes and imperatives of food purchases resulted in widespread indebtedness that white farmers then used to extract repayment in labor (Lambert 1989: 387). Faced with diminishing access to land and increasingly harsh terms of labor tenancies, large numbers of people sought refuge on African freehold land. By the early twentieth century, many African landowners were shifting from agricultural production to taking on rent-paying tenants, and freehold land increasingly came to play the role of a catchment for people dispossessed of land elsewhere.

The Natives Land Act, passed by the new Union parliament in 1913 and aimed at restricting African production outside the reserves, gave official backing to what had been happening for some time in Natal as well as in other provinces. The 1913 Land Act delimited reserves in the country as a whole, and made land acquisition outside their boundaries subject to the approval of the Governor-General-in-Council – permission which, as Brookes and Hurwitz (1957: 13) note, was not readily given. It confirmed the reserves in Natal and Zululand as they stood (see Table 2.2), but excluded most of the existing African freehold land from areas defined as reserves. In principle, the Act outlawed rent tenancy or sharecropping by Africans outside the reserves. In practice, it left open a number of loopholes favorable to *rentier* interests. In Natal and the Transvaal, only new arrangements became illegal; existing ones could be renewed (Slater 1975: 280).

Many analysts identify the 1913 Land Act as a decisive watershed in the development of capitalist agriculture – a process initiated by the mineral discoveries of the late nineteenth century that, in turn, created a domestic market for agriculture. Morris (1976), for example, viewed the 1913 Land Act as a victory for Boer landlords that cemented a Prussian path of agrarian transition in South Africa. Both he and Bundy (1979) maintain that the Act signaled the end of African peasant production, and reinforced labor tenancy as the dominant relation of exploitation in agriculture. By the 1980s growing numbers of historians were calling into question efforts to develop general models of agrarian transition, focusing instead on finely grained local and regional histories.[10] A number of these studies documented the widespread persistence of cash tenancy and sharecropping well into the twentieth century, as well as the tenacity with which African peasant producers in different parts of the country held on to that status. Either implicitly or explicitly they cast doubt on claims that the 1913 Land Act brought peasant production to an abrupt halt, and insist on far more complex, varied, and uneven processes of agrarian transition.[11]

In an incisive assessment and summation of these debates, Helen Bradford (1990) maintains that it is impossible to cram the transition to capitalist agriculture into the 40-odd years after the mineral discoveries, and unhelpful to presume that it followed in an automatic fashion from the establishment of internal markets. Labor power still had to become a commodity, and this often entailed bitter, extended, and deeply racialized – as well as gendered – conflicts. Rather than a specific turning point, agrarian capitalism took hold through spatially uneven processes that were often prolonged and fiercely contested.

Holding Out for the Land: Regional Accumulation and Agrarian Politics

> Many prominent and progressive farmers have already endeavoured to introduce a system of cash wages in lieu of land, but without success . . . the Native holds out for a piece of land which he may call his own. (Neveling 1931 cited by Harris 1994: 248)

In contrast to the lush semi-tropical coastal regions and the misty rolling hills of the Natal Midlands, nature has imposed quite harsh limits on human efforts to wrest livelihood and profits from the soil of northwestern Natal – and has also played into the shaping of agrarian social relations. Much of the northern interior of the province is dominated by medium-quality grassland, but cultivation is limited by scorching summers and lack of rain in winters that are often bitterly cold by South African standards.[12] In large swaths of the region, extensive stock farming has long been the dominant activity. The generally harsh environment and distance from the main centers of colonial settlement also meant that land was relatively cheap. A high proportion of white ranchers were Free State and Transvaal farmers who had acquired farms in northwestern Natal for winter grazing and as a source of labor. By the turn of the century, the majority of Africans living in northern Natal were resident on white-owned farms under various forms of absentee ownership (Harris 1994). Africans who had acquired freehold rights through land purchase constituted the second major group.

Nature's limited endowment of agriculture in the region has been compensated to some degree by rich coal seams. The rapid expansion of gold mining on the Witwatersrand pulled the coal industry along in its wake – particularly after 1895, with the completion of the railway line linking Durban to Johannesburg via Ladysmith and Newcastle (Guest 1989). Wealthy Natal sugar barons were among those who invested in the coal industry, and this alliance of sugar and coal in turn spearheaded the transformation of the *rentier* colonial economy (Lambert and Morrell 1996). Much of the wealth generated by coal was siphoned from northwestern Natal. Yet expansion of the regional economy generated by the railway and coal mining, combined with the continuing backwardness of white agriculture, created conditions in which many Africans were able to retain a hold on the land and evade being pressed into labor service or wage labor to a greater degree than in other parts of Natal.

In the mid-1890s, for example, some African farmers with accumulated capital weathered the crisis in agriculture, and some even managed to continue to acquire land. Many were located in Klip River County around Ladysmith, Newcastle, and Dundee, where white agriculture remained backward and where there was already a high proportion of *kholwa*-owned land. In addition, as the railway pushed northwards and coalfields opened in the mid-1890s, there was growing demand for produce in the towns that few white farmers could meet: 'Despite the continuing opposition of stockfarmers, *kholwa* syndicates were steadily increasing their land purchases, and were taking advantage of the more favorable opportunities created by the extension of the railway' (Lambert 1995: 117). In Natal as a whole the amount of land privately owned by Africans decreased between 1916 and 1926, while the number of people on it increased from 39,000 to 81,000 (Marks 1986: 65). Yet the situation continued to be different in northern Natal, where the extent of African-owned land increased in the same period (Lambert and Morrell 1996: 73). Marks cites a representative of the Klip River Agricultural Society in 1917 who claimed that 'Natives will go the [land] sales and buy in such a way that no Europeans will be able to buy . . . Two hundred may find the money, but only one need buy the farm' (Marks 1986: 50). Some of the land purchased after 1913 was bought by syndicates organized by chiefs for communal occupation as protection against proletarianization; *kholwa* purchasers, even those who formed syndicates, saw this land as the basis for accumulation (Marks 1986: 50).

In northern Natal, Harris (1994) argues, the capitalization of agriculture was slow and uneven, while the Native Land Act's restriction on 'squatting' was relatively easy to avoid. 'Squatting' was a term deployed by the Native Affairs Department and white farmers to define (and undermine) Africans who avoided labor tenancy or wage labor by living on white-owned land and paying rent. In Natal, the Natives Land Act did not demand the immediate eviction of squatters, but only the restriction of new contracts. There were also forms of labor tenancy that overlapped with rent tenancy. Harris (1994: 245) cites the prevalence in northern Natal of a system by which 'when the farmer owns two farms, for example, he may abandon one entirely to Native agriculture; and in return for such occupation, the Native residents pay rent not in money or kind but in labour.' The Elandslaagte Farmers Association of Klip River reported that 'there were many "kaffir farms" in the district, rents in most instance being collected in the guise of dipping fees' (Harris 1994: 246). He documents the widespread persistence of a variety of forms of rent-cum-labor tenancy in Klip River, Newcastle, and other northern Natal districts well into the 1930s, and contends that it was the gradual capitalization of agriculture rather than the operation of the Native Lands Act that explains the squeeze on so-called 'squatters.' Even so, tenants often staged fierce resistance to efforts to erode their rights in land and livestock:

> Initial resistance took the form of refusals to accept increased wages in return for reduced rights in land and livestock, and refusals to abide by landowners' limitations on the latter. The final step was to leave and search for a farmer prepared to offer more attractive terms, or more desirably, a landlord who would not demand any labour services. (Harris 1994: 248)

Particularly after the mid-1930s, labor tenancy was being eroded not only by white farmers intent on stripping away African tenants' rights in land and livestock, but also by gender politics – specifically, the rebellion against their elders by young African men and women, many of whom were moving to jobs on the mines and in the towns.[13] Yet despite the multiple forces that acted to undermine them, various forms of labor and rent tenancy persisted in northern Natal well into the apartheid era.

For a brief period in the late 1920s rural grievances and conflicts generated by capitalist transformations of the countryside found organized expression in the Industrial and Commercial Workers' Union (ICU) which, despite its nominal urban focus, expanded very rapidly in rural regions all over South Africa. The ICU gathered particularly wide support in northern Natal and the Midlands where, as Marks (1978: 184) noted, 'rural relationships were being restructured for the first time.' In her superb study of rural organizing by the ICU, Helen Bradford (1987) argues that 'far from invariably acting as the moving force behind the resistance it evoked, the ICU often merely channelled protest which was already coalescing in other localized institutions' (Bradford 1987: 16–17). The promise of land, she argues, was the single most important factor enabling the ICU to take the countryside by storm. For large numbers of labor tenants, organizing was as much about access to land and resistance to proletarianization as it was about improved wages and working conditions. In the Umvoti district south of Ladysmith, for example, labor tenants were often more militant than casual workers hired from the reserves:

> Unquestionably . . . it was labour tenants who were in the vanguard of this form of protest [strikes and stoppages]. As happened so often, the fact that they related to farmers not only as proletarians but also as peasants actually enhanced their

militancy. For one thing, their bumper harvests increased their ability and inclination to resist demands on their labour power. For another, they sorely resented being paid less for more work than hired hands, and desperately needed higher wages to compensate for the 'squeezing' suffered over the years. (Bradford 1987: 198–199)

The ICU disintegrated in the 1930s for a variety of reasons, along with organized rural resistance more generally. Although the ICU had 'articulated popular grievances and fuelled protest to an unprecedented degree' (Bradford 1987: 147), nationally organized movements – most notably the ANC and the Communist Party of South Africa – failed to build on the lessons of rural struggle attendant upon the rise and fall of the ICU. Bundy (1987) attributes this failure to the class character of the national leadership as well as to the complexities of rural politics: 'Despite the realities of resistance and unrest in the countryside, the national movements – physically located in urban centres, ideologically concerned either with the vanguard role of the proletariat or with wringing political concessions for modernisers – were structurally ill equipped to respond to the inchoate and murmurous patterns of peasant resistance' (Bundy 1987: 281).

In her account of the failure of the South African left to come to grips with the agrarian question, Alison Drew (1996) points as well to cleavages on the left, within and between communists who retained allegiance to the Comintern, and South African Trotskyists who split from it. The latter developed by far the more sophisticated theoretical understanding of the agrarian question, spurred in part by Trotsky's direct intervention in South African agrarian debates in 1935.[14] Framing his argument in terms of the theory of permanent revolution and the combined and uneven development of capitalism, Trotsky made a compelling argument for the necessity of linking urban-based proletarian movements with peasant uprisings around the land question. Yet, as Drew points out, the Trotskyist groups by and large were organizationally quite weak. This was certainly the case in northwestern Natal. For example, a strongly committed Trotskyist group formed in the 1930s in Dundee, a small town north of Ladysmith, with a keen interest in linking the poorer strata of the peasantry with the urban proletariat. Yet like Trotskyist groups in other regions, they failed to translate these ideas into practice.

Among communists aligned with the ANC there were some important exceptions to the general neglect of the politics of the agrarian question. A leading figure who sought to impress on the ANC the need for rural mobilization that addressed concrete local conditions and grievances while also linking with larger movements was the writer and political activist Govan Mbeki. As a young man in the Transkei, Mbeki had been exposed to the ICU when he worked with his uncle, a major ICU organizer. When I first met with him in 1999, he described how he became drawn to agrarian questions in theory as well as in practice:

In 1930 while a student at Fort Hare I started writing a book on the Transkei. I was influenced by the readings – Marxist readings – including a lot of papers that were coming out of Russia after the first five-year plan, 1928–33. The Soviet Union used to then put out volumes of propaganda on the situation in Russia. That book I gave the title 'The Transkei in the Making.' From that early age I had to find an explanation – why was there so much poverty in the Transkei? It boiled down to the reserves being too small. Then they introduced rehabilitation measures to cull the stock so it could be borne by the land. One of my arguments then was this is no cure. People are increasing by the day. The problem is shortage of land. When one saw people being stripped of their land . . . the problem was clear. It was land shortage. But how was it to be solved?

During the Defiance Campaign [in the early 1950s], I was in the Transkei. An old man – a peasant who was a member of the ANC in the 1920s – talked to me about the Defiance Campaign. In the Defiance Campaign we said we are non-violent, we are going to break the law and allow ourselves to be arrested. We will not pay fines. We will serve our period in jail. This peasant is carrying a greatcoat – an army coat, second-hand. He folds it up. He sits on it. He says to me, 'What are you doing? You say you are going to break the law, land in jail. You think you are going to convince the white man to give you your rights? Don't be silly. You are merely tickling the boer. You are not going to move the white man until you find guns. You must meet him on the battlefield.' I could give no answer except to say tactically we had to be non-violent. In the end we resorted to arms against the boer.[15]

In *South Africa: The Peasants' Revolt* (1964), Mbeki documents resistance and rebellion in rural areas between 1946 and 1962, focusing particularly on the Pondo revolt in 1960:[16]

The Pondo movement succeeded by example in accomplishing what discussion had failed to do in a generation – convincing the leadership of the importance of the peasants in the reserves to the entire national struggle. The leaders realized at last that a struggle based on the reserves had a much greater capacity to absorb the shocks of government repression and was therefore capable of being sustained for a much longer time than a struggle based on the urban locations . . . The struggles of the peasants start from smaller beginnings, build up to a crescendo over a much longer time, are capable of pinning down large government forces, and are maintained at comparatively much lower costs. *A proper blending of the peasant and worker struggles, therefore, coupled with skillful timing of joint action, is a matter which must engage the serious thinking of the leadership.* (Mbeki 1964: 130–131; emphasis added)

In his article on popular rural protest, Colin Bundy points out that since the early 1940s, Govan Mbeki had sought to impress on the ANC leadership the need for the nationalist movement to recognize and support rural struggles. Bundy quotes from Mbeki's correspondence with Dr A.B. Xuma, the President-General of the ANC from 1940–49, appealing for support from the national leadership:

> Our fears here are that we may work up the people only to find that the rest of the country does not attach much significance to its resolutions. Country people have a way of being honest. We have already lost face in the Anti-Pass Campaign which was just dropped when we were working up the people . . . (letter from Mbeki to Xuma, 27 June 1947 cited by Bundy 1987: 271)

Yet, as Bundy notes, 'There is little evidence that Mbeki's clear-headed urging elicited any notable response from the urban leaders of the ANC before 1948. Xuma's own lack of enthusiasm for rural mobilisation was observable at several points during the 1940s' (Bundy 1987: 271).

In 1948 the Transkei Organised Bodies (TOB), which Govan Mbeki had been instrumental in bringing to life, was effectively taken over by the All-Africa Convention (AAC), a constituent body of the Trotskyist Non-European Unity Movement (NEUM) led by I.B. Tabata. Govan Mbeki described his view of the AAC to me in the following terms:

> *I did not agree with them. They came into being after 1936. In 1935–36, Professor D.D.T. Jabavu convened the All African Convention to oppose the Hertzog Bills. At that moment the ANC was alive, but in its very weak stage. Jabavu called on the AAC to fight these bills. They were passed in 1936. The work of the AAC was finished. A group of people led by Tabata said the AAC continues . . . They didn't have a very long history. They were interested in rural questions. But they never got to grips with the struggle. They never got into action on the ground. In 1949 I left the TOB. They took over the secretaryship of the TOB. It didn't lead to much. It collapsed, although there are still remnants of it. I left because I found it difficult to work with them.*

Disillusioned by his efforts to get rural organizing off the ground and the lack of support from the leadership of the ANC, Govan Mbeki decided to return to teaching. He applied for a position in Natal where he was less well known than in the Eastern Cape, and in 1953 was posted to Ladysmith where he was actively engaged in organizing for nearly two years. While there, he exercised a profound influence in shaping popular understandings of the agrarian question and opposition to dispossession. In Ladysmith Mbeki also formed a close alliance with Dr Achmad Sader, a leading member of the Natal Indian Congress and an heir of Gandhi's legacy of active organizing in this area in the late nineteenth century. This alliance, as we shall see, was particularly significant in the light of racial tensions that had erupted between Indians and Africans in Durban in 1949. Mbeki's sojourn in Ladysmith also coincided with intense grassroots mobilization leading up to the Freedom Charter and contributed to the formation of powerful oppositional capacities in the Ladysmith township of Steadville and surrounding rural areas.

Before delving more deeply into these processes, we need to attend to another key set of forces shaping the politics of dispossession and how they carried over into relocation townships – namely the role of the African landowning class in the formation not only of the early ANC, but also the first Inkatha.

The African Bourgeoisie and the Rise of Zulu Ethnic Nationalism

Although the 1913 Land Act did not immediately halt African land acquisition, one of its longer-term effects was to increase differentiation between the long-established landowning class and the evicted peasantry who sought refuge on freehold land (Marks 1986: 63–64). In the first half of the twentieth century, many *kholwa* were transformed into *rentiers*, and some of the settlements that had flourished in the nineteenth century came to operate like the reserves as a bare base of reproduction for households caught up in migrant labor. For many *kholwa*, the most immediate and powerful effects of the 1913 Land Act were in the sphere of organized politics. Influenced by Gandhi and the Natal Indian Congress, leading *kholwa* (including John Dube, Albert Luthuli, Pixley Seme, and H.S. Msimang) formed the Natal Native Congress (NNC) in 1900 to press their interests – primary among which were extension of the franchise on the same terms as whites and individual land tenure. Following the unification of white South Africa in 1910, John Dube became president of the South African Native National Congress (SANNC), the precursor of the ANC, which sprang to life following the passage of the 1913 Land Act.[17] Shula Marks observes that the multi-faceted nature of the Land Act enabled the African landowning class and intelligentsia to present their class interests as the general interest, and to speak on behalf of the general community.

Efforts by members of the African landowning class to constitute themselves as a political force in the face of dispossession intersected with several other struggles, conflicts, and alliances that took shape in the 1920s and 1930s: the rise of militant labor movements; efforts by the state and settler capitalists to contain these threats by refurbishing communalism and invoking patriarchal and chiefly authority; and the complex, multifaceted formation of twentieth-century Zulu nationalism and ethnic identity. These struggles not only overlapped and informed one another but were also, as Shula Marks (1986) points out, highly ambiguous.

In their efforts to contain the threats that rising militancy posed to accumulation and racially entrenched privilege, members of the white establishment resorted increasingly to segregationist discourse: Africans had to be 'protected' from the influence of 'detribalized agitators' (Cope 1990; Dubow 1989). One of the chief architects of segregation in Natal, G.N. Heaton Nicholls, put it quite succinctly: 'If we do not get back to communalism, we will most certainly arrive at communism' (quoted by Marks 1989: 217). Beginning with the Native Affairs Act of 1920, a series of legislative measures – which built directly on the Shepstone system and the Natal Code of Native Law – were designed to divert African political activity from urban areas, and contain it within a separate territorial and social sphere of rural 'traditionalism.'

At precisely the point that segregationist efforts to freeze 'custom' and deploy a deracinated form of tribal authority were intensifying, new forms of Zulu nationalist sentiment were taking shape in other realms. Zulu popular nationalism in the 1920s emerged in the context of intensified class conflict and social differentiation, and was deployed by very different – and often sharply opposed – social forces:

> More than once in the 1920s, different elements of the Zulu-speaking population whose political objectives were then in open conflict, nonetheless equally perceived themselves to be acting for a higher Zulu national cause, and ultimately in the name of 'King Solomon.' The principal political division to emerge within Zulu-speaking society was between radicalised popular movements and Inkatha, and both sides invoked historic national and royal symbols in the course of their struggles. This did not simply highlight that Zulu nationalism could mean different things to different people. It also clearly showed how Zulu nationalism, because of its popular appeal and potential for large-scale political mobilisation, had itself become a site of struggle as contending class groups sought to define its political content. (Cope 1990: 434–435)

Despite these struggles over the multiple meanings and deployments of Zulu nationalism, the dominant ideology in the 1920s was that promoted by Inkatha; and Inkatha, as Marks (1978, 1986) and Cope (1990, 1993) have shown, grew out of an alliance between the Zulu royal family and leading *kholwa* landowners along with other members of the African petty bourgeoisie. In short, an important fraction of the class that had explicitly distanced itself from 'tribalism' in the nineteenth and early twentieth centuries, played an active role in fashioning new expressions of Zulu nationalism.

That leading members of the petty bourgeoisie sought rapprochement with the Zulu aristocracy reflected the multiple pressures to which they were subject. On the one hand, they were directly threatened by the radicalization of labor, and on the other hand by tensions within *kholwa* communities as avenues of access to upward mobility were closed off to younger generations. These conflicts and tensions found expression within Congress politics, as the older and more conservative generation were increasingly marginalized and ousted from positions of power. At the same time, increasing segregationism dashed *kholwa* hopes of being enfranchised and incorporated into a non-racial South African middle class (Cope 1990: 439). Yet segregationist efforts to divert African politics into a tribalized rural sphere seemed to open up opportunities – albeit highly circumscribed – for influence and access to resources. Thus, for example, the 1920 Native Affairs Act, which made provision for 'native councils' in rural areas, was greeted with enthusiasm by John Dube and other leading *kholwa*. Cope suggests that the first moves towards the alliance with the tribal aristocracy came from *kholwa* in the Vryheid district of Northern Natal, just north of Newcastle, who proposed the establishment of a 'co-operative agricultural scheme' in an adjacent area of Zululand:

> The proposals were essentially an attempt on the part of local Zulu *kholwa* living near the royal epicentre [Nongoma in western Zululand], to cooperate with tribal chiefs to take advantage of the 'progressive provisions' of the 1920 Act. The intention of the agricultural scheme was to buy land and farm it for commercial purposes. *Inkatha was in this way initially seen as a means through which commercial agricultural production could be set under way on land ostensibly bought by a 'tribe' – non-tribal landbuying syndicates having been practically outlawed since the 1913 Land Act.* (Cope 1990: 444; emphasis added)

Cope warns against too stereotyped an understanding of Inkatha as simply a strategic 'marriage of convenience' between the conservative old guard of the NNC and the Zulu aristocracy. The ethos of individual accumulation and private property was, he argues, 'softened by certain ideas of broader "social welfare" – influenced variously by Christianity, Victorian liberalism, the "self-help" and "co-operative" schemes of contemporary black consciousness, and traditional Zulu notions of social solidarity' (Cope 1990: 451). In addition, the international Pan-African movement played heavily into petty bourgeois understandings, identities, and definitions of political objectives. Nor was the emergence of Inkatha simply a product of segregationist engineering. While those such as George Heaton Nicholls, Member of Parliament for Zululand and President of the South African Planters' Union, actively encouraged the alliance between the petty bourgeoisie and the Zulu royal family, segments of the segregationist establishment – particularly within the Natal Native Affairs Department – opposed the resurgence of Zulu royalty (Marks 1978; Cope 1993).

In short, Zulu ethnic identity and nationalism emerged in the early decades of the twentieth century as a distinctively modern, multifaceted, and multiply-contested set of political forces. These forms and practices of modernity, woven together out of a variety of elements in changing circumstances, are crucial to understanding the multiple manifestations of Zulu ethnic nationalism later in the century. They also compel us to rethink categories like 'decentralized despotism' that seek to read politics off institutional structures. In a particularly useful contribution, Carolyn Hamilton (1998) warns against viewing the invocation of custom and tradition simply or primarily as top-down forms of colonial control. In Natal, she argues, colonial discourses of tradition not only changed over time; they were also 'shaped by pre-existing indigenous discourses, themselves far from homogeneous' (Hamilton 1998: 27). The colonial worldview was not simply imported from the metropole and imposed on the colonized; nor did colonial authorities, segregationists, or Zulu nationalists simply invent traditions and deploy them to their own ends. Rather, modern forms of Zulu ethnic nationalism emerged out of extremely complex historical processes of transformation, rearrangement, and struggles over meaning. The power and resilience of notions about 'tribal' identity and custom among those whom Mamdani (1996) terms 'subjects,' she argues, is located in deep entanglements of indigenous and colonial concepts. In addition, of course, the widespread popular appeal of Zulu nationalism among radical popular movements as well as the petty bourgeoisie, unsettles sharply drawn distinctions between citizens and subjects.

In later chapters I show how the concept of decentralized despotism also obscures the multiple and varied ways that Zulu ethnic nationalism has articulated with class and other processes in northwestern KwaZulu-Natal during the apartheid era as well as beyond it. In particular we shall see how Madadeni, the relocation township outside Newcastle, emerged as space of modernity and urban opportunity, embodying key hegemonic dimensions of the apartheid project that resonated closely with the elitist orientation of the first Inkatha – and how precisely this articulation of class with Zulu ethnic nationalism helped to call forth a particularly militant youth movement that vehemently opposed 'traditional' authority. In Ezakheni, the township outside Ladysmith, large segments of the dispossessed land-owning class sharply opposed official manifestations of Zulu ethnic nationalism in bantustan institutions and the revival of Inkatha under Gatsha Buthelezi in the 1970s. Yet, as in the 1920s and 1930s, discourses of custom and tradition entered into the formation of the particularly militant and well-organized labor movement in and around Ladysmith.

In other words, far from being hardwired into a determinate form of decentralized despotism, Zulu ethnic nationalism articulated with class (and, as we shall see, gender) through practices and processes that were not only multiple and multi-layered, but that also actively shaped divergent local trajectories. These processes of place formation, in turn, were profoundly shaped by specific experiences of dispossession. Accordingly, before moving on to trace these trajectories in greater detail, I want to conclude this chapter with some reminders of how the broad contours of agrarian change in the late nineteenth and early twentieth centuries defined the terrain on which apartheid-era dispossession and displacement took hold.

Dispossession under Apartheid

Rural removals got going in the 1960s, and gathered force through the 1970s. In the country as a whole, according to the SPP, just about half of the 3.5 million people displaced between 1960 and 1983 were from rural areas, 65 percent from white-owned farms and 35 percent from African freehold land (Platzky and Walker 1985: 10). In Natal, some 745,000 people were subjected to removals between 1948 and 1982 (Table 2.4). According to SPP estimates, at least 300,000 people were evicted from farms during this period; 'black spots' accounted for another 105,000 removals, and a further 245,000 people remained under threat of removal from 'black spots' in 1982.

The groundwork for removals had been laid early in the century. Official recognition of the inadequacy of the reserves defined under the 1913 Land

Table 2.4 Estimated number of removals in Natal, 1948–82.

	Moved	Under threat
Farm evictions	300,000 Abolition of labor tenancy; mechanization	?
'Black spots'	105,000 109 African freehold communities 14 missions	245,000 189 African freehold communities 14 missions
Consolidation	10,000 Reserve 6; Part of Reserve 4	300,000 Reduction of 48 scheduled and released reserve areas to 10
Urban relocation	17,000	61,000
Infrastructural	15,000 Dams, development projects, game preserves, forestry	? Sodwana Bay, Inanda Dam, Myumase Dam; Umfolosi Dam, Mkomanzi Dam
Strategic	3,500 Missile range, northern boundaries, and coast	? Ingwavuma?
Sub-Total	450,000	606,000 +?
Group Areas	295,000	?
Total	745,500	606,000 +?

Source: SPP (1983) Table 8, p. 53 (Question marks in original)

Act was reflected in the appointment of the Beaumont Commission (1916) whose purpose was to delimit additional areas in which Africans could acquire land. Various bills embodying its recommendations failed to pass parliament, and it was only in 1936 with the passage of the Natives Trust and Land Act that provision was made for expanding the reserves. Drawing on the system of Trust tenure developed in colonial Natal, the 1936 Act created the South African Native Trust (subsequently renamed the South African Development Trust) in which ownership of the reserves was vested. In addition to defining the existing ('scheduled') reserves, the Act created a new category of 'released' land – namely, land released from the prohibition of African acquisition outside the area of scheduled reserves. It specified a quota of released land for each province, to be purchased by the Trust for African settlement. The scheduled and released areas together amounted to 13 percent of the land area of South Africa that came to form the bantustans under apartheid rule, although by 1974 more than 20 percent of the released land had not yet been bought (Platzky and Walker 1985: 92).

The 1936 Act also in effect created what came to be termed 'black spots' by specifying two classes of African freehold property – namely those pieces of land included in the reserves, and those not. The former were specified in an additional schedule of released land, and included the Driefontein block of farms north of Ladysmith and some farms east of Newcastle; these became defined as reserves, and subsequently part of the KwaZulu bantustan. Freehold land excluded from the additional schedule subsequently became defined as 'black spots' that had to be removed. In Natal, these 'black spots' amounted to 42,226 hectares, of which half (and later more) was concentrated in northwestern Natal (Brookes and Hurwitz 1957: 23).[18]

Although white farmers formed a major part of the National Party alliance, significant tensions arose between large groups of white farmers and apartheid state officials over rural removals. Particularly in central and northern Natal, there was considerable ambivalence and conflict within the white farming community over state-sponsored abolition of labor tenancy and the costs of shifting to wage labor arrangements. Rapid mechanization of white agriculture fuelled by heavy state subsidies lowered the demand for agricultural labor nationally. Between 1947 and 1961, for example, the number of tractors increased from 22,000 to 122,218; by 1980 it had reached 300,000 or four per farm (Beinart 1994: 193). Yet many white farmers in central and northern Natal remained adamantly opposed to the abolition of labor tenancy: 'The tenant system is still in operation because it is the only one many farmers can afford,' commented the President of the Natal Agricultural Union in 1966 (cited by SPP 1983: 71). It was only in the 1970s that tenant evictions moved into top gear in this area.

White farmers also held up the process of removals by refusing to sell land to the South African Development Trust (SADT) for resettlement of displaced people. Although often viciously opposed to 'black spots' – whose residents were by and large able to resist low-wage agricultural labor – white farmers argued that making more land available for reserves would exacerbate their labor problems. 'The huge squatter population which lives on the Native farms must be removed with all its belongings,' argued the Farmers' Association for Elandslaagte (outside Ladysmith) in the Natal Agricultural Union's newsletter of May 11, 1954, and went on to suggest how these people should be dealt with:

> A number could find abode on European farms. The balance should be taken to townships created for Natives at a railhead, so that they could work in industries. Those who remained must be controlled, and if they could not succeed, they must quit. (cited by SPP 1983: 40)

As with the abolition of labor tenancy, it was the capitalization of agriculture that finally enabled the SADT to persuade white farmers to relinquish land at what was typically a handsome price.

Farm evictions took place in two phases: initially a large-scale state-sponsored effort to eliminate labor tenancy and 'squatting' on white farms and, particularly after about 1975, actions taken by individual farmers against people living on farms (SPP 1983: 70). Data by district are not available, but by far the largest concentration of labor tenancy and other forms of occupancy of white farms was (and still is) in the Weenen district south of Ladysmith. Although it is difficult to specify numbers, quite a large proportion of the increase in population in northwestern KwaZulu-Natal since the 1960s (Table 2.1) probably represents tenants displaced from farms in Weenen; for example, many of the people in the Waaihoek camp described in the first part of this chapter were from Weenen. The pace of evictions accelerated after 1990 when the main political parties were unbanned, and white farmers anticipated land claims by tenants – many of whom have been living in these areas since the nineteenth century, and whose occupancy predates white ownership.

Farm evictions were in many instances 'removals of a quiet kind' (Donald 1984), carried out by white farmers with varying degrees of coercion, but always with the backing of the state. In many cases, Mabin (1989: 5) suggests 'rural people saw the writing on the wall and moved to avoid eviction, as well as to secure places to live ahead of those who would otherwise be fellow evictees.' Yet, as he notes, the history of displacement from the farms and experiences of displacement remain largely unwritten: 'Little research [has] actually examined private or state practices surrounding evictions of farm dwellers, or the resistance of the latter; hardly any authors trace changing patterns of farm life and labour in sufficient detail to allow an understanding of relocation from the farms to emerge (Mabin 1989: 5).' According to the SPP, resistance to farm evictions was typically fragmented, localized, and individualistic:

> There are still no worker organisations straddling farm boundaries. Meetings, access to farms by outsiders, communication between farm workers and resource organisations are all enormously difficult undertakings. The KwaZulu government has not attempted to tackle the problems of farm workers who, as it points out, do not come under its jurisdiction anyway. Farm workers are generally dismissed as individuals now, making organised action even more difficult than in the past when large numbers of people in a single district faced the same crisis at the same time. Workers who have not been given notice are generally too intimidated to support those who have; they know how vulnerable they are. (SPP 1983: 81)

Yet there were, undoubtedly, innumerable instances of what Scott (1985) calls 'everyday forms of resistance'; many people passively resisted eviction, and had to be forced out by hut burnings, bulldozers, arrests, and prosecution (SPP 1983: 74). In one particularly notable example, a group of evicted tenants whom the government intended to relocate in Madadeni hid their possessions and loaded trunks and packages filled with stones on the removal trucks. As soon as they had been offloaded at Madadeni, they found their way back to the Weenen district, and many returned to their former land (SPP 1983: 74).

The heavy concentration of African freehold land in northwestern Natal accounts, of course, for the intensity of 'black spot' removals in the subregion. In addition to white farmers, the coal mining industry was also a major force behind forced removals in the region. The SPP (1983: 103–104) estimated that at least 30 of the 66 'black spots' in northern Natal had quite high quality coal deposits. According to the SPP data, some 48 of the 109 'black spot' removals were in the areas around Ladysmith and Newcastle. Since some of the 'black spots' in this sub-region were relatively large, the proportion of people removed is probably closer to 50 percent; in addition, most of the 245,000 threatened with removal at the time of the SPP study in 1982 were in the Ladysmith district of Klip River.

At the time of my research in the mid-1990s, many former landowners were in the process of reclaiming land and their stories are infused with the politics of memory: indeed, this is an important part of what the restitution process is about. Most landowners I met were professionals, the large majority of them teachers. Several key themes run through their stories. First, they all talked in some detail about how their ancestors bought land in the second half of the nineteenth and early twentieth centuries, and about how the proceeds from agriculture were used to educate children, often at elite church schools. They also painted vivid pictures of the churches, schools, clinics, carpentry workshops, and so forth constructed in these communities, and of the wanton destruction of property and deep financial losses they suffered through the removals. The graves of ancestors also featured prominently, and many told of returning regularly to their former lands to tend graves. In recounting their experiences of moving to the townships, all complained bitterly of the small, cramped houses they were allocated. Yet several former landowners living in Madadeni also told of the strategies they deployed to acquire additional property in the townships, of their confrontations with white officials, and of the help they gave to people who 'infiltrated' their land just prior to removals to gain access to township housing.[19] Older people in particular alluded to shifts in intergenerational relations as parents were no longer able to allocate land to children. In addition, important dimensions of social distinctions in some freehold areas emerged from comments such as 'there was a loss of respect; we had to mingle with people who were not of our standard.'

There are also common themes threading through the narratives of former tenants, relayed in far greater detail in the following chapter. For men, many of whom worked as migrants at the time of removals, the loss of cattle and other livestock in which they had invested most of their savings is typically a source of intense anger and frustration. Women almost always spoke of the shock and stress of having to pay for everything and the imperatives of generating cash income.

The way former landowners and tenants experienced and dealt with removals, and their relationships with one another, varied significantly in different places and over time. Quite often, tenants crossed swords with landowners who were fighting removals by opting for the relative security of a township house. Yet in some instances, tenants and landowners joined forces to oppose removals. While the experience of each community is distinct in its own way, there are also clearly discernible patterns: by and large, removals in the Ladysmith district were far more strongly contested than those in the surroundings of Newcastle, where there was comparatively little open opposition. One key indication is that, by 1982, all but one of the rural 'black spots' in the northern area (Newcastle, Dannhauser, and Dundee) had been removed. In contrast, 15 'black spots' remained – albeit under threat of removal – in the Klip River district of Ladysmith. It is to these discrepant patterns of dispossession and their longer-term significance that we now turn.

CHAPTER 3

Losing Ground and Making Space
Dispossession and Township Formation

SHIFTING NOW FROM a broad regional history of agrarian transformation, this chapter focuses on specific local dynamics of dispossession. We explore how divergent experiences and practices of resistance and
acquiescence have defined the character of relocation townships; and how
ongoing processes of place-making both reflect and shape social relations
and political subjectivities. As the title suggests, the chapter is composed of
two sections. 'Losing Ground' traces the sharply different ways in which
dispossession and displacement took place in the areas surrounding
Ladysmith and Newcastle, and situates these differentiated responses
within wider historical and political-economic contexts. 'Making Space'
traces the divergent political dynamics and translocal connections through
which seemingly similar relocation townships have taken shape as strikingly different places.

Losing Ground: Divergent Experiences of Dispossession
At the end of Chapter 2 we noted sharp differences in the pace, character,
and extent of removals in areas around Ladysmith and Newcastle. That
opposition to removals of so-called 'black spots' was in general more
openly contested in the Ladysmith district than in the areas around
Newcastle is partly a matter of timing. The relocation townships of
Madadeni and Osizweni were established on the sites of Duckponds and
Mountain View, two innocuously named white farms in the vicinity of
Newcastle that the SADT was able to acquire relatively early on. Removals
into these townships began in 1963, and one of the last freehold areas to be

removed to Madadeni was Milton Farm (about 11 km from Newcastle) in 1971. Building in Ezakheni only started in 1972, and most of the 'black spot' removals from the Klip River (Ladysmith) district into the township only took place after 1975. Differential timing of removals is highly significant, because of the larger political context. The 1960s was a period of extremely tight political repression in South Africa more generally, following the Sharpeville massacres and the banning of the ANC and the Pan African Congress (PAC). The main thrust of removals of Newcastle thus occurred at a time when any sort of organized opposition was extremely difficult, and outside support for opposition to removals was limited to individual church representatives like Cosmas Desmond and, in some areas, small white liberal groups like the Black Sash.

At the time of the Klip River (Ladysmith) removals the larger political climate was changing dramatically, along with the sorts of connections that threatened communities could forge with outside groups. Soon after its formation in 1975, Inkatha became embroiled in supporting several communities trying to oppose removals, although these initiatives were fraught with tensions, and several backfired. In 1979, the Association for Rural Advancement (AFRA) based in Pietermaritzburg was formed as an affiliate of the National Land Committee with the specific purpose of providing support to communities opposing removals, and linking them with international sources of support.[1] This was also the period of the Botha reforms, and of growing fissures within and between different levels of the state.[2] In short, the height of removals in the Ladysmith district coincided with a period in which the larger political room to maneuver was far greater than it had been in the 1960s, and agents of the apartheid state were operating under a tighter set of constraints than in the period when the Newcastle removals took place.

While shifts in the larger context of struggle between the 1960s and the 1980s played into divergent patterns of resistance to removals in the areas around Ladysmith and Newcastle, historically sedimented differences in political culture and oppositional capacity are also crucially important. My own understandings of these differences have been shaped by the accounts of local politics in the 1950s in the two places by older ANC members. In the early 1950s, as we saw in Chapter 2, Ladysmith and some of the surrounding freehold communities became major centers of a newer, less elitist form of ANC organizing led by Govan Mbeki. In their recollections of this period, several older residents of Ezakheni, Steadville (the municipal township outside Ladysmith), and nearby freehold areas emphasized the importance of Govan Mbeki's presence in Ladysmith in the early 1950s. One veteran of the struggle described how his experience of the ANC changed between the late 1940s and the 1950s:

> *In 1948–49 I was just a supporter of the ANC. I was not a proper member, just a supporter here in Ladysmith where I used to visit Dr Sader [a prominent member of the Natal Indian Congress] and others. I was not very happy because we were told that meetings were run by educated people. Ordinary people like me were not allowed to join. There was that feeling that the movement belonged to the elite . . . [Things changed when] Mbeki was transferred here in the 1950s. He taught at Steadville [the municipal township] and also at the Ephumakeni school in Roosboom [a freehold community about 10 km from Ladysmith]. In his part time he would go and organize the workers in the coal mine at Platberg. He was also our teacher. We had meetings with him, although this was not allowed in public. There were also certain groups and we met regularly with him. We also met with Dr Sader. Comrade Albert Luthuli used to pay us visits. J. Nyembe also used to pay us visits. Another one of our teachers was Stephen Dlamini. In the 1950s the ANC changed. The Nat Party introduced various laws intended to divide us, but the people came together.*

In Newcastle, it was extremely difficult to locate older people willing to talk about ANC politics in the 1950s. Younger ANC activists led me to an elderly man, who described a dramatically different political culture in Lennoxton and Fairleigh, two freehold areas close to Newcastle in the 1950s:

> *I've been a member of the ANC since the 1950s. But most people didn't want to show their politics, even before the ANC was banned . . . Newcastle is unique. I don't know why. Even in 1960 there was no political activity in Newcastle. I don't see why people didn't get active – we had a lot of tenants. Maybe because the ANC was seen as for high class people. The culture of resistance is just not here. At the time of the first removal, people didn't stand up. We said we'll get lawyers to help us, but they just weren't interested.*

The character of oppositional politics in and around Ladysmith emerges in an interesting way from different accounts of one of the first 'black spot' removals in northwestern Natal, which began in the early 1950s. The state acquired Hobsland, a white-owned farm adjacent to the Driefontein block that was redefined as part of the reserves, and set about moving the freehold community of Khumalosville. Writing in 1969, Cosmas Desmond describes the removal in terms that only allude to the sustained campaign against the removal that lasted for almost a decade:

Hobsland [renamed Vulandondo] is a settlement about nine miles from Ladysmith to which a number of African landowners from Khumalosville, sixteen miles the other side of Ladysmith, were moved in 1963 with great hardship, despite the efforts of their legal representatives. The people bought the farm at Khumalosville in 1908 and divided it into 2-acre plots; at the time of the removal 91 of these were owned by Africans. They were told in 1952 that the Government wanted to buy the farm but that they would be given a bigger place elsewhere. They were led to believe that they would be given four-acre plots at Hobsland and the rest of the farm as commonage. When they were eventually moved they were given compensation for land, improvements and 'inconvenience', and free 1/2-acre plot at Hobsland, and the right to buy another 1/2 acre for R110. The Government offered R42 per acre at Khumalosville and charged R220 an acre at Hobsland. They refused to go for some time but were finally told in September 1963 that if they had not moved by 2 October they would be arrested. They were taken to Hobsland in Government lorries and given a tent and half a bag of mealie meal. (Desmond 1970: 78–79)[3]

A fuller – albeit carefully edited – account of early opposition to removals is contained in a talk given by Elliot Mngadi at a meeting held in Ladysmith in 1981, and recorded by AFRA:

. . . in about 1956, the government first started moving people from these 'black spots'. One of the farms they started with was Besters [another name for Khumalosville]. At that time I was an organiser of the Liberal Party and I was also one of the landowners at Roosboom, near Ladysmith. It was during this time, as part of my work, that I had to organise the African landowners in Natal to form a body of their own. In 1955/6 we formed a body called the Northern Natal African Landowners Association. I don't know whether fortunately or unfortunately, but I was elected Secretary of that body. The main function of that body was to help people resist these removals. We tried very hard at Besters, as some will remember, and I think it took 5 or 6 years before they were moved. Next was Besterspruit, out at Vryheid. We tried to help those people there, but then, of course, the Government steamrollered the whole thing and in 1963 the people were moved to Mondlo. The same with Kingsley, the same with Gardensville, Crane Valley, Kopij Alleen, Waagalles, Siwang Farm. This last farm was owned by Mr Nyembe who was Vice-President of Chief Luthuli's ANC. (reprinted in SPP 1983: 348)

In his fleeting allusion to 'Chief Luthuli's ANC,' Mngadi carefully sidesteps the way the ANC and the Liberal Party collaborated in the formation of the Northern Natal Landowners Association (NNLA). When the national state of emergency was proclaimed in 1960, Mngadi was declared a 'threat to the state' and imprisoned. At that time too, the NNLA collapsed.

Shortly after a resounding ANC victory in the Ladysmith local government elections in 1996, I met with a former tenant from Besters/

Khumalosville, who recounted a far more radical version of the struggle against removal:

> At that time [in the late 1940s and 1950s] I was staying in Besters, which was also
> known as Khumalosville. Besters was the place of landowners. I didn't own land,
> but there were people there who had bought lands. When we talk about land we
> must realize that land, people, and politics go together. In those days there were
> the laws of the color bar. They said we are a black spot in a white area. That's
> when the struggle started at Besters, in the 1950s when the Afrikaners said we must
> move away. We opposed this. We organized ourselves as the Umviko [Protection]
> Party. There was a link with the ANC . . . By that time the ANC organization was in
> its worst time – the government was trying to destroy it. We requested assistance
> from the Liberal Party, especially Peter Brown who was from Pietermaritzburg.
> We requested them to guide us through the Umviko Party. We had to request these
> people to help us. We could not use the ANC.

The eventual removal of the Besters/Khumalosville community to Vulandondo in 1963 coincided with the collapse of organized support and tightening political repression. That same year, the first 'black spot' removals in the Newcastle district got underway. In Osizweni, I was able to meet with a group of people who were among the first to be moved. All were tenants on Esididini, an African freehold farm near Dannhauser (about 20 km from Newcastle) whose inhabitants were removed in 1963 to make way for the expansion of the Durban Navigation Colliery. The SPP (1983: 103–104) estimated that at least 30 of the 66 'black spots' in northern Natal have quite high quality coal deposits, but could not document the compensation paid to landowners. I was unable to meet any of the landowners; former tenants claimed that their erstwhile landlords received land as compensation and had moved away.[4]

These former tenants testified to the harshness of their experience of removal to Osizweni, and the combined sense of anger and helplessness. The removal happened very swiftly; several people remember being given 24 hours notice that they were to be moved, and that they would have to sell their cattle; others recall a week. Men were particularly bitter about the forced sale of cattle – their primary store of wealth; one described how, when they were first informed about the removal they were told that they could take cattle, but that two days before the move they were made to sell their animals. Shortly before the move, stock merchants appeared who bought cattle and sheep at ridiculously low prices. In South Africa more generally, forced stock sales were a major cause of impoverishment of tenants removed from 'black spots' as well as labor tenants evicted from white-owned farms. Former Esididini tenants claimed that they received no compensation at all.

At the time of the removal, what was to become Osizweni was a white-owned farm acquired by the SADT. Mrs D. described the removal as follows:

> *We were told that a special place had been prepared for us. We came to Osizweni and found just tents . . . We could not afford to resist – we were frightened. They told us, 'we have to get rid of you.' Under threat we had to get into the trucks. We were told that we wouldn't have to pay rent. But we had to pay, and lost a lot of property because there was not enough shelter. We were never compensated for our houses.*

Several people describe being offloaded in a mealie (maize) field that had not yet been cleared, and the discomfort of having to sleep with stalks sticking into their backs before they had time to uproot them. These removals took place in the middle of winter in a year people remember as being particularly cold, and a number (especially children) suffered from illnesses for which they could not afford treatment. Many could also not afford coal. One woman described how, in a bitterly ironic wordplay, her mother called Osizweni 'Osizini,' the place of misery. They lived in tents for more than a year before being issued with tin shacks. In *The Discarded People* (1970), Cosmas Desmond documents similar conditions in many other parts of South Africa.[5]

In describing how their lives changed after the removal, women in particular placed great emphasis on higher rents, and the rigors of having to shift from a largely subsistence to a commodified economy:

> *Before when we were farming we didn't have to buy food. We had cattle and sheep. We didn't even have to buy coal. The only problem was water – we had to dig deep holes. When we came to Osizweni we had to buy everything. Also, the rent was much higher.*

Women who had been largely engaged in agriculture came under considerable pressure to earn cash, as men's wages from migrant labor were inadequate to meet cash needs and sometimes also unreliable. Some women went to work as domestics, but the Newcastle economy in the 1960s was quite sluggish and there were few jobs. Others tried moving to Johannesburg and Durban. Mrs D.'s story is probably not unusual:

> *When I came here I had to work because of poverty. My husband was not sending back regularly. I tried to live in Johannesburg and worked as a domestic worker. But I decided to come back because I wanted to be with my children. I also wanted*

to build a house and be close to the people I knew. [When I came back to Osizweni]
I tried to get a job at Veka [a clothing factory that moved to Newcastle in 1969]. I
didn't get a job immediately. Lots of people wanted to work for Veka. A man from
Charlestown was selecting workers. The employers treated us well but the pay was
very little – only R3.75 a week. Transport was a big problem. They gave us bus
coupons, but deducted them from the wage.

Over the following decade, during which most of the removals from areas
around Newcastle took place, there was very little organized opposition.
The SPP report provides a cryptic description of removals from Lennoxton
and Fairleigh, two African freehold areas in the municipal boundaries of
Newcastle whose residents were moved to Madadeni in the 1960s: 'No
organised resistance to removal although people did not want to move.
Pressures such as closing school, cutting off water applied' (SPP 1983:
118). Cosmas Desmond's description of the removal to Madadeni of people
from Alcockspruit in 1969 sounds a similar note:

> The people, as usual, were resigned to their fate; many seemed just bewildered by
> the whole thing. They had never seen Madadeni and had no idea what to expect
> there. All they knew was that they would not have any land nor cattle. A Bantu
> Affairs Department official told them that it would be good for them to have to find
> jobs as they had become lazy living off the land at Alcockspruit.' (Desmond 1970:
> 75)

Former landowners in Alcockspruit described a more informed and
strategic response, albeit one that was heavily circumscribed. Some
landowners did, they claim, attempt to oppose the move but, as one put it,
'the government was very determined and there wasn't much we could do.'
By the late 1960s facilities in Madadeni were expanding, and former
landowners told of the strategies they deployed to acquire additional
property in the township, of their confrontations with white officials in
gaining access to township resources, and of the help they gave to people
who 'infiltrated' their land just prior to removals to gain access to township
housing.

By the mid-1970s, when removals in the Klip River (Ladysmith) district
accelerated, the broader political climate was changing along with growing
sources of support for opposition to removals. Yet the ways particular
groups and classes in different communities forged outside connections,
and the sorts of opposition they were able to mount, were shaped by locally
specific histories, class configurations, and social dynamics. Mmutlana
(1993) provides a fascinating comparative account of historical forces that

shaped resistance to removals in Steincoalspruit and Roosboom, two large Klip River freehold communities that confronted expropriation in the mid-1970s.

According to Mmutlana, the freehold area that came to be known as Steincoalspruit was purchased in the 1870s by a group of *inboekselings* (indentured servants of Boer farmers) who escaped servitude and joined a Protestant mission station in Ladysmith. Mmutlana describes them as an elite group of 'affluent "oorlam"-cum-Christian Africans, of whom the majority were non-Zulu speaking' (Mmutlana 1993: 23).[6] In the late nineteenth century the Natal Steam and Coal Company entered into a joint venture with the landowners to exploit the rich coal seams. Large numbers of workers and tenants moved into the area, while the original owners and their descendants flourished on mining royalties and some commercial farming. In the 1930s the Elandslaagte Farmers Association labeled Steincoalspruit 'a menace to white farmers,' and pushed for its expropriation. In 1939, however, the Native Affairs Commission assured the Steincoalspruit people that 'they would not be expropriated nor their rights interfered with in view of the special circumstances attached to their farm' (cited by Mmutlana 1993: 40). Threats of eviction reappeared in the 1950s, and materialized in 1977 for reasons, Mmutlana argues, that were as much about the changing imperatives of the coal mining industry as politically driven 'black spot' removal. In 1978, 11,000 tenants were moved to Ekuvukeni. Landowners were deeply divided. Some (especially descendants of the original owners who were living elsewhere) accepted compensation, while others fiercely opposed the move. They formed the Steincoalspruit Committee of Management, and mobilized all the resources at their disposal – including, very importantly, connections with the IFP and the KwaZulu government. It was precisely their non-Zulu origins, Mmutlana argues, that drove them in this direction:

> The source of IFP inclinations in Steincoalspruit can be traced from the 'oorlam' status acquired by the predecessors of the present landowners. On their arrival in Natal they strove to identify themselves with the predominant Zulu tradition in the area. The formation of the IFP in the 1970s tended to provide a home for their aspirations, because this organisation, through its leader Chief Buthelezi, was appealing to Zulu history and tradition for legitimation. (Mmutlana 1993: 54)

Soon after its formation in 1979 AFRA also became engaged in the struggle, at times in conflict with Inkatha. Throughout the 1980s Steincoalspruit landowners held tenaciously to their land, deploying both

Inkatha and AFRA in their battle with the apartheid state.[7] Deep tensions between Inkatha and AFRA surfaced at an event to celebrate the withdrawal of expropriation orders in 1991. Divisions within the 'community' were also manifested in ongoing struggles in Steincoalspruit – including moves to evict tenants in the name of 'development' and conflicts of interest within the landowning class.

Roosboom, another freehold area in the Klip River district with a population of about 11,000 that was targeted for removal in the mid-1970s, presents a very different picture. Located only 10 km from Ladysmith, Roosboom was acquired in 1908 by a syndicate of Zulu-speaking people whom Mmutlana (1993: 76) defines as a 'truly *kholwa* community' who, unlike their *oorlam-kholwa* counterparts in Steincoalspruit, had little interest in identifying with Zulu nationalism. Churches and missionary activity were to Roosboom what mining was to Steincoalspruit. Anglican and Methodist churches established influential schools in Roosboom that in turn produced an educated elite, many of them longstanding supporters of the ANC in its original, petty bourgeois form. This included Elliot Mngadi, the key organizer for the Natal Native Landowners' Association, whose father was one of the original syndicate members.

The official local history of Roosboom in the AFRA archives tells of how in the first few decades of the century Roosboom was a reasonably prosperous agricultural community that posed a competitive threat to white farmers who pushed for expropriation.[8] The turning point came in 1936, when Roosboom was effectively defined as a 'black spot' in terms of the 1936 Native Trust and Land Act. Insecurity combined with increasing hostility from white farmers resulted in declining investment in agriculture – although some Roosboom residents claim that they continued to bring produce to market in Ladysmith until the 1950s. Large numbers of new tenants moved in, and Roosboom evolved into what the SPP (1983) termed a 'peri-urban suburb of Ladysmith' housing large numbers of commuters. White farmers intent on the removal of Roosboom insisted that 'shack farming' posed a health threat to Ladysmith. In 1958 the Inspector of Squatters recommended that no newcomers be allowed to settle in Roosboom; in 1959 Verwoerd visited Roosboom to declare the closure of St Hilda's Girls School; and in 1960 Roosboom was placed under the control of the Local Health Commission. At first, according to Mngadi, landowners approved this move: 'We thought it would help to entrench us in the area, because we knew that they would spend a lot of money sinking boreholes and so on.' By the mid-1960s, however, the Health Commission started numbering houses, and refusing permission to build or extend houses. At the same time, tenants continued to move into Roosboom. By the early 1970s, pressures from white farmers for the removal of Roosboom reached a crescendo. A 1974 memo from the Ladysmith and District Farmers Association to the member of parliament (MP) for Klip River identified Roosboom as the top priority for removal to Ezakheni, then in the early stages of construction. Roosboom was not only the site of uncontrolled squatting and a 'permanent source of danger to health in Ladysmith'; in addition, the memo invoked its dangerous political history:

> In the event of terrorism, this Black Spot lies on both sides of the Durban-Johannesburg national road, and is within easy reach of the main Durban railway line. (Nelson Mandela addressed several meetings there in 1963, during the eleven months before his imprisonment) (cited in SPP 1983: 347)

In early 1975, Roosboom residents were served with expropriation orders and by 1976 all but three families had been moved to Ezakheni.[9]

Landlord-tenant relations feature prominently in Mngadi's history of the removal from Roosboom. He describes how landowners called a meeting to oppose the expropriation orders, 'only to find that the majority of the tenants told us "no you landlords can keep your land, we are going" ' (SPP 1983: 350). The rift between landowners and tenants was, he argued, the result of restrictions imposed by the Health Commission:

> Seeing that the tenants had no stake in the land, as far as they were concerned it was now better to go than to stay at a place where they could not make extensions for their children. For them – the quicker they went, the better; the sooner they were removed, the better . . . That's how hard it is to be a leader. Many people were really surprised and disappointed. They had expected resistance, especially where I was. I'd been involved in resisting removals at Besterspruit, Besters, Kingsley, and all over, but when it came to my own area, nothing happened. As far as I'm concerned, we were softened by this Local Health Commission. ('The Removal from Roosboom,' reprinted in SPP 1983: 349–351)

Although unable to oppose expropriation, Roosboom landowners set about organizing to reclaim their land soon after being moved to Ezakheni. Divisions among them were far more muted than in Steincoalspruit, and their strategies clearly reflect changing constraints and opportunities. One of the first efforts was in 1976, when they went through established white liberal channels to arrange for P.C. Kershoff of the South African Institute of Race Relations to write a letter to Helen Suzman, the Progressive Party MP, about the Roosboom expropriation (Mmutlana 1993: 107). In the late 1970s and 1980s as organized support for opposition to removals took shape, the Roosboom landowners mobilized Mngadi's connections to tap into AFRA, which in turn publicized the Roosboom case internationally. Following the unbanning of the ANC in 1990, Roosboom landowners moved swiftly to reoccupy their land.

Unlike their Steincoalspruit counterparts, Roosboom landowners did not operate through Inkatha. On the contrary their relations with Steven Sithebe, the key Inkatha figure engaged in opposing removals, became increasingly hostile. In the late 1980s this hostility erupted in open warfare, when Sithebe brought heavily armed troops of young men from an adjacent reserve into Ezakheni, and unleashed them in the section of the township occupied mainly by former Roosboom tenants. This overt and indiscriminate violence, discussed more fully below, stands in sharp contrast to the more strategic and sharply focused violence that took hold in Madadeni.

The sort of oppositional capacity evident in the Khumalosville struggle in the 1950s re-emerged in Umbulwane and Matiwane's Kop, two freehold communities near Ladysmith threatened with expropriation in the late 1970s. Although Umbulwane is a small peri-urban extension of Steadville (the municipal township adjacent to Ladysmith), and whereas Matiwane's Kop is a very large community with strong agrarian roots, political organization in both places bridged the divide between landowners and tenants, and posed a defiant challenge to different agents of the apartheid state.

In Umbulwane, brutal moves by the Ladysmith local authorities – including smashing houses of people defined as 'squatters' while they were away at work in August 1980 – were met with growing opposition. A significant dimension of the struggle in Umbulwane was that the Resident's Committee included both landowners and tenants – indeed the chair of the committee was a tenant – and two of the particularly active landowners on the committee were women. In times of crisis, most landlords and tenants attended general meetings and participated in discussions of various options for action. They also contributed to a reserve emergency fund.

In December 1980, in consultation with community leaders from Steadville who had been active in the struggles of the 1950s, the Residents' Committee of Umbulwane prepared a memorandum protesting the proposed removal and the demolition of houses, and pointing out that they paid

municipal rates but received no services at all. The memorandum was sent
to the Ladysmith Town Council, district and regional authorities, and Piet
Koornhof, the Minister of Co-operation and Development. In March 1981
Koornhof's office replied, reiterating the impending removal and maintaining that people were squatting illegally. The Umbulwane Residents'
Committee's reply in June of that year, composed after a great deal of
consultation, went far beyond local issues to address the broader political
confrontation taking place in South African society at large:

> The Government states that illegal people must go back to their place of origin yet
> people were expelled from white farms and most of those farms were taken by the
> Government. Some of these people were aiming to settle in Steadville which is the
> urban Black settlement, but due to the fact there was no housing, people became
> tenants of Umbulwane.
>
> We do not believe that we can only live in KwaZulu. We know that we owned
> a lot of large pieces of land all over Natal (that do no fall in KwaZulu) and this has
> been occupied a hundred years or more before the Whites came to Natal and took
> land for themselves.
>
> We know we can ask for rights in South Africa. We can ask for jobs, pensions,
> justice, and more in South Africa. (reprinted in SPP 1983: 526)

In addition to democratic practices, the Umbulwane struggle was informed
by increasingly sophisticated understandings of fissures within and between different branches of the state. One of these was a disagreement
between the Ladysmith Town Council and the Drakensberg Administration
Board (DAB) on the future of African housing in Steadville. Undoubtedly
aware of the furore that would erupt if they attempted removal, officials
within the DAB were prepared to consider allowing a permanent African
population to remain in the municipal township; the Town Council,
however, wanted to eliminate both Umbulwane and Steadville entirely. At
the same time, however, they were being held back by constraints
emanating from the Department of Co-operation and Development, headed
by Piet Koornhof (SPP 1983: 521). A key figure in the Botha reforms,
Koornhof was engaged in an effort to soften the image of the apartheid state
in the early 1980s. Framed in full knowledge of Koornhof's project, the
Umbulwane letters held his feet to a well-publicized rhetorical fire – from
which he, in turn, backed off in 1982.

Those engaged in the struggle against removals in Matiwane's Kop also
invoked Koornhof's reconciliatory statements. As one of the key participants explained to me:

Matiwane's Kop became a sore thumb, and we pushed Koornhof into a corner. We were doing everything to embarrass them. The government had to be very careful because they knew the whole world was listening. People from Germany and other places would go back and shout.

The title of Chapter 2, 'The Land of our Comfort,' is borrowed from a memorandum to Koornhof in 1980 protesting the proposed removal from Matiwane's Kop. The 'ever running streams and innumerable springs with crystal clear and cool waters' forms part of an environmental history of Matiwane's Kop, which tells of how the 'Shabalala Tribe' purchased the farm in 1870, after it had been rejected by white farmers as being 'unproductive and watery':

> These previous owners were White – they abandoned the farm because it was not productive – not arable – they failed to make a living out of it – it was therefore abandoned and 'forgotten' for White men's habitation. The Natal Land and Colonization Co. Ltd. then took it in trust, until some adventurer could take a chance on it. Nobody was forthcoming among the Whites because word had gone round that is was a 'White man's grave' . . . The Matiwaneskop Tribe has worked up the farm and made it productive and comparable with any other farm with the same population density per kilometre. (Memorandum prepared by the people of Matiwane's Kop for presentation to the Minister of Co-operation and Development, 1980)

Shortly before the memorandum was written, officials from Pretoria and Ladysmith had tried to use a young and inexperienced chief in Matiwane's Kop to help leverage the removal. The chief reported these developments to his councilors. They immediately called a general meeting in Matiwane's Kop, after which they marched unannounced into the local commissioner's office in Ladysmith to inform him that they were the legitimate representatives of the community, and that he and other representatives of the state would have to deal with them as a body and not the chief as an individual (SPP 1983: 454). The official history of Matiwane's Kop contained in the memorandum tells a pointed story of how the Shabalalas, who had been working for white farmers, bought the farm in 1870 to protect their young chief who was being abused by a white farmer.

The invocation of chieftancy and the tribal character of the community is also significant in light of the connections that the Matiwane's Kop leadership forged with Inkatha. The SPP report remarked somewhat disparagingly on how most of the leaders were a relatively privileged rural elite, who were also members of Inkatha: 'This has encouraged a dependency on Ulundi which may, in the long term, serve to undermine rather than enhance the community's campaign' (SPP 1983: 457). Leaders of the Matiwane's Kop struggle whom I met in 1997 described a more strategic relationship with Inkatha as well as with AFRA. When the threat of removal first loomed, 'Inkatha was the only organization seen as speaking for the people; it was said if we join Inkatha we would be protected'; there was also some debate over the relative merits of Inkatha and AFRA. The balance of opinion shifted in favor of AFRA when Matiwane's Kop landowners discovered that the title deeds had been transferred to the state, apparently with the collaboration of the KwaZulu government. At that point, they went back to Inkatha and insisted on a meeting with Steven Sithebe:

> *Instead of explaining, he said we've been going behind his back. There was a lot of shouting, but no explanation. From that day we became enemies with Sithebe. That was when we started up again with AFRA.*

This history was recounted to me within the context of deep divisions between IFP and ANC-aligned groupings within Matiwane's Kop, with the former invoking the chieftancy to assert their position and the latter recalling their centrality in the successful resistance to removal.

Direct connections with organized labor form a key part of this history. When the Dunlop factory, described in Chapter 4, was established in Ladysmith in the early 1970s, men from Matiwane's Kop – including members of the landowning class with lineage connections to the chieftancy – came to constitute a major segment of the workforce. With the development of union activity in the late 1970s and early 1980s, some of them rose to prominence as shop stewards in MAWU (Metal and Allied Workers Union). Widely seen as one of the most 'workerist' unions, MAWU was also at the forefront of developing practices of consultative workplace democracy. Workplace organizing informed resistance to removals at Matiwane's Kop as well as vice versa, and such synergy helps to illuminate the apparent anomaly noted by the SPP report – namely that, despite the existence of a 'relatively privileged rural elite' with links to Inkatha, Matiwane's Kop 'has acquired a useful reputation of militancy; this and the adroit manner in which community opposition has been mobilised by its leaders have encouraged other threatened communities in the area to adopt a stronger position against being moved as well' (SPP 1983: 457). One of the particularly significant articulations between land and labor struggles was the way landowners and tenants were able to present a united front, and to extend these strategies to other communities. For example:

In early 1982 a dispute arose over rents between an individual landowner and his tenants at Jonono's Kop. When it reached the commissioner in Ladysmith, he informed the tenants that the land no longer belonged to their landlord but to the state, and that they had no need to pay any rent at all. This of course threatened to set landowners and tenants against each other. The community has managed to weather this storm by agreeing to continue with the rent arrangements as traditionally fixed and thus far there has been no further comeback. At the meeting at which this was decided (attended by people from Matiwane's Kop and also by the local KwaZulu member of the Legislative Assembly (MLA)) a special committee was elected to represent Jonono's Kop in any further dealings with officialdom over removals. (SPP 1983: 455).

The overlapping land and labor movements in and around Ladysmith represent a locally specific form of social movement unionism that flies in the face of claims that the articulation of workplace and community politics was a distinctively urban phenomenon. They also call into question Mamdani's (1996) dichotomy between urban civil society and rural decentralized despotism. We turn now to the sharply divergent political dynamics through which Madadeni-Osizweni and Ezakheni took shape over the course of the 1980s, focusing on the dangers inherent in efforts to read the character of political struggles off structural conditions.

Making Space: The Differentiated Dynamics of Township Formation

Newly formed relocation townships like Madadeni-Osizweni and Ezakheni took shape in relation to – and were partly constitutive of – several broader political-economic processes. First was state-sponsored industrial decentralization, discussed in far greater detail in Chapter 4. In the 1970s, both Newcastle and Ladysmith became the locus of several large heavy industries – the expansion of which coincided with the explosion of labor protest in Durban in 1973. After 1981, the apartheid state offered substantial subsidies for light industries to set up in and near relocation townships. The rapidly expanding industrial workforce in the vicinity of Newcastle and Ladysmith formed an obvious focus for the resurgent labor movement. Yet industrial labor organization assumed quite different forms in Ladysmith and Newcastle – a reflection not only of the character of the industries, but also political dynamics of the townships arising in part out of local histories of dispossession from the land. Over the 1970s and 1980s, decisive differences in workplace politics in the two places in turn interacted with politics in the townships to produce the divergent local dynamics that have become clearly evident in the post-apartheid era. As we shall see below, these divergent local political practices and trajectories are also gendered in very different ways.

A second, closely related set of processes turned around the formation of the KwaZulu Legislative Assembly in 1972, the massive expansion of the bantustan bureaucracy in the 1970s and 1980s, and the reworking of Inkatha as the vehicle of Zulu ethnic nationalism and patriarchal authority (Maré and Hamilton 1987; Mzala 1988; Bonnin et al. 1996). For apartheid architects and their African collaborators, large and comparatively well-resourced relocation townships like Madadeni and Ezakheni represented key sites for the development of an African petty bourgeoisie and entrepreneurial class, conjuring up the close involvement of members of the landowning *kholwa* elite in the earlier manifestations of Inkatha in the 1920s and 1930s. These hegemonic dimensions of the apartheid project are notably missing from flattened categories like 'decentralized despotism.' So too are the ways that Zulu ethnic nationalism and its relationship to class formation assumed distinctive forms in the two townships – as did manifest-ations of violence in the late 1980s and early 1990s.

Third, oppositional politics in Madadeni-Osizweni and Ezakheni ar-ticulated differently with the national liberation movement and its changing dynamics over the 1970s and 1980s, through translocal connections that both reflected and shaped local political practices and dynamics. The differential connections that youth activists forged with the exiled ANC-SACP, the United Democratic Front (UDF), and with organized labor were in turn closely related to locally specific and class-inflected forms of Zulu ethnic nationalism and patriarchal authority, as well as to divergent and differentially gendered practices of organizing in the workplace and in the community.

A particular irony attaches to these divergent processes of place-making, especially if one subscribes to dichotomized understandings of 'the urban' and 'the rural' that equate the former with vibrant civil society and the latter with decentralized despotism. Although structurally similar, the Newcastle-Madadeni-Osizweni complex became significantly more urban than Ladysmith-Ezakheni, in part because of the establishment of a giant heavy industry in the early 1970s. In addition, the Newcastle townships were formed through a more complete process of dispossession than their Ladysmith counterparts. Madadeni in particular became a showpiece of the apartheid state, widely touted as a protected enclave of urban modernity within which an African petty bourgeoisie could flourish. Ezakheni, in contrast, has remained far closer to its agrarian roots, both through proximity to an old rural reserve, and because of the survival of nearby African freehold areas like Matiwane's Kop and Driefontein that resisted or evaded removals. Yet Madadeni has come to be governed by a politics of fear, while in Ezakheni there has taken shape a form of substantive democracy that some would call 'social capital' but that is far more usefully understood in terms of ongoing, power-laden practices in multiple, interconnected arenas.

Madadeni-Osizweni: 'Urban Opportunity' and the Politics of Fear

In the early 1960s, Osizweni was one of the first relocation settlements for people forcibly removed from 'black spots' in coal-rich areas in the vicinity of Newcastle. In his report on conditions in 1969, Cosmas Desmond (1970) labeled Osizweni a 'sub-economic' township with far fewer facilities than the adjacent township of Madadeni:

> It has about 20,000 inhabitants and more are arriving all the time; it is 'planned' for 72,000. They are all either completely indigent or of a very low income group. 'Squatters' from White farms are usually settled here rather than at Madadeni; some choose it because the rent is lower. About two-thirds of the houses are one-roomed, asbestos-under-iron structures, which measure 12 feet by 9 feet. The other one-third have two rooms of about the same size, one of brick, the other all corrugated iron. Whole families, up to fifteen people, live in these. Some have added shacks of corrugated iron, others have built mud huts, which is all illegal and adds to the slum-like appearance but at least provides more living space. Rows upon rows of these tiny 'houses' make a most depressing sight. (Desmond 1970: 76–77)

Desmond went on to note the exceptionally high rates of malnutrition in Osizweni, and the inability of many residents to afford coal to warm their houses in the freezing winters. In official documents Osizweni was described as a 'self-building' township with rudimentary infrastructural services, intended for former tenants, unemployed and unskilled 'squatters' and poorer urban dwellers (Todes 1997). By the mid-1990s Osizweni remained far poorer than Madadeni, although middle-class enclaves of comparatively large brick houses had sprung up, occupied mainly by teachers and nurses. Over the years Osizweni also earned a reputation as a more militant place than Madadeni although such militance was far more diffuse and disorganized than in Ezakheni.

Cosmas Desmond's description of Madadeni in 1969 is quite instructive:

> Madadeni is eight miles from Newcastle and, as townships go, is rather a superior one . . . There is a two-year waiting list for houses. The houses are mainly four-roomed with toilet and water outside for which the rent is R4.23 a month. There are shops, schools and the usual township facilities. A Training College is being built there to replace St. Chad's, the former Anglican college near Ladysmith [which was forced to close in the late 1960s]. There is a large hospital for chest diseases, but while a General Hospital is being built, the people still have to go to Newcastle for general medical treatment. (Desmond 1970: 76)

Apartheid planners described Madadeni in more glowing terms. It was destined to become a 'model township' designed by a prominent town planner with one of the first urban home ownership schemes for Africans (Todes 1997). Entrepreneurial opportunities would abound in this new space of urban modernity that represented the ultimate legitimation of 'separate development.'

These claims were bolstered by the booming local economy in the first part of the 1970s, when a plant of the state-owned Iron and Steel Corporation was established in Newcastle. The huge infusion of resources and population made Newcastle and Madadeni-Osizweni the most rapidly growing urban area in the country. 'It was the real buzz town,' recalled one man whose father moved back to the region from the Reef to establish his own business; 'lots of people saw Madadeni as the city of the future where there would be successful black businesses.' He described how many actual and aspiring African entrepreneurs like his father with roots in the region – many of them descendants of the landowning *kholwa* – flocked back to grasp these new opportunities. There are interesting parallels with the 1920s and 1930s, when concern over access to agricultural land was the key force that propelled the African petty bourgeoisie into alliance with Zulu traditionalists. By the 1960s agricultural opportunities had closed down, and trading had become the key avenue of accumulation. 'People knew they were taking part in a bantustan experiment,' commented another resident whose parents had also moved back to the region from the Reef in the hopes of establishing a trading business.

In practice, the course of accumulation was far more limited and problematic than these aspiring entrepreneurs anticipated. Particularly in the initial period, white local officials exercised bureaucratic and often paternalistic controls. Alison Todes' archival research is revealing:

Hawking of products other than milk was forbidden as it might undermine businesses on designated sites. Traders who had operated in Lennoxton or Fairleigh [the municipal 'locations' that were removed to Madadeni in the 1960s] had to apply for sites and were not necessarily granted them. For example, Zacheus Mack Gumede was turned down on the grounds that his understanding of business was too limited. By contrast Mr H.T. Madonsela, a trader who owned an eating house in Fairleigh and wanted to set up several larger businesses (including cinemas and garages) in Madadeni was informed that a principal of 'one man one business' applied. (Todes 1997: 313)

With the formation of the KwaZulu Legislative Assembly (KLA) and Inkatha in the 1970s, the dynamics of accumulation in Madadeni and other relocation areas became closely intertwined with bantustan politics, and brought many aspiring traders into conflict with efforts by bantustan authorities to forge connections with large-scale capitalist interests.

These clashes in turn illuminate some of the profound contradictions of the petty bourgeois base of support for Zulu ethnic nationalism. In one of its early policy statements in 1973, the KLA 'firmly rejected any policy . . . which could have the tendency and/or ultimate result that the wealth, resources and commercial opportunities of KwaZulu would no longer be reserved and developed exclusively for us' (cited by Maré and Hamilton 1987: 109). Trading interests in the KLA spoke specifically of the need for KwaZulu 'to purchase all shops owned by Non-Bantu in KwaZulu and lease them to Zulus' (cited by Maré and Hamilton 1987: 109). Such statements expressed key hegemonic dimensions of the apartheid project, manifest most clearly in places like Madadeni. Yet in practice they ran into head-on conflict with Gatsha Buthelezi's strategy of forging alliances with large-scale national capital through the mechanism of tripartite companies, know as tripcos.

Tripcos entailed three-way business deals among white capital, the bantustan authority, and the Bantu Investment Corporation (BIC), an arm of the apartheid state that sought to promote 'separate development' in the homelands.[10] Most of the white business interests entering these agreements were large-scale retail and food-processing arms of national conglomerates. With the formation of large commuter townships like Madadeni-Osizweni that compelled the commodification of livelihood, national retail chains were concerned to capture growing markets.[11] Initially, at least, tripcos were portrayed as a means for 'the people' to gain a potential share of wealth by increasingly acquiring shares (Maré and Hamilton 1987: 100). A relatively small group of African traders with close political links to bantustan authorities and the BIC became directly involved in tripco arrangements, and reaped substantial profits. At the same time, as national retail chains took hold in the townships, large segments of those who aspired to accumulation were effectively excluded. 'Halfway through we felt as though the rules were being changed,' commented the son of an aspiring grocer who was pushed out of business; 'we were very discontented and angry. There was no way a small business could match competition from the Madadeni Checkers [a national supermarket chain].' Maré and Hamilton (1987: 109) describe how, in their efforts to challenge Buthelezi's power bloc and its alliance with white capital, opponents of the tripcos sought alliance with the Zulu king; and how, in turn, they were out-maneuvered by Buthelezi.

Transport between the townships and Newcastle was another key source of tension, which exploded in September 1975 when Trans Tugela Transport (TTT) – a bus company owned by the BIC with a virtual monopoly of township routes – raised roundtrip fares between the townships and the 'white' town from 50c to 60c. According to a report in *Work in Progress* (Anon. 1980), bus fares had increased by 400 percent over a two-year period and consumed 17 percent of average wages in Madadeni-Osizweni compared to 5 percent in Durban. TTT had been formed when the BIC took over an African-owned bus company that had been established with BIC loans, but failed to weather increasing fuel costs. Working-class anger over increasing fares thus coincided with growing resentment of segments of the petty bourgeoisie who had been excluded from the tripcos. 'When the BIC moved in as TTT, this was seen as a change from black to white ownership. In the same way, the building of Checkers in Madadeni was seen as a loss of black empowerment,' I was told. Class-based coincidence of resentment found expression in one of the rallying cries of the bus boycotters: 'We want Mhlaba [one of the owners of the failed company] back!'

The bus boycott dragged on for five weeks, during which there were tense and sometimes bloody confrontations with police, and many white residents of Newcastle purchased firearms (Anon. 1980). There were also significant tensions within the Madadeni township council between the mayor Dr Frank Mdlalose, a close ally of Buthelezi's, and the rest of the council which called for the removal of the TTT (Anon. 1980). One of my informants commented that in Osizweni 'there was a lot of militancy against that Mdlalose – he really sold us out.'[12] The boycott ended following an announcement that the BIC and the KwaZulu government would take over TTT on a 50-50 basis: 'We were told that the buses were now ours,' recounted one of my informants with a cynical smile. The new company 'rationalized' routes – which amounted to charging lower fares for shorter trips, and a differentiated fare structure. People who lived closest to the main roads were better off than those in more remote parts of the township, which in turn created divisions between those who wanted to continue the boycott and those willing to stop. In addition, my informant noted, the price increases did not stop, and Mdlalose subsequently became director of the new KwaZulu transport company.

Most ANC activists were too young to recall the 1975 bus boycott, and most of the older township residents whom I met were hesitant to speak about it. ANC activists led me to an elderly man, who framed his history of the bus boycott in the context of his broader experience of very low levels of political activity in Newcastle and its environs. This history of apathy, he said, made the 1975 bus boycott all the more remarkable:

> Our [bus] strike really was unique. They [i.e. the police] tried to get the leaders, but there were no leaders – we were all leaders. It was quite spontaneous. We only had one public meeting.

The 1975 bus boycott was also a one-time event. In September 1979 when oil prices spiked, bus fares between Newcastle and Madadeni-Osizweni increased by 25 percent but elicited no overt response. Similar fare increases in Ladysmith-Ezakheni sparked an extremely militant boycott that ended, according to *Work in Progress* (Anon. 1979), 'with a temporary victory for the working class in that fares have been reduced.'

Despite their apparent political quiescence – particularly, as we shall see, in comparison to Ezakheni – Madadeni and to a lesser extent Osizweni became major recruiting grounds for Umkhonto we Sizwe (or MK), the armed wing of the ANC, in the 1980s. A former ANC youth activist from Madadeni put it this way:

> In terms of mass mobilization, we were not in the spotlight. But in terms of creating more of a military than a political base, we were hitting very hard. The ANC couldn't organize in Madadeni and Osizweni, but they pulled people into the underground structures.

Ironically, just as Madadeni's reputation as a 'model township' attracted aspiring entrepreneurs, it also contributed to conditions for emergence of a militant youth movement. Particularly after the Soweto uprising of 1976, many parents in major metropolitan centers sought to send their children to seemingly quieter and safer regions. For those with roots in Northern Natal, Madadeni was an obvious choice – combining newly constructed schools with traditional Zulu authority. In practice, rather than submitting to patriarchal authority, many youngsters brought their militance with them. One of them described his experiences as follows:

> We students [from Soweto] were very active and vocal. We would sing about
> Mandela and Tambo – almost all the schools were mobilized by us. In 1982 there
> was a major student strike. It happened in a very coordinated way, and there were
> riots in the schools. We still had links to the Transvaal and the Soweto schools.
> That's what provoked the KwaZulu government to send guys in to suppress us. You
> could see then the deployment of a very aggressive KwaZulu police. In 1982 at the
> time of the big school boycott, our school was the base of resistance in Madadeni.
> We brought in people from the Transvaal and toyi-toyied to our school to demand
> that they open a new school. That's when the KwaZulu police came in to disrupt us.
> They identified what they called the sayinyova rebels by a special cream called
> 'Perm' that people from Soweto put in their hair. They forced us to kneel down and
> rub our heads in the sand.

These angry young rebels formed the pool from which MK recruited operatives in the second half of the 1980s. Most of my discussions on this topic were with young ANC activists in Newcastle in June and July 1997, when the Truth and Reconciliation Commission was preparing to hear testimony on political assassinations in Madadeni. In recounting the history of the involvement of young men from Madadeni in underground structures of the liberation struggle, these veterans stress how Madadeni came to the attention of the top leadership through the history of youth militance in the late 1970s and early 1980s. In addition, Siphiwe Nyanda – a prominent figure of MK who became Chief of Staff after Chris Hani's assassination in 1993 – was from Madadeni. Two other people figure prominently in these stories. One is Harry Gwala, a hardline member of the SACP who was released from detention in 1988 and played a central role in organizing anti-apartheid struggles from his base in Pietermaritzburg.[13] In local reconstructions of the history of this period, considerable importance attaches to Gwala's role in forging connections between military structures of the ANC-SACP and the Madadeni youth movement. Yet it is also clear that militant activism by a relatively small group of young men in Madadeni predates Gwala's release from detention.

The other centrally important figure in these stories is Hlalanathi Sibankulu, known as Professor for his incisive intelligence. Professor Sibankulu matriculated from a Madadeni high school in the late 1970s, and went to Durban where he attended a technical college. In the early 1980s he returned to Newcastle, where he became deeply involved in both the labor and the youth movements. According to one of his former colleagues:

> *Prof could really speak politics – he had a mission of organizing. [In addition to union organizing] he also organized youth, especially during the period when the ANC called for ungovernability.*

In 1993 Professor Sibankulu was assassinated in Madadeni, apparently by the KwaZulu police. His murder was one of a series of highly targeted assassinations and arson attacks discussed more fully below.

Professor Sibankulu was by no means the only activist operating simultaneously on the youth and labor fronts. This pattern of joint engagement became a distinctive feature of the way the struggle unfolded in Madadeni-Osizweni, along with close links to the military wing of the exiled liberation movement. It also set in motion interacting dynamics that continue to reverberate in local politics, and that are deeply entwined with key dimensions of national politics.

First and most obviously, the forms of resistance that took shape in Newcastle-Madadeni-Osizweni represent particular local manifestations of the vanguardist tendency in the national liberation struggle, carried forward through a distinctive set of understandings and political practices. While organizing took place simultaneously on the labor, youth, and underground fronts, it was always clear that the labor movement was subordinate to the broader liberation struggle. Local ANC activists with whom I spoke articulated these points with great clarity in contrasting their *modus operandi* with those of more 'workerist' trade unionists:

> *Politics from the trade unions were very different from those of the UDF and the liberation movement. Trade union politics are more workerist. Everything should be approved by the general membership. In the broader liberation movement you assume you know what needs to be done, and take far-reaching decisions . . . There were trade unionists [in Newcastle] who were mainly interested in labor and not as broadly politicized as you would expect. That category of trade unionists were politically empowered by MK cadres.*

One of the other consequences of the ways in which labor and liberation politics were linked was that divisions within the youth movement spilled over into the labor movement. An intense crisis erupted in 1988, when a group of Osizweni labor organizers-cum-youth activists attempted to form a breakaway group. Tensions generated in the course of this political struggle in turn carried over into the labor movement, and further undermined its effectiveness. These weaknesses within the labor movement, generated by the ways in which it articulated with the liberation movement, were compounded as we shall see in Chapter 4, by the character of the major industries that took hold in Newcastle.

The vanguardist character of political culture and practices that took shape in the Newcastle townships was also deeply gendered, as are contemporary accounts of the history. Most obviously, very few women were directly involved in the intersecting labor, youth, and underground structures.[14] The predictable reason given in retrospect is that the work was simply too dangerous for women. Also in retrospect, there is an interesting tendency among ANC activists to talk about how, in contrast to the ANC, Inkatha had considerable success in mobilizing women through the Inkatha Women's Brigade – an observation sometimes linked with allusions to women not having a broad political understanding.[15] The 'pre-political character' of women workers also figures prominently in explanations of the problems of labor organizing in Newcastle. Women's involvement in the labor movement was very different in Ladysmith-Ezakheni – as were the ways in which many, if not most, women living in different townships experienced political violence in their everyday lives.

In 1994 when I started this research, Madadeni and Osizweni seemed miraculously to have evaded the civil war raging through KwaZulu-Natal. Ezakheni, in contrast, had just emerged from a period of intense violence. White local government officials described the Newcastle townships as 'very quiet places'; so too did many of the township residents whom Alison Todes and I met in the second half of 1994. Madadeni in particular was widely represented as a quiet, 'polite' place.

Former ANC youth activists present a very different picture. They describe how the Special Branch (the security division of the police force that dealt with political matters) set up its regional headquarters in Newcastle with the specific intent of eliminating them. In addition, they claim, Inkatha deployed a number of KwaZulu police recruits who were trained by the South African army in the Caprivi Strip for hit squad activities; a number of these men were recruited from Madadeni and deployed back there to carry out highly targeted actions to eliminate the leadership. The assassinations of Professor Sibankulu and other local activists were part of this strategy, as were firebombings of their houses.

In the second half of the 1980s, Newcastle also became the sub-regional headquarters of the national Joint Management Centre (JMC), the coordinating arm of the National Security Management System set up P.W. Botha and his 'securocrats' to manage the state of emergency declared in 1986.[16] JMCs were designed to contain dissent through the simultaneous deployment of state-sponsored violence and strategies aimed at 'winning hearts and minds' (WHAM) of township residents. All over the country, Community Liaison Forums of the JMCs focused on extending benefits and incorporating within their sphere of influence 'churches, youth groups, neighbourhood associations, vigilantes, traders, sports clubs, interest groups, journalists, opinion-makers, shebeen-owners, cultural groups, moderate political organizations, teachers, etc.' (Swilling and Phillips 1989: 83). Since the history of co-optation is so sensitive, I explicitly avoided asking questions about JMC activity in Newcastle. Nevertheless, a number of my conversations with ANC activists contained allusions to efforts by the Newcastle JMC to co-opt local activists and divide the youth movement.

From my own circumscribed position as a visiting researcher, the extent to which rifts within the youth movement of the 1980s were the product of JMC co-optation as opposed to internally generated tensions – or indeed some combination – remains a secret. What is clear, however, is that these divisions pulled the labor movement apart, and continue to reverberate in local politics. Together with local experiences of state-sponsored violence, they amplified the politics of fear that pervaded the Newcastle townships. The contrast with Ezakheni, where vibrant and broadly based forms of political mobilization took hold, is quite dramatic.

Ezakheni: Elements in the Formation of a Vibrant Civil Society
If Osizweni originated from the overt brutality of early forced removals and Madadeni from the hegemonic dimensions of apartheid, Ezakheni was forged in the crucible of escalating opposition to removals and the emergence of a militant and highly organized labor movement. Resistance to removals in Matiwane's Kop and surrounding areas, as we saw earlier, was closely linked with the labor movement and spearheaded by a scion of chiefly family with a broad base of support in an increasingly organized worker-peasantry. A significant proportion of the industrial workforce in Ladysmith has continued to be based in Matiwane's Kop and other

surviving freehold communities in the vicinity of the town. The more rural character of Ladysmith-Ezakheni compared to Newcastle and its adjacent townships stemmed also from its smaller size and from the proximity of Ezakheni to one of the original Shepstone reserves. This area, known as Umhlumayo, was also the base of Steven Sithebe, the KwaZulu MLA who, as we saw earlier, was actively engaged with some of the Klip River freehold communities resisting removals. Over the course of the 1980s, Sithebe earned a reputation as a notorious Inkatha warlord who deployed his control over young rural men defined as 'warriors' (*amabutho*) to launch vicious attacks on Ezakheni. Both of these more rural dimensions and connections that have gone into the making of Ezakheni have contributed to the emergence of a stronger and far more cohesive civil society than in the Newcastle townships.

Sithebe's position both as a rural warlord perched threateningly on the border of Ezakheni and as a prominent member of the KLA stood in sharp contrast to the petty bourgeois character of the Madadeni leadership of Inkatha. In addition to Frank Mdlalose, a medical doctor with a lucrative practice in the township, the KLA-linked leadership of Madadeni included a prominent lawyer, Richard Madonsela. They, in turn, were part of a relatively large and growing middle class, attracted by the promise of expanding urban opportunity. Ezakheni, in contrast, attracted no such middle class. Most of what could be termed a petty bourgeoisie in Ezakheni were from Roosboom. As we saw earlier, former landowners in Roosboom were deeply resentful of being moved into Ezakheni, had rejected Sithebe's intervention, and fought actively to reclaim their land. Indeed the first mayor of Ezakheni was Elliot Mngadi, a leading – but ultimately unsuccessful – figure in the effort to resist removals.

Ezakheni residents' accounts of violence in the late 1980s and early 1990s point repeatedly to Steven Sithebe as its chief source. These accounts are not only remarkably consistent; in addition, the readiness with which people were willing to launch into discussions of township violence with me contrasts sharply with the general denial of violence in Madadeni by all but a small group of ANC activists. According to these accounts, episodes of violence in Ezakheni frequently erupted on weekends, when busloads of young rural men from Msinga – reportedly mobilized and paid by Sithebe – would arrive in a particular section of the township occupied by former residents of a freehold area who had forged close links with Inkatha:

The base was in C Section. It was very well supplied with weapons. Sithebe had access to a lot of arms. We all knew he was getting weapons from the KwaZulu government. He didn't like the ANC.'

From this staging point, which was adjacent to an area occupied mainly by former Roosboom tenants, Sithebe's troops would move through the township killing indiscriminately – including, it is said, a number of Inkatha supporters. On several occasions, people recounting this history of violence insisted that I accompany them to the area of the township where fighting was intense and burnt-out shells of houses remained as dreadful reminders. Each person I spoke to provided horrifying accounts of brutality personally witnessed or experienced. Many of them also leveled accusations of participation by the KwaZulu police, as well as white police in blackface. Sithebe's troops, in contrast, are often portrayed as 'innocent people who didn't even know what they were coming for.'

These recollections of the horrors wreaked by Sithebe along with his *amabutho* and the police in the late 1980s and early 1990s remained central to local political dynamics later in the decade. In part, as we shall see later, these memories are deployed to bolster demands for resources for township reconstruction. In addition, and perhaps more importantly, they form a major ingredient in the ongoing production of social and political cohesion in what is, in practice, a highly differentiated community. One man put it very succinctly: 'By *moering* [murdering] us, Sithebe brought us together.'

There are two important ways in which people recall how cohesion worked in the past. First was the organization of defense units to ward off the Inkatha attacks. For example:

We took a resolution after experiencing an ambush when four people were killed. No-one would run away and leave their houses empty. We resolved to let the old people leave. When they [i.e. Sithebe's troops] came we fought – it was a hell of a fighting situation. We had two work shifts. It was do or die. We were very organized and they couldn't occupy any of the houses. Even people who weren't fighting were contributing money and help. Women were helping along with men to defend the township.

These stories are told mainly by people living in sections of the township where the attacks were focused. They also tell of how, initially, people in other parts of the township were shielded from and ignored the violence, but how they were increasingly drawn into contributing to the defense effort.

The second account is of an extraordinary peace accord between ANC and Inkatha supporters reached in mid-1994, following episodes of intense violence in the period leading up to the national elections in April of that year. All agree that the accord was made possible by Sithebe's severe illness and subsequent death. Church leaders played a central role in the process of negotiations. Those with whom I spoke placed considerable emphasis on how their political neutrality gave them the legitimacy to negotiate with both sides. Both they and ANC supporters argue that the indiscriminate violence of Sithebe's troops had severely eroded Inkatha's relatively small base of support in Ezakheni. In October 1994, shortly before I began my research in Ladysmith-Ezakheni, the process of negotiations culminated in what was by all accounts an extraordinary peace rally in the section of Ezakheni where violence had been most intense. Many people described how several cows were slaughtered for a communal feast and how, amidst prayers and blessings from the *bafundisi* [priests] of all the main churches, both sides in the conflict made commitments to maintain peace. As one person described the rally, 'it was really like a church situation.' The rally continues to reverberate in local politics, where invocations and memories of it constitute a key resource both for making claims and for smoothing over conflicts. In the years since the rally, peace has prevailed in Ezakheni.

The sharp contrast between Ezakheni and Madadeni-Osizweni in forms of violence must be set in the context of broader political culture and everyday practices, manifest most clearly in the interaction between the youth and labor movements in the 1970s and 1980s. Earlier we saw how the youth and labor movements in the Newcastle townships were closely linked with one another, and with involvement of key figures in the underground structures of the liberation movement – and how struggles in these arenas were both informed by and reinforced vanguardist political practices. In contrast, putatively 'workerist' industrial unions prevailed in Ladysmith. While there was a clear separation between workplace organizing and the youth movement, the latter was shaped in important ways by the culture and practices of shopfloor democracy.

Chapter 4 contains a far more detailed account of how powerful industrial unions took hold in Ladysmith, and the difficulties they encountered in Newcastle. For purposes of the present discussion, the key point is that both MAWU and NUTW (National Union of Textile Workers) – two of the most militant independent unions – established a strong presence in

Ladysmith factories in the late 1970s. Both unions maintained an explicit distance from Congress politics, and both actively sought to recruit Inkatha members. Most importantly, both subscribed to consultative practices on the shopfloor and to the creation of a substantial stratum of shop stewards which, in the case of NUTW and its successor SACTWU (South African Clothing and Textile Workers Union), included women.

The experience of one woman who was also deeply engaged in the youth movement is instructive:

> *SACTWU was not empowering to women – all the top leadership was men. But it was the first union that really opened my eyes. It was really something lovely. They gave seminars, they gave workshops, we learned what it is to really be a shop steward. I'm still using that now – I learned what are my rights, I learned how to organize, and I'm still using that now. In SACTWU I was a worker. But it also pertained to being a youth and a woman.*

Her account of the relationship between the labor and youth movements is also illuminating:

> *SACTWU was saying to us don't get involved in politics. There was a big debate at that time (1986–89). They said we don't need to adopt the Freedom Charter – we must be proper workers and focus on worker issues, not the UDF. SACTWU believed that the ANC would dominate workers ... But the union was not punishing what you do at home. When I was at work I was a worker. But when I was in the location I was jumping all over the streets as a youth. When we were at home we forgot we were workers.*

Yet, as she readily conceded, she did not forget the political practices – and sense of self-confidence – she learned as a shop steward. Like a number of other women trained as shop stewards in Ladysmith factories, she went on to assume positions of prominence in local and provincial politics in the 1990s. Indeed, virtually all the women ANC members elected to the Ladysmith-Ezakheni local council in the 1996 local elections are former shop stewards.

This woman's experiences embody distinctive features of the youth movement in Ladysmith-Ezakheni, and its relationship to organized labor. Unlike Madadeni, there was no direct connection to the youth movement in Soweto. Yet a group of militant young activists emerged in the early 1980s who, in the words of one observer, 'went straight for Buthelezi's throat.' The KwaZulu police and the Special Branch responded by arresting a number of them. Former political prisoners whom I met described in graphic detail the torture they suffered in detention. Ezakheni and Steadville appear not to have been the targets of the sort of co-optation strategy deployed through the JMC in Newcastle. Along with Sithebe and his troops, the security arm of the apartheid state based in Ladysmith confined itself to open brutality.

In their accounts of this period, some former youth activists describe a close relationship with the unions. They tell of how unions allowed them to use office facilities, and indeed often sheltered them in union offices; and how they in turn supported the unions in strike activity. Present and former union leaders portray the relationship in far less symmetrical terms. They describe how, particularly in the first half of the 1980s, they formally distanced themselves from the UDF while at the same time providing indirect support and training to young activists:

> *We isolated from the UDF, but at the back we sympathized with the youth. We were working with them, but not directly. At the time when a lot of them were getting arrested, we had a ruling from the unions to try to contain the youth. We tried to educate them about how to formulate structures. We used to meet secretly with them, and teach them about how structures worked. At the back we were also helping them with things like transport.*

The contrast with the overlapping labor and youth movements in Newcastle is, of course, dramatic.

In response to a question about how and why the relationship between the youth and labor movements in Ladysmith differed from that in Newcastle, a union organizer who had been closely engaged with support of the youth movement made a telling observation:

> *Newcastle is not as old as Ladysmith. Many people here are still in the places where they were born. Our resistance to forced removals brought us together. People in Newcastle were moved earlier – they were all in the location. Many places here [i.e. around Ladysmith] are rural – they can't be run by children. We are sort of behind them – but they are children, and under us.*

This statement and the practices it describes illuminate two important sets of issues. First, they focus attention on how political practices putatively labeled 'workerist' are constituted and articulated in locally specific ways. The 'workerism' that took hold in Ladysmith and its environs in the 1980s, and that shaped the course of the anti-apartheid struggle, wove together Zulu patriarchal sentiments and practices associated with an agrarian past with those that were startlingly new. In similar vein, Bonnin et al. (1996) make the point that

Zulu symbolism and culture were central in the construction of notions of exploitation, oppression, struggle, freedom ... Yet worker organisation and politics [also] allowed people who saw themselves as Zulu to question political mobilisation on a purely ethnic basis. (Bonnin et al. 1996: 172)

A second, closely related point concerns the problematic distinction between 'urban/civil society' on the one hand, and 'rural/decentralized despotism' on the other. The more urban character of Madadeni-Osizweni did not automatically strengthen the organizational capacity of civil society; if anything, both labor and community politics have become increasingly chaotic. By the same token, the historically and geographically specific processes and practices through which rural communities in the vicinity of Ladysmith resisted removals contributed in important ways to the emergence of a vibrant civil society and to the robust character of the local state in the post-apartheid era.

CHAPTER 4

Manufacturing Connections
Labor, Township, and Industrial Politics

JUST AS THE countryside bears the imprint of dispossession and removals, the industrial landscapes of northwestern KwaZulu-Natal yield clues into another of the grand projects of apartheid spatial engineering – industrial decentralization. Yet, as with removals, the process has been far from monolithic. Even on a quick trip through the sub-region, an observant tourist would notice that industrial decentralization has followed quite different trajectories in Ladysmith-Ezakheni and Newcastle-Madadeni-Osizweni.

The road from Ladysmith to Ezakheni traces the local history of industrialization. Closest to the town are some large textile and clothing factories, several of them closed, which bear witness to the withered vision of Ladysmith as the Manchester of Africa, conjured up by local planners in the 1940s and 1950s. Several kilometers further down the road one comes across the second phase of industrialization – a group of heavy industries (mainly tires and machine tools) established in the early 1970s following Ladysmith's official designation as a growth pole in 1969. About 15 km from Ladysmith, but separated by 5 km from the residential township, is the Ezakheni industrial estate, one of the showpieces of the KwaZulu Finance Corporation (KFC). Situated within a piece of what was KwaZulu, the Ezakheni estate exemplifies the national decentralization thrust launched in the early 1980s as part of the state's effort to revitalize and redefine the geography of racial capitalism. Although nominally a part of bantustan industrialization, in practice the Ezakheni estate is the product of close collaboration between the local state in Ladysmith and the white male executives based in Durban who ran the KFC. That this is a highly regulated and well-resourced environment is evident from the barbed-wire fencing,

127

the careful landscaping, and the post-modern architecture and bright colors of some of the buildings. Color-coded streets and signs provide a bizarre finishing touch to this anomalous collection of factories stuck in the middle of the South African veld.

The Madadeni industrial estate outside Newcastle is quite evidently the small, poor step-child of apartheid planners. Located on the edge of the residential township, it has none of the refinements of its counterpart in Ezakheni. Although the streets are also named after bright colors, the much smaller assortment of squat gray factory buildings merge with the dusty gray of the township. In fact, the KFC's relative neglect of Madadeni industrial estate prompted Newcastle local government officials to launch their aggressive pursuit of Taiwanese investment in the early 1980s.

On the road from Madadeni to Newcastle, one glimpses the real industrial heartland of the locality and inhales the heavy pall of smoke and air-borne effluent drifting towards the township. Dominating the horizon and belching forth filthy gray smoke are the cooling towers of Iscor – the Iron and Steel Corporation, a major state-owned enterprise with roots in the 1920s that established a huge plant in Newcastle in the 1970s prior to its privatization in the 1980s. Iscor is located some distance from the main industrial district where, if one ventures in, a far more differentiated picture presents itself. The most assertive elements of this picture are a set of heavy, resource-based industries (iron works, cement, and so forth), some of which have clearly been around for some time, and several very large clothing factories, including what used to be called Veka where Mrs D. in the previous chapter worked in the late 1960s. Veka and another big clothing company, originally based in Charlestown, about 50 km north of Newcastle, moved large parts of their operations to Newcastle in the late 1960s when people living in the 'black spot' in Charlestown were removed to Osizweni.

Scattered among these industrial behemoths in the industrial area are large numbers of much smaller buildings, many adorned with signs painted in Chinese characters along with names like 'Happy Knitting,' 'Lucky,' 'Taiphoo,' 'Ying-Wei,' and 'Chance.' Further indications that Newcastle operates very directly as part of the global economy appear as one moves through the town. In addition to small Chinese industries in the side streets, Chinese characters appear on numerous shop fronts on the main commercial streets. In the mid-1990s one of the industrialists described his vision of building a large Taiwanese-style shopping mall, a glittering palace that would stay open evenings and weekends and become the commercial center of the town. The bright pink shopping mall that actually materialized turned out to be more modest. Yet it exemplifies what seems to be a broader shift from industry to trade in Newcastle as tariff barriers tumbled in the mid-1990s, as well as the enduring presence of significant numbers of Taiwanese in the town.

If the built form of Newcastle seems to be yearning towards a global future – albeit one that is ferociously contested by a variety of social forces – that of Ladysmith speaks far more directly of its colonial past. Newcastle is a thoroughly modern town that was basically rebuilt in the 1970s when Iscor was established. At that point, a local historian declared, Newcastle effectively became part of the Transvaal, where it has always belonged. In Ladysmith, much of the British colonial architecture has been carefully preserved, including the elaborately domed town hall which probably has replicas in towns all over India. Ladysmith has another important connection with India. In the 1890s when Gandhi was establishing the Natal Indian Congress (NIC) he spent substantial amounts of time in Ladysmith, and the Indian community in the town formed a significant base of NIC support. Important links developed between the NIC and some members of the African landowning elite in the freehold areas around Ladysmith, which found expression in the Natal Native Congress. This network of relationships simply did not exist in Newcastle.[1]

A North American visiting the area for the first time shortly after the new government in South Africa assumed power in 1994 wrote:

Whether in the Drakensberg, at the KFC in Ezakheni, at the Ladysmith Town Hall and Siege Museum, or Lourie's Restaurant in Newcastle, there is everywhere an apparent nonchalant ease among ordinary white South Africans about their current and continuing wealth and comfortable life-styles. In the daily affairs of life, white control seems quite unchanged. (How this was historically contested between British and Boer is dramatically portrayed in the Ladysmith Siege Museum, but this seems a lost or largely buried issue now.) Strikingly, no blacks at all are depicted in the Ladysmith Museum or Town Hall; from the numerous photos and drawings on the walls, the Anglo-Boer [South African] War could have been fought in the rolling hills of England. Nor are any blacks depicted among the 100 plus years of town fathers (and one mother) of Ladysmith – though as of 1992 an Indian community group gets a picture, the first in color, on the wall. (David Szanton, Notes, 4 July 1994)

The town fathers (and occasional mothers) whose portraits adorned the Ladysmith and Newcastle Town Halls at the time were the elected town councilors, most of them part of the local business elite, from whom the mayor was chosen. The central fulcrum of power in local government is not the mayor, however, but the town clerk who appears in the annual pictures wearing elaborate ceremonial garb and a solemn expression befitting his responsibilities. As head of the executive branch of the local state, town clerks and other senior bureaucrats have historically wielded enormous influence, and sought actively and aggressively to create the conditions for capital accumulation. Many were also directly implicated in forced removals, particularly those that involved efforts to eliminate municipal townships and move residents into relocation townships like Madadeni, Osizweni, and Ezakheni. The pivotal role of white local government officials intensified in the 1980s when they were at the forefront of marketing labor in the relocation townships, but local state entrepreneurialism had been going on for some time. At least since the late 1940s local bureaucrats and politicians in Ladysmith and Newcastle competed fiercely with one another to forge connections with different branches of capital, and with different levels and agencies of the state apparatus.

By the time of the National Party electoral victory in 1948, the Klip River district centered in Ladysmith had become the traditional seat of the leader of the National Party in Natal, providing local bureaucrats and politicians with privileged access to provincial centers of power. Yet Newcastle had more powerful links into the ruling bloc of the National Party in the person of Willie Maree who won the Newcastle seat with a small majority in 1948, and subsequently became a national cabinet member. Differential local connections into the apartheid state at provincial and national levels are central to understanding trajectories of industrialization – and the lucrative land deals on which they were, quite literally, grounded. Iscor for example is situated on land previously owned by Willie Maree. The different forms of industrialization described earlier testify to the ways that local strategies shifted over time, partly in response to changing phases and configurations of wider political-economic forces, but always mediated through locally specific connections. It was, for example, the contraction of heavy state-owned enterprises like Iscor in the late 1970s, combined with weaker provincial connections than their counterparts in Ladysmith, that propelled Newcastle local authorities into developing their strategy of by-passing the central government to forge connections in Taiwan. In short, industrial landscapes in the two places reveal quite clearly the locally specific forms and dynamics of relations among apartheid state agents and different fractions of regional, national, and transnational capital.

What these landscapes conceal are sharply divergent capital-labor relations. Industrial ensembles in Newcastle are larger and more elaborate than their counterparts in Ladysmith. Yet it was in Ladysmith that a militant and highly organized industrial labor movement took shape in the 1970s and gathered force in the 1980s, while industrial labor relations in Newcastle have in general been quite chaotic. The particular industries drawn into the two places in different phases are partly responsible for these diverse patterns, but they are by no means the whole story. Part of my purpose in this chapter is to highlight how industrial workplace struggles – and forms of acquiescence – in the two places have intersected with the divergent local histories of dispossession and township politics that formed the focus of Chapter 3.

The locally specific dynamics of industrial, labor, and township politics traced out in this chapter speak directly to debates over industrial decentralization. According to a widely held neoliberal consensus, industrial decentralization was the politically driven invention of apartheid spatial engineers seeking to turn back the tides of economic logic by 'artificially' locating heavily subsidized factories in the middle of nowhere (DBSA Panel of Experts 1989; Urban Foundation 1990). An important dissenting voice that challenged this neoliberal consensus was Bell's (1983, 1986) contention that the movement of labor-intensive industries to non-metropolitan regions particularly in the 1970s and 1980s was not simply the result of apartheid policies that distorted incentives. Instead he argued that what he called 'spontaneous decentralization' was driven by industrialists' search for lower production costs in the face of intensified global competition and the growing power of the trade union movement.

Spatial dynamics of labor-intensive industries in the 1990s, as we shall see, lend *prima facie* support to Bell's argument. Yet 'spontaneous decentralization' by itself is inadequate, both because it abstracts from the historically specific processes through which the workforce was constituted, and because an emphasis on 'economic' as opposed to 'political' factors is misleading. Processes of industrial dispersal may in part reflect capitalists' search for lower costs of production, but they are not simply 'spontaneous.' Rather, they are socially, politically, and historically constituted in particular localities, and generate quite diverse outcomes. The question, therefore, is not one of politics versus economics, but of grasping the interlocking dynamics of dispossession and industrialization.

The primary material in this chapter is based on the first phase of my research in 1994–95 conducted jointly with Alison Todes and focused primarily on Newcastle, although I did interview white local government officials, unionists, the Chamber of Commerce, and the KFC in Ladysmith on their versions of the industrial history of the town. In the second half of 1994, Alison Todes and I offered to conduct an industrial survey for the Newcastle municipality, which at that time still retained its old apartheid form. Through this somewhat Faustian bargain we gained entrée to both Taiwanese and South African factories. While significant, such access drew us into deeply compromised positions. A fairly junior white municipal official made the appointments, and accompanied us on many interviews. Although we were always extremely careful to explain our research project and university affiliations, it was clear that the majority of industrialists simply assumed we were secretaries. With some notable exceptions, Taiwanese industrialists almost immediately launched into bitter complaints about the unwillingness and/or inability of local bureaucrats to discipline labor, and into extended, often animated narratives of the laziness, ineptitude, and dishonesty of African women workers, and the evils of trade unions. South African industrialists and managers, by and large, smugly congratulated themselves on their superior, paternalistic labor relations, which they contrasted with the Eastern despotism of the Taiwanese. Our *de facto* association with local government officials rendered us uncomfortably complicit with these multiply-racialized discourses.

Equally discomforting was my own sense of complicity in encouraging apartheid state officials to recount their life histories. These interviews happened just as the local state was about to be dismantled, at a moment of radical uncertainty about how new forms of local governance would play out in practice. Particularly when read in conjunction with other narratives and sources of information, these interviews were deeply revealing of translocal connections through which the local state had been made in different ways in Ladysmith and Newcastle, and of how local bureaucrats in both places competed with one another. They also yielded extraordinary insights into how municipal bureaucrats defined their relationships with local councils, and their intense unease at the prospect of the new democratic dispensation. For all the insights that emerged, some of these interviews were also deeply uncomfortable. Not only was I complicit in a retelling of history to suit the needs of the present. In addition, in order to extract as much as possible, I deliberately refrained from challenging parts of the story. A notable example was an interview with an official who had played an active role in a particularly brutal forced removal, the documentary evidence of which I had reviewed before our meeting. In the course of our discussion, he devised an elaborate explanation of how he had been acting in the interests of 'the people.'

The literature on feminist ethnography is rightly critical of what Gibson-Graham (1994) aptly terms an extractive or mining model of research, advocating instead that researchers engage in 'speaking with' the subjects of their research. Yet this rich literature has remarkably little to say about the ethics and politics of working with subjects who are relatively and problematically powerful.[2] At the time, I coped by defining what I was doing as a sort of investigative reporting-cum-detective work but, as Alison Todes was quick to point out, this strategy simply evaded the ethical and political dilemmas. An unpleasant yet telling episode forced us to confront some of these issues. One evening in a restaurant in Newcastle we encountered the manager of a large South African firm whom we had recently interviewed, drinking heavily with a local bureaucrat. The inebriated pair insisted that we go back with them to one of their homes, and were clearly infuriated when we refused. Later that evening they arrived at our motel even drunker and angrier, and tried to break into our room. At the time I reacted with pure rage. In retrospect I came to see the episode as an aggressively sexualized effort to put us in our place, perpetrated by white males whose pedestal of race-class power was crumbling. Yet it remains an unsettling reminder of the ambiguities of power that course through and disrupt the research process.

This chapter unfolds chronologically, organized around a periodization of major phases of industrial accumulation and state policy between the 1940s and mid-1990s. After outlining reconfigurations of larger political-economic forces in each key period, I show how they were constituted and reworked in locally specific ways through overlapping, spatially extended struggles, strategies, and forms of acquiescence in multiple, interconnected arenas. Throughout the chapter we move back and forth across transnational, national, and regional sites, as well as industrial workplaces, town halls, local government and union offices, and retrace our visits in the previous chapter to the townships where workers not only renewed themselves but were also caught up in varied and changing oppositional practices.

Early Industrial Dynamics

State sponsorship of industrial decentralization was not, in fact, the invention of apartheid spatial engineers. Moves in this direction began under the Smuts government in the early 1940s as part of the national import substitution strategy, and were actively pursued by the Industrial Development Corporation (IDC). At the time, the state confronted the joint and contradictory imperatives of creating the conditions for industrial expansion and evading the threat posed by an increasingly militant urban African proletariat, many of whom were moving into skilled operative jobs reserved for whites. Particular pressures arose in the textile industry. Prior to the Second World War most yarn had been imported, but severe shortages during the war made spinning and weaving a priority area for IDC involvement. The solution posited in 1942 by A. Cornish Bowden, the IDC's technical adviser, in a report entitled 'Location of the Cotton and Wool Spinning Plant,' was that the spinning and weaving stages of textile production should be 'almost entirely a native industry,' but that it must be located in an area where color bar restrictions on the use of African operatives could be evaded.[3] He dismissed rural locations near white farms which 'would create competition with farm labour' and suggested instead an area with a 'settled native population in the vicinity upon which to draw, and a large hinterland of native reserves, etc., which can be drawn upon in the future and in which products could be marketed.' To avoid the impression that his proposals had anything to do with improving economic conditions in the reserves, he concluded by noting that 'it must be remembered that our job is first and foremost to promote efficiency in the spinning and weaving of cotton and wool. To mix this job too intimately with the broader issue of the national development of the natives is undesirable in that it will detract the attention of the management from the issue of industrial and technical efficiency.' These proposals were taken up by the IDC, which decided in 1944 to locate a large cotton-spinning plant outside King William's Town in the Eastern Cape 'within native territories on land to be leased from the Native Trust.' The Trust agreed to build a 'model settlement village' nearby to relieve the IDC of the cost of housing.[4] The Good Hope Textile factory was established in 1946 with a very short-lived monopoly of the domestic market. In addition to cheap Japanese textiles that flooded the market after the war, a number of new competitors entered domestic production.

Prominent among these was the Frame company, which followed the IDC's lead and set up a plant of the Consolidated Lancaster Cotton Company in Ladysmith in 1948.[5] Philip Frame rented an empty munitions factory located just outside the town that had closed after the war for one pound a year, brought in old machinery from England, and hired 1,300 workers (mostly African men) at wages well below those in urban areas.

That Frame established in Ladysmith was the result of active and aggressive initiatives of the white local government. Lester Clarence, a prominent town councilor in Ladysmith, operating in alliance with the chief planner of Natal, proposed the Thukela Basin initiative in the 1940s. Modeled on the Tennessee Valley Authority, the initiative was a massive water control project designed in part to draw industry from the Transvaal into northern Natal. Although the initiative received strong backing at the provincial level, it failed to gain the support of the central government. Clarence's grand visions failed to come to fruition, but he was actively engaged in trying to create the conditions for industrial capital – including, in Frame's case, nominal rent.

Cheap labor was somewhat more problematic. In 1950 African workers in Consolidated Cotton in Ladysmith went on strike, angered by poor wages and harsh working conditions. One of the workers at the time remembers the strike in these words:

> *Working conditions at Consolidated Cotton were very hard. We only earned 15 shillings a week. In 1950 there was a big strike at CC. We never had any union at that time – we just organized ourselves. The strike went on for two weeks and was very violent. They brought police from Dundee, Colenso, all over. The police used firearms with sharp points. They chased us up from the factory, all the way out of town to Limit Hill. Most of our workers were being pushed right out of town. People were chased out to the army base. At that time I had no knowledge of sabotage. But because of that ill-treatment, I collected some sacks. I went to buy dark glasses and hand gloves. In my mind I was trying to go and burn that factory. After I had collected all those things, I saw I could not manage to burn it all because there were a number of separate buildings, and I could not burn it completely. I wanted to burn it so that nothing could be left. I didn't wish to involve any other person. It was my secret. My anger was very great. Since this plan failed, I decided to go to Durban and forget everything about Ladysmith.*

In practice, he did not forget everything about Ladysmith. When he was working in Durban he would return to Ladysmith, and became actively involved in the land struggle at Besters-Khumalosville described in the previous chapter. When asked about the relationship between labor and land struggles, he replied:

> *Automatically a person is involved in both. Many people from Ladysmith were at work in factories in Johannesburg and Durban. In those days many belonged to SACTU [South African Congress of Trade Unions]. They came back here in December and worked on the land issue.*

Many of them were also involved in the newly radicalized ANC which, as we saw in Chapter 3, was highly organized in Ladysmith and deeply influenced by Govan Mbeki. The Good Hope Textile factory in King William's Town was similarly disrupted by strikes in the early 1950s, and there were also close connections across the politics of production, the conditions in which workers lived, and larger political movements.[6]

In 1960 the apartheid state initiated its own border industrialization policy, with the stated aim of stemming African urbanization. In 1956, Verwoerd had rejected the Tomlinson Commission's (1955) recommendations that large numbers of white-owned industries be brought into the reserves: 'The Government adopts the attitude that private White undertakings – important, big undertakings – will make no contribution towards keeping the Native areas truly Bantu' (cited by Lazar 1993: 374). Instead, Verwoerd argued, white industries requiring large numbers of African workers should be located 'in suitable European areas near Bantu territory.' In addition to exemption from industrial council wage determinations, the border industry incentives included tax concessions, low interest loans, transport subsidies, and tariff protection. The IDC also offered to erect buildings according to specifications, lease premises, and buy shares in border industries (Glaser 1987: 34). As forced removals and farm evictions gathered momentum through the 1960s, the state constructed huge townships like Madadeni-Osizweni on patches of bantustan land adjacent to growth points.

Large-scale industrial capitalists based in metropolitan areas were predictably opposed to border industrialization. In 1959, for example, the Federated Chamber of Industries (FCI) issued a 'grave warning against artificial and forced development of industries in particular areas, involving discrimination against existing industries and the conduct of harmful and expensive experiments in industrial development' (cited by Glaser 1987: 34). In border areas, including Ladysmith and Newcastle, the concessions were greeted with considerable enthusiasm. Large-scale industrialists subsequently complained bitterly about the favoritism allegedly enjoyed by small Afrikaner firms (cited by Glaser 1987: 34).

Another source of opposition to border industries was the white working class:

> In June 1958, the MPs for Alberton and Pretoria West, Marais Viljoen and P.J. van der Walt, visited factories in Charlestown, Ladysmith, and Durban. In a private memorandum to Verwoerd, they argued that the establishment of border industries paying lower wages would inevitably lead to the closure of factories in the white urban areas, and that, under these circumstances, the 'days of the white clothing workers were numbered'. To avoid a clash between the policy of protection of the white worker, on the one hand, and the border industry policy, on the other, the government must intervene to extend job reservation to decontrolled areas, and to ensure that only goods of a lower quality were manufactured in the border factories. (Lazar 1993: 377)

Earlier that year, in a tour of border areas in Natal, Anna Scheepers and other leaders of the white Garment Workers' Union asked the Minister of Labour, Jan de Klerk, to refuse registration to clothing factories in Natal and the Orange Free State that employed cheap black labor. The union claimed that thousands of white garment workers in the Transvaal were 'walking the street, hungry and out of work' because factories had moved to 'decontrolled' border areas – a move that began *prior* to the inception of state-sponsored industrial decentralization (Bell 1983).

The border industry policy remained intact, but De Klerk conceded to organized white labor by closing several of the offending factories, including Veka in Charlestown, just north of Newcastle. Veka is particularly interesting, because it exemplifies the development of Afrikaner national capital. Financed initially by the savings of farmers in the Orange Free State, it originally established in Johannesburg in the 1930s employing Afrikaner women at wages below those prescribed by the Industrial Council. As O'Meara (1983: 163) has observed: 'A major thrust of the ideological elaboration of the period was to "prove" to Afrikaner workers that their intensified exploitation by Afrikaner capitalists was in their own interests as part of the volk.' In the case of Veka these efforts failed, and the Industrial Council forced the company to raise wages. Veka subsequently opened a plant in Charlestown, 50 km north of Newcastle, where there was a large African freehold community, and employed African women workers at much lower wages. In response to the closure of Veka in Charlestown, the owner sent a revealing letter to

Labour Minister De Klerk noting that, because of unemployment in the garment industry on the Rand,

> everyone's venom was directed towards Veka in Charlestown and our closure would be the solution . . . My feelings go even further. What must one do when one feels crushed between two or three government departments? You know that we informed you that we were urged by the Department of Native Affairs to open a factory in Charlestown as soon as possible. We asked that the wage question first be resolved. That department answered – and I have it in writing – that it would delay the issue too long. There would be no difficulty in setting a satisfactory wage . . . Now it looks as if we should not have allowed ourselves to be talked around. We have also read that one Minister said that some industries – perhaps referring to us – acted too quickly. At that time this Department was his. The hurry came from another quarter. But then Departments should really work together and not let a specific factory be the victim of their differing internal workings . . . We read that it is government policy to decentralise industries. We thought that we would be performing a service to our people. (Cited by Lazar 1993: 390)

Veka's invocation of its 'service to our people' succeeded, and it reopened. In 1968 it set up a large plant in Newcastle, following the removal of the freehold community to Osizweni. Another large clothing company located in Charlestown followed suit.

In the latter part of the 1960s and early 1970s, Newcastle emerged as a major center of the clothing industry. Veka and several of the other clothing factories that moved into Newcastle received government contracts for uniforms, in addition to the border industries subsidies. There is an interesting contrast with Frame in Ladysmith in the 1950s, which was moving into an intensely competitive segment of the textile market. Mrs D.'s experience of working in Veka – 'the employers treated us well but the pay was very little' – parallels that of several other former workers.[7] The other key contrast, of course, is that in the 1950s Frame was drawing on a militant and politicized male workforce with a base in freehold communities, while by the 1960s Veka and the other large clothing and textile firms in Newcastle had access to huge numbers of women recently wrenched from the land and desperate for cash income. Not only was this a period of intense political repression more generally; in addition, people living in the relocation townships came under the sway of reconstituted traditional authorities – although this did not stop many of them from joining the bus boycott in 1975. There was evidently very little labor militancy in these factories until the 1990s. Yet 3,000 women workers in the original Veka factory that had remained in Charlestown came out on strike in 1973, and were thus at the forefront of the resurgence of labor militancy in the 1970s (*Sechaba* June & July 1973).

The Era of Heavy Industrialization

Over the course of the 1960s the extent of industrial decentralization in South Africa as a whole was in practice quite limited, and did little to stem the pace of African urbanization. Towards the end of the decade the apartheid state stepped up its efforts to reconfigure industrial geography, and mesh it with 'self-governing' bantustans where forced removals and farm evictions were producing massive concentrations of dispossessed people. The Physical Planning and Utilisation of Resources Act of 1967 placed strict controls on industrial expansion in the main metropolitan areas, with the exception of Durban, and enabled the state to restrict directly industrial employment of Africans. A year later, the Promotion of the Economic Development of Bantu Homelands Act sanctioned the entry of white private capital into the bantustans and, over the course of the 1970s, the state offered increasing incentives to industrialists to invest in bantustan and border areas. Although explicitly linked to bantustan policy, these intensified efforts to reshape the industrial space economy found ready legitimation in the global discourse of scientific regional planning in ascendance at the time.[8]

Yet regional planning was far from simply a 'top-down' imposition of the apartheid state. Alliances between the local state and business interests in Ladysmith and Newcastle eagerly tapped into the opportunities provided by this new round of industrial decentralization policies, but they did so through very different sets of networks and connections. The town clerk of Ladysmith at the time informed me with great pride that on December 5, 1969, Ladysmith was declared the first growth pole in South Africa. He was quite clear about the reason: the mayor's son was a political correspondent for *Die Burger*, the official organ of the National Party. *Die Burger*, in turn, was closely allied with the Broederbond, the secret 'society of brothers' that launched the project of Afrikaner national capitalism in the 1930s (O'Meara 1983).

The IDC, which by that time was acting mainly to support private capital rather than engaging in production directly, acquired 630 hectares of land from the Ladysmith Town Council, 240 hectares of which was developed and fully serviced as an industrial area which came to be known as Danskraal. According to the town clerk at the time: 'It cost Ladysmith nothing for the infrastructure.' To attract industry to Danskraal, local officials and locally based politicians drew on their provincial connections. As noted earlier, Ladysmith had become the traditional seat of the National Party in Natal. Within just over a year, the Dunlop Tyre Company headquartered in Durban established a large plant in Danskraal, followed by Lasher Tools, several other heavy industries, and some clothing factories as well. Between 1970 and 1980, according to Population Census data, industrial employment in Ladysmith jumped from 3,800 to well over 10,000. The provincial networks and promises of lower production costs through which Dunlop was brought in were similar to those that had attracted Frame. Ironically, when the Durban strikes broke out in 1973, Dunlop and Frame in Durban were two of the most militant bases of the resurgent labor movement.

With still tighter connections into the heart of the central state and Afrikaner national capital, Newcastle hauled in a much larger industrial prize – a plant of the state-owned Iron and Steel Corporation, described at the beginning of this chapter. For promoters of industrial development in Newcastle, it is only natural that the Iscor plant was located there in 1970. Those in Ladysmith remember it as a bitter defeat. The former town clerk of Ladysmith explained to me how, in the late 1960s, circulars went round to all the towns in the area announcing Iscor's intention to locate its third plant in northwestern Natal. 'We tried very hard for it,' he said; 'At that time Ladysmith was the third largest town in Natal. But Willie Maree was the MP for Newcastle, and we didn't have a chance.' The story of how Iscor was built on land bought from Willie Maree at a huge price was repeated to me several times by different citizens of Ladysmith. In short, place-based competition in the 1970s took the form of who had what contacts into the apartheid state.

Iscor unleashed an unprecedented boom in Newcastle, making it the fastest growing town in the country (Todes 1997, 1999). Between 1970 and 1980, the massive state-owned enterprise injected R5 billion (in 1989 prices) into the local economy. In the first half of the 1970s the town's white population increased by 360 percent, and the value of building plans passed by the municipality jumped by nearly 900 percent. Although Iscor itself generated few direct industrial linkages, the number of industrial establishments in Newcastle grew from 29 in 1970 to 57 in 1979 (Harrison 1990: 91). According to Population Census data, industrial employment soared from under 5,000 in 1970 to over 21,000 in 1980.

Iscor brought with it to Newcastle a history of tightly regulated labor practices stretching back to its origins in the 1920s, and its huge size and market dominance placed management in an extremely powerful position *vis-à-vis* labor (Clark 1994). From its inception, Iscor had operated under the contradictory imperatives of keeping labor costs low, and implementing a 'civilized labor' policy of employing a high proportion of relatively highly paid white workers. Its strategy was to placate white workers, while simultaneously undermining union power and employing as much low-wage black labor as possible. In the 1940s, the board of directors of Iscor withdrew from the Industrial Council for the Engineering Industry, and established a separate industrial council with Iscor as the sole employer.[9] In the apartheid era, Iscor adopted an explicit strategy of defining jobs in racial terms, and classifying all Africans as 'general laborers':

> These jobs – as with the position accorded the white operatives and artisans – would command a wage based on race rather than skill; in fact, skill could be considered irrelevant to wage level. In such capacities, they performed jobs that could rightfully be considered at least semi-skilled, yet their title and pay were defined by the color of their skin. (Clark 1994: 152)

In contrast to Dunlop and the other heavy industries that moved into Ladysmith, white men comprised a relatively large proportion of Iscor's workforce – which accounts for the large increase in the white population of Newcastle in the 1970s and the strength of the Conservative Party in Newcastle in the 1980s and 1990s.

In constituting the African workforce, the managers of Iscor in Newcastle not only used Iscor's convenient system of racial classification; they also invoked Zulu nationalism and 'traditional' notions of masculinity. During the 1970s the African workforce was composed mainly of men brought in from rural areas, rather than those who had been moved to Madadeni and Osizweni. They were housed in tightly regulated hostels adjacent to the plant, and a prince of the Zulu royal house was employed as personnel manager. Although Iscor established in Newcastle at precisely the time that organized labor was gathering force in other parts of South Africa, MAWU and later NUMSA (National Union of Metal Workers of South Africa) were unable to gain a foothold in Iscor. As one NUMSA official who was engaged in organizing in northern Natal at the time put it: 'Ladysmith was always very strong, but we could never break Iscor.' Another noted that the Zulu prince who preached an anti-union gospel was always a stumbling block. Iscor's labor strategies shifted over time towards employing men from Madadeni and Osizweni, and offering relatively high wages and benefit packages. Particularly in the 1980s and 1990s there was also considerable downsizing and Iscor jobs came to be highly prized. Although the reasons have shifted over time, Iscor still remains beyond the reach of NUMSA.

A significant feature of labor organizing in the 1970s and early 1980s, particularly in Natal, was a very specific focus on workplace issues and on building organization within the factories. The new independent unions affiliated under the umbrella of the Federation of South African Trade Unions (FOSATU) explicitly distanced themselves from the Congress movement and community politics.[10] Among other things, they were fearful of the repression that had been visited upon the ANC-linked South African Congress of Trade Unions (SACTU) in the early 1960s. In addition, by steering clear of township and ANC-linked politics, the 'workerist' FOSATU unions were able to organize and incorporate migrants and, in Natal, people who identified with Inkatha and Zulu nationalism. Even though Inkatha members were implicated in attacks on students and other protesters in Durban townships in the late 1970s and early 1980s, and in collaborating with the police, the trade unions maintained a distance from township politics: 'FOSATU, which organised the majority of these workers, had adopted a position of non-involvement in political organizations and of caution towards Inkatha' (Meer 1988: 83). Prominent in FOSATU were the metal and textile unions, focused on precisely the industries that were most prominent in Ladysmith and Newcastle.

The fragmented and generally disorganized character of the industrial labor movement in Newcastle derives partly from the dominance of Iscor, but the particular forms of township politics in Madadeni and Osizweni were also important. In Chapter 3 I called attention to the generally quiescent character of politics in these townships in the 1970s and 1980s, but also traced the emergence of a small but extremely militant youth movement in the late 1970s, part of which was conscripted into MK, the military wing of the armed struggle. We also saw how, by the early 1980s, leaders of the youth movement sought to connect with organized labor. These were not, however, FOSATU but rather general unions which identified far more closely with oppositional politics, and focused far less on everyday practices of workplace democracy than the FOSATU unions.

We shall return in the following section to draw out the significance of these connections – and the contrasts with connections between youth and labor movements in Ladysmith.

That the trajectory of labor politics in Ladysmith was so dramatically different stems in part from the provincial links that brought Frame and Dunlop to the town, as well as perhaps greater proximity to Durban. A strike by workers in a Frame plant just outside Durban in January 1973 sparked actions in other Frame factories throughout Natal, and was a key force behind the massive resurgence of organized labor in South Africa more generally after the quiescence of the 1960s.[11] Although Frame in Ladysmith did not go out on strike in this initial phase, all Frame factories in Natal closed down in February and opened again only after wage concessions had been won. From then on, Frame plants throughout Natal became major targets of the newly formed NUTW linked to FOSATU.

During the 1970s, the Dunlop plant in Durban also became highly organized (Sitas 1984). By the end of the 1970s, according to a former MAWU organizer, Dunlop was the most militant factory in Durban. A former worker in Dunlop's Ladysmith plant described how, as part of his job as a truck driver, he became closely familiar with the organizational tactics in the main factory in Durban, and brought this knowledge back to his fellow workers in Ladysmith. Yet there was more to the Dunlop militancy than just proximity to Durban: agrarian struggles were also crucially important. A number of the men working in the Ladysmith Dunlop plant were from Matiwane's Kop where, as we saw in Chapter 3, the fight against forced removals was accelerating in the late 1970s and early 1980s. Shopfloor stewards describe vividly how struggles in Dunlop carried over into opposition to forced removals, as well as vice versa, and how their own formation as political subjects was profoundly shaped by these intersecting struggles. When Dunlop in Ladysmith instituted a mass dismissal in 1981, organizing began in earnest and overlapped with worker actions that were gathering force in Frame. Employers and the police responded with coercion; this further politicized workers and reinforced labor militancy that spread to other factories.

Formal avoidance of community politics continued to characterize the FOSATU-led labor movement in Ladysmith as it took shape in the late 1970s and early 1980s; indeed some of the key figures continue to promote what they still call workerist strategies. Thus, for example, the bus boycott of 1979 described in Chapter 3 was not taken up as a labor issue at the time.

In addition, organized labor in Ladysmith maintained a formal distance from the youth movement that emerged in the early 1980s under the umbrella of the UDF which, as we saw in Chapter 3, was far more broadly based than its Newcastle counterparts. Yet in practice – and in sharp contrast to Newcastle – democratic practices forged on the factory floor carried over into, and informed township politics. What this formal distancing meant, however, was that union leaders were able to infiltrate and organize factories drawn in by a new round of industrialization in the 1980s even though, as we shall see, union activity was technically banned.

Regional Restructuring in the 1980s

In 1981, just as spatial policies were becoming discredited in most of the capitalist world by the rise of neoliberalism, P.W. Botha's administration unveiled a new regional strategy as part of its 'reformist' thrust that was, in turn, part of an effort to tame the growing power of organized labor and oppositional politics in the townships. The Good Hope plan dramatically increased incentives for industrial decentralization, with the emphasis shifting from tax concessions to direct cash subsidies. Subsidies were graded according to location, with 'industrial development points' in more distant bantustan locations receiving higher levels than 'deconcentration points' on the peripheries of metropolitan areas (see Map 1). Some bantustan administrations such as the Ciskei added extra incentives like extended tax holidays, thereby creating what was widely seen as the most generous package of incentives in the world. At the national level, the huge increase in incentives was financed by windfall revenues from a sharp increase in the gold price in the early 1980s.

Yet the Good Hope strategy was far from just an intensification of Verwoerdian political geography. In their insightful analysis, Cobbett et al. (1987) argue that regional restructuring represented an abandonment of the political and territorial premises of apartheid – although not necessarily of race or ethnicity – in preparation for the future reincorporation of the bantustans into a single national state: 'the devolution of power, the partial "deracialisation" of administration, and the proposed federalist system are being developed as an alternative to "majoritarianism" and all that the ruling groups fear would accompany majority rule: bureaucratic breakdown, social disruption, inter-communal conflict, welfare statism, socialism' (Cobbett et al. 1987: 21). The Good Hope strategy also reflected a new rapprochement between the state and metropolitan capital. Its discourse centered around 'teamwork with big business' and 'promoting the forces of free enterprise' – although, as we shall see later, tensions between the state and big business over industrial decentralization intensified during the 1980s.

The architects of regional restructuring redrew the map of South Africa to encompass eight (later nine) 'functional regions' that incorporated both bantustan and 'white' areas – the so-called 'soft borders' approach advocated by the Buthelezi Commission in 1980 (Map 1).[12] Planning and advisory bodies that cut across bantustan borders were established within the new regions, including Regional Development Advisory Committees (RDACs) on which business interests were heavily represented. The nine provinces in post-apartheid South Africa in fact conform quite closely to the regions defined by the Good Hope plan.

Particularly in metropolitan areas, regional restructuring was accompanied by the withdrawal of the central state from local finances. A new third tier of government was created, financed by payroll and turnover levies in urban areas. These Regional Services Councils (RSCs) established in the late 1980s were designed to link black and white municipal areas, and redistribute resources from the latter to the former in a rather desperate bid to localize and depoliticize the provision of municipal services and stabilize black townships. At the same time, restrictions on industrial expansion in metropolitan areas imposed in the late 1960s and 1970s were lifted. The consequence was that metropolitan-based capitalists were confronted with the choice of either decentralizing their industries, or contributing to the 'upgrading' of urban townships (Glaser 1987: 46). Within metropolitan areas, the system of deconcentration points created incentives for industry to move into the peripheries of metropolitan conurbations where the state sought to direct and contain new African settlement.[13] Thus the apartheid vision of reversing the flow of Africans to urban 'white' South Africa gave way to a discourse of 'deconcentration' through which, in the words of the Kleu Report (1983), 'the benefits of agglomeration of the metropolitan areas will be spread over a wider area without aggravating pressure on the metropoles' (cited by Cobbett et al. 1987: 10).

The provision of massive subsidies to industries to move into non-metropolitan 'industrial development points' (IDPs) seemed, on the face of it, to contradict greater accommodation to the imperatives of accumulation in metropolitan areas. No less than 49 localities became designated IDPs, with the largest subsidies going to the most remote and under-resourced bantustan areas where industrialists were least likely to locate. In practice, as Glaser

(1987: 44) points out, the designation of IDPs was largely a sop to bantustan elites, and a far smaller subset of IDPs was fully serviced with infrastructure.

This was certainly the case in KwaZulu-Natal, where the bulk of resources deployed through the 1982 Regional Industrial Development Programme (RIDP) was concentrated in Ezakheni, Newcastle-Madadeni, and a new industrial estate in Isithebe, approximately 100 km north of Durban on the main road to Richards Bay. Industrial development in the three key patches of former KwaZulu was orchestrated by the KFC, which promoted itself as the most professional of the bantustan development corporations. Despite nominal representation of KwaZulu bantustan officials on its board, the KFC was run by white men based in Durban, and operated quite independently of KwaZulu authorities. The racial and gender composition of the KFC is, as we shall see, extremely important to understanding how its strategies meshed and clashed with those of local government officials in Ladysmith and Newcastle.

For these officials, the RIDP could hardly have come at a more opportune time. In 1977, Iscor's directors not only cancelled plans for expansion, but also implemented large-scale retrenchments. By the early 1980s the workforce of 12,000 had been reduced to 9,600, and 2,500 disgruntled white workers moved out of Newcastle. At least 600 houses stood vacant, as did 2,000 serviced lots (Harrison 1990: 92). The rise and fall of Iscor coincided with a more general boom-bust pattern in mining and agriculture in the sub-region. During the 1970s, the oil crisis and the construction of the large harbor in Richards Bay provided a major stimulus to the coal industry in northwestern Natal. Coal demand fell sharply after 1982, and a number of mines closed down. Agriculture, which had also expanded rapidly in the 1970s mainly in response to huge increases in cheap credit for white farmers, collapsed at the same time. Many farmers borrowed heavily to finance both mechanization and expanded operations, and a number switched from diversified cropping to maize monoculture. Record harvests were reaped in 1980/81, but the 1982/83 crop in the sub-region was devastated by drought and was only one fifth that of the previous year. Agricultural employment, which had dropped by 35 percent between 1968 and 1980 as a consequence of mechanization, fell still further. Declining maize prices and rising interest rates through most of the 1980s resulted in widespread bankruptcy in white agriculture in the sub-region (Harrison 1990: 62–63).

Evictions of wage laborers and tenants from white-owned farms in the sub-region also escalated during this period. The SPP documented approximately 300,000 farm evictions up to 1982 in the province as a whole, but numbers in northwestern Natal undoubtedly increased sharply through the 1980s. Large numbers of these people moved into relocation townships outside Ladysmith and Newcastle, as well as 'informal' settlements like Blaaubosch. Population census data confirm these patterns: in Madadeni, for example, population grew at 3 percent per annum in the 1980s compared with a natural increase of just over 2 percent. Particularly in Ezakheni, the population was not only growing but also becoming more militant both in the workplace and in the townships; the 1979 bus boycott in particular sent ripples of anxiety through the normally complacent white town.

In the face of these combined pressures and opportunities, local government officials in Ladysmith and Newcastle moved quickly – and in direct competition with each other – to take advantage of the RIDP. As in the past, external linkages were crucial, but by the 1980s they assumed different forms from the direct political connections of the 1970s. In keeping with Ladysmith's historically closer connections at the provincial level, local officials forged close relationships with the KFC and garnered the lion's share of resources for the Ezakheni industrial estate (Table 4.1).

Table 4.1   Industries and employment in the Ezakheni and Madadeni industrial estates.

	Ezakheni		Madadeni	
	No. industries	*Employment*	*No. industries*	*Employment*
1983	2	1,566	1	51
1984	4	1,927	1	51
1985	22	4,963	3	1,160
1986	32	7,611	5	1,168
1987	44	8,464	9	2,084
1988	57	9,469	13	2,596
1989	70	10,475	14	2,559
1990	75	11,930	16	2,702
1991	76	13,758	18	2,737
1992	74	10,109	22	1,498
1993	62	10,844	16	1,596
1994	62	10,790	16	1,808

Source: Data supplied by KwaZulu Finance Corporation

The Ezakheni estate was not only larger but also more diversified, with women comprising an average of 68 percent of the workforce in Ezakheni as opposed to 84 percent in Madadeni. Most of the industry in Madadeni was Taiwanese-owned, and concentrated in clothing, footwear, and simple plastic products. A senior KFC official explained the industrial mix in the former bantustan estates in the following terms:

> *We took a deliberate decision to stop attracting clothing companies from the Far East. Some of them had the seven-year syndrome – they were footloose. [The RIDP incentive package in the 1980s was for a seven-year period.] We were afraid of that. We were also afraid that they would saturate the market with clothing.*

When it became clear to local state entrepreneurs in Newcastle that the Madadeni industrial estate had lost out to Ezakheni, they reached directly into the global economy to lure industrialists into the town. Taiwanese clothing industries eschewed by the KFC were precisely those that the Newcastle local government was able to attract to the town. By 1990, according to data supplied by the Newcastle municipality, there were 34 Taiwanese industries employing somewhere in the vicinity of 3,700 workers, the large majority of them women. Some 90 percent of these firms were textile/clothing producers, with the large majority clustered around knitwear production. In 1991, a further nine Taiwanese industrialists (eight of them knitwear producers) established in the town.

There are, needless to say, conflicting versions of the story about how and why the local state in Ladysmith came to forge particularly close links with the KFC and push the Ezakheni industrial estate far ahead of that in Madadeni. The discursive strategies employed by key actors in reconstructing this piece of local history are quite instructive. In answer to the question why Ladysmith had a far closer link with the KFC than Newcastle, the former town clerk of Ladysmith replied:

> *Ladysmith realized we had to cooperate with the KFC. Newcastle ignored the KFC. We built up good relations with Marius Spies [director of the KFC]. Newcastle tried to do it on their own. I am good friends with Spies and Peet Marais [another senior KFC official]. KFC brought people into Madadeni; they were stolen by Newcastle. This was not acceptable to the KFC. Marketing is a strange thing. It's done by a few people. I did the marketing for Ladysmith and Ezakheni. The council [i.e. elected representatives] just left it to me and I did it. Most councillors spend 4–5 hours a month on council business. What they know about the affairs of the town is minimal . . . Here the town clerk is the executive officer and controls everything. Local executives determine the way things work.*

Emphasizing still further his personal connections, he went on to describe how, in the mid-1980s, he accompanied KFC officials on trips to Europe and Asia to drum up business. These trips no doubt afforded further opportunities for male bonding.

When asked why the KFC set up a much larger operation in Ezakheni than in Madadeni, a senior KFC official whom I interviewed in 1994 put it this way:

We didn't decide – it happened. There was good industrial land in Ezakheni. Newcastle had industrial land already developed. We didn't want to duplicate the cost structure [in Madadeni]. But Ladysmith didn't have industrial land. We could develop Ezakheni in a more disciplined manner in which you can manage the estate. In Ezakheni we could develop up to 1,000 hectares. Ezakheni is just an industrial suburb of Ladysmith. You can't have separate economies. They must develop in a holistic manner. Newcastle didn't have that philosophy. Ladysmith was more open.

That Ladysmith did not have industrial land is a point of dispute. A report in the *Natal Witness* of March 14, 1980, for example, notes that the outgoing president of the Ladysmith Chamber of Commerce described Danskraal, the industrial estate on the outskirts of the town as 'undeveloped' and reported how for years they had been pleading with their public representatives to go out and find industrialists to occupy it. Local industrialists in Ladysmith were, in fact, adamantly opposed to the Ezakheni expansion, and at least one large clothing firm moved to QwaQwa, a bantustan estate adjacent to Harrismith in the former Orange Free State.

Evidently, the 'more disciplined' manner in which Ezakheni could be developed was a prime consideration not only for the KFC, but also for Ladysmith local bureaucrats who assumed – erroneously as we shall see – that the KwaZulu government would take on the task of disciplining the militant labor movement.

To explain why Ladysmith-Ezakheni and Newcastle-Madadeni followed such different paths, Newcastle officials invoke Ladysmith's political connections. 'Ladysmith is a big problem for us,' declared one: 'We really are the regional capital, but they grab all the goodies because they have political connections in the province.' The story of how the Newcastle foreign investment strategy was launched, told to me by the local state official most directly responsible for it, runs as follows:

The foreign investment strategy started in 1983 when Newcastle suffered economic decline because of Iscor and had to look to other avenues to promote development and growth. The council realized that to broaden the economic base of Newcastle and not depend on Iscor and Karbochem they would have to make a commitment to smaller labor-intensive industries. At that time the government was undertaking industrial development under the auspices of the Economic Development Corporation [EDC – the precursor of the KFC]. They started with developments in certain parts of Natal. Newcastle approached them to do something for Madadeni and Osizweni. They decided to start off with a development program of R500,000 – but this wasn't even a drop in the bucket. The idea for Newcastle starting its own initiative came at a meeting with the Economic Development Corporation.

The teller of this story made clear that the idea was his, and that it occurred to him when it became evident that the EDC/KFC was refusing to expand investment in Madadeni. Around this time the bantustan development corporations were beginning to travel abroad to draw in foreign investment. He made contact with Plant Location International, a firm in Belgium that connected prospective European investors and non-European investment sites. This European strategy produced no results, and it was then that he decided to look eastwards.

The link into Asia came from a KFC-sponsored firm in Madadeni, a Hong Kong-based clothing producer. The owner of this firm organized seminars for the Newcastle delegation in Taiwan and Hong Kong, and began to operate as an investment consultant. When US sanctions took hold in 1986, her factory was hit very hard; it had been set up to take advantage of the quota-free clothing exports from South Africa to the United States. She then sold the factory to another Hong Kong investor who moved it into Newcastle to produce for the domestic market (with a fresh set of incentives), and became a full-time investment consultant for the Newcastle municipality. As local officials in Newcastle tell it, their strategy succeeded beyond their wildest dreams:

We concentrated on Taiwan. Sixty-five factories have come in, bringing 10,000–11,000 new jobs and a capital investment of R120 million. They have had a tremendous impact on the town. Property values have soared and there has been a commercial boom. Also, related service industries have been established. The economy of the town has grown by 3 percent per year, and South African companies have also established in Newcastle. Also, Taiwanese firms have moved here from Isithebe and Botshabelo [other bantustan industrial estates].

While these numbers are undoubtedly inflated, there is no question that Newcastle became a major locus of Taiwanese investment. In addition to RIDP incentives and large labor pools, cheap real estate was a key element of the strategy Newcastle officials used to lure Asian investors. When the Iscor expansion failed to materialize, the town was left with about 600

empty houses – some of them very large and luxurious. Local lore (particularly in Ladysmith) has it that Asian industrialists who moved to Newcastle
were given houses free of charge; Newcastle officials are evasive on this
point, but concede that luxury houses were 'very reasonably' priced. In any
event, it is clear that there has been extensive property acquisition by
Taiwanese investors, and they themselves agree that one of the chief
attractions of Newcastle was the housing market. The consequence has
been powerful processes of social agglomeration, with Newcastle becoming a major node in a worldwide Taiwanese diaspora.

How Taiwanese industrialists took hold in Newcastle forms the focus
of the following chapter which tells of the ambiguous relations between
Taiwanese industrialists and local state officials, tensions among competing factions of Taiwanese industrialists, resentment towards them on the
part of South African industrialists and, most importantly, the deeply
conflictual relations between Taiwanese factory owners and African
women workers. In addition, as we shall see in the following section,
Taiwanese industrialists continued to move into Newcastle in the early
1990s despite a sharp reduction in subsidies, establishing a network of
factories engaged in different elements of knitwear production that closely
resembles the satellite factory system that helped to drive the spectacular
pace of industrialization in Taiwan.

First, though, we must turn our attention to the changing dynamics of
labor and township struggles in the late 1980s. By the mid-1980s, just as
local strategies of tapping into RIDP resources and attracting labor-
intensive industries to decentralized industrial development points were
moving into top gear, townships in most of the main metropolitan centers
were literally exploding. It was also at this point that organizers of rent,
consumer, and other boycotts in urban townships, many of them operating
under the umbrella of the UDF formed in 1983, were joining forces with
union organizers to create what has come to be known as social movement
unionism.[14] For many industrialists, escalating protest in the metropolitan
centers no doubt enhanced the attractiveness of decentralized areas. In
addition to subsidies that covered most if not all of the wages bill, workers
were at least in principle under the control of traditional authorities. Indeed,
as we saw earlier, this was an important part of the reason why Ladysmith
local authorities pushed hard for the industrial estate in Ezakheni. When
Newcastle local officials went to Taiwan, they undoubtedly extolled the
control exercised by Inkatha in Madadeni and Osizweni, and were careful

to differentiate these 'peaceful' and non-unionized places from the chaos of Soweto. In practice, of course, industries attracted by the RIDP moved into local contexts shaped by their own specific histories of opposition and acquiescence. Over the course of the 1980s, struggles in the factories and the townships intensified, although they assumed locally specific forms that reflected far more complex and varied dynamics than the simple linking of township and workplace protests.

Ladysmith local officials' hopes that the ban on unions in the Ezakheni industrial estate would undercut labor militancy quickly evaporated. Just as the new industrial estate was setting up in 1984, both Dunlop and Frame folded under labor pressure and signed union recognition agreements. Fresh from their victories in Ladysmith, union leaders sprang into action to organize the factories moving into Ezakheni. In some cases management acceded quite quickly, thus flying in the face of the official ban on union organizing in the estate. Those that recognized unions tended to be branch plants of firms based in Durban and Pietermaritzburg that were already organized. The majority, however, put up a fierce fight. Particularly in the metal working industries, organizers of MAWU actively deployed the workerist strategies developed in the 1970s in order to incorporate members of Inkatha. Former MAWU (now NUMSA) officials tell of how one factory dismissed all the workers who had signed up with MAWU, and recruited Inkatha men from rural areas whom they housed in a hostel in the township. MAWU leaders infiltrated the hostel, and won over the workers by stressing their independence from Congress/UDF politics and their emphasis on purely workplace issues. More generally, NUMSA officials argue that their success in organizing Ezakheni factories hinged crucially on maintaining a formal distance from politics in the townships – in particular, from the UDF movement that emerged in the 1980s.

Systematic organizing in the clothing and textile factories in the Ezakheni estate only took hold in the late 1980s. As in the metal industries, a small group of South African branch plants signed union agreements, but the majority of industrialists fiercely opposed organized labor. According to SACTWU organizers, a number of them brought in women workers from Lesotho who were extremely difficult to organize. Some factories did go out on strike in the 1980s, including a large Taiwanese yarn producer that then tried hiring white workers but quickly abandoned the experiment. Fearful of the militancy of workers living in Ezakheni, the firm resorted to a strategy of selecting what they hoped were more docile workers from rural communities like Driefontein and Ekuvukeni, whom they would bus into the factory. In a strategy borrowed from urban areas, SACTWU then used the buses as a locus for organizing.

Relationships between labor and community organizing in Ezakheni and surrounding rural areas in the late 1980s present an interesting and significant irony. The two key industrial unions held fast to a workerist stance, continuing to maintain a formal distance from the UDF despite the official national affiliation. Yet in practice, as we saw in Chapter 3, organizational capacities and democratic practices and identities forged on factory floors carried over into township struggles, as well as vice versa. At the same time, unionists provided effective (albeit covert) support for the youth movement. The coincidence in the late 1970s and early 1980s of opposition to forced removals with the rise of organized labor was also significant. So too was the violence that wreaked havoc in the township in the late 1980s and early 1990s, but effectively united township dwellers – particularly those living in the working-class section of the township. In short, the formal distance between organized labor and the youth movement was accompanied in practice by closely synergistic relationships.

Connections between community and labor organizing in Newcastle, Madadeni, and Osizweni could hardly have been more different. We have already seen how, in the late 1970s and early 1980s, industrial unions failed to gain a foothold in Newcastle factories, and also how the smaller but more militarized youth movement in Newcastle sought to connect with general unions that were closer to the Congress movement. Labor organizing in Newcastle factories remained haphazard through the 1980s. Not only did NUMSA remain stymied in its efforts to penetrate Iscor. In addition, as we shall see in Chapter 5, SACTWU was confronted by fierce opposition from Taiwanese industrialists, and peculiarly South African forms of paternalism from their South African counterparts. The forms and dynamics of township politics were also important. Over the course of the 1980s, youth movements in Madadeni and Osizweni were torn apart by internal conflicts and co-optive strategies of the local JMC (see Chapter 3). These tensions and connections remain sensitive and difficult topics for an outside researcher to probe. What does seem fairly clear, though, is that dissensions within the youth movement carried over into the sphere of labor organizing, and further undermined the development of a coherent industrial labor movement. At the same time, the politics of fear described in Chapter 3 that coursed beneath the apparent quiescence of township politics more generally stood in sharp contrast to broadly based mobilization underway at the same time in Ezakheni.

In short, by the time of the historic events of early 1990, the interlocking dynamics of industrial, labor, and township politics – and the processes of formation of political subjects – were playing out in quite different ways in the two places.

Reconfigurations: Capital, Labor, and the Local State, 1990–95

From the perspective of places like Ladysmith and Newcastle, a more dramatic set of macro political-economic changes than those of the early 1990s is difficult to imagine. With the unbanning of the liberation movement, the balance of power of course swung sharply in favor of those engaged in oppositional struggles. Yet particularly in KwaZulu-Natal, this was a period of intense and escalating state-sponsored violence – albeit spatially uneven – between supporters of the ANC and Inkatha. There was also considerable uncertainty about how local government restructuring would unfold, although it seemed likely that the power of white local bureaucrats would be sharply curtailed. In response, a number of strategically based municipal officials were making moves to shore up their positions, and forge new translocal connections.

The ground was also shifting under the feet of local capital. Neoliberalism assumed a harsh official guise in 1996, but the dismantling of protective barriers behind which industries in Ladysmith and Newcastle had grown seemed increasingly likely in the early 1990s. Some of the clothing producers whom Alison Todes and I met in 1994 bravely proclaimed that they were about to break into the export market, taking advantage of the lifting of sanctions and cheaper imported textiles. Yet barely six months later, as we shall see in the following chapter, the knitwear industry in Newcastle was reeling under the impact of identical items flowing in from China at prices which were, some industrialists claimed, below the costs of production in Newcastle. More generally, it was clear that places like Ladysmith and Newcastle would increasingly be exposed to fiercely competitive global forces.

A powerful indication of neoliberal impulses came in 1991, with the slashing of industrial subsidies provided through the RIDP since 1982. The revised RIDP linked these drastically reduced incentives to productivity rather than inputs.[15] Unlike the 1982 RIDP, it was in large part spatially neutral.[16] These revisions were the product of political compromise. A strong neoliberal lobby called for total abandonment of any attempts to influence industrial location, but they were opposed by those representing different regional interests.

Revision of the RIDP stemmed from a strident critique of apartheid industrial decentralization policy spearheaded by metropolitan capital in the second half of the 1980s. In 1986 the captains of industry based in Johannesburg succeeded in their campaign to lift influx control, and turned their attention to industrial decentralization policies. The Private Sector Council of the Urban Foundation commissioned a series of critical studies, and soon thereafter the Development Bank of Southern Africa (DBSA) assembled a 'Panel of Experts' – several of whom had been closely involved with the Urban Foundation initiative, and who were allied with increasingly neoliberal technocrats in the DBSA.[17] Running through both reports is a powerful elision between apartheid/state intervention on the one hand, and dismantling apartheid/neoliberal reform on the other. It was, of course, precisely these discursive strategies that were so influential in shaping the ANC's neoliberal turn in the 1990s.

In development discourses more generally, places like Ladysmith and Newcastle that had figured so prominently in the apartheid era simply fell off the map. The revised RIDP formed part of a broader consensus that South Africa's post-apartheid future lay in the main metropolitan centers, and that any diversion of resources from these centers represented a distortion of natural tendencies. Articulated most forcefully by large corporate interests, the metro-centric consensus extended to include important segments of organized labor. Helping in effect to cement this alliance, a group of academics associated with COSATU conjured up visions of a high-tech, high wage industrial future. In the early 1990s, as we shall see in Chapter 6, the main challenge to this metro-centric view of the future came from a faction within the World Bank that set forth an alternative vision of a small-farmer path for South Africa, whose way would be paved by market-led land reforms. For all of these visionaries, decentralized industrial sites represented unpleasant relics of apartheid spatial engineering, destined to 'bleed away,' as one observer put it, once the plug was pulled.

In their preliminary evaluation of the revised RIDP, Wilsenach and Lichthelm (1993) noted with some alarm that a large proportion of industries were continuing to locate in old decentralization areas, thus flying in the face of 'natural' tendencies of urban agglomeration.[18] To explain this seemingly puzzling phenomenon, they pointed to ongoing activities of bantustan development corporations as key factors 'inhibiting the full realisation of the objective of concentrated industrial development at locations with natural potential for industrial development' (Wilsenach and Lichthelm 1993: 361). The problem, they asserted, was that development corporations had well-established institutional capacity, whereas local authorities in the metropolitan areas were still in the process of making the necessary institutional arrangements to attract industry. Once metropolitan authorities had their acts together, they implied, 'natural' agglomeration tendencies would spring into action.

Meanwhile, as we saw in the Introduction, it was in fact white local authorities in peculiar little places like Bronkhorstspruit who were springing into action in the early 1990s to emulate – if not surpass – the Newcastle strategy of bypassing both the national government and bantustan development corporations by luring not only Taiwanese industrialists but also Buddhist monks and nuns, along with religious tourists. Like their Newcastle counterparts, they proffered real estate with swimming pools along with access to labor pools in adjacent townships. Metro-centric proponents were either unaware of these and other spectacular strategies emanating from the ruins of apartheid, or they dismissed them as pipe-dreams. More prosaically, they failed to take account of what Bell (1983, 1986) had called 'spontaneous decentralization' – namely, industrialists moving into decentralized areas in search of lower costs.

The ongoing dispersal of labor-intensive industries into such areas in KwaZulu-Natal in the first half of the 1990s emerges clearly from a study by Harrison and Todes (1996), which encompassed both an analysis of projects approved under the new RIDP, and a set of case studies. According to RIDP data, the three key decentralization areas created during the apartheid era – Ladysmith-Ezakheni, Newcastle-Madadeni, and Isithebe – together accounted for 35 percent of projects approved under the new RIDP between 1991 and 1995 in the province; these relatively labor-intensive industries account for 46 percent of employment generated by RIDP-supported industries in the province, but only 23 percent of capital investment. The tendency for new foreign investment to locate in old decentralization areas since 1991 is even more marked. According to data supplied by the Department of Trade and Industry, Ladysmith-Ezakheni, Newcastle-Madadeni, and Isithebe were designated to receive 80 percent of projects, 91 percent of employment, and 63 percent of capital investment in the province generated by foreign investments approved under the RIDP between 1991 and 1994. In addition, *all* the prospective Asian investment – which accounted for two-thirds of the foreign investment projects approved in KwaZulu-Natal between 1991 and 1994 – was destined for these three areas. Taiwan formed by far the most important source of new foreign investment in this period – nearly 80 percent of Asian projects – although several projects from Mainland China were in the pipeline, most of them destined for the Ezakheni estate outside Ladysmith. The case studies, which included the survey that Alison Todes and I conducted in Newcastle, revealed numerous small firms – most of them clothing producers – setting up in decentralized areas *without* RIDP subsidies. They include, as we shall see, a group of small Taiwanese knitwear producers, many of whom moved into Newcastle behind the backs of white local authorities, but with credit from a large Taiwanese yarn producer based in Ezakheni.

According to data supplied by the KFC, the Ezakheni industrial estate contracted somewhat in the first half of the 1990s, but it certainly did not 'bleed away' (Table 4.1). Between 1991 and 1994, the KFC claims, 19 of the original 76 firms either closed or moved out, but another five moved in with the reduced RIDP incentives. The most dramatic decline was in the clothing sector, where seven firms closed and total employment fell by 50 percent from 4,600 to 2,300. Several of these were large South African firms that had relied on government contracts which were withdrawn. Some smaller Taiwanese clothing firms also closed but at least some of them seem to have reopened in Ladysmith. Apart from the decline in the clothing industry, the picture conveyed by these data is one of remarkable stability.

These types of data are always questionable, and the KFC had a vested interest in denying industrial decline. Yet the broad trends accord with the assessments of union officials, managers of the six largest industries, and the chamber of business in Ladysmith. Broadly speaking, what seems to have been happening in Ezakheni in the first half of the 1990s was a sorting-out process by which firms either left the estate, or were in the process of adjusting to union pressures. A number of Ezakheni firms that had adamantly opposed unions in the 1980s and early 1990s had either signed union recognition agreements by the mid-1990s, or were in the process of doing so. This includes several large Taiwanese textile firms that had long been targets of union activity. Management in these firms described their plans to deal with unionization by increasing capital intensity and reducing the workforce as much as possible.

This process resembles what happened in the Ladysmith industrial area in the 1980s when several large clothing firms closed, while Dunlop, Frame, and other industries signed union recognition agreements, and then proceeded to reduce their workforces and substitute capital for labor. A survey of a sub-set of firms in Ladysmith in 1996 by Kabelo Reid, a researcher at the University of Natal Durban, suggested that a number of them were trying to deal with intensified competition by seeking out niche markets and increasing productivity – with varying degrees of success.[19] In contrast to Newcastle where there were rapid and large-scale retrenchments in industries undergoing restructuring, the downsizing of the workforce in Ladysmith appeared more gradual and governed by union agreements. The managers with whom I spoke in Ladysmith were all careful to emphasize their smooth working relationships with the unions. In short, the relative strength and capacity of the union movement played a key role in shaping the trajectory of industrial development in Ladysmith and in the Ezakheni estate in the first half of the 1990s.

Yet this is by no means the whole story. While some segments of industry capitulated and were adjusting to organized labor, others – among whom clothing producers figure prominently – were trying to circumvent it. At least some of the clothing producers who moved out of Ezakheni appear to have set up in Ladysmith without RIDP incentives. Both Reid and I came across small, undocumented clothing operations in the suburbs of Ladysmith.

A particularly spectacular effort to circumvent organized labor emerged in 1995, in the context of local government restructuring. As explained more fully in Chapter 7, the IFP held more seats than the ANC alliance on the Transitional Local Council, which was established in late 1994 in preparation for local government elections that eventually took place in June 1996. Early in 1995 the IFP mayor and several prominent white businessmen in Ladysmith sought to emulate the earlier Newcastle strategy by sending a delegation to Taiwan. They managed to bring in a group of 10 Taiwanese clothing producers, who were set up in an empty factory vacated several years earlier by an industrialist who had gone off in search of more docile labor. The Taiwanese were promised a non-unionized workforce through a strategy designed to kill several birds (including SACTWU) with one stone: prospective workers were invited to come to the IFP office, register with the party, and obtain a ticket which would guarantee a job in the new factory complex. This strategy did indeed influence the outcome of the elections, but in a way that was totally at odds with the original intentions.

In short, industrial dynamics in Ladysmith-Ezakheni in the first half of the 1990s were not only molded and shaped by historically and locally specific arenas and forms of struggle. They also unleashed new rounds of struggle that reconfigured these local arenas, and indeed the form of the local state. We shall return to this theme in Chapter 7, which tells of how industrial, labor, and township politics interacted even more dramatically to shape processes of local state formation.

These recursive dynamics also emerged with great clarity in Newcastle-Madadeni in the 1990s, although the particular forms and trajectories are distinctly different. In October and November of 1994, as mentioned earlier, Alison Todes and I surveyed most of the industries in Newcastle and Madadeni in conjunction with the Newcastle municipality. By drawing on data from an earlier municipal survey, we were able to construct a broad picture of industrial trends in the first half of the 1990s. Two patterns stand out with particular clarity. First there was a sharp decline in heavy industries, where employment – almost exclusively male – appears to have fallen from around 9,500 in 1990 to approximately 6,800 in 1994. This shrinkage came about both through the closure of several firms, and fundamental restructuring of those that remained in business. Managers described how, in the face of intensified competition in the 1990s, they flattened managerial hierarchies, brought in new technologies, and moved swiftly to streamline their workforces by firing workers who did not conform to the new profile. They were able to strip away 'surplus workers' quite quickly because, unlike most of the heavy industries in Ladysmith, Iscor and other Newcastle industrialists by and large were not bound by union agreements. Some managers emphasized their efforts to implement more progressive labor practices, whereas others were quite frank about trying, as one put it, 'not to depend too heavily on people.' For workers – virtually all of them male – restructuring meant a sharp differentiation between those retrenched, and those who became far more incorporated into and identified with corporate structures than in the past. Some workers were unionized, but many were not. In practice, unionization seemed to make relatively little difference to wages and working conditions.

Second, our survey found that mainly female employment in clothing and textiles probably remained more or less unchanged in total (approximately 9,000 workers), although there was a proliferation of very small firms employing less that 30 workers. One quite surprising finding was that several large South African firms – including those that had in the past received heavy subsidies and operated in highly protected segments of the market – survived the vicissitudes of the early 1990s. Some of these firms closed down in the early 1990s, but others were restructured and their managers proclaimed that they had significantly increased productivity and efficiency.

Among foreign, mainly Taiwanese, firms about 75 percent of those established since the mid-1980s with RIDP incentives still existed in mid-1995.[20] In addition, between 1991 and 1994, at least 14 new Taiwanese knitwear firms were set up without incentives, although most of them received credit from a large Taiwanese acrylic yarn producer in Ezakheni.[21] They form part of the knitwear production network that took hold in Newcastle in the 1990s, the contentious dynamics of which form the focus of the following chapter.

As a prelude to the discussion that follows, let me conclude this chapter by recounting a horrendous and widely publicized incident on December 1, 2001. Nokhutula Hlatswayo, a worker in a Taiwanese clothing firm, gave birth to twins on the factory floor during a nightshift. She received no medical assistance because the factory was locked, and both babies died. In the public outrage that ensued, officials of the Department of Labour moved in and closed down a number of Taiwanese factories in Newcastle for gross violations of labor laws – wages well below the legal minimum, as well as appalling working conditions. Taiwanese industrialists responded by threatening to move to Lesotho. Press reports at the time made clear the desperation of workers terrified of losing their jobs, along with the frustration of SACTWU officials at a workforce unwilling to unionize. The incident also prompted a national soul-searching about the meaning of foreign investment and, implicitly at least, the neoliberal logic of GEAR. In an article in *Business Day* (December 14, 2001: 3) entitled 'Dickensian fiction brought to life,' Nicola Jenvey concluded:

> As a decentralised zone, Newcastle has attracted a wide range of predominantly Taiwanese investors who are seeking low-cost regions in which to ply their trade. Their interest has created jobs, but in the light of these levels of working conditions, the question is, at what price? If this is direct foreign investment, perhaps it is not the kind that SA needs.

Notably missing from this righteous indignation and national condemnation of Taiwanese as 'bad capitalists' was any critical reflection on the forces that had produced and perpetuated a deeply impoverished population for whom a job, however poorly paid and exploitative, had become – as one SACTWU official put it – 'a matter of life and death.' Yet, as I will try to show in the following chapters, the presence of Taiwanese industrialists in Newcastle offers an extraordinary opportunity for shedding new light on precisely these questions.

Part II

Transnational Trajectories

CHAPTER 5

Taiwanese Networks in Newcastle
The Production of Knitwear and of Difference

(T)hat which becomes spread or distributed 'globally' cannot be unproblematically deposited on one blank place-slate after another. It cannot avoid being locally superimposed upon already existing circumstances, cannot avoid being encountered by people already engaged in situated practices and their associated power relations, meanings and forms of knowledge and experience, and therefore cannot avoid being reworked in particular ways. (Pred 1995: 1076)

Battlegrounds of Capitalism

ON THE ROAD into Newcastle, a large sign – perhaps better described as a monument – welcomes visitors in Chinese. The sign not only proclaims the transnational character of the town; it also testifies to the political ambitions of the leader of one of the rival Taiwanese business groups whom I shall call Eddie Liu. At the end of 1994, Liu attached himself to the IFP in an effort to take over the local state. Confronted with intense labor conflict, he intended using his political clout to transform Newcastle into an export-processing zone in which unions were banned. Other signs on the road into Newcastle describe the town as the gateway to the region's main tourist attraction – the Battlegrounds Route, described in Chapter 2. In effect, this site of major colonial wars of the nineteenth century has been reconstituted as a battleground of contemporary capitalism.

The most visible and violent confrontations take place between Taiwanese industrialists and representatives of SACTWU, whose leader announced to me in 1995 his intention to 'eat these fly-by-nights for my breakfast.' At that time, SACTWU had over 30 labor disputes pending with Taiwanese industrialists in Newcastle, the majority for failure to pay minimum wages. When SACTWU did manage to drag Eddie Liu and his compatriots into court, they were represented by a lawyer who was for a time also head of the local branch of the ANC. On more than one occasion, when mutual fury between union representatives and Taiwanese industrialists threatened to erupt in physical violence, the local peace monitors – whose formal role, ironically enough, was to avert clashes between IFP and ANC supporters – were brought in to mediate.

These predominantly masculine sword-flashing episodes punctuated an ongoing series of skirmishes that took place every day on the factory floor between Taiwanese owner-managers and the African women who constituted the large majority of the workforce. A striking feature of Taiwanese factories in South Africa is their architecture: many, particularly the larger ones, are reminiscent of a panopticon. In her brilliant analysis of space and discipline in Chinese silk factories, Lisa Rofel (1999) reminds us how, in *Discipline and Punish* (1977), Foucault took the panopticon as a metonym for systems of surveillance in which, subject to an anonymous 'disciplinary gaze,' subjects take responsibility for disciplining themselves. Intended as a design for prisons, the original panopticon was a circular building with a guard tower in the centre; inmates of individual cells around the perimeter of the building cannot see the guards, but they are aware of being visible at all times from the central observation point.

The physical design of the Taiwanese industrial panopticon is rather different from Foucault's prison, but the intent is identical. Instead of a central guard tower, the point of surveillance is a set of offices on the second floor with internal windows looking over the factory floor, and a second-floor balcony from which all parts of the factory floor are visible. Yet the way this spatial arrangement works is directly at odds with the intent. Rather than creating hardworking, self-disciplined subjects, Taiwanese systems of labor control and surveillance in South Africa more often produce a powerful and palpable resentment that hangs like a pall over the factory floor, and is immediately evident when one enters the production area. With some key exceptions, the majority of Taiwanese industrialists complained incessantly about 'low productivity,' which they attributed to laziness, low levels of education, and ingratitude: 'We come here and make jobs,' shouted one, 'but they don't want to work!' Both on and off the factory floor, women workers express their deep resentment not only of low wages and poor working conditions but also, as one of them poignantly put it, the way 'they treat us just like animals.'

The battles going on in Taiwanese factories – as well as in the courtrooms, local government offices, and streets of Newcastle – assume locally specific and sometimes idiosyncratic forms, but they are far more generally significant, and illuminate a much larger set of issues. When Newcastle local government officials set up seminars in Taipei in the mid-1980s they were, quite unwittingly, tapping into one of the more remarkable dimensions of late twentieth-century capitalism – the emergence of Taiwan as one of the major sources of foreign direct investment, partly as a consequence of the phenomenal proliferation of lilliputian industries organized around familial and network forms of production. Between 1966 and 1986, the number of registered enterprises escalated by over 300 percent; by the early 1980s, there were over 700,000 registered firms in a population of 20 million – approximately one 'boss' for every eight adult males (G. Hamilton 1998: 48). In 1981, 87 percent of registered enterprises had fewer than 30 workers and only 4 percent employed more than 100 people (Greenhalgh 1994: 764). Since large numbers of enterprises were not registered, the incidence of petty capitalism was even more spectacular. It also created the conditions for its own destruction. By the early 1980s, escalating wages, land prices, and exchange rates were forcing large numbers of petty industrialists out of Taiwan.

In common with many other places around the globe, Newcastle became a node in a worldwide Taiwanese diaspora. By the mid-1990s, the organization of Taiwanese industries in the sub-region had come to resemble the network forms of production (or satellite factories) that are the predominant organizational form in Taiwan. Some 70 percent of the industrialists in Newcastle produced knitwear, and they constructed flexible production networks in which small- and medium-sized firms were linked to one another through subcontracting and a variety of other inter-firm linkages, as well as to a large Taiwanese acrylic yarn firm in Ladysmith.

Efforts to explain rapid and relatively egalitarian growth in Taiwan have increasingly come to assign pride of place to the proliferation of just such small-scale family firms and complex sub-contracting networks.[1] In addition, some observers (see for example Orru 1991) point to close parallels and structural similarities between Taiwanese forms of industrial organization and the small-firm complexes in north-central Italy that have come to epitomize 'flexible specialization' (Piore and Sabel 1984). More generally, 'network production' has become a metaphor for the organizational logic of contemporary capitalism, and part of a recognition of the rise of the Asian Pacific region as a major locus of industrial dynamism in the global economy (Castells 1996).

On the face of it, at least, the Taiwanese knitwear complex in Newcastle bears a close resemblance to forms of network production that have flourished in Taiwan. Yet network production in this context provides no guarantee of the sustained and relatively equitable growth that many observers regard as synonymous with small-firm production complexes. On the contrary, the knitwear production network in Newcastle both generates and is undermined by intense labor conflict. By the mid-1990s, it seemed to be in the process of unraveling.

For many South Africans of quite different political persuasions, the reasons are clear: Taiwanese industrialists are inherently super-exploitative. These stereotypes of 'bad Chinese' as greedy, opportunistic and lacking in social conscience, find their mirror image in notions of 'good Chinese' imbued with ancient, timeless traditions of familistic collectivism, harmony, and hard work. Since the late 1980s, a burgeoning literature emanating primarily from business schools and conservative think-tanks invokes precisely these positive stereotypes, framed in terms of Confucian cultural programming, to explain the success of Chinese family firms and network production.[2] For example:

> The Chinese networks derive their legitimacy and attraction from certain cultural predispositions, most of which are traceable to Confucian values. The very success of these networks encourages other cultural predispositions, such as patrimonial authority patterns, which give high organizational influence to key individuals, and an ethic of trustworthiness, which provides discipline and moral justifications to the system. This reciprocation releases other forms of efficiency, which can be explained technically in terms of low transaction costs, strategic flexibility, and a capacity for innovation, all of which facilitate a continuation of the successful recipe in the future. (Redding 1990: 46)

These celebratory narratives of Confucian capitalism represent a sort of inverse Orientalism (Greenhalgh 1994). They are also picked up and deployed by political and economic elites in different parts of Asia in strategies of what Ong (1997) calls 'moral management.' She points to 'a move beyond the simple reiteration of Chinese (Confucian) values to the articulation of a pan-Asian humanitarian model that is based on ahistorical and homogenizing descriptions of Asian cultures to legitimize overall state policies of capital accumulation, labor control, and social control' (Ong 1997: 191).

A large body of academic writing on network production in general and Asian forms of economic organization in particular explicitly rejects explanations cast in terms of cultural predispositions and mentalities, and focuses instead on the structure of social relations.[3] The central claim, is that 'cultures manifest themselves fundamentally through their embeddedness in institutions and organizations' (Castells 1996: 151).[4] Sometimes dubbed 'the new economic sociology,' this sort of neo-Weberian social structuralism traces to Granovetter's (1985) exposition of the embeddedness of economic institutions in social life.[5] Institutionalists portray Asian forms of network production in terms of the organizational logics embodied in the structure of social relations. Biggart for example explains that 'by "organizational logic" I mean a legitimating principle that is elaborated in an array of derivative social practices. In other words, organizational logics are the ideational bases for institutionalized authority relations' (Biggart 1991: 222). Thus Japanese firms enact a communitarian logic, Korean firms a patrimonial logic, and Taiwanese firms a patrilineal logic: 'Although all are network logics, they differ qualitatively and have important implications for how workers are organized, the character of subcontracting relations between firms, investment patterns, and a host of other economic relations. Each of these logics informs not only business relations, but social relations in other institutions in each society' (Biggart 1991: 222). In what is probably the most influential exposition of network production, Castells (1996) draws directly on this typology.

In practice, this structural portrayal provides very little room for understanding crucial questions of dynamics: how networks change, and what happens when they travel. While making claims about the flexibility of network production, it derives from singularly rigid and inflexible conceptions of power and culture that reduce social action and the meanings of social action to pre-given rules and structures of logic. Thus hierarchies such as those of gender are assumed to be given and fixed. By the same token labor discipline is simply taken for granted, or it is treated as a natural and unproblematic concomitant of familial forms of production and/or patriarchal authority relations. There is, in short, no possibility for change emerging from processes of negotiation, contestation, debate, and conflict.

An alternative, processual understanding associated with the concept of multiple trajectories outlined in Chapter 1 suggests a very different way of understanding network forms of production. Cultural meanings in this view are not simply imprinted in organizational logics and played out in authority relations, but are actively produced and contested in everyday practice in multiple, interconnected social arenas at different spatial scales. Accordingly, instead of simply asking *what* are the rules embodied or embedded in particular institutional forms, the focus is on *how* negotiation takes place within and among social arenas – the emphasis, in other words, is on practice, process, and the exercise of power rather than on pre-given logics.

These different conceptions of meaning and practice are extremely important to the way one goes about understanding what happens when particular forms of production relocate in different contexts. Within a structuralist framework, it is difficult to go beyond simply juxtaposing two different sets of organizational logics and authority relations – a sort of billiard ball model of relocation. In the case of Taiwanese forms of production in Newcastle, all one could say is that different logics are smashing up against one another. Recognition that conflicting material practices are simultaneously practices of meaning-making – that, in this particular case, the contention around the production of knitwear simultaneously involves the production of meanings, definitions, and identities – opens up far more interesting and useful lines of inquiry. In particular, it enables us to see how material struggles – over wages, working conditions, productivity and so forth – simultaneously produce understandings of racial, ethnic, and gender difference, as well as people's understandings of themselves as political subjects. It also sheds light on how struggles in the workplace intersect with those in other social arenas, and on how these overlapping processes both reflect and reconfigure local and regional histories.

To the extent possible with secondary sources, I will first try to locate Taiwanese industrialists in their own histories and their telling of these histories, and then explore key dimensions of their engagements with the white local government officials, African women workers, trade union officials, and white industrialists whose histories we have traced in part in earlier chapters. In short this chapter suggests how, through an intensifying spiral of conflict, the production of knitwear and the production of difference have reinforced one another.

Producers of Miracles: Narrations of Taiwanese Modernity

[Cultural identities] . . . come from somewhere, have histories. But far from being eternally fixed in some essentialised past, they are subject to the continuous 'play' of history, culture, and power. (Hall 1990: 225)

With a Taiwanese population of about 1,500 Newcastle had, by the mid-1990s, become a node in a worldwide Taiwanese diaspora.[6] Who are these people who, by the mid-1990s, defined Newcastle as home? One (or at most two) of the larger industrialists could be described as sophisticated, highly educated global operators with links to Hong Kong and investments in other parts of the world, a few had connections with relatively large industries in Taiwan, but the large majority came from the substantial class of self-made 'bosses' and their families that emerged since the 1960s in large part from the peasantry.

In a telling remark, a Newcastle local official described how, when he first went to Taiwan to recruit industrialists, he looked at the audience and asked himself 'are these the kind of people we want in Newcastle?' He described having visited scruffy little factories with no lighting and poor safety conditions, and claims he told prospective investors that they would have to shape up in South Africa.

In their insightful discussion of Chinese transnationalism, Nonini and Ong (1997: 9) note that idioms of Chinese culture, family values, forms of reciprocity (or *guanxi*), and Confucian capitalism do not merely explain Chinese identity, networks, and economic activity; rather such discourses and their connections to power in large part *constitute* Chinese identities and transnational practices (see also Yang 1994). In addition, invocations of 'Chinese culture' – strong families, loyalty to elders, discipline, frugality, work ethic and so forth – provide the raw materials for different narrations of modernity and for pointed critiques of the West (Ong 1997). Yet these narrations of Asian modernity contain many elements of Western discourses since they are produced in negotiation with Western domination: 'I therefore use the term *alternative modernities* to denote not so much the difference in content from Western ones as the new self-confident political reenvisioning of futures that challenge the fundamental assumption of inevitable Western domination' (Ong 1997: 195).

For Taiwanese in South Africa, confronted not only with racist stereotypes but also with the stigma of association with apartheid, there are additional layers of complexity. Taiwanese industrialists did indeed deploy Orientalist constructions of themselves – both to contest negative stereotypes, and to underscore the inherent laziness and economic backwardness of South Africans, white and black alike. In addition, in the course of their struggles with local government officials, union representatives, and workers, they drew heavily on particular narrations of the Taiwanese 'miracle' – and of themselves as producers of it. Particularly in the mid-1990s, 'lessons from elsewhere' – including, quite prominently, East Asian tiger economies – were being widely invoked to chart the way forward in post-apartheid South Africa (see Chapter 1). Accordingly, these narrations of Taiwanese miracles became a key medium through which labor conflicts in Taiwanese factories came to articulate with larger debates about adjustments to 'globalization' in the post-apartheid order. In addition, they formed key components of the political currency with which Eddie Liu was able to buy his way into the IFP and associate himself with Zulu ethnic nationalism.

The stories Taiwanese industrialists told about themselves and about post-war Taiwanese history combined several key elements. In addition to their own capacity for extremely hard work – in contrast to the inherent laziness of South Africans – they consistently invoked unfettered markets as the secret of Taiwanese success. Time and again, Alison Todes and I were regaled with accounts of how unions were responsible for South African economic backwardness, and how this – or indeed any – sort of interference with natural market mechanisms would never be countenanced in Taiwan.[7] The constant refrain was that, if South Africa wanted to develop, unions must be eliminated and other markets had to be deregulated. In practice, as we shall see later, there was a significant retreat from invocations of free trade when cheaper commodities produced in China started flowing into South Africa. In general, though, neoliberal narratives formed a central thrust of their construction of the Taiwanese miracle, and a key point of contrast with the economic morass into which South Africa had fallen as a consequence of union activism and state interference.

These constructions of the Taiwanese miracle cast in terms of the unleashing of market forces articulated with the growing influence of neoliberalism in national policy arenas in the mid-1990s (see Chapter 1). A spate of articles in the popular South African press, for example, expounded on how free markets had propelled East Asian economic successes, and these arguments were also widely deployed in national debates. In

KwaZulu-Natal, the dynamic of articulation was even more direct: as I will argue more fully later, Taiwanese narratives of neoliberalism provided a key means by which Eddie Liu's incorporation into the IFP was made possible.

The stories told by Eddie Liu and his compatriots about Taiwanese economic success in terms of free markets are also closely analogous to those deployed by proponents of neoliberalism in the late 1970s and early 1980s (see for example Galenson 1979; Balassa 1981; Kreuger 1981) – several of whom were actively engaged in pushing the World Bank to embrace structural adjustment policies, justified in terms of East Asian economic success. It was precisely these interpretations that prompted a series of vigorous rebuttals by Amsden (1985), Gold (1986), Wade (1990), Pang (1992), Evans (1995), and others, who provide detailed accounts of the interventionist character of the state in post-war Taiwan.

In reaction to what he sees as an excessively state-centric emphasis of this literature, Gary Hamilton (1998: 71) argues that 'Taiwan's capitalism is not state-led capitalism; instead it is *guanxi* capitalism, a capitalism built up and extended out from networks embedded in Chinese society.' Thus, Hamilton contends, the Taiwanese state has to contend with and ultimately accept the established patterns and economic momentum that exist within the society, the very patterns that arise out of Taiwan's horizontal economic networks. Hamilton's ideal-type model posits two key network structures, vertical and horizontal. Vertical networks operate mainly between fathers and sons, and govern inheritance through patrilineal systems. Horizontal or *guanxi* networks occur outside spheres of direct family control; they are based on norms of reciprocity, have broad horizontal spans of control, and are marked by low degrees of hierarchy. The defining feature of these relationships is personal trust: 'One does not normally think of personal trust as an organizational principle, but in Chinese businesses it is . . . Trust binds people together by obliging them to act according to set rules of social relationships' (G. Hamilton 1998: 62).

Taiwanese industrialists in Newcastle would heartily endorse this effort to restore them to center stage. Indeed, part of the stories they told about themselves revolved around forms of industrial organization that enabled them to outcompete South Africans whom they portrayed as not only inherently lazy, but also disorganized second-rate capitalists. My first exposure to such narratives came in January 1991 on a visit to the Dimbaza industrial estate in the Eastern Cape (Map 1). One of the Taiwanese industrialists whom I shall call Mr Wong described to me how, from raw cotton, he produced shirts identical to those of Da Gama, an Anglo-American Corporation subsidiary down the road, for precisely half the cost – even though both paid extremely low wages to the predominantly female workforce.[8] The secret, claimed Mr Wong, lay in his lean and flexible system of management. Da Gama employed large numbers of well-paid administrators and managers who enjoyed frequent games of golf during working hours. Mr Wong explained how he, in contrast, had no formal managerial structure. Rather, he had brought six 'technicians' from Taiwan who knew every aspect of the business. He and they worked incredibly long hours, and could substitute for one another on virtually any task. Industrialists in Newcastle were unable to make such direct comparisons, since none were in precisely the same line of production as South African firms. Yet they also made consistent claims about their capacity to outcompete South African firms on the basis not only of hard work, but also more efficient forms of management structured around familial relations, along with ties of trust and reciprocity to technicians and other industrialists. In short, this dimension of their self-presentation of success is closely consistent with those of academic interpreters who accord primacy to familial and network forms of industrial organization.

Feminist critics in particular have pointed to some key missing elements in these stories. First and most obviously, these forms of production are deeply gendered, and operate very differently for women and men. Ethnographic research in different parts of Taiwan by Hsiung (1996), Greenhalgh (1994), and Gallin (1984) illustrates with great clarity the centrality of gendered practices and meanings in shaping how network forms of production operate, and the way they change over time. Gender is important not only in intra-familial relations, but in other social arenas as well – including, very importantly, the exercise of labor discipline. Similar considerations pertain to *guanxi* relations of reciprocity. What's missing from representations of these relations in terms of trust and harmony are the exclusionary principles through which they operate:

> The tactical practices of family and *guanxi* euphemized in discourse show amoral tactics of domination, violence, exploitation, and duplicity, both outside this relationship and within it. Outside it: *guanxi* discourse demarcates various relationships of comity and privilege with specific kinds of people ('brothers,' classmates, people with the same native place). But this by implication excludes numerous

others with whom one has an acknowledged relationship . . . These people can be legitimately taken advantage of, exploited, disciplined, abused, or cheated. Within it: Most *guanxi* relationships are articulated between putative status equals . . . Yet the supposed equality or benign status difference euphemizes relations of domination where de facto differences in power and capital are misrecognized or not acknowledged in public by both sides. (Nonini and Ong 1997: 22)

Particularly from a transnational perspective, key questions revolve around *how* these relations are reworked over time and in different contexts. Thus, for example, it is not sufficient to simply replace a cultural determinist model of benevolent paternalism with a structural model of patriarchal authority. Rather we need to ask *how* gendered definitions and identities both inform and are shaped by everyday practices, and how these change and are reconfigured in different contexts. As far as *guanxi* relations and their exclusionary logic are concerned, the key questions are how boundaries between insiders and outsiders are constructed and maintained, who has the capacity to engage in these practices, who is included and excluded, and what are the conditions that either encourage or undermine the construction of boundaries.

To grasp how and why Taiwanese network forms of production work so differently in South Africa, it is also important to situate the emergence of these forms – and the subjectivities of the industrialists who forged them – in relation to the historical specificities of larger configurations of political and economic power in post-war Taiwan. Although any such account is obviously partial, two dimensions seem particularly important and salient – and notably missing from most accounts of Taiwanese miracles. First are the exclusionary ethnic politics practiced by the Kuomintang (KMT) nationalists who fled to Taiwan and took control of the state following their defeat by the Chinese communist forces on the mainland. The second dimension, taken up in greater detail in Chapter 6, concerns the particular path of agrarian transformation in post-war Taiwan, characterized by rapid industrialization without dispossession.

Ironically, the Taiwanese industrialists who moved to South Africa form part of an ethnicized majority that was subjected to systematic state-sponsored discrimination in the post-war period. Fragments of this history emerged in interesting ways in the course of my research in Newcastle. One industrialist, for example, noted that '1948 people (i.e. KMT nationalists who took over the state) are like Americans; they don't work so hard but have big businesses; people like us (i.e. ethnic Taiwanese) are like the Japanese – we work very hard.' This comment is fascinating for what it does – and does not – say about the historical processes that gave rise to huge numbers of small-scale industrialists in Taiwan, as well as the way this history is being invoked to drive home claims of industriousness. The reference to Japan is particularly interesting when one recalls that Taiwan was colonized by Japan from 1895 to 1945, when the island was returned to China.[9] What is most revealing, however, is his counterposition of '1948 people' and ethnic Taiwanese.

In discussing how ethnic difference has been produced and perpetuated in Taiwan, Gates (1981) and Hsiung (1996) identify four main ethnic groups: the aborigines, the Hakka, the Taiwanese, and the mainlanders. The aborigines, the first inhabitants of the island, are of Malayo-Polynesian descent; they lost their independence and predominant role in Taiwan to immigrants from China more than two centuries ago, and have been further marginalized under KMT rule. The Taiwanese and Hakka are descendants of Hokkien and Hakka speakers who migrated from Fujian and Guandong provinces in China in the seventeenth century. They constituted the bulk of the peasantry and, by 1980, owned and operated approximately 85 percent of small-scale enterprises in Taiwan (Gates 1981). Mainlanders – the '1948 people' – are the 1,020,000 troops and refugees who arrived in Taiwan with the KMT between 1947 and 1949, following their defeat by Mao Tse-tung's Communist Party in China. Mainlanders took control of the state, and monopolized control of state resources.

Hsiung describes ethnic relations as follows:

> Not only does each of these four ethnic groups have its own dialect, but the roughly nine aboriginal tribes also speak different dialects. Relations among these four major ethnic groups have been covertly divisive in the last thirty years. Toward the aborigines, the Taiwanese, Hakka, and mainlanders form a single interest group. In Mandarin, the dialect of the mainlanders which is also the official language, the aborigines used to be called *Gaoshanzhu*, meaning literally 'the mountain tribes' or 'the mountain race.' The Taiwanese call the aborigines *Whan-a*, meaning 'the barbarians.' The tensions between the mainlanders and the Taiwanese and Hakka majority dates back to the early years of the KMT takeover and has scarcely diminished since then. Seen by others and themselves as outsiders, the mainlanders are normally referred to as *Waishengren* (people from other provinces), as opposed to *Benshengren/Taiwenren* (people of the local/Taiwan province, including the Taiwanese and Hakka). By 1990, 1.7 percent of the population consisted of aborigines, 15 percent were mainlanders, and the rest Taiwanese and Hakka. (Hsiung 1996: 24–25)

Resentment of the Taiwanese and Hakka majority towards mainlanders was initially fomented in the period in the late 1940s that Gold (1986) terms a 'chaotic interregnum.' Following the retrocession of Taiwan to China after the Japanese defeat, mainland nationalist officials and soldiers pillaged the island for private gain and in support of the civil war against the communists. In February 1947 mainland soldiers shot a woman peddler accused of selling cigarettes illegally, and Taiwanese resentment erupted in popular uprisings throughout the island; KMT troops responded by killing between 2,000 and 20,000 Taiwanese/Hakka: 'While on one level the killing seemed indiscriminate, a pattern is discernible: the Nationalists intended to liquidate the Taiwanese intellectual and social elite. They went after ... teachers, students, newspaper editors, lawyers, and anyone considered critical of the government' (Gold 1986: 51).[10]

The KMT continued to claim sovereignty over the mainland and monopolized state power in Taiwan, holding strongly to the position that Taiwan was simply a province of China. At least until the late 1980s when martial law was lifted, Hakka and Taiwanese were disproportionately disadvantaged because the KMT distrusted and excluded them from the bureaucracy (Hsiung 1996: 25).[11]

> The exclusion and derogation of the Taiwanese was justified in terms of the government's 'sacred mission' of national reunification. By claiming to represent all of China, the mainlander government could argue that Taiwanese did not deserve to occupy a place of power because in the grand scheme of Chinese history they represented only one province, and a small one at that. (Greenhalgh 1994: 766)

Excluded from access to state jobs and advanced educational opportunities, ethnic Taiwanese were allowed to go into business – but in a context deliberately designed to disperse the economic power of the private sector. These limits included state control over upstream industries supplying raw materials and intermediate inputs, party control of the stock exchange, and tightly restricted access to the state-run banking system (Wade 1990). For their part, ethnic Taiwanese devised myriad informal means to pursue their economic interests beyond the purview of their rulers, primary among which was the mobilization of family, kinship, and other personalistic forms of social relations:

> Kept out of jobs in government and state-run institutions, ambitious Taiwanese had little choice but to invest their energies in business. In this ethnically bifurcated

society, entrepreneurship meant ethnic entrepreneurship, more concretely, exploiting Taiwanese kin and community networks to mobilize business resources such as
labor, capital and information . . . My own informants operated within a largely
Taiwanese sociobusiness world. For business associates, they favored family
members over suprafamily kin, suprafamily kin over other Taiwanese, and other
Taiwanese over Japanese. In an irony that escaped no-one, they preferred to do
business with Japanese – their former colonial rulers – than with mainlanders.
(Greenhalgh 1994: 766)

In Chapter 6, we shall attend more closely to the spatial as well as the social
processes of industrial dispersal in post-war Taiwan, in particular the
emergence of small-scale industrialists from the peasantry. For purposes of
the remainder of this chapter, it is important to recognize that while every
aspect of agriculture was very tightly controlled, industry provided a means
of escape from state scrutiny:

> In a sense, small-scale decentralized industrialization, including household fact-
> ories as well as some of the larger villager-owned enterprises, constitutes a form of
> underground economy at the micro-economic level. A certain proportion of
> production is unreported, and hired labor is often paid in cash, enabling both
> workers and employers to avoid taxes . . . the very structure of this type of
> economic activity enables local entrepreneurs to exercise greater political auto-
> nomy over their lives, and in the process, to make a political statement . . . In a
> country where the government is actively involved in trying to manage economic,
> social, and cultural change, decentralized, small-scale industrialization has allowed
> postpeasants a remarkable degree of autonomy. Given the restrictive political
> climate in modern Taiwan, this is undeniably an attractive side benefit of small-
> scale industrialization in rural areas such as Zhonge. (Niehoff 1987: 306–307)

This account ignores the gendered micro-politics through which familial forms
of production operate, and different experiences of power and autonomy. It
does, nevertheless, illuminate male industrialists' understandings of themselves
as operating in the interstices of the economy, beyond the purview of a
politically repressive state. In an interestingly ambiguous metaphor, Lam
(1989) labels this modus operandi 'guerrilla capitalism.' It was precisely these
guerrilla capitalists whom Newcastle local government officials encountered
when, in the mid-1980s, they launched their own guerrilla-like strategy of by-
passing both the central government and the KFC.

Signs of Tension: Taiwanese Industrialists and the Local State in Newcastle

In portraying conditions in Taiwan as messy, overcrowded, and chaotic,
Newcastle local government officials were quick to provide contrasting

images of their own town as a place of order, cleanliness, and superior amenities, and of themselves as the guarantors of a well-ordered society. The stories they told about Taiwanese typically revolved around their peculiar habits and insularity on the one hand, and their capacity for brutally hard work on the other. The proclivity of Taiwanese to snap up luxury houses figured prominently in the stories to which I had access. As we saw in the previous chapter, a large stock of luxury housing was standing vacant in the early 1980s in Newcastle when a planned expansion of Iscor failed to materialize; cheap real estate, along with good schools, hospitals, and so forth were key selling points that entrepreneurial local government officials deployed in luring Taiwanese to the town, along with lavish supplies of labor and generous subsidies. I was regaled with stories of how Taiwanese are 'fussy about funny things': no number 4 in the street number (one official explained that he had changed street numbers to accommodate Taiwanese purchasers); front and back doors could not be opposite; and the fence could not have steps. Once these criteria had been met, I was told, Taiwanese just grabbed up houses, often fully furnished – and had placed sharp upward pressure on housing prices. Another set of stories revolved around Taiwanese demands that required skirting around zoning restrictions, which once again required the deployment of discretionary power for the good of the community as a whole. In these and other ways, local government officials used their stories about encounters with Taiwanese to portray themselves as rational, helpful men who, in their concern for orderly growth of the town, had to deal with distinctly peculiar, almost child-like beings who had to be humored at every turn.

Late in 1994, Alison Todes and I were inadvertent witnesses to a particularly revealing encounter. We were sitting in the office of a senior bureaucrat when a huge commotion broke out in the corridor. An agitated secretary came rushing in, saying that Eddie Liu was extremely angry and insisting on meeting immediately. The bureaucrat groaned and grimaced, but left the room straight away. For the next 10 to 15 minutes, Eddie Liu berated the bureaucrat about the delay in erecting the Chinese 'Welcome to Newcastle' mentioned at the beginning of this chapter. 'I paid for this sign,' he shouted, 'but you people are too lazy and slow. Why can you never get anything done?' With barely suppressed rage, the bureaucrat explained that he had to get the approval of white town councilors – whom, it turned out, were not enthusiastic about publicly proclaiming the Chinese identity of the town. As it happened, the sign was only erected in 1995 when the old white town council had been replaced by the Transitional Local Council, on which Eddie Liu was a representative of the IFP.

The Chinese sign represented not only an effort by Eddie Liu and his compatriots quite literally to ground their identity in a reconfigured image of the town; it was also a lightning rod of multiple, overlapping struggles, at the center of which was intense and escalating labor conflict in Taiwanese factories. When Newcastle local government officials launched their transnational strategy in the mid-1980s, a key selling point was the large supply of cheap and supposedly docile labor. The relative quiescence of industrial labor in Newcastle in the 1980s was not simply a matter of official repression. As we saw in the previous chapter, it was at least partly a product of a local history of labor disorganization and political conflict in the townships, and contrasted sharply with conditions in Ladysmith. When union activity and overt labor conflict did emerge in Newcastle in the 1990s, it was exacerbated by the labor practices of the large majority of Taiwanese industrialists. In addition, the history of labor disorganization resulted in several unions competing with one another, and being played off each other by industrialists.

By the mid-1990s, labor in Newcastle was in a state of chaos – in the face of which local government officials were largely helpless. They were also under intense pressure from South African industrialists, who expressed their resentment of Taiwanese industrialists and their labor practices in no uncertain terms. Ironically, as mentioned in the previous chapter, mutual resentment towards Taiwanese enabled some union leaders and South African industrialists to downplay cross-cutting differences of class and race in their own relationships and understandings of one another.[12] In short, by the mid-1990s, Newcastle local government officials were in an embattled position, engaged both in defensive constructions of Taiwanese industriousness – and, by extension, of course, their own strategy – and in dramatizing peculiar Taiwanese habits.

Early in my research, I recounted to a senior bureaucrat in Newcastle the story told to me by the Taiwanese industrialist in Dimbaza about the superior efficiency of Taiwanese relative to South African firms. His face lit up, and he offered to take me on a tour to illustrate precisely that point. First he took me to a Taiwanese factory – in fact, quite an unusual one – where the bureaucrat did indeed have a fairly close relationship with the owner. In this highly automated clothing firm, which was not part of the knitwear network, employment had been minimized and tight discipline exercised through a combination of carrots and sticks. We then visited a large South African clothing firm where managers were indeed sitting around in offices drinking tea, and the atmosphere on the factory floor was relatively relaxed. In the car on the way back to the office, I was treated to a lecture about differential efficiency in the two firms. My informant also noted that when he wanted to meet Taiwanese industrialists he would simply go to the factory floor, whereas South African managers would typically be found on the golf course. It subsequently turned out that the manager of the South African firm was among the most vociferous critics of Taiwanese industrialists in general, and the actions of one of the Taiwanese business associations in particular.

What also became evident was that Newcastle local government officials in practice had very little understanding of the modus operandi of Taiwanese industrialists, and were anxious to get a better grasp on what was happening. It was in this context that Alison Todes and I offered to assist with an industrial survey, and our offer was quickly accepted. As I mentioned earlier, a fairly junior municipal official made appointments with industrialists, and accompanied us on most – although not all – of the interviews. In each of these interviews, Alison Todes and I were careful to explain our university affiliations and engagement in research. By and large, however, most industrialists, both South African and Taiwanese, probably defined us as secretaries of the municipal official. Although the context of these encounters was quite constrained, most industrialists seemed to welcome the opportunity of an audience before whom to vent their anger and frustration. Without exception, Taiwanese industrialists complained bitterly and at great length about the inability of the local government to deal with labor conflict. Those who had come in the 1980s through initial personal contacts with local government officials talked about their sense of betrayal; they had been promised a large, cheap and docile labor force, and were now being threatened with court actions by militant unions and regularly closed down by hostile workers. Why, they wanted to know, was the local government so incapable of taking any action? Most Taiwanese industrialists made it clear that they regarded local government officials as dishonest in their representations of docile labor; and either incompetent or lazy for their failure to take any action. For their part, local government officials were forced to admit their helplessness in the face of chaotic labor conditions.

These constructions by local government officials and Taiwanese industrialists of one another, and the tense relations between them, need to be situated in the context of changing conditions of accumulation between the mid-1980s and the mid-1990s. When Taiwanese industrialists first started coming to Newcastle in the mid-1980s, local government officials mediated access to key resources. These included organizing applications for the extremely generous subsidies offered under the 1982 RIDP, assisting with access to very cheap luxury real estate, obtaining permits for skilled male 'technicians' whom industrialists brought with them from Taiwan and other parts of Asia, and easing zoning restrictions. By the early 1990s, RIDP subsidies had been cut back very sharply. Although Taiwanese industrialists continued to move into Newcastle in the 1990s, they did so without subsidies. Indeed, a number of them came in without residence permits and, as one local government official put it, 'we pick up the problems.' In short, Taiwanese settlers were increasingly mobilizing their own resources to bring in new industrialists. In the process, strategically placed local patrons were positioning themselves as brokers, and Taiwanese industrialists in general were becoming less reliant on relations with the local state.

By the time that Eddie Liu came storming into the town planner's office in Newcastle in late 1994, relations between Taiwanese industrialists and the old local state had frayed almost to breaking point. It was in this context that Eddie Liu made a major bid to take over the local state – with the unintended consequences described in Chapter 7.

Engendering Networks

> Whether as members of the contingent workforces of subcontractors or as technocratic elites, diaspora Chinese have found themselves in novel social arrangements. The newness of these arrangements has largely gone unnoticed . . . because they take the guise of 'traditional' patterns of family and of networking based on *guanxi* particularism. (Nonini and Ong 1997: 11)

Deteriorating relations between Taiwanese industrialists and local government officials reflect the deeply contradictory dynamics of industrialization that took hold in the late 1980s and first half of the 1990s. Transplanted to Newcastle, Taiwanese network production unleashed a powerful growth dynamic, while at the same time creating the conditions for its own destruction.

The majority of Taiwanese in Newcastle come from two regions of the island, both major centers of knitwear production: Tainan in the south and Shulin, a town outside Taipei in the north. In the mid-1990s, two mutually antagonistic Chinese business associations more or less reflected these spatial origins, although there were some defections that intensified the conflict. The northerners regarded themselves as far more sophisticated than the southerners whom they defined as rather crass.

The sort of knitwear produced in Taiwanese factories in Newcastle – with acrylic yarn produced in Ladysmith – is enormously popular in South Africa more generally. A typical jacket would be made from brightly colored, boldly designed fabric, woven on a computer-driven machine. It may well be lined and shoulder-padded, and would almost certainly be decorated with metallic buttons and elaborately embroidered pockets. Items like these are attractive, practical, and cheap. In a climate where winters can be bitterly cold and a society where large numbers of people command low and often shrinking incomes, these warm and decorative jerseys (as they are called) are broadly attainable objects of desire. At least until mid-1995, when identical knitwear from China started flooding the market at prices below costs of production in Newcastle, Taiwanese industrialists were catering to a large segment of the South African market. Indeed, some claim that they created the broadly based mass market for this type of knitwear in South Africa. Whether or not this claim is true, it does seem to be the case that until the middle of 1995 Taiwanese knitwear producers had cornered at least a sizable segment of a growing and fairly protected market.[13]

By the mid-1990s, knitwear production in Newcastle-Ladysmith had increasingly come to resemble network or satellite production in Taiwan. In the Newcastle segment of the network, firms became smaller, more specialized, and more tightly connected with one another since the early 1990s. Some firms did nothing but knit acrylic fabric; these tended to be quite small. Larger firms did both knitting and assembly, although at times of peak orders they subcontracted knitting to specialized firms. Other firms specialized in zippers, seam binding, shoulder pads, buttons, and other components of the final product. There were also very small firms that did nothing but embroidery. By early 1995, several of the new firms that came in were importing machine parts and assembling new machines. Firms within the Newcastle network were hierarchically ordered, with a firm's position determined by access to markets and the capacity to generate orders. Smaller and more specialized firms tended to be owned by people whose lack of English and contacts meant that they had to rely on others for obtaining orders. The large acrylic yarn producer in Ladysmith had also come to form an increasingly important element of the network; in addition to supplying materials, this firm played a key role in the extension of the network by providing credit to small new firms that started up without incentives.

This growing resemblance to forms of production in Taiwan is the product of several quite contradictory processes. Taiwanese industrialists were able to replicate some of the practices that drove rapid industrialization in Taiwan – most notably familial forms of management and male employees splitting off to form their own firms. At the same time, their efforts to discipline African women workers generated enormous resentment that placed limits on their capacity to expand. These racialized processes were also deeply gendered. To understand how they took hold in Newcastle, one must first attend to the centrality of gendered practices and identities in shaping the way superficially similar networks operate in Taiwan.

Young men's spinning off to form their own firms forms a key element of the endogenous growth dynamic of satellite factory systems in Taiwan. Several studies document how subcontracting firms are frequently started by former employees who establish subcontracting relationships with their former bosses:

> Employers would often encourage such departures and even invest in firms started by their best and most capable employees in order to develop the subcontracting network. Although it is counterintuitive, such encouragement of and investments in potentially competing firms create a satellite assembly system capable of achieving economies of scale on a temporary basis without enlarging the size of existing firms and without making large capital investments in labor and machines that might not produce at capacity or may not produce very long. Investment capital is put into people who will repay at a premium, and who will likely remain morally bound to their former bosses and economically anchored in their satellite assembly systems, at least as long as business orders hold out. (G. Hamilton 1998: 66)

A key point, however, is that the 'people' into whom this investment capital is put are almost always male; the bonds that sustain inter-unit relations are, as Hsiung (1996) points out, those of brotherhood. Ethnographic studies in Taiwan consistently point out how, for young men, industrial work is typically an apprenticeship on the way to self-employment. Young men often prefer jobs in small factories, despite the far lower (and frequently non-existent) benefits and physically unpleasant working conditions, precisely because they afford greater opportunities for learning multiple dimensions of the business and establishing potentially useful relationships

(Stites 1985; Harrell 1985; Niehoff 1987). For large numbers of young men industrial work is, as Stites (1985) puts it, an entrepreneurial strategy; describing his work in a small spinning and dyeing factory he remarks that '[male] workers viewed extraordinary demands [for work intensification] with an equanimity that would have been embarrassing to an American unionist.' He goes on to note that appearances of worker complacency are deceiving, but that rather than publicly criticize conditions in the factory and disrupt a fragile social relationship that might be useful later on most workers simply change jobs:

> Chinese workers are not mindless workaholics, nor are their attitudes easily comparable to those found in American factories. Hard work, lack of interest in the unions that do exist, and a superficially close relationship with the employer are combined with an ambivalence about depending too much on one employer. The consequence is high labor turnover, but for many workers this is only a preliminary stage to an eventual goal of self-employment. (Stites 1985: 237)

In similar vein, Shieh (1992) argues that the satellite factory system generates 'opportunities for workers to set up their own manufacturing workshops' and so reduces the confrontational clashes between bosses and workers on the shopfloor. Yet the 'opportunities' that Taiwan's satellite factory system provides to men are very different from those available to women: 'although most male skilled workers may have the option for "exit" to become their own bosses, many married women are destined to become the unwaged family workers whose labor is crucial in assisting their husbands to set up small businesses' (Hsiung 1996: 21).

The Mandarin term for the owner of a small factory (*taogei*) is, Hsiung (1996: 87) points out, the same as 'head of household' – a position that affords considerable authority over women and subordinate males. Family firms are not unified entities bonded by the glue of family sentiment (Greenhalgh 1994: 750); rather, they are highly differentiated labor hierarchies based on inequality of opportunity and reward along gender and generational lines. The family/firm head exercises formidable power to command the loyalties and skill of different family members that is grounded in control over property and in gendered meanings. 'Traditional Confucian culture' is not simply a set of rules to which family members automatically adhere, but part of a cultural repertoire that constitutes a key resource in the gendered exercise of power and discipline, the mediation of conflict, the construction of loyalty and trust, and the division of rewards:

> Taiwanese businessmen garnered family labor for their firms by promoting cultural constructions of enterprise work as part of family obligation. They filled the full range of positions by exploiting traditional family hierarchies and cultural expectations about appropriate roles for men and women. Building on traditional inequalities, they fostered the formation of a stratified workforce in which women held high-trust but low-power jobs that did not interfere with their reproductive tasks, while men worked at high-trust and high-power jobs that advanced their careers. (Greenhalgh 1994: 759)

The process by which women became incorporated into the management of 'family firms' is clearly a key component of the Taiwanese 'miracle' to which remarkably little attention has been given.

These familial forms of management and masculine avenues of upward mobility are precisely those that many Taiwanese industrialists who moved to South Africa were able to replicate. The first round of industrialists brought with them, as noted earlier, multi-skilled male 'technicians.' In addition to operating and maintaining machines, technicians were often involved in labor discipline and other production tasks. Their relationship to the firm/family head was often one of fictive kinship; one industrialist, for example, explained how he treated his technicians as his 'sons' and trusted them accordingly. Others talked about the importance of maintaining 'smooth' relationships with their technicians, and of the way they plied their technicians with gifts. Once when I inquired about the costs of these gifts I was told, 'Oh but you don't understand; I can't bargain with these people.' For their part technicians were also, of course, aspiring capitalists – many of whom had plans to settle permanently in South Africa. It was indeed the promise of cheap real estate, good schools, and so forth that drew many of them to South Africa in the first place. As one of their bosses noted, 'they want to come because you can live like a king in South Africa.'

Technicians who split off to form their own firms were the chief source of industrial growth in Newcastle in the first half of the 1990s. At least until mid-1995 when cheap imports posed a major threat, it seemed as though a powerful dynamic of expansion was taking hold. Although some technicians split off from firms based in Newcastle, others came from former bantustan industrial estates in places like Isithebe, QwaQwa, and Botshabelo. They were drawn to Newcastle both by the knitwear network and, it seems, by ongoing processes of social agglomeration. Although I cannot substantiate this directly, it is possible that part of the attraction of Newcastle was a sort of growing informalization in the 1990s, which enabled industrialists to operate more or less independently of the white local government. The decline in subsidies after 1991 meant that industrialists were far less dependent on local government officials than they had been in the 1980s, and were increasingly operating in ways that circumvented the local state. In short, conditions that in certain respects more or less approximated the relatively deregulated spaces of small-scale industry in Taiwan seemed to be taking shape in Newcastle in the first half of the 1990s. Aspiring new industrialists were both attracted by these conditions of accumulation, and acted in ways that expanded and reinforced them.

On the face of it, this endogenous growth dynamic appears remarkably similar to that which drove rapid industrialization in Taiwan. Yet relations between bosses and their former technicians were not always the smoothly functioning *guanxi* ties that feature so prominently in the literature on Taiwan. Nor were former technicians necessarily subordinate elements of a hierarchical satellite structure. On the contrary, several of the technicians who set up on their own were in the process of outcompeting their former bosses – one of whom described his ex-technician as an 'industrial enemy!' Another former technician had established himself at the center of a new set of satellite firms, and was challenging the dominant position of one of the most influential bosses in Newcastle. What distinguished this relatively successful new round of industrialists was that they were far better able than their original bosses to exercise labor discipline – or, as Burawoy (1979, 1985) might put it, to manufacture some degree of consent.

The gendered and racialized practices through which labor control is – or is not – accomplished are missing from many accounts of network production in Taiwan and elsewhere; but they are central to understanding how it operated in Newcastle.

The Production of Difference

In taking questions of labor discipline for granted, structuralist accounts of network production appear to assume – either implicitly or explicitly – that women workers who make up the bulk of the industrial workforce are governed in an unproblematic fashion by patriarchal authority relations. A growing body of feminist research in Asia and elsewhere – much of it based on participant observation on factory floors and in the communities where workers live – challenges these easy assumptions. A consistent theme running through these studies is that even the seemingly most despotic and coercive low-wage factory regimes are, to some degree, negotiated orders – albeit highly asymmetric ones. While workers are certainly subjected to an array of powerful disciplinary forces, they often construct alternative interpretations and definitions. Such 'cultural struggles' (Ong 1991) do not necessarily have direct political effects; in some circumstances they may, indeed, become part of a process of accommodation or even partial consent to industrial work discipline and familial pressures. A key point, however, is that these processes can and do vary markedly, even in settings and conditions that appear structurally quite similar.[14] A great deal depends on *how* cultural and symbolic resources are deployed and reconfigured through everyday practice not only on the factory floor, but also in other intersecting social arenas both local and translocal.

A particularly interesting example of this type of approach is Lee's (1995) comparative study of management practices and worker strategies in two factories owned by the same company, one in Hong Kong and the other in Shenzhen (just over the border in China). Lee shows how gendered practices on the shopfloor were very different, and how this in turn reflected differences in the historical constitution of the workforce, as well as in the everyday conditions and practices of social reproduction. Most of the workers in China were young, unmarried women migrants, whereas those in Hong Kong were mainly older married women. Participant observation enabled Lee to illuminate the varied ways that the local communal institutions within which workers were situated became incorporated in shopfloor practices:

> Localistic networks in Shenzhen and family and kin in Hong Kong mediated the supply of labor and provided resources that neither the state nor employees offered to women. Incorporating localism and familialism into the respective factory regimes reduced management's financial burden, legitimized management control, and satisfied workers' mundane interests. (Lee 1995: 394)

While management manipulated the gendered hierarchies of localism and familialism to exercise greater control, workers invested them with their own understandings and used them to temper and mitigate managerial domination. These practices also reflected a set of meanings which, while contested, were sufficiently shared to provide the basis for negotiation – as well as worker acquiescence.

Research in the early 1970s in large-scale factories by both Diamond (1979) and Kung (1976) reported that Taiwanese women workers defined resentments arising in the workplace in terms of social problems of dealing with supervisors and foremen. While there were indeed episodes of labor militancy among women workers in China in the 1920s and 1930s, these did not carry over to Taiwan. Diamond (1979) suggests that the issues which led an earlier generation of women workers in China to labor actions were resolved through paternalistic practices in Taiwan: 'There is no need to strike over issues of corporal punishment, absence of a lunch period or washroom facilities, kickbacks of pay to foremen or hiring agents and so on.'

Hsiung's (1991, 1996) research based on participant observation in unregulated small-scale factories in Taiwan provides a more finely grained understanding of paternalism as an ongoing product of constant struggle and negotiation on the factory floor. In many of these factories, married women from the local community have come to constitute a large proportion of the workforce. In the course of working in such factories, Hsiung observed considerable conflict between workers and employers. Workers' resistance was, however, informal, individualized, and clandestine, and articulated in the idiom of paternalism: 'because pre-existing family/kinship systems are intertwined with the production unit, the conflict of interest between the factory owner and waged workers often takes the form of familial disagreement. The construction of paternalism illustrates the constant struggle between those who own the means of production and those who sell their labour . . . ' (Hsiung 1991: 148–149). Both owners and workers were deeply invested in personalistic constructions. Workers invoked the concept of 'help' to drive home that they were not simply selling labor, but also providing a personal commitment in return for which they expect a variety of favors; employers for their part engaged in petty acts of 'goodwill,' which doubled as personal debts that were reclaimed when owners made excessive demands on workers (Hsiung 1991: 186–187). Rather than simple coercion, labor relations were constantly renegotiated in the idiom of familial obligation. Some employers also deployed appeals to ethnic pride. In short, gender, kinship, local community, and ethnic identity provided the cultural raw materials from which production relations and work experiences were fashioned in satellite factories.

To understand how and why a superficially similar form of industrial organization operated so differently in Newcastle, one would ideally engage in this sort of participant observation in order to experience shopfloor dynamics at first hand. Such activities were simply not an option for me. In addition, it was impossible to talk with workers in a factory setting. My main contact with workers was in the townships, and over the course of my research I was able to meet with close to 50 women who had worked in Taiwanese factories.

Virtually all the workers with whom I met spoke bitterly of their sense of ill-treatment in Taiwanese factories. All complained about low wages and of being driven to work unreasonably hard through the 'score' system – a minimum level of production that workers have to meet. In almost all of these discussions, however, workers talked most fully and eloquently about everyday practices and conditions in the factories that they found demeaning – one of the most consistent complaints being about poor toilet and kitchen facilities which, many of them said, showed their employers' lack of concern about them as people. One woman provided a particularly interesting example of how she had gone about trying to shame her employer. She described how she had complained about respiratory problems caused by fluff from acrylic yarn. When her employer ignored her complaint, she wore a surgical mask to work not only to facilitate her breathing; her purpose, she made clear, was to demonstrate the level of pollution in the factory, and to assert her humanity. In one way or another, all of the workers with whom I spoke expounded on this theme of inhumanity, expressing a profound sense of affront at being 'treated just like animals.' Their bitter complaints about harsh treatment by Taiwanese industrialists resonated with how industrialists frequently constructed workers in terms such as their having 'not yet entered civilization.'

Language – or, more precisely the lack of a means of constructing any sort of common meaning or basis for negotiation – constitutes one obvious way of interpreting the failure of many Taiwanese industrialists to manufacture even a modicum of consent. On a number of occasions I was witness to factory owners and managers barking monosyllabic commands in heavily accented English. Yet the question of language by itself leaves open the question of why many industrialists – including those who had moved to Newcastle in the 1980s – had failed to improve their language skills, and why several of those who spoke relatively good English were among the most problematic employers.

The depth and intensity of conflict was not just a matter of miscommunication but, more fundamentally, of the way racial and sexual difference were being constructed in close relationship to one another. An important clue, I suggest, comes from a question posed by Donna Haraway (1991): what happens to the idea of gender, she asks, if whole groups of women and men are positioned *outside* the institution of kinship altogether? In addressing this question, Haraway draws heavily on Hazel Carby's (1987) compelling discussion of gender in the context of slavery. Carby in turn calls into question claims by Catherine Clinton (1982) that white slave-owners used similar methods of keeping blacks and women excluded from spheres of power, and employed near-identical ideological warfare against them. Pointing to the limits of claims that elide differences among women, Carby (1987: 25) makes the crucial point that 'if women, as an undifferentiated group, are compared to blacks, or slaves, as an undifferentiated group, then it become impossible to see the articulations of racism within ideologies of gender and of gender within ideologies of racism.' Thus black women were not constituted as 'woman' in the same way white women were. Instead – and this is where Haraway borrows from Carby – 'black women were constituted simultaneously racially and sexually – as marked female (animal, sexualized and without rights), but not as women (human, potential wife, conduit for the name of the father) – in a particular institution, slavery, that excluded them from "culture" defined as the circulation of signs through the system of marriage' (Haraway 1991: 145). I suggest that something very much along these lines was happening on factory floors in Newcastle. The majority of Taiwanese industrialists, who had come from a setting in which negotiations with women workers are conducted in the idiom of kinship and family, constructed African women workers as so different that they had no means at all of invoking and deploying these idioms. The anger and resentment that African women experienced is captured very precisely in the phrase I heard a number of times – namely their sense of 'being treated just like animals.'

The centrality of kinship idioms as the currency of negotiation between male managers and women workers is a consistent theme in the ethnographic literature discussed earlier. Some of these studies also yield insights into very different articulations of racial/ethnic and sexual/gender difference. Ong (1987) for example describes how managers of Japanese firms in Malaysia emphasized their racial and national superiority *vis-a-vis* Malay women workers. At the same time, they invoked a familial discourse that defined women workers as 'children' who should 'obey their parents.'

The racialized spaces in which South African workers live is probably also a key element of the ongoing construction of racial difference. Low-wage factory regimes in different parts of Asia very often involve industrialists

being actively involved in regulating the conditions of reproduction of the
workforce: workplace and residence are typically not separated, so that
labor management is just as much involved with controlling the workers
when they are not at work as with supervising the labor process itself (Smart
and Smart 1993: 29). Far from regulating workers' living conditions, most
Taiwanese industrialists in South Africa (as indeed most white South
Africans) regard the townships where workers live as distant and dangerous
places over which they have no control. These qualities of distance and
danger are, of course, also deeply racialized. A corollary of this physical
and metaphorical distance is that most industrialists seem to have very little
sense of who workers are in terms of their age, familial status, or
positioning in their communities; they are, in other words, largely deper-
sonalized. What this in turn means, of course, is that gendered constructions
of localism and familism that are central to the way managers and workers
negotiate with one another in different parts of Asia – such as those
described by Lee (1995) – are simply unavailable. At the same time, they
did not have in place supervisory personnel to police production. Racially
defined mistrust made most Taiwanese industrialists in South Africa fearful
of employing black supervisors who, as one of them put it, would simply
side with the workers. The very low level of supervisory personnel in
Taiwanese factories in South Africa is in fact quite striking, and contrasts
quite dramatically with conditions in Taiwanese factories in China,
discussed in Chapter 6.

In short, the particular ways in which many Taiwanese industrialists
produced understandings of racial difference undermined their capacity to
engage with workers on anything other than openly coercive terms. Yet
these dynamics were neither uniform, nor cast in stone. By 1994, a small
but significant group of industrialists were engaged in an effort to
manufacture consent through strategically constructed paternalistic practices.

(Re)-Inventing Paternalism

In the course of conducting the industrial survey, Alison Todes and I were
struck by how a small group of Taiwanese industrialists actively distanced
themselves and their labor practices from those of their compatriots, and
declared themselves quite satisfied with worker productivity. They also
waxed eloquent in describing their own ingenuity. Unfortunately, it was not
possible to elicit workers' experiences of and reactions to the strategies that

industrialists describe. Even so, their representations of these practices are quite telling, as are the origins of those who claim the status of 'good bosses.'

With one key exception, all were former technicians who came to South Africa to work for the first round of industrialists, and had considerable experience on the factory floor. All started on a very small scale, and since expanded – in sharp contrast to their original bosses, most of whom had contracted the scale of their operations. Indeed, in several cases they were engaged in direct competition with their former bosses. Nevertheless, their capacity to expand their scale of operations appeared limited by precisely the strategies that they deployed to elicit worker consent.

Several common threads run through the stories these industrialists told about their methods of coping with workers. First, they claimed a familiarity with workers' living conditions in the townships, together with careful selection of workers. Some claimed that they had visited workers' homes, and one described how he selected his workers from different townships; that way, if there was trouble in one of the townships he would be assured of workers from the others.

Second, they portrayed their relations with workers in the language of generosity, paternalism, and keeping workers happy: 'If you help these people you can help yourself,' declared one; 'we're very free here.' Often quite explicitly, they contrasted their generosity – encompassing higher wages, as well as parties, loans, sick pay, leave pay, and other 'gifts' – with the tight-fistedness of their compatriots from whom they actively distanced themselves. As is typically the case in clientilistic relationships, gifts often came with surveillance and other strings attached to them. For example, one industrialist explained how, if a worker said she was sick, he sent a driver to her house to check that she really was sick; if so, he sent her to hospital and paid the bills. Compassion and familialism also had its limits. While declaiming that everyone in the factory was like a family, and his willingness to grant leave to workers for family crises, one industrialist stipulated 'one father, one mother dead only once!'[15]

Wages and work effort were also described in terms of gift-giving: 'I give you the right money, you give me the right job.' But the carrot of higher wages was combined with the stick of enforcement built into the forms of work organization common to all these factories. In all cases, workers were organized into mutually competing groups that were presented with a daily or weekly production quota. Group monitoring was the key enforcement mechanism: if a group failed to meet the quota, all workers were penalized even if only one or a subset of individuals failed to perform to the required standard. If they met the quota, they could either leave early or earn bonuses for additional production.

In effect this was a modified piece-rate system, which these industrialists claimed they were able to put into effect because their workers abjured unions. In other Newcastle factories piece-rates were, indeed, the source of intense conflict between employers and unions. The self-proclaimed 'good bosses' were just as opposed to unions as their more openly exploitative compatriots; several declared that if unions came in, they would leave. For the time being, however, they seemed to have devised a paternalistic barrier against union organizing – a point to which union leaders conceded.

There is another dilemma that the evident capacity of capital to transform itself is likely to present to organized labor in the future. One of the industrialists in this group subcontracted part of his operation to a black man with whom he had worked since he was a technician, and whom he brought with him when he set up on his own. At the time of my interview with him in 1994, the industrialist had handed over 30 mechanical knitting machines to the subcontractor, to whom he also provided materials, designs, and machine servicing. The subcontractor, who was unlicensed and operated out of an old grain storage facility, hired and managed labor and paid the rent. This was a pure piece-rate system, in which the subcontractor received R4 (just over US$1 in 1994) per piece, of which workers (all of them women) were paid R1.30. The workday was 10 hours during which, he claimed, workers could produce 12–15 pieces; at this rate, the weekly wage would more or less approximate the minimum laid down by the Wages Board, but the hours worked and intensity of work effort were considerably greater than in a typical factory. The beauty of the system, according to the industrialist, was that the subcontractor spoke Zulu, could maintain discipline, and would not be touched by the unions. He was not afraid that the machines would disappear because, as he put it, only Chinese people could afford to buy them, and they would not buy from a black man. In fact, he said, all the other Chinese thought him crazy: 'How can you give to a black man?' they asked – but he knew better, and was convinced that this was the trend of the future. In a number of Taiwanese factories, mechanical knitting machines just like these were sitting idle because of labor conflict. Whether or not this particular system becomes more widespread remains to be seen, but it exemplified the broader forces of informalization taking hold in the context of intensified global competition. It also illustrated the limits on expansion built into paternalistic and personalistic strategies of labor discipline.

Just as some industrialists began to discover ways of recreating paternalistic strategies of labor control, a new source of instability appeared in the form of identical knitwear produced in China. The competitive threat appeared suddenly and without warning. In the second half of 1994 when Alison Todes and I did our first round of research in Newcastle, imports were not an issue at all. When we returned in mid-1995, the Newcastle knitwear industry was in a state of siege. Most industrialists blamed the influx of knitwear on corrupt customs officials, but they also conceded that it was a portent of things to come as trade liberalization took hold. Even the most enthusiastic proponents of free markets were adamantly opposed to the lifting of tariff barriers whose protection they had enjoyed. 'If this government opens up the gates they kill all business,' declared one; jumping out of his chair, he demonstrated vividly how 'they take a big wire and tie it around our neck; they take a big rock and drop it on our foot!'

Perhaps the ultimate irony was that the competition came from compatriots of Newcastle industrialists who moved to the southern coastal regions of China. Newcastle knitwear producers claimed that their counter-parts in China could produce essentially the same commodities at prices below the costs of production in Newcastle.[16] We shall pick up this theme in the following chapter, which traces what happens when Taiwanese industrialists move to small towns in southern China. Before we leave Newcastle, however, there is a seemingly small but highly significant matter that demands our attention.

Postscript: Battlegrounds Revisited

In 1998, the monument (or sign) described at the beginning of this chapter was once again a lightning rod of conflict between Taiwanese industrialists and the local state. Following local government elections in June 1996, the composition of the town council changed dramatically – including Eddie Liu's becoming Deputy Mayor representing the IFP (see Chapter 7). His standing for the IFP probably contributed to the unexpected (albeit narrow) victory of the ANC in the Newcastle local government elections – a vivid illustration of how struggles on the factory floor reverberated and helped to remake the local state. The position of the Taiwanese community was further weakened in November 1996, when the South African government recognized Mainland China in place of Taiwan.

In April 1998, ANC councilors on the Corporate Services committee recommended that the Chinese monument be removed, on the grounds that Chinese was not one of the 11 official languages provided for in the constitution. They also recommended the removal of a statue of a British soldier in front of the town hall. The statue was a memorial to colonial forces who had died in the battle of Rorke's Drift in 1879 when Zulu armies, fresh from their defeat of the British at the battle of Isandlwana, were themselves defeated by the British. In a multiply-ambiguous statement, the ANC councilors on the committee declared the history of the British soldier to be a 'good one,' but wanted it removed to the Fort Amiel museum.

An enraged letter published in the *Newcastle Advertiser* of May 8, 1998 speaks volumes about the ongoing production of racial and ethnic difference:

> Sir – We the Southern African Chinese Factory League who represent approximately 60 Chinese Industrialists manufacturing and trading in Newcastle, do hereby wish to record our serious objections to the proposed removal of the Chinese Welcome Monument which was erected a couple of years ago on the corner of the Volksrust and Memel roads.
>
> We would like to point out that the aforesaid monument was donated and paid for by the Chinese community of Newcastle during 1995. Your Council's consent was obtained for the erection of same and at the time we expressed our appreciation for the co-operation which we received from your Council.
>
> It must also be borne in mind that the then Premier of KwaZulu-Natal, Dr Frank Mdlalose officiated the ceremony.
>
> The monument portrays a significant occurrence in the history of Newcastle, namely the settlement of Chinese industrialists in Newcastle with their families and it signifies the warmth and confidence of the Chinese community comprising of more than 1200 people in Newcastle.
>
> The Chinese community has made a significant contribution to the economy of Newcastle creating employment for 3000 Zulu speaking people.
>
> Why must the Chinese community then be slapped in the face by the proposed step of the removal of this monument? Is this the kind of democracy by ANC Town Councillors in Newcastle?
>
> Why must we be insulted in this way when we have displayed confidence in Newcastle?
>
> Should your Council proceed with their intention it would most definitely lead to a review of our investments both present and future in this country and will obviously force us to embark on a National Media Campaign which will have disastrous effects for not only Newcastle, but for the country as such.

Inviolably we must draw attention to both the Government of Taiwan and the Government of Mainland China to this nonsensical step.

In view of the fact that the monument was built and erected with private money, you are hereby given notice that should any steps be taken for the removal, we will not hesitate to apply for an interdict in a proper court of law to prevent such a step.

(Signed) P.L. Cheng – Vice Chairman

The anger and frustration that come across so clearly in this letter form the point of departure for the next chapter.

The China Connection
Agrarian Questions in an Era of Globalization

A T THE END of the last chapter we left Eddie Liu and his compatriots in Newcastle fuming over multiple indignities: their incapacity to discipline labor; the cheap knitwear flooding in from China; the disintegration of Eddie Liu's vision of using his association with Zulu ethnic nationalism to turn Newcastle into a free trade zone and ban unions; the South African government's recognition of Mainland China in place of Taiwan; and the humiliating threat that the Chinese 'Welcome to Newcastle' sign would be torn down. In bemoaning their fate, several expressed the wish that they had instead gone to China.

What might have happened had they indeed gone to China is an extremely interesting question because it compels a spatialized understanding of transnational flows, as opposed to the 'impact' model or disembodied spatial metaphors such as deterritorialization. It would be ideal, of course, to trace the shift to China of knitwear producers from the same regions in Taiwan as those who moved to Newcastle. Although such direct tracking was not possible, You-Tien Hsing (1996, 1998) has provided a detailed study of similar Taiwanese industrialists who moved to Fujian province on the southern coast of China in the late 1980s and early 1990s. Hsing's industrialists produced fashion footwear rather than knitwear, but had also moved into small towns, forging direct connections with local government officials and by-passing the central state. This spatially dispersed pattern is not at all unusual; on the contrary, small towns in southern coastal provinces in China have received massive flows of capital and industrialists from Taiwan since the late 1980s.

On the face of it, these direct connections between transnational capitalists and local state officials in China bear an eerie resemblance to those in Newcastle. Yet Hsing's study reveals striking – and instructive – differences in how Taiwanese industrialists forged relations with local government officials, and their strategies to mobilize and discipline labor. By comparing the dynamics of Taiwanese investment in Newcastle and Fujian, we can see how the production of footwear – like that of knitwear – simultaneously entails ongoing struggles over meanings, definitions, and identities, and the centrality of gender, ethnicity, and other dimensions of difference. It also makes clear how categories of difference are produced – and to some degree dissolved – through the deployment of supposedly 'traditional' practices that are both strikingly new, while at the same time shaped and inflected by particular historical geographies. Rather than just 'path dependence' or institutional 'lock-in' as some would have it, these divergent trajectories exemplify what Burawoy and Verdery (1999: 7) call the creative and resistive processes of everyday practice.[1]

What also emerges is how Taiwanese investors in China derive major benefits from redistributive reforms and social investments that remain from the socialist past – while also drawing down these investments. In other words, tracing the practices of Taiwanese industrialists in China focuses our attention to the relationships between production and the conditions of reproduction of labor, as well as to *how* these relationships have been forged in multiple arenas of practice, and with what consequences.

To pursue these questions, we shall shift from the southern coastal provinces to other regions of China where, at least in the early to mid-1990s, labor-intensive industries in towns and villages were also growing rapidly but with much lower levels of foreign investment. During a visit to the inland provinces of Sichuan and Hunan in 1992 I was struck by how much of the stunning economic growth in China was being generated in small towns and villages, as well as by claims that a large proportion of these so-called Township and Village Enterprises (TVEs) were collectively owned and operated by local governments.[2] In some cases collective ownership was clearly giving way to more concentrated forms of ownership and control, with local government officials converting collective enterprises to private stock companies and forging relations with foreign investors. In others, however, it seemed that collective process were functioning well, with at least part of the surplus from industry retained, reinvested, and redistributed within local circuits, and directed towards schools, clinics, and other forms of collective consumption. I was also struck by what seemed to be the relatively egalitarian distribution of agricultural land among households, and by the diversified forms of livelihood through which men and women combined intensive cultivation of tiny plots with industrial and other forms of non-agricultural work. On returning to Berkeley, with the help of China scholars I scoured the literature on these TVEs, and later in this chapter I try to distill key patterns and debates.

Despite vast diversity in the forms and dynamics of TVEs – partly shaped by particular configurations of local power and translocal connections – a key force propelling their growth is that, unlike their urban counterparts, they do not have to provide housing, health, retirement, and other benefits to workers. In effect, much of the cost of reproduction of labor has been deflected from the enterprise – but, at least in some instances, is being supported through redistributive mechanisms. Accordingly, two issues seem crucial: the local political dynamics that shape whether and to what extent industrial surpluses are collectively controlled and plowed back into collective forms of consumption, and the history of agrarian transformation, going back to Mao's mobilization of the peasantry, and the continuing salience of agrarian questions. What is distinctive about both China and Taiwan – and dramatically different from South Africa – are the redistributive land reforms beginning in the late 1940s that effectively broke the power of the landlord class. The political forces that drove agrarian reforms in China and Taiwan were closely linked and precisely opposite. Yet in both socialist and post-socialist China, and in 'capitalist' Taiwan, the redistributive reforms that defined agrarian transformations were marked by rapid, decentralized industrial accumulation *without* dispossession from the land.

A central argument of this chapter is that the retention of peasant property – along with other state-sponsored subsidies securing the reproduction of the workforce – have been both underappreciated and absolutely central in defining the conditions of 'global competition' emanating from both Taiwan and China, underwriting the massive mobilization of industrial labor post-Second World War. To the extent that the relationship between the conditions of reproduction of labor and industrial accumulation in East Asia has been recognized, it has focused on housing in the city states. In *The Shek Kip Mei Syndrome* (1990), Manuel Castells and his colleagues pointed out that state-subsidized public housing in Hong Kong and Singapore operated to lower the money wage while maintaining the social wage, and contributing substantially to industrial competitiveness.

These are, however, two small city states. In societies with large, and largely impoverished rural populations, urban housing cannot perform this function without tight restrictions on access. This is precisely what happened in socialist China, where a form of influx control was necessary to guarantee urban dwellers' access to housing and other forms of social security.[3] Beyond the city states and urban China, connections between industrial production and the conditions of reproduction of labor have been forged in small towns and villages in China as well as in Taiwan.[4]

That some of the most spectacular instances of industrial production in the second half of the twentieth century have taken place without dispossession of peasant-workers from the land not only sheds light on the distinctively 'non-Western' forms of accumulation that underpin global competition. These trajectories also have a powerful and direct bearing on South African debates, *not* as models that could be emulated but rather because they denaturalize dispossession. To appreciate their wider significance and political potential, we have to revisit classical political economy debates, and revise the teleological assumptions about 'primitive accumulation' through which dispossession is seen as a natural concomitant of capitalist development. East Asian connections and trajectories underscore the ongoing salience of agrarian transformations in shaping the conditions of reproduction of labor, thus helping to thrust histories of racialized dispossession in South Africa to the forefront of attention. While dramatizing the radical inadequacy of post-apartheid land reforms and the liberation movement's historic neglect of agrarian questions, they also suggest alternative possibilities.

'Squeezing the Sponge to the Last Drop': Taiwanese Investment in China

> As a Taiwanese shoe manufacturer in Dongguan in the Pearl River Delta put it, 'China is like a sponge full of water, you just have to squeeze it hard until you get the last drop.' (Hsing 1998: 83)

Ironically, it was the Tiananmen Square massacre in June 1989 that helped to propel the sharp increase in Taiwanese investment in Mainland China in the early 1990s (Hsing 1998; Ong 1999). In reaction to the decline in Organization for Economic Cooperation and Development (OECD) investment following Tiananmen, the Chinese government put together lucrative packages to lure Taiwanese investors. These moves coincided with a financial crisis in Taiwan that enhanced the attractiveness of such inducements. By the end of 1994, according to one estimate, nearly 25,000 Taiwanese companies had invested something in the order of US$16 billion in Mainland China, and formed the second largest source of foreign direct investment after Hong Kong.[5] Particularly in the first part of the 1990s, most Taiwanese investment was concentrated in the southern coastal provinces of Fujian and Guangdong. Although export-processing zones such as Shenzhen attracted numbers of Taiwanese investors, many of them moved into small towns and villages in the southern coastal provinces. In the process, a highly localized pattern of transnational capital flows has taken shape, with local government officials and Taiwanese industrialists by-passing the central state to forge direct relationships with one another.

Guangdong and Fujian have in fact enjoyed the most generous fiscal policies *vis-a-vis* the central state.[6] Hsing (1998: 134) points to several additional powers that enhanced the capacity of local government officials to negotiate with foreign investors: authority to grant permission to transfer profits; relax rules on foreign exchange balances; reduce fees for water, power, and rent; grant exemptions for import licenses; provide cheap loans; relax restrictions on hiring non-local labor; exempt social welfare contributions; and reduce taxes on items designated 'high tech' or 'special.' These are, she argues, reflections of politically rather than constitutionally defined relationships between different levels of the state, with high levels of ambiguity that provide space for flexible local interpretations and implementation of central government policies:

> Local Chinese officials since the imperial period have been skillful in avoiding the scrutiny of the central government while not creating direct conflicts with it. They were able to make decisions based on what higher level officials would not oppose rather than what they would allow ... [These practices] blossomed in the institutional context in which opportunities for local accumulation, including local governments' increasing fiscal authority and influx of foreign capital, were present. Under stated policies that were supposed to be implemented universally, the actual investment arrangements were mostly tailor-made for individual foreign investors. As a Taiwanese investor forthrightly put it, 'No favorable investment policies issued by Beijing could be as favorable as the special deals I made with the local officials. (Hsing 1998: 132–133)

Practices of gift exchange or *guanxi* have formed the primary means through which Taiwanese industrialists and Chinese local government officials established and cemented their relationships. The art of gift exchange entails a fine balance between material favors and expressions of friendship and loyalty: 'What matters is not just the gift itself, but also the message revealed in the presentation of the gift' (Hsing 1996: 2253). *Guanxi* is also a continuous process that also calls for considerable investment of time and effort, rather than simply material expenditure. Linked together through these relationships, Taiwanese industrialists and Chinese local government officials do not see public and private domains as clearly bounded entities: 'A Taiwanese investor commented that the best way to maintain and enforce the relationship with an official is to offer the opportunity for him or her to gain personal benefits, while simultaneously benefiting his or her institute' (Hsing 1996: 2255). Finally, she argues, language is crucial. What is spoken is often less important than what is left unsaid, and each of the participants in a gift exchange require 'both technical understanding of the spoken words and cultural understanding of the hidden meaning to grasp fully the expectations of the other participant' (Hsing 1996: 2256).

In her study of the pervasiveness of *guanxi* in post-reform China, Mayfair Yang (1994) shows how the multiple meanings and uses of *guanxi* have been reworked over time, and how the extent of *guanxi* has shifted in different historical conjunctures since the late 1940s.[7] At the same time Yang argues that *guanxi* is distinguished by a particularly powerful appeal to shared identities, the symbolic breaking down of boundaries between persons, and the redefinition of 'outsiders' as 'insiders':[8]

> Guanxi exchange cannot take place without first establishing the basis of 'familiarity' in the relationship between two parties. The logic of guanxi tactics is expressed in the attempt to transform the other into the familiar, to bridge the gap between the outside and the inside . . . Familiarity is born of the fusion of personal identities. And shared identities establish the basis for the obligation to share one's wealth and to help with one's labor. (Yang 1989: 40–41)

In other words, the gift exchanges that bind Taiwanese industrialists and Chinese local government officials to one another are also, very importantly, about the dissolution of difference between them – in sharp contrast to the ongoing production of difference between Taiwanese industrialists and Newcastle local government officials described in the previous chapter.[9]

Close relations between Taiwanese industrialists and Chinese local government officials in turn helped to consolidate their power *vis-à-vis* the predominantly female workforce. In their eagerness to accommodate foreign investors, local government officials were willing to loosen labor regulations and evade inspections of labor conditions in Taiwanese-owned factories (Hsing 1998: 83). Connections with local government officials also facilitated Taiwanese industrialists' access to migrant workers from poorer regions – predominantly young, unmarried women in their late teens and early twenties. Workers from poor, inland provinces were not protected by the local government and, Hsing suggests, their lack of local social connections and urban experiences made them more compliant with the demands of management than local workers. A further constraint on labor organizing was a system akin to influx control: migrants were only permitted to stay in more prosperous regions if they had jobs, and risked not only dismissal but also losing residency rights if they protested. Hsing documents extremely long working hours, wages one-eighth to one-tenth of those in Taiwan, and systems of piece-rate payments that effectively placed part of the burden of risk of fluctuating orders on workers. Most of the low-wage female migrant workers were accommodated in tightly regulated dormitories, in which paternalistic modes of discipline and familial idioms overlapped with those on the factory floor – along with rampant sexual harassment. Taiwanese industrialists also deployed explicitly militaristic techniques as key elements of labor discipline.[10] Hsing's research revolved primarily around interviews with Taiwanese industrialists, and did not encompass workers' understandings of themselves and the conditions in which they found themselves.[11] Even so, representations of labor relations set forth by Taiwanese industrialists are quite revealing:

> Many Taiwanese industrialists interviewed emphasized that Taiwanese workers were brighter than their Chinese counterparts and more willing to take initiative. Among Chinese workers, the Cantonese were considered brighter than their counterparts from the inland regions. However, most Taiwanese managers admitted that Chinese workers were 'easier to manage' than Taiwanese workers. Chinese workers, especially those from inland regions, were more compliant and willing to work overtime without complaints. A manager claimed that he could shout at his Chinese workers and use 'military-like management' without worrying too much about worker reaction. He emphasized that if he treated his Taiwanese workers the same way, they would 'protest immediately.' Plus, Taiwanese workers were 'too spoiled and were not willing to work overtime, and they demanded too many holidays.' For the Taiwanese managers, the compliant attitude of Chinese workers and their willingness to work long hours and overtime also made up for the lower productivity. (Hsing 1998: 91)

Another key factor that seems to contribute to this compliance – and that distinguished Taiwanese industries in China from those in both Taiwan and

South Africa – is an elaborate stratum of supervisory and managerial personnel, made up of ambitious and highly educated young Chinese men and smaller numbers of women. Taiwanese industrialists who moved to China were unable to recruit Taiwanese technician/managers to bring with them; ambitious young Taiwanese men looked with disdain upon what they saw as low-grade labor-intensive industries, as well as the prospect of working in semi-rural regions in China. Yet on arrival in China, industrialists encountered large numbers of young Chinese professionals eager to move into supervisory and low-level management positions in Taiwanese firms. Their absorption into Taiwanese firms has given rise to forms of industrial organization that are dramatically different from the 'lean' managerial structure that characterized much of the industrial growth in Taiwan – and that their counterparts in South Africa invoke to underscore their efficiency relative to South African industrialists (see Chapter 5). Large numbers of dedicated, well-educated and comparatively low-paid supervisors and low-level managers have also enabled Taiwanese firms in China to expand far beyond the modal size in Taiwan – or, for that matter, in Newcastle.[12]

Hsing documents how Chinese first-line managers put in incredibly long hours – often longer than their Taiwanese bosses – and assumed significant responsibilities.[13] In their efforts to get ahead, they also became standard-bearers of capitalist virtues:

> The ideology of capitalist production, like the moral implications of hard work and the value of efficiency, was also a part of their education in the Taiwanese ventures. The Chinese low-level managers, in turn, helped to pass this ideology on to the Chinese operators [workers]. During my visits to the factories, I often saw groups of operators standing at attention in the courtyard of the factory building while being reprimanded by the Chinese coordinator for the poor job they did and their lack of devotion to the factory. (Hsing 1998: 98)

Some of them also engaged in active critiques of state-owned industries in China, particularly their inability to dismiss workers and their commitment to paying benefits and housing: as one of them noted, 'that's why the state-owned enterprises lost their competitiveness.'

A particular irony attaches to this critique. Not only did the bulk of these managers and supervisors come from the state sector; many of them were also able to retain access to state-sponsored social security (Hsing 1995: 23–24). One device was a system constructed by local government officials who set up 'employment centers' that enabled state employees who found employment in foreign firms to register, and have the time spent working in the private sector count towards his or her seniority and pension plan provided by the state. The more common strategy to maintain job security was for the manager or supervisor to take a leave of absence, and retain access to housing and other benefits provided by the original work unit. Yet another strategy was for a husband to shift permanently to working for a foreign firm while his wife kept the 'iron rice bowl' in the state sector in order to ensure retention of state-sponsored housing, health care, and other benefits. In short, the capitalist values that Chinese managers and supervisors so enthusiastically espoused were underwritten – indeed heavily subsidized – by precisely the 'inefficient' and much-maligned state sector.

More generally, Taiwanese investors in China have derived huge benefits from social investments set in place during the socialist era. In addition to social security guarantees that effectively subsidized wages of low-level managers and supervisors, Taiwanese investors had access to another key legacy of the socialist era – a huge pool of highly educated workers. Hsing shows how families in impoverished communities that were the source of migrant labor sent the best educated and brightest young women out to work in the hopes that they would return with some resources.

The irony of the sponge-squeezing strategy, of course, is that the highly exploitative, low-wage labor practices tend to run down precisely the social investments that seem to have bolstered the social wage. Yet there is evidence from other parts of China showing how part of the surplus from rural industries has been plowed back into various forms of social welfare. It is within this context that the forms and dynamics of rural industrialization in regions that are less exposed to foreign investment assume particular interest and significance.

Neither Capitalist nor Socialist? Local State Corporatism in China

On the surface at least, rural industrialization in post-reform China appears very similar to that in Taiwan. In many areas, huge numbers of tiny factories – along with some quite large ones – nestle in fields of rice and other crops, as well as in and around small (albeit often rapidly growing) towns. To an even greater degree than in Taiwan, these seemingly modest little outfits have driven a growth process that 'is so outstanding by world

historical standards that it does not seem unwarranted to label it spectacular' (Weitzman and Xu 1994: 130). According to official statistics, the
number of rural industrial enterprises shot up from 1.5 million in 1978 to
23.3 million in 1993. Over the same period, rural industrial employment
(including seasonal and part-time workers) expanded from 28 million to
over 100 million, and by 1997 rural industrial employment stood at well
over 130 million (Sun 2000). Output of rural industries grew by about 30
percent per year, and by the early 1990s constituted more than 40 percent of
China's industrial output and a rapidly expanding share of exports (Sun
2000). These and other numbers must be read with caution. The category
'rural' encompasses many areas that are effectively peri-urban. In addition,
the process has been highly uneven within and among regions. There is no
question, however, that the lives of millions of Chinese peasants have been
fundamentally transformed in a very short space of time by countless
factories that have mushroomed in the fields.

What makes this process even more extraordinary is that a huge
proportion of industrial growth has been generated by factories owned and
operated by local governments in villages and small towns. Zhang (1999)
describes how these collectively-owned TVEs have arisen from the
'backyard furnaces' of the old communes (now townships) and brigades
(now villages). By the early 1990s, according to widely cited figures, TVEs
accounted for 75 percent of rural industrial output, and about 60 percent of
employment in rural industries (Bowles and Dong 1994).[14] Sun (2000)
reports that between 1992–97 the real growth rate of TVE value added was
22 percent per annum, and that in 1998 and the first half of 1999 this growth
rate was still over 15 percent despite deflation and the East Asian economic
crisis. Between 1988 and 1997, TVE's shares in national exports rose from
17 to 46 percent, an annual growth of 26.5 percent in terms of US dollars
(Perotti et al. 1999). Not surprisingly, spectacular TVE statistics are the
subject of intense dispute.[15] Some observers argue that many TVEs are
actually private firms in disguise: 'many collective firms are actually family
businesses whose owners registered their firms as collective in order to gain
access to factor resources, bank loans, markets, political protection, and tax
subsidies and to circumvent regulatory hurdles that discriminate against
private firms' (Nee 1992: 17). In some regions, this practice known as
'buying a red hat' does indeed seem to be widespread. Official statistics
may well be problematic, masking wide variations as well rapid transformations in institutional arrangements. Yet a number of local level studies

document not only the widespread, direct, and very active role of local government officials in initiating and operating industrial enterprises, but also redistribution of the surplus.[16]

Most observers trace the explosive growth of TVEs and rural industrialization more generally to fiscal reforms initiated in the mid-1980s.[17] Until then, each level of government received an annual budget and had to surrender any surplus to the next higher level. The reforms, designed to reduce the fiscal burdens of the central government, constructed a bottom-up system of revenue sharing through which local authorities were required to submit a contractually specified portion of their revenues to the next highest level of government, and could keep the residual. The fiscal reforms also created new sources of extra-budgetary funds that were not included in the revenue base to which fiscal contracts applied, and accrued wholly to the local jurisdiction. Despite variations in the precise formulae for revenue sharing, the system creates powerful incentives for local governments to generate income sources over which they can retain discretionary control.

Ironically, it was a study by the World Bank that – at least in the literature in English – first identified TVEs as a remarkable institutional innovation, combining collective ownership with market discipline (Byrd and Lin 1990). The Bank study not only confirmed that local government officials have indeed been the driving force behind rapid industrial growth in some areas, such as Jiangsu province in the Yangzi delta adjacent to Shanghai. In their comparison of rural industrialization in Jiangsu with conditions in relatively poor regions – many of them remote areas of hardscrabble agriculture – Bank researchers also found that 'backward areas are being forced to turn away from traditional [i.e. pre-reform] community enterprise development strategy and actively encourage or at least permit the emergence of a large private enterprise sector . . . (whereas better-endowed areas) will continue to develop the traditional TVE sector' (Byrd and Gelb 1990: 383).[18]

The growth and performance of TVEs seem to contradict not only the main tenets of property rights theory, but also the basic shibboleths of neoliberal orthodoxy. How TVEs are interpreted and understood therefore carries quite far-reaching implications. Very broadly speaking, the debate is between those who argue that TVEs do indeed represent an institutional innovation that combines collective ownership with market discipline and embodies a distinctive redistributive logic, and those who deny the collectively-owned character of TVEs and ascribe their performance to market (or market-like) forces unleashed in the 1980s.

The most influential arguments for the institutionally distinctive character of TVEs place primary emphasis on the structure of incentives for local government officials generated by fiscal reforms.[19] Jean Oi (1992, 1999) locates the emergence of what she calls local state corporatism in efforts by local government officials to 'maintain their patron-client networks and personalized systems of authority' that took shape in the centralized distribution system of the Maoist period. She argues that rather than threatening the power of township and village officials, the development of collective industry provided new resources to replace those lost with decollectivization and it thus enhanced the power of those officials at the township and village levels. Income derived from local government-led growth is redistributed to citizens in return for compliance with local corporate control, and the redistributive elements of socialism are coupled with fostering growth and competition – what Oi calls a new form of redistributive corporatism.[20]

The contrary position is that TVEs are not really state-owned – rather they are 'quasi-private' or 'quasi-marketized hybrids' – and distinctly different in ownership form from the large state-owned enterprises (SOEs) dating from the Maoist period that dominate the economies of large cities; in addition, rural industries are more dynamic than old urban industries because they are more fully exposed to markets and competition.[21] Nee (1992), for example, explains TVEs in terms of transaction costs arising from weak market structures and incomplete institutional foundations such as the lack of private property rights and contract enforcement mechanisms. As market institutions become more predominant, Nee argues, the cost of 'hybrid government structures' will increase and the costs of transacting for private firms will decrease.

In an interesting contribution to this debate, Walder (1994, 1995) argues that characterizations of TVEs as 'hybrid property forms' (Nee 1992) or a 'nonstate sector' (Sachs and Woo 1994) are misleading. Instead, he argues, county-, township-, and village-owned enterprises are under a form of public ownership fundamentally similar to that of the large state firms in urban areas, and that these government rights are if anything clearer and more actively exercised than in the urban sector. The key point, Walder notes, is that state-owned industrial enterprises in China are not all owned by the central government but by thousands of separate government jurisdictions that range from ministries of the central government down to all but the poorest township and village governments. As a result of decentralization drives from the 1950s through the 1970s, ownership and control of state firms was gradually shifted away from the central government to lower tiers of the state apparatus, leading to a high degree of regional autarky.[22] This trend intensified in the 1970s, when communes were pushed to develop their own industries. Thus, Walder argues that China embarked on the reform era as a nested hierarchy of hundreds of government jurisdications, each with its own set of enterprises whose activities they directed and planned and whose earnings contributed to local revenue. These government-owned firms are divided into two legal types: state and collective. In terms of property rights – defined as a bundle of rights to manage, control income flows, and transfer assets – they are essentially similar; in both state and collective enterprises, the salient level of government has the right to hire and replace managers or allocate contracts to lease assets; the government also has the right to all income flows from the asset, except those allocated to managers or to taxes to higher levels; and it also has the right to sell off an asset.

Walder maintains that local governments in townships and villages with relatively small industrial bases are in a far stronger position to run industrial enterprises effectively than those at higher levels of the hierarchy who run large SOEs. Local government officials in villages and townships (i.e. the collective sector) not only have clearer financial incentives and constraints, but also greater capacity to monitor and enforce their interests, and fewer regulatory constraints. Key among these constraints, it seems, is provision of social services:

> One of the most important ways in which the state sector is more heavily regulated in relation to the collective sector is in the legal requirement that state firms provide health insurance, disability insurance, death benefits, and pensions according to national standards and that the enterprises write these costs directly into costs of production . . . Collective enterprises are not required to provide the same benefits to the same level. Among public enterprises designated as collective, moreover, there are wide variations in the degree of regulation. The administrative category 'large collectives,' predominantly the larger collective enterprises held by city and county governments, are required to provide similar though less comprehensive insurance and retirement benefits. The smaller collective enterprises, especially those established by the lower ranking government jurisdictions in the 1980s, are subject to almost no regulation, and usually provide few if any benefits of this sort.

The impact of this closer regulation is illustrated by the fact that some 40 percent of the difference in profitability between state and collective enterprises is due to social overhead costs of this kind. (Walder 1994: 11)

In other words, not having to supply benefits provides TVEs with an enormous cost advantage *vis-à-vis* urban state-owned enterprises.[23] Similarly, Perotti et al. (1999) cite a World Bank study in the early 1990s that 40 percent of the difference in profitability between SOEs and TVEs can be attributed to SOEs' welfare provision obligations. Christiansen's (1992) study of the links between urban SOEs and rural TVEs in Jiangsu province provides a fascinating example of how the two ends of the hierarchy have, in practice, become closely connected through subcontracting.[24]

The question remains, however, as to who controls the surplus, and how it is used. Studies of TVEs in different parts of China have documented an extraordinarily wide array of different sorts of arrangements – ranging from highly exploitative patterns of surplus extraction, to those that appeared to be actively redistributive. In a further contribution to the debate, Alan Smart (1998) points out that Walder's intervention fails to distinguish rights of property that extract profit from those that extract rent, and goes on to suggest how this distinction helps illuminate enormous diversity in local conditions of accumulation and relations of production.[25] At the same, Smart warns against being too impressed by the variety of local systems – the view that economically 'anything goes' as long as local actors are convinced of its viability. Thus, he suggests, one commonality might be the need to keep labor costs down and productivity up. An attendant factor 'given the socialist heritage and the ability of Chinese citizens to make effective discursive use of this heritage to criticise the emergent managerial elite, is being able to keep labour costs down without setting off local dissatisfaction heavy enough to derail development' (Smart 1998: 444).

Both points seem crucial. The question of labor costs links directly, of course, with Walder's argument that the key cost advantage of TVEs derives from their not having to pay social benefits. Clearly there is a profound distinction between more genuinely collective arrangements in which local workers have rights to a share of the profits, and conditions in which migrant workers receive minimal wages. In addition, a number of studies call attention to an insider/outsider phenomen, whereby local residents receive a variety of benefits, while migrant 'outsiders' are subject to far harsher conditions. Yet despite these and other caveats, prior socialist redistribution has clearly played an absolutely critical role in providing what is, in effect, a form of social wage. I return to this argument in the following section to insist on the importance of locating the formation of the social wage in relation to specific histories of agrarian transformation and forms of peasant political mobilization.

Smart's point about local hegemonic processes appears vital but, with a few key exceptions, it remains remarkably underdeveloped in much of the literature in English on township and village industries to which I have had access. Yet local power dynamics are clearly crucial. Lu (1997), for example, documents a growing incidence of 'unruly exaction' from peasants by local state agents. Wang (1997) goes further, pointing to how the growing economic power of local officials and cadres – and attendant tensions in cadre-peasant relations – was producing a serious crisis of legitimacy and governability in many rural regions of China by the early 1990s. In their survey of TVEs in the 1990s, Perotti et al. (1999) observe that 'in townships and villages where the development of grassroots democratization has lagged behind, the problem of who monitors the monitors has become increasingly serious.' This allusion to 'grassroots democratization' refers to formation of committees of villagers to hold local officials accountable. Wang (1997) describes the emergence of locally based villager committees in different parts of China in the 1980s and shows how, by the early 1990s, the Central Committee of the Chinese Communist Party was actively supporting forms and practices of local democracy in the face of growing tensions in peasant-cadre relations and the resurgence of traditional authorities. He explains the irony of an authoritarian central state promoting local democracy as follows:

> To change this adverse situation and to maintain political stability, the state had to rejuvenate grassroots political institutions and scale back the arbitrary power of local state agencies so as to resume both governability and legitimacy. It was obvious that the state alone could not complete this substantial engineering. It had to find allies in society. Ironically, the state found that the only force it could appeal to was just what it tried to hold control over. The state had no other choice but to encourage peasant participation. (Wang 1997: 1436).

The question of how forms and practices of local democracy are entangled with industrial dynamics assumes particular significance in light of tendencies towards new ownership forms documented in recent studies that stress intensified competition as a driving force (for example

Perotti et al. 1999; Sun 2000). The dominant form of ownership restructuring, according to Sun, is the joint stock cooperative, in which both managers and workers hold a majority of shares and a fixed proportion of profits is earmarked for distribution to shareholders. Whether or not there is a community or collective share varies. In some areas it appears that collectively-owned enterprises are being converted into more privatized joint stock companies, a process that I observed in areas outside Chengdu in late 1992. In such circumstances, one would expect surplus appropriation to become far more concentrated, and for a chunk of it to be pumped out of local circuits. Whether and how these presumably more exclusionary systems work, and the sorts of pressures and opposition they evoke, are incredibly important and as yet not widely understood. While competitive pressures may well be a key driving force, local configurations of power and translocal connections almost certainly mediate the actual forms of institutional change.

How then do TVEs illuminate decentralized industrialization in South Africa, and how – if at all – do they speak to the possibilities for alternatives? Most obviously, they illustrate the enormous diversity of institutional forms and dynamics, along with at least the possibility for more collective productive relations. At the same time, they do *not* represent 'models' that can be emulated or conjured out of thin air. While institutional innovations may well be possible, they have to be grounded in existing conditions, but move in new directions. The diverse forms and dynamics of TVEs suggest strongly that configurations of local state power are likely to be crucial to any such process.

Second, we have seen how socialist-era redistribution underpinned rural industrialization, operating in effect as a social wage. Likewise in 'capitalist' Taiwan, land redistribution created key conditions for rural industrialization. These East Asian agrarian transformations are hugely significant because they represent rapid industrial accumulation *without* dispossession of peasant-workers from the land. Yet in both China and Taiwan these processes are heavily debated and subject to multiple interpretations. To draw out the broader relevance of such processes and debates for South Africa, I want to circuit briefly through classical political economy debates on 'primitive accumulation,' and to attend as well to the politics of the agrarian question – in particular, Mao's mobilization of the Chinese peasantry.

Accumulation without Dispossession: East Asian Agrarian Debates

> The capitalist system pre-supposes the complete separation of the labourers from all property in the means by which they can realise their labour ... The so-called primitive accumulation is nothing else than the historical process of divorcing the producer from the means of production ... (T)hese new freedmen became sellers of themselves only after they had been robbed of all their own means of production, and of all the guarantees of existence afforded by the old feudal arrangements. And the history of this, their expropriation, is written in the annals of mankind in letters of blood and fire. (Marx [1887] 1954: 667–668)

> The present upsurge of the peasant movement is a colossal event. In a very short time, in China's central, southern and northern provinces, several hundred million peasants will rise like a mighty storm, like a hurricane, a force so swift and violent that no power, however great, will be able to hold it back. They will smash all the trammels that bind them and rush forward along the road to liberation. (Mao Tse-tung [1927] 1967: 24–25)

In using the term 'so-called' to preface primitive accumulation, Marx was deliberately distancing himself from Adam Smith's naturalized account of the accumulation of landed property by capital as 'previous' to the division of labor. Perelman (2000: 25) notes that Marx translated Smith's word 'previous' as *'ursprunglich,'* which Marx's English translators in turn rendered as 'primitive' – but which in German is far closer to Smith's neutral language. So-called primitive accumulation plays about the same role in political economy as original sin in theology, Marx remarked – an anecdote of the past that is supposed to explain its origin. What the early political economists portrayed as the 'eternal laws of Nature' of the capitalist mode of production – the transformation of the mass of the population into the 'free labouring poor' – were in practice established through concrete historical processes of expropriation in which 'capital comes dripping from head to foot, from every pore, with blood and dirt' (1954: 712). Further, Marx insisted, 'The history of this expropriation, in different countries, assumes different aspects and runs through its various phases in different orders of succession, and at different periods' (1954: 669–670).

In a fascinating discussion of what he calls 'the secret history of primitive accumulation' in classical political economy, Perelman (2000) calls attention to a deep tension within Marx's critique of Smith and other political economists. On the one hand Marx insisted on an historically (and geographically) grounded account in which colonial conquest, plunder, and slavery in Africa, Asia, and the Americas were central to 'classic' English primitive accumulation that he took as the focus of his own historical account. Yet he also downplayed primitive accumulation to focus on modern capitalist accumulation. His analytical focus in *Capital* was on the 'silent compulsion' of economic relations, rather than on crude methods of primitive accumulation: 'Marx did not want his readers to conclude that the ills of society resulted from unjust actions that were unrelated to the ills of a market society' (Perelman 2000: 30). Fierce debates over forced removals in South Africa in the 1970s and 1980s, outlined in Chapter 2, echoed precisely this concern. The fear on the left was that attributing the brutality of forced removals and farm evictions to 'apartheid' would detract from an understanding of capitalist dynamics, and undermine the possibilities for a socialist future driven by the urban working class. The irony and the tension is that primitive accumulation then becomes relegated to the status of a naturalized one-off event, not dissimilar to the Smithian account against which Marx railed so passionately.

There is a vitally important distinction, Perelman reminds us, between primitive accumulation construed as an event as opposed to an *ongoing process*. This latter understanding, in turn, compels attention to the ongoing processes and conditions of unwaged work – much of it, of course, performed by women within the household – through which the labor force is produced and renewed on a daily basis. Marx of course recognized that 'the maintenance and reproduction of the working class remains a necessary condition for the reproduction of capital,' but went on to note that 'capital may safely leave this to the workers' drives for self-preservation and propagation.' This easy dismissal of the reproduction of labor has not only earned him the wrath of feminists. It also obscures the multiple, interconnected forms and dynamics of accumulation that are far from just earlier stages of the 'classic English case.'

The cultural politics, practices, and conditions of labor reproduction are inseparably linked with specific historical geographies of primitive accumulation understood as an ongoing processes. Primitive socialist accumulation in China, accomplished through land reforms in the early 1950s and subsequent collectivization of agriculture, diverged sharply from Stalin's forced collectivization in the USSR 20 years earlier. The politics of peasant mobilization that propelled this divergence also precipitated US-led land reforms in Taiwan, Japan, and Korea.

This brings us to Mao's famous 'Hunan Report' (1927) that sets forth the basic tenet of Maoist theory and practice – the revolutionary potential of the peasantry – and flies in the face of the similarly fundamental Marxist-Leninist tenet that only the urban industrial proletariat can lead the socialist revolution. One common interpretation has been to label Mao an agrarian populist, a sort of Chinese Narodnik produced by conditions of extreme pre-capitalist backwardness.[26] Meissner (1982), for example, draws parallels between Mao and the utopian socialists on whom Marx and Lenin heaped considerable scorn. He attributes Mao's inversion of the relationship between town and countryside to the imperialist domination of Chinese cities: 'This was a perception that bred powerful antiurban biases and, correspondingly, a strong agrarian orientation; the city came to be identified with alien influences, and the countryside with "the nation"' (Meissner 1982: 61).

In a more nuanced and historically grounded analysis, Isaac Deutscher (1984) points out that Maoists were far more broadly based in the peasantry than the Russian Narodniks had ever been: 'Mao and his colleagues have spent the best part of their lives in the midst of the poorest peasants, hiding with their Partisans in the mountains, sleeping in the caves, fighting, marching, and starving together ... ' (Deutscher 1984: 207). Deutscher also underscores the complex and changing forces and conditions that shaped Mao's 'withdrawal from the cities' in the late 1920s, and how the Japanese invasion and destruction of industrial plant in Shanghai and other cities in the late 1930s vindicated the strategy of 'surrounding the cities with the countryside.' The deeply ambiguous connection with Stalinism and the USSR was also crucial:

> (T)he Chinese revolution could not – and cannot – be dissociated from the Russian. Although the Partisan armies received little or no Stalinist support and had overthrown the rule of the Kuomintang in the teeth of Stalin's obstruction, Red China, born into a world split into two power blocs and herself confronted by American hostility and intervention, could not but align herself with the USSR. In this alignment, Maoism found another potent motive for carrying the revolution beyond the bourgeois phase ... With the Chinese proletariat almost dispersed or absent from the political stage, the gravitational pull of the Soviet Union turned Mao's peasant armies into agents of collectivism. No Marxist textbook has or could have foreseen so original a concatenation of national and international factors in a revolution: Maoism does not fit into any preconceived theoretical scheme. (Deutscher 1984: 201)

The connections between the communist triumph in China and Taiwanese land reforms were particularly powerful and direct. Fresh from their defeat by Mao's peasant army, the KMT nationalists who fled to Taiwan in the late 1940s were determined to pre-empt any sort of rural opposition or uprising.[27] Mainlanders did not own land, and the KMT was not allied with Taiwanese landlords, the largest of whom had been active Japanese collaborators (Gold 1986: 65). Urban terror unleashed by the KMT in the late 1940s also helped to contain opposition from landlords (Gold 1986: 65). Particularly after 1950, the KMT received substantial support from the US; American advisors (who had just pushed through a land reform in Japan) supplied experts, advice, and funds to back land reforms, channeled through the Joint Commission on Rural Reconstruction (JCRR).[28]

That rapid industrialization has taken place in large part without dispossession in both China and Taiwan is not subject to dispute. Instead, the controversy in both cases revolves around whether agrarian reforms reflected broadly based state support of the peasantry, or whether eliminating the landlord class facilitated state extraction from the peasantry.

One widely held view is that China under Mao Tse-tung embarked on a pro-peasant path that broke decisively with Stalin's forced extraction from the countryside in the USSR (see for example Amin 1983). The comparable argument for Taiwan is that a smoothly egalitarian process of agrarian transformation was facilitated by an enlightened and pragmatic state. According to this interpretation, often termed the growth linkage model, rapid agricultural growth within an egalitarian farm size structure generated multiplier effects that drove the expansion of small-scale, labor-intensive non-agricultural enterprises located largely in the countryside.[29]

Selden and Ka (1993) vigorously dispute pro-peasant interpretations of agrarian transition in both Taiwan and China. There are, they contend, fundamental similarities that illustrate the common imperatives of state-driven 'original accumulation' (or primitive accumulation) inherent in late industrialization:

> In neither China nor Taiwan did the dispossession and proletarianization of rural producers provide the driving force in, or coincide with, original accumulation, though in each case original accumulation was predicated on transformation of rural social relations and the formation of a small industrial working class. Nor were the market and commercialization central. On the contrary, in both cases the state deliberately (and devastatingly) curbed both domestic and international market activity in early phases of original accumulation. China and Taiwan reveal

the decisive role of state-driven processes of accumulation predicated on the transformation of ownership and production relations in agriculture and industry. What is particularly striking is the preservation of household-based agriculture in Taiwan under Guomindang rule, and [in China] the conscious rejection of dispossession (and proletarianization) of rural producers in favor of a strategy of land reform followed by collectivization and population controls that restrained rural producers from leaving the land . . . In both [China and Taiwan], land reform transformed the principal axis of class conflict in the countryside, the conflict between landlord and tenant, resulting in the elimination of both social classes; in both, the state fostered original accumulation in ways that exacerbated sectoral conflict between rural producers and urban industry and between countryside and city. (Selden and Ka 1993: 113–114)

Both sides in these debates rely heavily on aggregate survey data to support their claims; indeed, in the Taiwanese debates several observers use the *same* sources to arrive at opposite conclusions. More recently, Karshenas (1995) has reworked key sets of data for both China and Taiwan to call into question the story of victimized peasants set forth by Selden and Ka, while at the same time suggesting a more complex and interesting set of stories than a simple pro-peasant path. In a nutshell, Karshenas argues that extractive moves by both the Chinese and Taiwanese states were offset by rising levels of non-agricultural income in rural households, derived increasingly from rural industrialization.

This is, of course, precisely the point made earlier about the importance of understanding primitive accumulation in terms of ongoing processes that are historically and geographically specific, and closely linked with the complex of forces that shape the reproduction of labor. Yet what's missing from Karshenas' story are the social processes and power relations – including, very importantly, gender and kinship – that propelled these trajectories, and shaped what are in practice highly diverse forms of rural industrialization. In the discussion that follows I sketch the broad contours of these debates, drawing wherever possible on longitudinal ethnographic studies.

In the case of Taiwan, Selden and Ka base their claims about state extraction on estimates of intersectoral capital flows by Lee Teng Hui (1971).[30] According to Lee, net capital outflow from agriculture increased at an annual rate of 3.8 percent in the pre-war period of Japanese colonial rule; in the first decade of KMT rule (1951–60), net capital outflow escalated at an annual rate of 10 percent. During the Japanese colonial period, rents and land taxes were the main sources of extraction from agriculture. Under the KMT, the single most important mechanism of resource extraction was an obligatory barter system in which peasants were forced to hand over rice to the state in exchange for high-priced fertilizer. In addition, the state exacted land taxes, other compulsory procurements, and land repayments in kind. Between 1950 and 1960, the government collected more than 50 percent of rice sold and more than 30 percent of total rice produced, a percentage that surpassed landlords' share during the colonial period (Lee 1971: 81). Here, Byres (1996) observes, was primitive accumulation with a vengeance: an agrarian transition whose passage and sustaining have required a very powerful and repressive state. Selden and Ka (1993: 113) make a stronger claim that 'the conflict over resources between industry and agriculture and between investment and consumption pitted small family farms against urban industry and a state committed to industrialization.' This, of course, is a direct contradiction of claims that egalitarian agricultural growth generated consumption linkages that stimulated non-agricultural expansion.

A key issue in these debates is whether and how a demand-led stimulus from agriculture is possible in the face of extraction of this magnitude. Proponents of the growth linkage model, drawing on Lee (1971), argue that 'sustained agricultural productivity growth in Taiwan made possible the large net transfer of resources to the nonfarm sector as well as the broadly distributed and rapid increases in rural income and consumption' (Park and Johnston 1995: 121). Selden and Ka (1993: 120) also invoke Lee to argue that 'throughout the 1950s, the state tightly restricted peasant consumption and directed the surplus to the industrial sector and the cities.' If one allows Lee's 'facts' (about which he is quite circumspect) to speak for themselves, they refuse to support either set of claims.[31] Karshenas (1995) has reworked Lee's data to suggest that increases in *non-agricultural* income of rural households between 1950 and 1960 amounted to more than twice the rent payments and easily offset all the agricultural taxes. In other words, Taiwanese peasants were able to fend off the depredations of state extraction from agriculture in the early stages of industrialization not simply through increasing agricultural productivity as growth linkage proponents would have it, but rather through deploying increasing amounts of labor to rapidly growing non-agricultural sectors while holding on to the land. Conversely, as Gates (1979) suggested some time ago, the costs of reproduction of the industrial workforce were in large part passed on to the peasantry:

... there must be something distinctly peculiar about the social reproduction of Taiwan's proletariat. To a very large extent, the working class does not reproduce itself. Rather, industry relies for recruits on the temporary labor of the children of other classes; it is the sons and daughters of the petty bourgeoisie who form Taiwan's industrial reserve army. The whole pattern of peasant and small business family life conduces toward the supply of large, but elastic numbers of laborers who will never demand pensions, seniority raises, substantial medical benefits, or even a wage which will support a family, because most will leave factory work to marry and enter their permanent occupations after a few years of 'selling their youth to the company'. The costs of reproducing an industrial workforce are neatly passed on to a class characterized by (among other things) large families whose members practice mutual economic support and extremes of self-exploitation. (Gates 1979: 396)

A series of longitudinal ethnographic studies traces how, in the late 1950s and 1960s, growing numbers of young women and men from rural households started moving into industrial and other non-agricultural jobs.[32] Although this often entailed migration to urban areas, parents typically maintained close ties with their children – particularly daughters. Indeed, parents frequently dictated where their daughters would work and appropriated a large proportion of their earnings. These earnings in turn contributed significantly to high levels of household savings – and hence to non-agricultural investment in rural areas. Although women's wages at that time were only about 60 percent that of men's, parents' (perhaps fathers') greater capacity to control their daughters' earnings meant that young, unmarried women became 'more effective engines of household capital accumulation' than sons, as Niehoff (1987: 293) graphically put it.

Shifts in the spatial pattern of industrialization are an important part of this process. During the import substitution phases of Taiwanese industrialization in the 1950s and early 1960s, industrial growth was concentrated in the main urban centers.[33] Shih (1983) cites data suggesting that between 1956 and 1966, the period in which agriculture was growing rapidly, the chief increases in rural non-agricultural employment were in the services sector; the share of manufacturing in total rural employment remained fairly stable and was concentrated mainly in food processing.[34] With the rise of export production in the 1960s, important industries that were originally urban-based began dispersing into rural areas; these included textiles, leather, chemicals, rubber products, basic metals, metal products, and transport equipment.[35] The recession of 1974, when large numbers of urban factories closed and competition from other low-wage areas intensified, produced a fresh round of decentralization propelled by familial forms of production, and the proliferation of the satellite factory system described in Chapter 5.[36]

In short, when cost-pressures hit in the early 1970s, large numbers of incipient peasant-industrialists were waiting in the wings. As we saw in Chapter 5, the exclusion of ethnic Taiwanese from the state went hand-in-hand with a complex of institutions, policies, and measures that worked to fragment private-sector business and disperse economic power (Greenhalgh 1994: 765–766). For peasant-industrialists, the political economy of agriculture *vis-à-vis* industry further reinforced these processes.[37] Even after 1973 when there was a shift to agricultural subsidies, the KMT continued to exercise strict control over agriculture; the long arm of the state reached down to regulate how virtually every farm family used their land.[38] Small-scale industry, in contrast, provided far more room to maneuver beyond the scrutiny and regulatory control of the state. For villagers, tiny factories represented a space in which it was possible to evade the tight state regulation that applied to agriculture and larger industries.

Several ethnographic studies provide further insights into the way gender practices and kinship relations have shaped the trajectory of rural industrialization. In particular, they show how senior males used industrial enterprises in an effort to bind their sons and reinforce filial obligation.[39] The distinction between inherited and acquired property is particularly crucial in agrarian settings. Inherited property – notably land – is owned by the male descent line as a whole, with fathers holding family property in trust for their sons who have equal rights of inheritance at the time of partition in terms of customary law. Property *acquired* through industrial activity is under the discretionary control of senior males, and provides them with tremendous leverage in intra-familial negotiations (Greenhalgh 1994). From this perspective, rural industries provided not only a route of escape from state scrutiny, but also a means by which senior males sought to revitalize their control over the younger generation in a context of land fragmentation and rapid decline in the relative importance of agriculture.

In sum: what emerges is neither a simple extraction nor a pro-peasant story of agrarian transformation, but more complex, multi-layered, gendered struggles that shaped interlocking trajectories of agrarian transformation and rural industrialization.

What, then, of China? In the early stages of land reform in China (1947–52), Selden and Ka concede that elimination of the landlord class yielded important gains to former tenants and smallholders. After 1953, however, state-imposed restriction of market activity stripped smallholders of income from sideline activities. Particularly in the period following the collectivization of agriculture in 1955 and the intensified drive for heavy industrialization in the cities, Selden and Ka claim, agricultural resources were channeled to industry and the cities at the expense of both rural consumption and investment. Dismissing claims about communist China's pro-peasant path, they argue that the collectivized peasantry, trapped in the countryside, paid for urban industrial accumulation and the privileges of urban workers through the state's ruthless squeezing of agriculture.

As in the case of Taiwan, Selden and Ka use aggregate data on intersectoral resource flows to support their argument. These include data on agricultural taxes from Ishikawa (1967), and Lardy's (1983) estimates of the meager share of centralized investment allocated to agriculture relative to industry. Yet, as in the case of Taiwan, some of the same data sources are consistent with quite different interpretations. Karshenas (1995) also uses data presented by Ishikawa (1967, 1988) to argue that real intersectoral commodity flows favored agriculture between 1953 and 1980; in addition, Karshenas contests the argument that the agricultural sector's share of investment was relatively low, claiming that it underestimates price subsidies on investment goods in agriculture, investment financed by internal funds of communes, and deployment of labor in construction and land improvement.

As in the Taiwanese debates, conclusions about intersectoral resource transfers hinge crucially on whether and how non-agricultural incomes of rural households are taken into account. Karshenas for example points out that there was a large inflow of wage income from the non-agricultural activities of farm households, due to the growing importance of commune-managed non-agricultural enterprises in rural areas. In other words, in China – as in Taiwan – part of the reallocation of resources from agriculture to industry took place *within* increasingly diversified rural households, as well as through communal arrangements. Yet at the same time, increasing non-agricultural rural production supported expanding consumption. Unlike Taiwan where at least part of this process entailed rural-urban migration, in China it was spatially confined by restrictions on mobility. These restrictions, in turn, intensified huge regional disparities in income (Riskin 1987).

In the post-reform period, linkages between agriculture and industry forged at the level of the household and local community have remained a key component of industrial accumulation. The decollectivization of agriculture in China after 1978 is often portrayed in the mainstream literature as the triumph of individualized forms of production, private enterprise, and the market. Others emphasize that decollectivization entailed a highly egalitarian distribution of land rights, combined with an absence of private property rights in land.[40]

Several historical ethnographies illuminate these transformations in different places.[41] Huang's (1990) fascinating longitudinal study of a village in the Yangzi Delta suggests that the significance of the return to household organization in farming lay not so much in the supposedly superior incentives powering increases in crop yields, but rather in the capacity to make more efficient use of labor for diversifying the rural economy. In collectivized agriculture, Huang argues, the workpoint system encouraged not only large labor surpluses, but also what he terms 'loitering labor.' The shift to the household responsibility system was accompanied by a sharp decline in labor use in grain agriculture (despite substantial price increases), combined with diversification of labor into what in China are termed sideline activities such as poultry, rabbits, silkworms, vegetable production, fishponds, and so forth. Hence, he argues, the key difference between collective and family production units is the latter's motivation and 'superior ability to diversify into low return and/or high risk sideline activities' (Huang 1990: 221). Huang's otherwise rich ethnography yields disappointingly few insights into the intrahousehold dynamics and power relations through which what he revealingly terms 'auxiliary and spare-time labor' is mobilized, and how the product of this labor is claimed and used. Even so, his and other studies underscore a key feature of agrarian transformation in the post-reform period: the rapid expulsion of labor from foodgrain agriculture and accelerated diversification not only into sideline activities – but also, of course, rural industries – has continued to take place in large part without dispossession.

Rural industrialization supported by post-Second World War land reforms was more limited but nevertheless important in Japan and South Korea.[42] In Japan, for example, Mary McDonald (1996) shows how between the mid-1960s and the mid-1980s, the number of farms declined from 6 to 4 million, while the number of farm residents engaged in off-farm work rose from 4 to 6 million. During that period, farm residents accounted for 34 percent of new construction jobs and 22 percent of new manufacturing jobs in the Japanese economy. The large majority of these new industrial workers were women who, through 'an elaborate choreography of farming and factory work' in multi-generational farm households were drawn into factories that moved into rural regions at relatively low wages. McDonald also shows how this process of dispersal was not simply driven by market forces, but was orchestrated and facilitated by central government agencies and local state authorities.[43] In other words, profitability and industrial competitiveness in Japan were underwritten in crucially important ways by agrarian conditions and agricultural subsidies that, in turn, enabled industrial capital to mobilize low wage, predominantly female labor.

More generally I am proposing that Mao's mobilization of the Chinese peasantry in the first half of the twentieth century laid the seedbeds for spectacular and distinctively 'non-Western' trajectories of industrial accumulation later in the century. These processes, accomplished through complex concatenations of power-laden practices at different levels of society that took different forms in different places, not only underscore the contemporary and ongoing salience of agrarian questions to grasping the conditions of global competition. Most importantly, for my purposes in this book, they enable us to revisit South African agrarian debates, and to shed new light on them in a way that bears directly on questions of future possibilities.

South African Agrarian Debates Revisited

Direct connections between production and the conditions of reproduction of labor in Taiwan and China compel attention to the ongoing significance of agrarian dispossession in South Africa, as well as to the character and pace of post-apartheid land reforms. When Taiwanese industrialists moved to places like Newcastle and other decentralized regions of South Africa, they encountered a workforce expropriated from the land and thrust into radically commodified forms of livelihood. The intensity of labor conflict unleashed by these forms of production derives, I suggest, not only from the inability of the majority of Taiwanese industrialists to deploy gendered forms of negotiation on the factory floor, but also from the absence of the sort of wage subsidy that characterized Taiwanese and Chinese industrial trajectories. One rough indication of this point that I discuss more fully elsewhere (Hart 1995) is that in 1995, when cheap knitwear produced by Taiwanese industrialists in China began flowing into South Africa, wages in Taiwanese knitwear factories in Newcastle were nearly double those in

Fujian when calculated in terms of prevailing exchange rates. Yet real wages – calculated in terms of Purchasing Power Parity – were 30–40 percent lower. In comparing their situation with those of their compatriots who had moved to China, Taiwanese industrialists in Newcastle consistently complained not only about low worker productivity, but also how much higher wages were in South Africa. What was missing, of course, was any sort of recognition of the radical inadequacy of these wages – or of how they themselves were the product of East Asian agrarian reforms.

This misrecognition is particularly ironic, since part of what attracted Taiwanese industrialists to South Africa in the 1980s was precisely the availability of cheap luxury housing, as well as access to the appurtenances of white privilege – including educational, health, and other facilities. As one industrialist put it, 'you can live like a king in South Africa!' In addition, the English education that their children receive in South African schools enables them to become far more globally mobile than if they had been raised in Taiwan. There is, in fact, a double irony since it was precisely the converse of these racialized subsidies – namely dispossession – that has, at least in part, undermined the accumulative capacities of Taiwanese industrialists.

These claims have some important continuities with earlier debates, but with some new twists. A key argument in the race-class debate that raged during the 1970s was the reserve subsidy thesis, which posited that, at least until the first half of the twentieth century, capital latched on to women's labor in subsistence agriculture in the former reserves to subsidize low wages of male migrant workers. The functionalist tendencies in this argument came under attack from those who pointed out that the deeply gendered migrant labor system, at least in part, reflected a degree of agency by patriarchal societies resisting full proletarianization.[44] Despite this and other critiques, there is no question that mining capital, in particular, derived huge benefits from workers' access to land in the reserves, particularly in the earlier phases of capitalist expansion.

East Asian trajectories turn the reserve subsidy thesis on its head, underscoring the depth and extent of racialized dispossession since the 1950s that severely eroded the conditions of reproduction of labor. In the most sophisticated statement of the reserve subsidy thesis, Wolpe (1972) of course recognized that by the middle of the twentieth century the capacity of the reserves to provide subsistence had run out of steam. Yet at precisely the time that East Asian land reforms were taking hold in the late 1940s and early 1950s, the stage was being set for ongoing, massive dispossession of black South Africans from land in rural 'white' South Africa through farm evictions and 'black spot' removals (see Chapter 2). To grasp the ongoing significance of these histories of dispossession, it is essential that we move beyond the 'politics versus economics' debates of the 1970s and 1980s, and attend as well to the politics of the agrarian question in South Africa.

It is in this context that Govan Mbeki's contribution remains powerfully relevant. His political engagement with agrarian questions, it will be recalled from Chapter 2, grew out of his early involvement with the Industrial and Commercial Workers' Union that was sweeping the South African countryside in the late 1920s – precisely the point at which Mao was expounding on the revolutionary potential of the Hunan peasantry. Yet Mbeki's theoretical and political emphasis transcended rural versus urban, or peasant versus proletarian debates to insist on historically specific *connections*, and on linking struggles in multiple social and spatial arenas. Hence his appeal to the leadership of the liberation movement for 'a proper blending of peasant and worker struggles . . . combined with skillful timing of joint action' (Mbeki 1964: 131). In this sense he had much closer affinities with Gramsci than with Mao or Lenin, both as an organic intellectual *and* in his conception of the agrarian question concretely located within historically and geographically specific conditions. Yet as we saw in Chapter 2, neither his appeals nor his practical engagements in linking peasant and worker struggles had much effect on the largely urban-oriented ANC and SACP. Mbeki's insistent focus on everyday material conditions and practices was also at odds with the liberation movement's two-stage theory of revolution, outlined in Chapter 1.

Within the South African liberation movement there has long been a profound tension between the powerful emotive force of the 'land question,' and the relative neglect of agrarian questions in practice. This tension was clearly evident at a workshop organized by ANC activists in Lusaka, Zambia in February 1990 to discuss future land and agrarian policy.[45] According to Heinz Klug, a member of the ANC's Land Commission that was established at that workshop:

> . . . all the participants . . . seemed to assume that nationalization of existing land holdings, given a history of dispossession and the vast inequalities in land holdings between black and white, would be high on the agenda of an ANC government. This shared assumption was based in no small part on our commitment to the 1955 Freedom Charter . . . Despite our assumptions and the liberation movement's

general rhetoric on the 'Land Question,' activists at the workshop had a realistic view of the low priority rural issues had on the mainly urban-based ANC's political agenda in the late 1980s. (Klug 2000: 124–125)

Nationalization of land was effectively abandoned during the constitutional negotiations, when the ANC accepted the principle of protection of property rights. The property clause of the bill of rights does, however, make provision for land expropriation with compensation based in part on the current use of the land 'for a public purpose or in the public interest,' which is defined to include 'the nation's commitment to land reform.' The more concrete commitment wrested through the negotiation process was to restitution of land expropriated since 1913.

In fact, it was a delegation from the World Bank that in 1993 set forth the most comprehensive proposals for a market-led land reform that would transfer 30 percent of agricultural land in rural 'white' South Africa into the hands of a newly created class of small-scale black agricultural producers.[46] Since such producers would 'saturate' the land with unpaid family labor, Bank economists asserted, the small farmer strategy would ensure higher yields than large white-owned farms. Drawing directly on the Taiwanese-based growth linkage model outlined in the preceding section, proponents of the peasant path for South Africa also made extravagant claims about how the multiplier effects of rapid agricultural growth would generate substantial growth of rural non-farm employment. Peddled at workshops around the country, the Bank proposals drew sharp critique. The magic figure of 30 percent of agricultural land to be transferred into black ownership within five years did, however, find its way into the RDP and other policy documents.

The land reform program actually set in place when the ANC assumed power in 1994 comprised three main elements: restitution of land to those deprived of land after 1913; tenure security; and land redistribution. Post-apartheid land reforms have now been extensively documented, so I will sketch only the broad outlines of the redistribution component.[47] In the first phase (1994–99), redistribution was aimed primarily at poor rural households with little or no land, rather than the formation of a small-scale commercial farming class envisaged by the World Bank. Households earning less than R1,500 a month (US$325 in mid-1996) were eligible for a Settlement and Land Acquisition Grant (SLAG) of R15,000 (later increased to R16,000) which they could use to purchase land on willing buyer-willing seller conditions. Cherryl Walker outlines the workings of the SLAG as follows:

By pooling their grants, groups of households could buy farms (generally with state
or NGO help) at market-related prices; the balance (usually only a small amount)
could then be spent on preparing a development plan and on limited infrastructural
development on the land. Because of the high cost of farm land relative to the
household grant, as well as strong social forces supporting group mobilisation of
prospective applicants, a major feature of the early period was the aggregation of
relatively large numbers of potential land reform beneficiaries into what might be
called project (in many cases, more accurately 'projected') communities. In some
cases there were strong historical or leadership ties holding these groups together;
in many cases they were held together more by the exigencies of the project design
or the aspirations of their leaders than by any compelling social or economic bonds.
(Walker 2001b: 10)

The SLAG crept forward at a sluggish pace, although it started picking up
speed in 1998/99.[48] Yet by the end of 1999, redistribution and restitution
programs *together* had transferred only 1.13 percent of agricultural land to
black ownership (Walker 2001b: 11).[49]

When President Thabo Mbeki came to power in mid-1999, he appointed a new Minister of Agriculture and Land Affairs, Thoko Didiza,
who immediately launched a sweeping review of land redistribution set in
place by her predecessor, Derek Hanekom. In early 2000 she imposed a
moratorium on the SLAG, calling for new directions in redistribution to
cater to black South Africans aspiring to become full-time commercial
farmers. At the end of that year, Didiza's office proposed a program entitled
Land Reform for Agricultural Development (LRAD) that resurrects elements of the World Bank's vision of the early 1990s – but without some of
the more 'welfarist' provisions of the original Bank proposal (Walker
2001b: 14): 'While paying lip-service to "food-safety nets" and the encouragement of a broad spectrum of producers, the new policy and the publicity
surrounding it is unambiguously aimed at promoting a class of full-time
black commercial farmers' (Lahiff 2001: 5). LRAD replaces an income
ceiling (R1,500 per household for the SLAG) with an income floor for the
grantee's own contribution (R5,000 per person to qualify for the lowest
grant level of R20,000). To qualify for the highest grant of R100,000, the
grantee has to come up with R400,000. All grants are conditional upon
agricultural production. Essentially, LRAD ties land redistribution to the
agenda of the national Department of Agriculture at a time when South
African agriculture has one of the lowest levels of state protection in the
world (Walker 2001b). LRAD only came on line towards the end of 2001.
For two crucial years, then, any sort of land redistribution beyond
restitution was essentially put on hold.

Budgetary data provide perhaps the most vivid indication of the extent to which redistributive impulses have fallen off the official map. In 2001, the Department of Land Affairs (DLA) received 0.38 percent of the national budget. Walker (2001b: 13–14) provides national treasury data showing that, while the national budget of the DLA is set to increase, the bulk of the increase will go to speeding up restitution. The actual allocation to redistribution and tenure reform programs falls from R421.9 million in 2001/02 to R339.5 million in 2003/04. The amount budgeted for transfer payments (the allocation that covers the actual purchase, planning, and servicing of land) in 2003/04 (R195.5 million) is substantially below the R360.8 million spent on transfer payments in the 1998/99 financial year.

Here, in short, is land reform on a very slender shoestring – in a context of escalating poverty and land hunger for settlement – exemplifying in a particularly intense form the profound tension between the historical and emotive significance of the 'land question' on the one hand, and minimal practical commitment on the other. In addition to the ANC's historic neglect of agrarian questions, its logic derives from the neoliberal imperatives of the post-apartheid order, the rise of a powerful, urban-based African bourgeoisie, and what are often termed implementation or 'capacity' problems – the complex struggles and negotiations between 'beneficiaries' and state agents at different levels, as well as among them. Particularly in the former bantustans another element in the mix is the ANC's political accommodation with 'traditional leaders,' expressed most clearly in recent proposals for tenure reform.[50]

Not surprisingly, NGOs and some academics have sharply attacked the narrow and miserly (re-)direction of land redistribution.[51] Much of this critique is directed at the radical inadequacies of LRAD in addressing demands by poor black South Africans for land for settlement – demands that SLAG, for all its limitations, went at least part of the way in addressing. One argument coming from the Programme for Land and Agrarian Studies at the University of the Western Cape is that 'land adjacent to the former homelands and townships, and in areas of acute landlessness, needs to be targeted and acquired by government, through a mixture of aggressive intervention in the market and selective expropriation' (Lahiff 2001: 5; see also Cousins 2001). The imperatives of land for settlement in urban and peri-urban areas are also becoming increasingly urgent, as we shall see in Chapter 8, with critiques of land policy coupled with those of housing. Increasingly as well, critical attention has come to focus on the imperatives for land redistribution programs that enhance the capacities of members of poor households – particularly women – to stitch together livelihoods from a multiplicity of sources.

I raised some of these broader issues of livelihood in an earlier phase of land reform debates, prompted in part by what I saw as World Bank economists' fallacious deployment of 'Asian models' and 'lessons from elsewhere' to make claims about the multiplier effects of the small farmer strategy. During the initial post-apartheid period (1994–96), before the SLAG had been set in place, the forms that land redistribution might take were still very much live issues.[52] At the time, I suggested the possibility of a 'multiple livelihood land reform' – namely, state-sponsored moves to expand access to land in areas adjacent to already existing non-agricultural activities, such as the so-called 'buffer zones' set up by apartheid planners to separate former white towns from black townships (Hart 1995, 1996a, 1996b). In this pre-GEAR period, I also sought to engage critically with those who invoked notions of 'flexible specialization' and visions of the 'Third Italy' to claim that South Africa's future lay first and foremost in high tech, high wage, 'high road' forms of industrial development.[53] It did not take a large leap of imagination to see how dangerously these formulations played into what Morris (1991) had called the '50 percent solution,' reduced more recently by Marais (1998) to 30 percent.[54] My 1995 article in the *South African Labour Bulletin* was an appeal to organized labor to take up the land question in moving beyond such exclusionary strategies. I also wanted to make clear that I was *not* proposing land reform as a way of subsidizing low-wage, highly exploitative forms of industrialization, but rather a broader strategy to secure livelihoods.

In retrospect I am aware of the lacunae in these arguments, influenced in no small part by Govan Mbeki's understanding of the agrarian question, as well as by the divergent trajectories of local political dynamics in Ladysmith and Newcastle on which my research has focused since 1996. What is missing from my earlier arguments – as well as from more recent critiques of land reform – is attention to *how* political and social forces might be constituted to press for more broadly based redistributive change that bridges the rural-urban divide. This question assumes additional significance and urgency in the present conjuncture in light of both the hardening of the ANC's conservative position and, as we shall see later, growing signs of discontent in a number of arenas. In short, appeals cast in terms of the centrality of land to sustaining livelihoods are important, but by themselves insufficient. The 'land question' in South Africa is not only about livelihood, but also histories and memories of racialized dispossession.

Precisely because of their deep and powerful resonances, these histories, memories, and meanings of dispossession are crucial to linking struggles in multiple social and spatial arenas – and hence to the formation of alliances to press for social and economic justice. Central to any such process is the idea of articulation outlined in Chapter 1, understood in the dual sense of the joining together of diverse elements, *and* the production of meaning. By denaturalizing dispossession and underscoring the ongoing importance of redistribution in shaping the conditions of reproduction of labor, the East Asian trajectories of agrarian transformation sketched out in this chapter point a way forward that turns around an extended definition of the social wage. What I am suggesting more specifically is a political strategy that *dis*-articulates the land question from agriculture, and *re*-articulates it in terms of the social wage, and the moral and material imperatives for basic livelihood guarantees.

A second, related proposition is that the local state forms a key terrain for such a strategy, both because of its rising importance in this era of neoliberal globalization, and because – as we shall see in the following chapter – the balance of forces, political dynamics, and the constitution of political identities take divergent and locally specific forms, even in places that are structurally very similar. In addition, new municipal demarcations set in place at the end of 2000 have effectively dismantled rural-urban boundaries, while also intensifying the slippages, openings, and contradictions inherent in the neoliberal post-apartheid order.

Part III

Post-Apartheid Possibilities

CHAPTER 7

Accumulating Tensions
Remaking the Local State

L OCAL GOVERNMENT RESTRUCTURING in post-apartheid ˙South Africa has, quite literally, entailed redrawing lines on maps to incorporate areas defined as 'white' and 'black' under the Group Areas Act as single geographical and administrative entities. These boundaries encapsulate the contradictory imperatives of the post-apartheid order in a highly condensed and intense form. The amalgamation of racialized spaces in the first phases of local government reform (1994–2000) has been particularly dramatic in places like Ladysmith-Ezakheni and Newcastle-Madadeni where, under apartheid, the huge resettlement townships were part of the KwaZulu bantustan, and where memories of dispossession and displacement remain vivid.

As we saw in Chapter 1, there is nothing unusual about the retreat of the central state from redistribution and welfare provision, and the devolution of these and other responsibilities to the local state. They represent precisely the sort of reconfigurations of territorial state power associated with neoliberal capitalism in many different parts of the world. What renders this process particularly explosive in post-apartheid South Africa is how the spatial dimensions of race, wealth, and privilege have become reinscribed within the local state. In principle, the presence of democratically elected and directly accountable local councilors has opened greater opportunities for township residents to exercise citizenship rights and press demands for material improvements. In practice, new cadres of local politicians find themselves perched precariously on seismic fault lines, confronted with direct and urgent demands for redistribution in the face of fiscal austerity and protections of white privilege and, simultaneously, with helping to guarantee the conditions of accumulation and attract investment. Particularly in the larger urban centers the privatization of municipal services has been the most overt source of conflict, generating fierce disputes between unions and municipal authorities, and often placing township councilors in a difficult position.[1]

These tensions are evident in the tortuous double-speak of the Local Government White Paper (1998), a document that paved the way for the final phase of local government restructuring that went into effect in 2000, and drew sharp critical responses from both the liberal right and the left.[2] Both critiques point to the White Paper's strategic omission of any mention of GEAR, and of the escalating demands being placed on the local state in the face of fiscal austerity. The response from the Centre for Development and Enterprise (CDE) – a business-funded think-tank, descended from the old Urban Foundation, that intervenes actively in policy debates – is interesting for its unequivocal statement of the contradictory imperatives that pervade the local state: in the short run, at least, 'the needs of the poor and the demands for an investment-friendly environment with world class infrastructure are very different' (Bernstein 1998: 300). In articulating the priority that must be given to accumulation, the CDE is disarmingly – if not brutally – frank:

> [W]hile any local authority in the new dispensation must be concerned about redress of the disadvantages suffered by poor areas as a consequence of Group Areas and other discrimination from the apartheid period, this must not in any way lead to a deterioration in the quality of administration and services as they impact on wealthier neighbourhoods. While this balance cannot be justified on a moral basis, it is a practical imperative and an essential precondition for the investment and employment creation which will eventually benefit the poor much more in the longer run than administratively-driven redistribution in the short run. (Centre for Development and Enterprise, 1998: 28)

The report goes on to note that, to the extent that the White Paper is concerned with ensuring the prerogatives of majority-based power, it fails 'to reassure potential investors that some kind of populist deviation in local government, with associated protests from other interest groups, can be ruled out' (Centre for Development and Enterprise 1998: 29). The question, of course, is how and by whom these protests and 'populist deviations' are to be suppressed, particularly since such protests are inflamed by precisely the measures that the CDE advocates. That the Local Government White Paper is riddled with contradictory claims and agendas is scarcely surprising. Essentially it represents a desperate effort on the part of elements within the post-apartheid state to grapple with the pulsating remains of apartheid geography in the face of jackboot neoliberalism, the sharp limits imposed by the negotiated settlement to end apartheid, and rapid exposure to the forces of global competition.

In the final phase of local government restructuring that went into effect at the end of 2000, a Municipal Demarcation Board slashed the number of local authorities from 830 to 284. The new demarcations not only vastly enlarge the size of municipalities, and incorporate rural and urban areas within single entities. They eliminate the disproportionate representation of former white areas that was part of the compromise in the interim phase of local government restructuring.

This chapter traces how the interim phase of remaking the local state played out in Ladysmith and Newcastle, and culminates with the second local government election in December 2000. Although privatization of municipal services was not an issue in Ladysmith and Newcastle during this period, three other key sites of struggle figured prominently: local taxes, service charges, and the formation of municipal budgets; the 'integrated development plans' required of local authorities by the central government; and the promotion of accumulation under the aegis of 'local economic development.' Each of these sites is shot through with contradictions operating at multiple levels; and tensions among them amplify the contradictions.

These structural tensions define the broad terrain of local governance, but they do not in any simple or direct way determine the course of local politics. On the contrary, as we shall see in this chapter, the contradictory imperatives of redistribution and accumulation are being constituted, contested, and redefined in distinctively different ways in Ladysmith and Newcastle. These divergent dynamics, as well as the limits within which they operate, are deeply revealing of what Gramsci (1971) termed 'the terrain of the conjunctural' – namely 'the incessant and persistent efforts' by political forces to defend and preserve the status quo, which in turn defines the terrain upon which the forces of opposition organize.

Reconstituting the Local State

My first inkling that the transition to new forms of local government was unfolding quite differently in the two places came in the second half of 1994. This was the so-called 'pre-interim' phase of local government restructuring, in which localities were required to form Local Government Negotiating Forums that would nominate pre-interim Transitional Local

Councils (TLCs) to serve until the local government elections. Both the national negotiations for local government restructuring and the local-level Negotiating Forums embodied dualist interpretations of the stakeholders in local politics: statutory and non-statutory. According to official definitions, statutory bodies (also known as 'establishment forces') were those from pre-existing government structures, as well as organizations representing officials, councilors, professional institutes, and so forth. The non-statutory side was defined to include 'all those who had previously been excluded from local government.'[3] At the local level, things were considerably more complicated. The pre-interim TLCs were to comprise 50 percent statutory and 50 percent non-statutory representatives, and were to take over local government from the apartheid structures. In addition to vigorous jostling for position, there were also some quite remarkable efforts by white politicians and organizations to insert themselves into the non-statutory side.

In Newcastle the white local government went even further, and tried to evade the TLC system altogether by defining Newcastle-Madadeni-Osizweni as a metropolitan rather than a local structure; the intent of this move was to maintain the town and the townships as separate sub-structures. Strategically placed township councilors – all of them holdovers from the old bantustan system and members of the IFP – concurred with this plan on the grounds that an integrated local council would have required reducing the number of township councilors; this was impossible, the councilors claimed, because their workload was so heavy. Provincial officials – including IFP representatives – overrode both the white local government and the township councilors, and intervened successfully to oppose the separate system. The resentment with which this decision was received in Newcastle is expressed very clearly in the mayor's report for that year:

> One is clearly left with the impression that a new form of altruism is being established which will make one sector of our town's population more dependent on the other and this will inevitably lead to the carrying of the brunt of the financial obligations by a small sector of our total population in the district of Newcastle. Unless the Provincial Government who [*sic*] has the tendency to interfere with the establishment of local negotiating forums who do not meet their approval, provide other avenues to financial resources, this new tendency is doomed. It is of paramount importance that the vast majorities [*sic*] of people acquire the culture of paying for services before such services are made available to them. Those who are keen to control the assets and the expertise of a municipality will first have to be educated in the basic principles of Local Government. (*The Mayor's Minute*, Borough of Newcastle, 1993/94: 1–2)

In Ladysmith, efforts to subvert the pre-interim TLC process in order to shore up white privilege took a different form. Several white groups – including the Ladysmith Ratepayers' Association and the Chamber of Commerce – tried to claim seats on the non-statutory side of the TLC. So too did a member of the National Party who maintained that under apartheid he had been excluded from campaigning in the townships! The intent of these moves, of course, was to restrict the number of seats available to township representatives. In contrast to Newcastle where the province intervened, this strategy was foiled by the local ANC representatives who sought to head off the infiltration of the non-statutory side of the TLC by creating an alliance with the IFP. In defining political interests in terms of town versus township, the local ANC was also attempting to create a rift between black IFP representatives and a strategically placed group of white businessmen who had joined the Ladysmith IFP. What made this strategy of ANC-IFP alliance particularly compelling was that, only six months previously, Ezakheni had been wracked with violent conflict when a local IFP warlord brought in busloads of young men from a nearby rural area to kill ANC supporters. A remarkable reconciliation process was set in motion after the general election, culminating in the peace accord described in Chapter 3. ANC representatives invoked this reconciliation in their efforts to isolate white IFP members and to circumvent the takeover of non-statutory seats by white groups. The strategy to maintain ANC-IFP representation on the non-statutory side was largely successful; perhaps even more significant were the accusations of opportunism leveled by the ANC against white IFP members, and the assertion of 'township interests.' In short, by the end of 1994 the ANC in Ladysmith appeared set for victory in the local government elections.

In mid-1995 when I returned to South Africa, local government elections in KwaZulu-Natal were shrouded in uncertainty. Ongoing violence in the province made it unlikely that the elections would be held that November, when the rest of the country was scheduled to go to the polls. Although there was no overt political violence in Ladysmith and Newcastle, conservative forces seemed to be in the ascendance in both places. Even in Ladysmith, the ANC representatives with whom I met were deeply pessimistic about their prospects in the local government elections. They explained that their efforts to seek common cause with the black IFP membership had been circumvented by a powerful IFP-National Party

alliance, in which white English-speaking IFP members were playing a
prominent role. It was also evident that the experience of operating within
the TLC had exposed divisions within the ANC alliance between an Indian-
led elite and 'the townships,' as well as between township groups coded as
'youth' and 'unions,' and within the Indian segment of the ANC. In
Newcastle, the ANC alliance appeared even more disorganized and deeply
divided; its key representative on the TLC was an Indian lawyer who had
defended Taiwanese industrialists on charges of violations of labor laws,
and whose relationship with township activists was problematic to say the
least. In both places, ANC officials talked anxiously about how few voters
they had registered compared with the IFP-National Party machine.
Provincial ANC officials were similarly pessimistic about their prospects in
Ladysmith and Newcastle. Indeed, one senior Durban-based official
declared that, since Newcastle is larger and more industrialized than
Ladysmith, the ANC's chances were better there. This observation reflected a more general presumption of a fairly clear urban-rural political
divide, in which the urban areas belonged to the ANC and rural regions to
the IFP. According to this simplistic calculus, Newcastle falls on the urban
side of the divide, Ladysmith on the rural.

When the KwaZulu-Natal local government elections finally happened
at the end of June 1996 they were remarkably peaceful, contrary to
widespread fears. As expected, the ANC won in the large urban centers
while the IFP was dominant in rural areas (Johnston and Johnson 1997).
What took most observers by surprise were the ANC victories in both
Ladysmith and Newcastle:

Table 7.1   Results of the 1996 local government election.

	Greater Ladysmith		Greater Newcastle	
	No. of seats	Percentage	No. of seats	Percentage
ANC	21	62	26	44
IFP	1	3	12	20
National Party	9	26	7	13
Independents	3	9	9	15
Conservative Party			3	5
Minority Front			2	3
Total	34	100	59	100

In reading this table, it is important to recall that 33 percent of the seats were reserved for former 'white' areas as part of the compromise that under-pinned the first phases of local government restructuring. In Ladysmith the ANC won 62 percent of the seats, decimating the IFP which emerged with only one seat. In Newcastle, even ANC organizers were stunned by the results, particularly in Madadeni, where the ANC won seven of the eight wards; in the eighth Madadeni ward the IFP was defeated by an independ-ent candidate. Overall the Newcastle ANC won 44 percent of the seats, more than double those of the IFP. The white vote in Ladysmith was captured exclusively by the National Party; as in other parts of the province, substantial white and Indian support for the IFP in the national elections simply melted away. In Newcastle, both white independents and the extreme right wing figured prominently – including a member of the Conservative Party charged with murder in Namibia!

In retrospect, one can see very clearly how these electoral results reflect the deeply sedimented local histories traced out in earlier chapters. Yet they also contain elements of contingency and surprise that would have been impossible to predict in advance. Most dramatic, perhaps, was the move by Eddie Liu – the most prominent and controversial of the Taiwanese industrialists in Newcastle whom we met in Chapter 5 – to align himself with the IFP, contributing generously to party coffers in the expectation of becoming mayor. When Alison Todes and I met with him in October 1994, his political ambitions were evident in two photographs on the wall of his office. In one he was handing a check to Frank Mdlalose, IFP premier of KwaZulu-Natal, and in the other, Nelson Mandela was the recipient of his generosity. During that meeting, he laid out his vision in no uncertain terms: he wanted to turn Newcastle into a free trade zone, build an airport, and ban all union activity. In practice, there is strong reason to suggest that his affiliation with the IFP contributed to the ANC victory. One indication is the relatively low turnout of registered voters in Newcastle (42 percent) compared with Ladysmith, where nearly 60 percent of registered voters went to the polls.

When Phelele Tengeni and I went to Newcastle shortly after the elections, we were regaled with two sets of stories that are suggestive of how Eddie Liu's involvement in IFP politics helped to win the election for the ANC. First was the staging of pro-IFP campaigns in some of the Taiwanese factories; given the extreme alienation of workers in the majority of Taiwanese factories, it is difficult to imagine a more effective way of undermining IFP support. Second was a rally held in Madadeni a week before the election. Large numbers of IFP members were invited, and issued with numbered tickets entitling them to win lavish prizes dispensed by Eddie Liu. Memories vary as to quite how large, elaborate, and numerous these prizes were; what is fairly consistent is the resentment that they provoked. If Eddie Liu is so rich, people asked, why doesn't he pay decent wages?

Taiwanese industrialists and their labor practices also played a role in the Ladysmith local government elections, albeit in a less direct and spectacular way. In 1995, National Party and IFP representatives on the pre-interim local council sought to emulate the earlier Newcastle strategy by sending a delegation consisting of the IFP mayor and several prominent white businessmen to Taiwan. They managed to bring in a group of 10 small Taiwanese industrialists, who were set up in a large empty factory vacated several years earlier by a South African industrialist who had gone off in search of more docile labor. The Taiwanese were promised a non-unionized workforce through a strategy designed to kill several birds (including the Clothing and Textile Workers Union) with one stone: prospective workers were invited to come to the IFP office, register with the party, and obtain a ticket that would guarantee a job in the new factory complex. The ANC promptly leapt on the issue of low wages and tense labor relations to brand the IFP as the lackeys of exploiters of the people. While there is no way of knowing to what extent these events influenced the outcome of the elections, there is little question that widespread resentment of Taiwanese labor practices became a distinct political resource for the ANC and a liability for the IFP.

In Newcastle, the election results reflect another dimension of local industrial history – the establishment of Iscor that brought in a substantial white working class. The downsizing of Iscor through the 1980s and 1990s contributed to an embittered and extreme right-wing presence in Newcastle. Support for the Conservative Party in the local government elections came almost entirely from the white working class suburb established by Iscor.

Along with deeply ethnicized and racialized industrial histories, the election results also reflect a series of interconnected struggles that assumed distinctively different forms in the two places. We have seen how forced removals were more fiercely contested in Ladysmith than in Newcastle for reasons related to longer histories of politicization; how labor politics were constituted in very different ways – with a far more organized and coherent labor movement taking hold in Ladysmith; how the interaction between the youth movement and the labor movement in the 1980s in the two places generated even more sharply divergent paths of struggle. The civil war of the late 1980s and early 1990s in KwaZulu-Natal also assumed different forms. In Ezakheni, the brutal attacks orchestrated by the Inkatha warlord had the effect of creating greater cohesion in what was already a far more organized and politically mobilized civil society. In contrast, targeted assassinations and house burnings in Madadeni and Osizweni – inflicted anonymously by what appears to have been some combination of the Special Branch and the KwaZulu police – further exacerbated political disorganization and intensified many peoples' fear of explicit identification with the ANC and SACP in these townships.

These very different political histories were clearly manifest in the process of candidate selection. ANC officials in Newcastle described how, with a few exceptions, the relatively few middle-class professionals who openly supported the ANC refused to stand as candidates; they were, they said, afraid of having their houses burnt down. Most of the candidates for both the wards and the proportional representation list were drawn from the group of activists who were prominent in both the youth and labor movements in the 1980s. The problem, several observers noted, is that many did not have broadly based support from their constituents. In Ladysmith, ANC ward candidates were elected by ANC branches through what many people described as an open, widely contested, and democratic process. Many of the first cadre of ward councilors – including most of the women on the council – had a history in the youth movement, and some had also served as shop stewards. Their experience of shopfloor democracy within the strong industrial unions carried over into their practices as councilors. Yet the industrial COSATU unions (notably SACTWU and NUMSA) had no formal representation on the Ladysmith council – a lacuna that turned out to be extremely significant.

Election results in Ladysmith and Newcastle also reflect complex and divergent local histories of political engagements by people of Indian descent. Of particular significance is not only the historical strength of the Natal Indian Congress in Ladysmith relative to Newcastle, but also the close alliance between Achmad Sader and Govan Mbeki in the 1950s. When tensions have emerged between African and Indian ANC members in Ladysmith, the invocation of this alliance has served as an important symbolic resource.

Emerging from the election results were important differences in racial configurations within political parties. The ANC in Ladysmith was not only bolstered by strong Indian support; in addition, the retreat of white residents from the IFP before the election and their clustering in the National Party meant that party political opposition to the ANC was split largely along racial lines. In Newcastle, the far smaller group of ANC councilors confronted a splintered but vociferous opposition. Although most of the white independents were closely aligned with the National Party, there were also some deep personal animosities arising from earlier histories of political competition. Both groupings were sharply opposed by Conservative Party councilors some of whom, through a particularly ironic twist, became aligned with a faction in the IFP led by Eddie Liu and a member of the Zulu royal family.

Relations between newly elected town councilors and the (mainly white) cadre of municipal bureaucrats also diverged sharply. Immediately following the local government elections, the town clerk (or 'chief executive officer') of Ladysmith resigned, along with at least six other senior municipal officials including the borough engineer, the town treasurer, and the chief of health services: 'Punch drunk municipal officials fed-up with being political scapegoats' declared the *Ladysmith Gazette*, a mouthpiece of the National Party, whose chairman described the departures as disastrous. The *Newcastle Advertiser* reported the resignations with self-congratulatory relish: 'Newcastle enjoys stable post-election municipal administration, unlike Ladysmith . . . (which) has lost virtually every senior official and is now struggling to find replacements.'

The resignations were prefigured in an interview I had in November 1994 with a senior white bureaucrat who had recently retired from the Ladysmith municipality, and was reflecting on how things would change under the new dispensation. He described how, until then, local government had been run entirely by municipal bureaucrats. 'We made all the decisions,' he declared; 'we set budget priorities, decided on appointments and so forth, and simply presented them to the councilors. They would approve our decisions in 10–15 minutes, and go off and drink. The chief executive was a very powerful man.' In future, he noted, the chief executive will not have nearly such a strong influence: 'the new councilors will want to exercise powers and rights – they will want more say. They will want to put in their people and have a say in appointments and budget priorities. The culture of the new councilors is to go back to the people. This will create delays and problems.' It was precisely the strains of coping with local democracy that prompted the departure of senior bureaucrats in mid-1996.

For newly elected ANC councilors, the resignations presented an extraordinary opportunity to reconstruct the upper echelons of the municipal bureaucracy. It also meant that councilors very quickly came to see themselves as employers and managers. Their efforts to construct a more racially diverse bureaucracy were partly successful; but the only qualified applicant for the key position of town clerk was a comparatively young white male Afrikaner. Defying stereotypes, he moved very quickly to reconstruct racialized understandings and practices within the local state. Soon after assuming office, he took municipal bureaucrats and town councilors on a retreat to the Drakensberg at which he insisted on racially mixed accommodations. Several white bureaucrats described to me their initial incredulity and opposition, as well as the shaking up of their racial identities: 'I'm a WAM (white Afrikaner male) and always will be,' one of them declared, 'but this guy really has forced us to change the way we think.' The ongoing renegotiations of racialized understandings in everyday encounters between councilors and bureaucrats form a central theme of the remainder of this chapter.

The contrast with Newcastle is dramatic. White bureaucrats in Newcastle were unpleasantly surprised by the ANC victory, but confident they could prevail: 'They [i.e. the ANC] don't have a majority in the council, so one party can't dominate,' declared one. When I asked how he thought the new council would operate differently, his reply was that little would change: 'There are rules and regulations, and even the new councilors will have to obey the rules.' Besides, he observed, 'there are a lot of guys on the council who understand the international market and they will basically be running things.' He went on to note that several representatives of Newcastle First (the white independent party closely aligned to the National Party) had orchestrated the industrial strategy in the past, and that Eddie Liu would pull in large amounts of new Taiwanese investment in the future. In short, Newcastle bureaucrats sailed into the new era arrogantly confident of their hold on power and monopoly of expertise. This hubris very quickly produced a major boycott of service charges in Madadeni and Osizweni that brought the town to the brink of financial crisis. In Ladysmith not only were growing numbers of township households paying their service charges, but an extraordinary process of community budget consultations had been set in motion. At the same time, a group of white residents of Ladysmith were threatening rates boycotts, claiming that they were victims of 'neo-apartheid' who had been deprived of their human rights!

Rates, Rights, Boycotts, and Riots

> South Africa is currently undergoing a major change within its public sector, in which government functions, virtually across the board, are being decentralized to the local level. District health services, municipal police forces, local housing programs, child care – name the department and there will be some or other function on its way down. Two forces are driving this decentralisation: a fiscal squeeze at national and provincial level, leading to the shedding of functions (and hence to what we call 'unfunded mandates' being dropped on local government); and a realisation that many functions can be provided more efficiently at local level. (Olver 1998: 289)

With stunning clarity, this statement by the then Deputy Director-General of the Local Government section of the Department of Constitutional Development lays out one of the central contradictory imperatives of the post-apartheid era: the escalating functions deployed to the local state in the face of neoliberal austerity. Compounding these contradictions are official discourses that designate the local state as the primary arena in which the injustices of apartheid must be dismantled. It is within this larger context that such seemingly mundane matters as municipal rates and service charges have become key sites of material and symbolic struggle.

In 1995, the new government launched a lavishly funded national campaign entitled Masakhane (an Nguni word meaning 'let's build together'), ostensibly aimed at building popular confidence in local government, and reconfiguring understandings of citizens' rights and responsibilities – in particular, service payment. In practice, Masakhane quickly became associated with an effort to reverse the 'culture of non-payment.' Yet the following year payment levels fell still further, and the amounts owed to local authorities continued to escalate, placing additional strains on already minuscule budgetary allocations from the central state. By 1997 there were widespread service disconnections, accompanied by public protests against municipalities which, in some areas, became extremely violent.[4] According to official figures, almost half the 843 municipalities faced financial problems in 1999, and a further 151 were in full-blown financial crisis.[5] In short, as a commodified national effort to manufacture consent, Masakhane has proved a resounding failure.

A quick tour through the changing terrain of local government finance is necessary in order to appreciate the importance of locally raised revenues. Under the old dispensation, white local authorities – which included areas designated 'Indian' and 'Coloured' under the Group Areas Act – derived their revenue primarily from rates on property and trading services (electricity, water, and so forth), while townships situated in areas designated as 'white' South Africa were typically in arrears. Swilling et al. (1991: 195) offer compelling evidence of how the fiscal system of urban apartheid facilitated the net transfer of resources from the townships to 'white' cities and towns, and helped spark the rent boycotts that began in the early 1980s. The apartheid state responded to the fiscal crisis in the townships through an ad hoc system of bridging finance, as well as through the system of Regional Service Councils (or Joint Services Boards).[6] Townships like Madadeni and Ezakheni situated in bantustan areas were subject to a different fiscal and administrative system. Formally, these townships (known as R293 areas) were the responsibility of the KwaZulu government. In practice they were administered by the central government's Department of Development Administration (DDA) which assumed responsibility for service delivery and exercised wide-ranging control over finance (Bekker 1991: 111). Township households paid a flat service charge for municipal services that did not, in fact, cover the costs of service provision. The shortfall was met by the DDA, which provided relatively large annual subsidies. These subsidies, in turn, meant that residents of townships located within bantustans paid lower service charges than those living in townships in so-called white South Africa (Becker 1991: 117).

Since 1996 newly reconstructed local authorities have received transfers from the central fiscus. In aggregate, these transfers amounted to R5.2 billion in 1996–97, an amount equivalent to only 10.8 percent of the total municipal budget; conversely, new local authorities remain responsible for raising on average nearly 90 percent of their revenues locally. In 1996/97, for example, the Ladysmith local authority received R12.4 million to subsidize operating costs in Ezakheni and Steadville, an amount equal to 14.5 percent of the total operating budget; this amount was substantially less than the minimum required to provide even basic services in the townships, and probably only one third of what would be required to provide services comparable to those in the white towns.[7] In the 1998/99 budget, the Department of Finance devised a formula for allocating an 'equitable share' of centrally raised revenues to local authorities, the bulk of which is designated as an operating subsidy of R86 ($14 at prevailing exchange rates) for each household earning less than R800 ($133) per month. Between 1998/99 and 1999/2000, the local government equitable share fell from R2.3 billion (1.1 percent of total expenditure) to R1.7 billion (0.8 percent of total expenditure).[8] These figures make clear how local government is being called upon to undertake fundamental tasks of redistribution in the face of radically inadequate resources. In the interim phase of local government restructuring, the prospect of higher rates and the diversion of resources to the townships rendered many residents of the formerly white towns apoplectic, while township dwellers were deeply resentful of poor and often non-existent services. Neoliberal austerity, in short, is conjuring up the ghosts of apartheid in a familiar spatialized form.

Within towns like Ladysmith and Newcastle, a second key axis of tension took shape in the mid-1990s. The Group Areas Act, which restricted the areas in which people defined as Indians and Coloureds could buy property, resulted in relatively high property prices, particularly in suburbs designated as Indian. Since rates are determined by property values, many Indians had argued for years that they were paying excessive rates.[9] Differential property rates in former Indian and white areas need to be set in the context of the particularly bitter history of the Group Areas Act in Ladysmith and Newcastle, and the removal of Indian traders from the central business district. Although they lived within the municipal boundaries of the town and paid rates, Indians and Coloureds were not represented on the town council. National constitutional changes in 1984 included the establishment of separate 'Local Affairs Committees' for Indians and Coloureds, but their limited powers did not encompass property rates.[10]

In the period immediately following the local government elections in June 1996, the new town councils in both Ladysmith and Newcastle effectively reduced rates in former Indian areas. Differential rates rebates provoked a certain amount of grumbling from some activist white rate-payers in Newcastle, but a veritable explosion of rage in Ladysmith. These discrepant reactions to similar adjustments of rates are revealing of larger reconfigurations of power in the two places, and are also closely connected with the politics of resource allocation between the towns and the townships.

The battle over rates reductions in former Indian areas of Ladysmith was waged not only in the council chambers, but also in the *Ladysmith Gazette* which enjoyed a sharp rise in circulation. The opening salvo was fired in the *Gazette* of August 9, 1996 with a front page article entitled 'It's Pay-Back Time':

> Rates for the so-called 'advantaged' areas in Ladysmith are likely to go up by 20% – the highest increase since anyone can remember. Meanwhile the 'disadvantaged' areas escape without any increase at all . . . 'The advantaged areas paid a lesser rate in the past – now it's pay back time,' said Cllr Khan [ANC].

Charges of racism are a key theme in the enraged responses, articulated most fully by a National Party member of parliament who excoriated the ANC for its 'neo-apartheid' actions in a letter to the *Gazette* a few weeks later:

> Since the ANC has been installed as the new government, law and order has collapsed, corruption is rife, merit and hard work are no longer cherished criteria and equally worrisome, they have introduced neo-apartheid in Ladysmith and other towns . . . Not only is the granting of rebates, Ladysmith style, unconstitutional, but the underlying motive, namely to bring colour into play, has brought shame to town.

The letter concluded with threats of rates boycott, which would cause the town 'to collapse into a financial mess and . . . suffer the humiliation of being placed under an administrator.' A spate of letters from other infuriated white residents also played the race card, charging ANC local councilors with racism and contrasting their actions with those at the national level: 'The local ANC's dismissive attitude to the concerns expressed by ratepayers is in stark contrast to our President's commitment to consultation, investigation and enquiry before decision making is concluded.'

One of the most poignant responses came from an Indian resident:

> It is a strange irony that the Nationalists, who for forty years had played such havoc with our lives, our country, and our town should today be offering advice on the matter of rates. The problem of rebates which Ladysmith faces today was, after all, directly caused by the Nationalists in their vain attempt to 'kick the Indians out of town'.
>
> It will likewise not have gone unnoticed that today's passionate critics of the TLC [Transitional Local Council] decision were not as passionate in their criticism of the Nationalists when non-whites were being hounded out of the central areas of Ladysmith. When, for instance, old Mr Sayed, with suit-case in hand and wife at his side, stood outside the family home in lower Murchison Street one morning in the early eighties and watched the bulldozers demolish his home, the good citizens (of all political persuasions) of this town were strangely silent. That week's edition of

the *Ladysmith Gazette* did not even devote a line to the matter! I mention these
things not out of any sense that retribution is justified but merely to remind those
whites who today also claim to have been victimised under apartheid that their
claim is, to put it mildly, disrespectful to the immense pain and suffering that
people like Mr Sayed and many, many others experienced under apartheid and the
Group Areas Act.

In early October of 1996, a group of about 100 indignant residents of
former white areas marched into the council chamber, and presented the
mayor with a petition protesting the differential rates system that contained
over 2,000 signatures.[11] The language of the petition echoed that of the
letters; it invoked the 'neo-apartheid' character of the differential rates
system, its discrimination against 'truly disadvantaged' people, and the way
it had divided the community into opposing ethnic factions. It also
reiterated the threat of a rates boycott which would put the town into
receivership: 'We would rather negotiate with an Administrator appointed
by the Province than an insensitive, arrogant and dictatorial council,' the
petitioners concluded. Yet directly beneath its report of the petition, the
October 4 edition of the *Ladysmith Gazette* carried a one-line article which
noted that 'ironically the Monday deadline saw municipal offices packed
with people paying rates, in spite of the threatened boycott.' In the months
that followed, both the council and the petitioners sought legal counsel on
the constitutionality of the differential rates system – which came to
precisely opposite conclusions. By mid-1997, an uneasy truce prevailed
while new assessments of property values were underway.

The underlying issue at stake in the 'great rates debate' was alluded to
in one of the many letters sent by white residents to the *Ladysmith Gazette*:
'One may justifiably fear that this is only the first step along a long road of
retribution, their sordid cry "It's payback time" being a ringing reminder.'
Although the redistribution of resources between the town and the
townships was never made explicit in the public debate, it constituted a
powerful subtext.

Conversely, the comparative complacence with which white residents
greeted the similar rates rebates in Indian areas of Newcastle reflected their
confidence that the balance of forces in the local council precluded the
diversion of resources to the townships. In a move that entailed simultaneous de- and re-racialization, white power-brokers defined the town
(including both white and Indian areas) as Newcastle West and the
townships as Newcastle East; the former characterized by a 'pay-culture,'

and the latter by a 'culture of non-payment.' The complacence of those who defined themselves 'ratepaying Westerners' traces, at least in part, to a decision made by the pre-interim Local Council in February 1996 that flat service charges would be eliminated, and township residents would be required to pay rates and user charges: 'Several members of the Newcastle Residents and Ratepayers Association expressed their satisfaction with council's approval of the proposal which will see all residents paying rates towards local government,' reported the *Newcastle Advertiser* of March 1, 1996. In fact, soon after the new local government was installed in July 1996, councilors from all parties – including the ANC – approved a budget that retained flat service charges in the townships for the following financial year – but increased them from R17 to R76 per month.

ANC councilors claimed that the increase in service charges took them totally by surprise. As one of them put it:

> *We were told in July that we must approve the budget immediately. They said if you don't approve the budget right now you won't have any money. We requested time to go through the budget document. They said no. We were not sure of the by-laws. We were very shocked when the accounts were sent out, and we discovered that rates and services had increased by nearly 600 percent.*

Several different councilors repeated this story of having been railroaded by municipal officials in almost precisely the same terms.

Not surprisingly, escalating service charges provoked explosion of resentment in the townships. The fury of township residents was compounded by the sharp deterioration of a series of services – roads, refuse removal, and so forth – in the townships over the preceding year. In fact, the Newcastle local authority only took over formal administration of the townships in March 1997, nearly nine months after the local government elections. The official reasons for the delay were complexities in working out the terms of incorporation of administrative staff in the township into the municipal bureaucracy. One senior white bureaucrat informed me with something of a smirk, 'Just before the 1994 elections Madadeni and Osizweni were transferred to the Ingonyama Trust; we can't do work on the King's property!' In practice the delay reflected ongoing efforts described above by powerful forces in Newcastle to prevent the amalgamation of the town and townships in a single local authority.

Protest first erupted in early October 1996, when township residents received their accounts for services. Later that month the ANC mayor tried to address a meeting of several thousand people in Madadeni, but was forced to take refuge in the police station after being pelted with stones in which people had wrapped their municipal accounts; others burned their accounts, and very soon there was an almost total rates boycott.

Organized protest coalesced in an organization called the Madadeni and Osizweni Concerned Residents Association. ANC officials describe the association as having been formed from a strongly anti-ANC wing of the IFP, with the encouragement of the extreme right-wing Conservative Party; but they conceded that it also contained disaffected former members of the ANC who were not appointed as councilors, and whose animosity towards ANC councilors was rooted in conflicts among youth-cum-labor activists in the 1980s. The Concerned Residents Association demanded reduction of the flat rate service charge to its former level, better services and roads, and the expulsion of township councilors. The Association also joined the Newcastle Ratepayers Association in complaining about councilors' having voted themselves allowances of R2,900 a month – almost double those in Ladysmith. Soon after its formation, the Association appealed to the Provincial Minister of Local Government to remove Newcastle councilors. In November 1996, according to the *Newcastle Advertiser*:

> Two bus loads of Madadeni Concerned Residents Association supporters were set to disrupt Tuesday's month-end council meeting. However, they were not aware the meeting had started at 2pm and it was all over by the time they arrived. The buses packed with people were parked outside the Farmer's Hall when councillors were leaving.

Earlier that month, nine Association members had marched into a meeting of the council's executive committee demanding to be heard. Further organized action took place in February 1997 when, according to the *Newcastle Advertiser*:

> A large group of Madadeni residents gathered on Sunday [February 16] to demand the resignation of their councillors and the implementation of a flat rate in the township. The people also called on the 'so-called' Newcastle West to stop paying Madadeni's councillors . . . Ironically Sunday's meeting was attended only by the Town Clerk, a Peace Accord representative, and two councillors, Cllr SJ Zulu [IFP] and Cllr LM Veenendal [Conservative Party]. Although invitations were extended to the Mayor and chairman of the executive committee [ANC], Cllr Zulu was the only Madadeni councillor to arrive at the meeting. A memorandum which was handed to the Town Clerk included issues such as employment, sewerage removal and flush toilet systems, an end to corruption and bribery, a flat rate of R16 for section 1–6, a flat rate of R5 for those who own sites and a writing off of arrears.

In a desperate attempt to cope with the rates boycott, the council voted in early January of 1997 to hire a firm I shall call Vumela Facilitation Services (VFS) – at a cost of R900,000. Both ANC and National Party councilors supported this quite stunning commodification of local politics; the key point of contention was which consultants would be hired. In its terms of reference, VFS consultants undertook to ensure a 100 percent payment rate. They pledged not only to 'change the attitude of the people from refusing to pay to that of being willing to pay for municipal services,' but also 'to ensure that people understand why their attitudes should be changed.' The proposal to produce consent includes surveys, workshops, media events, and 'slogans to capture "hearts and minds" of the community using children and the future as central themes.'

The Concerned Residents Association soon made clear that they had no intention whatsoever of allowing their hearts and minds to be captured. Deploying the language of the anti-apartheid struggle, the association vowed to make the townships impenetrable for the consultants, and 'to vehemently oppose them at every turn'; it also threatened 'rolling mass action' in the form of a consumer boycott in the central business district (CBD), work stay-aways, and a continuation of the rent boycott until demands for a rates reduction were met. According to the *Newcastle Advertiser* of May 16, 1997, the leader of the Concerned Residents Association also accused the ANC mayor of being a 'warlord' and alleged that members of the Association had received death threats.

ANC representatives dismissed these charges as ridiculous posturing. Yet they also conceded to the anger and alienation of township residents, as well as to their own inability to do much about it. One sympathetic but critical observer noted a 'huge vacuum between the ANC councilors and the community.' It was only in July 1997 that ANC councilors initiated direct consultation with their constituents. Attendance at these meetings was small, but the message was clear: 'We are prepared to pay, but let the councilors deliver.' Those attending the meetings apparently agreed that R43 a month was fair payment – but only in return for substantially improved services. Yet shortly before I left Newcastle in July, National Party representatives were proposing a moratorium on services until the rates boycott was lifted. There was also widespread speculation that the Newcastle townships would be brought under the control of the province.

The sequence and character of conflict in Newcastle following the local government elections reflect both the power of forces opposed to amalgamation, and the history of disorganized and fragmentary township politics described in previous chapters. Interestingly, the Concerned Residents Association represented overtly organized oppositional protest directed against the ANC, in which some disaffected township residents forged a somewhat bizarre alliance with their counterparts in an overtly racist segment of the white working class.

The contrast with Ladysmith was dramatic. In the first place, the interim local government in Ladysmith took over administration of the townships in February 1996 – a full year before there was grudging agreement to do so in Newcastle. It was clear that the provincial grant was inadequate to cover service charges. Yet instead of simply hiking up charges as in Newcastle, municipal bureaucrats and councilors representing the townships worked out a strategy to maintain charges at a relatively low level but increase payment rates.[12] Local government officials also embarked on a process of transferring ownership of all township houses, along with the provision for gradual introduction of municipal rates and metered services, while at the same time making allowance for a basic package of rudimentary services at a low, flat rate. Ladysmith also gained access to R1 million from a provincial fund earmarked for urban renewal in areas that had been affected by violence. These, along with other RDP resources, enabled small but noticeable improvements in township infrastructure. Between mid-1996 and mid-1997, according to the town clerk, payment of service charges in Ezakheni rose from 30 percent to 68 percent. At precisely the same time that the Vumela Facilitation Services was struggling to 'educate' township residents in Newcastle, the Ladysmith council was convening large and extremely lively open budget meetings at which residents were explicitly invited to educate the councilors about their priorities. In June and July of 1997 I was able to attend five of these remarkable encounters between civil society and local government officials, and also to observe – and in a very limited way participate in – some of the everyday practices through which the local state was being refashioned in a place with a long history of organized political mobilization.

Enacting Local Democracy: Everyday Encounters

On the first day of my return to Ladysmith in June 1997, one of the Ezakheni councilors whom I had met the previous year invited me to a ceremony in Steadville, the township outside Ladysmith that had resisted removal. Before the ceremony we met for lunch in town, during which he expressed his satisfaction with the municipal officials. 'You will see,' he said 'how these people are really quite cooperative.' We then walked over to the town hall, where he introduced me to the white official who was organizing the ceremony and explained that he had invited me. After an initial start of surprise, the young Afrikaner rose to the occasion: 'Of course, uncle,' he said to the older black man, a former Robben Island detainee, 'can I drive you both in my car?' On the trip to Steadville, the official engaged in a fascinating reconstruction of history. Pointing to hills from which Boers and British had exchanged fire during the Anglo-Boer (South African) war, he explained how the British had oppressed the Boers, how the Boers in turn had made the mistake of oppressing the Zulu, but how the Zulu had learned from the mistakes of both and were engaged in reconciliation.

The site of the ceremony was a well-equipped new library in Steadville recently built with RDP funds, and the occasion was the handing over of new houses to six families whose homes had been destroyed by floods earlier in the year. When we arrived, groups of white municipal officials and ANC councilors were standing around outside the library, chatting and waiting for the mayor. Once all the councilors and officials were assembled outside the library a large white Mercedes drew up, driven by a white chauffeur who jumped to attention as he opened the door for the mayor – a former UDF youth activist who had been detained and tortured in the 1980s. As on other public occasions, the mayor emerged wearing the gold chain of office that was, for generations, the symbol of white power in Ladysmith. A procession led by the mayor then moved into the meeting room in the library, where the recipients of the new houses and their families were waiting. Not surprisingly, the speeches were an opportunity for both councilors and bureaucrats to engage in self-congratulation. What caught me by surprise – and others too, judging by the murmur that rippled through the room – was the town clerk's speech. After claiming credit for raising funds and supervising construction of the new houses, he went on to note that the previous speaker – a Steadville councilor – had made him feel small; it made him realize, he said, that he had thought too much about the houses and not enough about the people and their suffering. After all, he said, development is not just about new buildings – it is about people. During the reception that followed the speeches, one of the Steadville councilors with whom I was talking noticed the town clerk standing nearby and broke off our conversation, explaining that she needed to talk to him about getting help with a survey she was conducting among her constituents. She returned a few minutes later, well satisfied. 'You see,' she remarked, 'with this guy we can really get things done.'

Over the course of the preceding year, I had wondered many times about how ANC councilors and municipal bureaucrats would deal with one another. The symbolic and practical reconstruction of the local state I encountered on that first day back was extraordinary. Yet in the following six weeks, the process through which new meanings and relationships were being forged was, if anything, amplified.

The story about Zulus, Boers, and British, for example, was clearly part of the stock-in-trade of Ladysmith municipal officials – and the smiles and glances it provoked among Zulu-speaking listeners suggested that they had heard it before. I heard it on three occasions delivered by different people – but triggered in each case by my arrival at an event with an ANC councilor. On the third occasion I acknowledged direct descent from the original sinners in the form of my maternal grandfather who had fought with British troops in the vicinity of Ladysmith, and helped to imprison Boer women and children in concentration camps. The municipal official who had initiated this conversation responded that his mother-in-law had watched her mother and baby brother die in a British concentration camp, and that she refused to speak English under any circumstances.

This exchange took place in the courtyard of the town hall, while we were waiting for the open budget meeting for residents of the town to begin. Just as we were speaking, one of the National Party councilors marched off in a huff. The reason, according to a press report the following day, was that he took offence to the banner 'Ladysmith/Emnambithi: Government by the People for the People' being in English only. According to a report in the *Times of Ladysmith* of July 8, 1997, he said 'Afrikaans was being "misken" [impoverished] by certain municipal officials and English was being shoved down everyone's throat.' Ironically, the official to whom he was referring was precisely the person who was at that very moment telling the story of his mother-in-law's refusal to speak English.

Perhaps a related part of the reason why the irate National Party councilor stormed out of the meeting was that his constituents had evidently refused to define themselves as part of 'Government by the People for the People.' When the open budget meeting in the town hall eventually began, municipal officials and ANC councilors outnumbered the residents; most of those who did attend were former township dwellers who had moved into town, and formed the Ladysmith Tenants Association. ANC councilors joked about the 'white-out'; several of them also offered sympathy to a National Party councilor evidently embarrassed by his constituents' boycott of the event.

The contrast between the open budget meeting in the town hall and those that took place in the townships was dramatic.[13] Like the Steadville ceremony described earlier, these events were joint productions by predominantly white municipal officials and ANC councilors – but on a far grander scale. They were held in school yards in different sections of the townships (four in Ezakheni and two in Steadville), and each meeting was attended by some 700 to 1,000 people. The deployment of mayoral symbolism was also intensified; at each meeting the mayor was led into the school yard by a marching band of drum majorettes, and on several occasions a group of women councilors commandeered my small red rental car to follow in procession behind the mayor's Mercedes. The meetings commenced with either a prayer or the singing of *Nkosi Sikelele i'Afrika*, followed by introductions of both municipal officials and councilors by the councilor in whose ward the meeting was being held. These introductions typically remarked on how the 'rainbow nation' was represented at the meeting – along with pointed references to the absence of National Party councilors, and suggestions that perhaps they were afraid of entering the townships.

These comments were followed with a speech by an Indian ANC councilor on what Nancy Fraser (1989) would call 'the politics of need interpretation.' He started off explaining how, in the past, officials simply sat in air-conditioned offices, and presumed they knew what the people needed. 'This government is different,' he declared; 'We are your servants, and we are here today so that you can tell us what your needs are. In the past councillors spoke for the people. Now we are coming to the people to learn from you.'

'The people' lost no time at all in stating their demands, well over half of which addressed needs for improvements of existing services. While each meeting had its own character, the more general message emanating from the open budget process was clear: 'We have put you in power, now you must deliver,' as one speaker stated succinctly. Speaker after speaker called attention to rutted roads that remained muddy for days after rain; to burst water pipes; to electricity failures; to leaking sewerage drains and rotting piles of garbage. Calls for crime reduction also figured prominently, along with complaints about the corrupt and inefficient police force, and calls to bring in the army. The second category of demands was for new facilities – mainly community halls, sports facilities, and libraries – frequently accompanied by comments that such facilities existed in Steadville or in other sections of Ezakheni; comparisons to facilities in the white town were never made. Instead, many speakers legitimated their claims in terms of the youth: 'The youth are becoming criminals because they don't have sports facilities; but other areas like Steadville which doesn't even compare with us in size has a sports stadium'; 'We really need a library here like the one in Steadville. Our kids have many talents, but there is nowhere they can go to upgrade their talents.' A third key theme of each meeting was the imperative for jobs, often accompanied by challenges to official discourses of 'cultures of non-payment.' 'We want to contribute to the running of this town, but we cannot because we are unemployed'; 'We don't want anything for free – we are willing to pay but we must have money' were typical comments.

Yet 'local economic development' was also the focus of intense anger. One meeting nearly broke up when a young man quivering with rage – clearly the spokesman for a large group – challenged the mayor on his trip to China, and uneasy murmuring ran through the crowd as an ANC councilor tried to take the microphone away from him. This challenge and the mayor's response are discussed at greater length later in this chapter.

Part of what made the township budget meetings so compelling was the power and passion with which many of the demands were delivered. A significant proportion of interventions were not simply challenges and demands, but also virtuoso performative events that often elicited enthusiastic audience participation. Cries of *yebo!* (yes!), and *hawu!* (an expression of disapproval), along with headshaking or laughter, punctuated many of the speeches – often to the noticeable embarrassment of both councilors and bureaucrats.

The character and intensity of the performances and the general tenor of the meetings were also quite varied, reflecting in large part the class composition and political histories of different areas of Ezakheni. By far the most intense and critical meeting was in C Section, the area of 'shack houses' in which former tenants were dumped at the time of forced removals and in which services are far more rudimentary than in A Section (the middle class area of the township), or B and D Sections where housing and facilities are less rudimentary. C Section was also the staging point from which heavily armed Inkatha men went on the rampage in the early

1990s, and where the most savage fighting and destruction took place. The charred remains of houses in C section bear witness to the civil war in Ezakheni. In making their demands for paved roads, drains, and jobs many speakers at the C Section meeting also talked of suffering through forced removals and the armed invasion. The brutal history of the area was present even when there was no explicit reference to it: 'When she was talking about her roof, that old lady [referring to one of the particularly eloquent speakers] was really remembering how her husband was killed by the Inkatha *impis* [troops],' one of her neighbors explained to me afterwards.

She and many others were engaging in what bell hooks (1990) calls the politicization of memory. They were also, in effect, demanding reparations – and holding local government responsible for ensuring they were made. A number of older speakers in particular reminded representatives of the local state that they had been forced to move into Ezakheni by the previous government. They issued ringing reminders of how they had been promised the amenities of urban life, and then dumped in inadequate houses and made to pay escalating fees for basic resources that had cost nothing in rural areas. Several also pointed out that people living in surrounding freehold areas that had resisted removals continued to live more comfortably, safely, and cheaply than they did in Ezakheni.

These statements are enormously significant. They represent township dwellers' staking claims on urban services in the language of rural rights, and invoking the history of forced removals to drive home their claims. The poignancy of these claims underscores an additional irony: to implement removals and bring large numbers of black South Africans under the sway of bantustan authorities, the apartheid state embroiled itself in a system of subsidizing relocation townships from which the post-apartheid state is now retreating. We turn now to exploring some of the contradictions generated in this process.

Enforcing Participation: Central Directives, Expert Discourses, Local Contentions

> It is in the interest of the nation that local government is capacitated and transformed to play a developmental role . . . In future developmental local government must play a central role in representing our communities, protecting our human rights and meeting our basic needs. It must focus its efforts and resources on improving the quality of life of our communities,

> especially those members and groups within communities that
> are most often marginalised or excluded, such as women,
> disabled people and very poor people . . . Where municipalities
> do not develop their own strategies to meet community needs
> and improve citizens' quality of life, national government may
> have to adopt a more prescriptive approach toward municipal
> transformation. (Section B of the *White Paper on Local Govern-*
> *ment*, March 1998)

If the strictures on local government finance disclose the pinched neoliberal
face of the post-apartheid state, its interventionist impulses emerge full-
blown in the planning exercises required of local authorities *en route* to
their metamorphosis into 'developmental local governments.'

In the interim phase of local government restructuring, two key pieces
of central legislation specified in great detail the terms and conditions of
'decentralization,' and confronted new local authorities with a dizzying
array of directives. First was the Development Facilitation Act (Act 67 of
1995), which emanated from the Office of Reconstruction and Development. The stated intent of the Act was to speed up implementation of
programs and projects under the RDP by requiring each municipality to
draw up a set of Land Development Objectives (LDOs) as a condition of
access to RDP funds; its subtext is the circumvention of apartheid planning,
and the reconfiguration of racialized geographies. The LDOs must provide
detailed information on demography and existing settlement patterns and
specify, *inter alia*, how poorer areas (i.e. townships and 'informal settlements') will be integrated into the area as a whole; how all residents will
gain access to basic services; how the environment will be used in a
sustainable manner; how bulk infrastructure for the purpose of land
development will be provided; what densities there should be in settlements; how land use will be coordinated and controlled; how to obtain
finance for land development; and how much housing will be built. LDOs
have to be approved by authorities in provincial government, after which
they become legally enforceable, binding all three spheres of government
as well as private developers (Pycroft 1998: 157). With the demise of the
Office of Reconstruction and Development in 1996, national-level responsibility for the Development Facilitation Act was transferred to the
Departments of Land Affairs and of Housing.

At the same time, the Department of Constitutional Development
issued its own set of directives to 'developmental local governments.' The
Local Government Transition Act of 1996 required all municipalities to

formulate Integrated Development Plans that not only incorporate the LDOs, but also specify institutional, financial, and communications plans in an 'integrated framework.'

Local government legislation is shot through with the language of 'participation' as a key condition of access to resources disbursed through provincial and central government departments. The Development Facilitation Act, for example, calls for 'community participation in land-use planning and development, and the empowerment of disadvantaged sectors of the community,' and requires provinces to set regulations regarding how communities assist in developing LDOs. The *White Paper on Local Government* (March 1998: Section B) also insists that 'municipalities should develop mechanisms to ensure citizen participation,' although the language is rather more circumspect than that of the Development Facilitation Act, and there is at least implicit recognition of conflicting 'stakeholders.' These and other constitutionally mandated efforts to regulate local authorities and enforce 'participation' are of course sharply at odds with the neoliberal thrust of the post-apartheid state. In effect, local authorities had to engage in detailed and costly planning exercises as conditions of access to very limited resources, over which provincial authorities exercised considerable control. At the same time, under the neoliberal imperative of 'right-sizing,' there was a hollowing out of the state at the provincial level.

What this in turn has meant is that avenues of access to central and provincial state resources have increasingly came to be patrolled by privately owned development consulting firms. In KwaZulu-Natal, provincial bureaucrats were offered large retrenchment packages, which some have then used to establish development planning consultancies – drawing of course on their connections within the provincial bureaucracy. A sizable chunk of the resources allocated by the central government to local government via the provincial administration was then channeled to development consultants. For example, R280,000 of the R1 million RDP fund that Ladysmith received for urban renewal was diverted to a firm that I shall call ExpertPlanners to draw up an Integrated Development Framework. In short, even though technically the bureaucracy is shrinking, the costs have simply been transferred elsewhere.

Opportunities for development experts are not simply a product of the post-apartheid order; on the contrary, there is significant continuity with the past. Planning firms have been active in this region since at least the immediate post-Second World War period, and worked closely with the architects of apartheid to delimit bantustan borders and push forward their agendas. In the 1980s and early 1990s, the Department of Development Administration which, as mentioned earlier, played a central role in administering townships that fell within bantustan borders, made extensive and increasing use of development consultants; so too did the Joint Services Boards (JSBs).[14] ExpertPlanners was appointed by the provincial government to oversee development planning in both Newcastle and Ladysmith. Yet articulations between these supra-local experts and the local state took shape in dramatically different ways that both reflect and reinscribe divergent configurations of power in the two places – and are quite revealing of how official discourses of 'participation' and 'development' play out in everyday practice.

In Newcastle, ExpertPlanners had a long-standing tie with an extremely powerful councilor. By mid-1997, ANC councilors saw him as being in effective control of local government – and themselves as effectively excluded from the circuits of power he had established with supra-local alliances of experts and anti-ANC forces in the provincial state.[15] That ANC local councilors felt unable to challenge these exclusionary practices was, in part, a consequence of the vulnerable position in which they found themselves; this in turn derived primarily from escalating opposition in the townships where, as we saw earlier, the ANC had effectively handed over political negotiation to the Vumela Facilitation Services. In addition, ANC councilors described how they were further marginalized by ExpertPlanners' deployment of expert discourses. For example, in August of 1996, ExpertPlanners conducted a socio-economic survey in Newcastle; its stated aims were to assess residents' ability to pay rates and service charges, and 'to give a picture of employment and unemployment levels in the area.' The ANC councilors with whom I spoke were convinced that the survey results underestimated unemployment and overstated income levels, but the study was cast in obscure technical language that made it difficult to contest.[16] They also noted that ExpertPlanners had made a presentation to the council that was similarly impenetrable. As one of them noted with wry cynicism: 'They [i.e. ExpertPlanners and their ally in the council] will just compile whatever they think is good.'

For ExpertPlanners, working in Ladysmith has been far more difficult: 'We've come up against certain bureaucratic and political blocks,' one of the planners told me, while also making clear that he would not divulge any more information until I gave him a full briefing of my research – which I declined to do.[17] That ExpertPlanners had a hard time in Ladysmith is scarcely surprising. ANC councilors complained bitterly about the way the firm had simply been imposed on them by the provincial administration: 'Suddenly one day we got a letter from Province saying [ExpertPlanners] will tell you what to do,' commented one; 'these top-down actions are a total abortion of everything we fought for.' The second bitter complaint was that ExpertPlanners had come up with a planning document without any consultation with 'the community' – or, for that matter, with councilors who represented them. The provincial official in question conceded that the decision to appoint ExpertPlanners to work in Ladysmith was his, and was based on his confidence in the firm. The problems in Ladysmith, he claimed, derived from the intransigence of ANC councilors who were determined to put a spanner in the works. In early July 1997, when ANC councilors invited me to attend a meeting at which ExpertPlanners were scheduled to present their report to the Executive Committee of the council, I accepted eagerly.

The meeting was held in the Council Chamber, presided over by the ANC chair of the Executive Committee who was seated on a raised dais and flanked on either side by senior municipal officials; ExpertPlanners and the provincial representative were seated together below the dais and to one side, facing the audience composed of other councilors and municipal officials. This spatial arrangement, it turned out, was directly expressive of underlying power relations and dynamics. The meeting commenced with a speech by the senior representative of ExpertPlanners:

> *In this report we are taking a multi-sectoral view in a holistic way. Once we are at one, we can move on. This is your plan; it is for you to guide us, to say 'we are happy' and move on.*

In addition to being 'holistic,' the plan embodied shared information, community participation, and sustainable development: 'We have taken a non-partisan approach; the outcome is not designed to favor any particular group or party.' He did concede, however, that 'some sectors might not like all of it.' He went on to note how, in the past, plans used to be blueprints; this plan represented a 'new wave in which the community is involved in planning'; this was a 'very open, cards-on-the-table approach . . . based on consultation with community structures and designed to initiate institutional capacity building.' Towards the end of the address, the language of participatory planning gave way to a sterner tone. This plan, the Expert-Planner explained, was

> *the first step in what the central government has in mind for future development planning process . . . If political structures can't communicate with the community, or there is lack of communication between political elements and line departments, then the plan won't get off the ground.*

The provincial official wielded more overt threats: he reiterated that the plan had to be approved immediately in order to move into the second phase, and that no money would be released until all three phases were completed: 'If your accounts are not processed by September 30, you are in trouble. You have to work with the consultants, communicate with them, and move forward.'

The next presentation was by a firm I shall call Khuleka Development Consultants, to which ExpertPlanners had subcontracted the job of 'community consultation and capacity building.' The head of the firm, who had worked with ExpertPlanners in his previous job as a KwaZulu government official, described how his efforts to convene meetings in the townships had failed:

> *When we tried to hold a meeting on June 3, the meeting was not successful. We were advised to come back to the council. We want to know how you are going to arrange this.*

It became clear, in short, that the much-vaunted process of participatory planning had, in practice, turned out to be a disaster.

The Ladysmith contingent – including municipal officials and councilors on both sides of the political divide – responded in unison, driving home two key points. First a number of speakers pointed out that, through the open budget process, the council was engaging in community participation and had been extremely successful in accomplishing what ExpertPlanners and their subcontractors had failed to do. 'We don't make decisions for the community,' was a typical comment; 'they do so themselves. We've had our ear to the ground from day one.' Second, the proposed plan could not be ratified by the Executive Committee: 'This plan can't be approved without community participation; we won't just rubber stamp it.' ExpertPlanners were told that it was imperative that they attend the remaining open budget meetings in order to observe participation in action, and that 'no plan will be supported unless you sit around a table with key role players.'[18]

The chief ExpertPlanner responded that 'in an ideal world we would endorse this methodology, but there are budget limitations to the degree of participation . . . we would want to meet with each of these organizations individually, but we would have to review the budget.' The more efficient alternative, he suggested, was that these different organizations be co-ordinated by the Executive Committee and the results channeled to ExpertPlanners. A storm of protest ensued: 'If you say public participation you have to do it,' expostulated one infuriated ANC councilor; 'Public participation is quite different from representative participation.' A great deal of angry attention was also turned to the question of the budget. ExpertPlanners were forced to concede that they had already spent R110,000 of the R280,000 allocated for the entire planning process, to which one bureaucrat responded 'we got nothing for our money' and an ANC councilor backed him up with pointed remarks about extravagance. At this point the provincial representative intervened, saying: 'You have got something for the money. You have got documentation. The purpose of the first phase was gathering existing information, not necessarily informa-tion from the communities.' 'Yes,' added the chief ExpertPlanner, 'people have information. Now they can make objective decisions. There will be intensive community participation in the second phase.' 'Oh,' responded a councilor, 'are you now telling us that community participation was not necessary in the first phase?'

For the remainder of the meeting, both ANC and National Party councilors and municipal officials ignored ExpertPlanners and the provin-cial representative, and discussed the logistics of distributing the planning document and convening meetings. The town clerk rejected a suggestion that only six copies of the report be distributed – four to Steadville/ Ezakheni and one each to the Chamber of Business and the Ratepayers' Association: 'Everyone [i.e. all the councilors and an extensive list of organizations] must get reports and be empowered,' he declared. He also rejected an offer by the chief ExpertPlanner to prepare an executive summary for more broadly based distribution: 'No; the whole report [must be distributed] so no-one can say you planned for us – that's my fear,' was his revealing reply.

These sharply contrasting experiences in Ladysmith and Newcastle represent locally specific reworkings of the contradictions generated by the post-apartheid state's assertion of redistributive social justice, and its simultaneous retreat under the imperatives of austerity and neoliberalism.

Contradictory central state directives have been reconfigured at the provincial level, and then experienced and fought over in quite diverse ways in different local arenas. Part of what makes the episode in Ladysmith so interesting is how, at a particular moment, contesting political forces and the bureaucracy were able to coalesce around a common understanding of Ladysmith as a special place defined by participatory democracy, and unite against what they perceived as intrusive external forces. In this particular moment, at least, the stated intent of central state directives was being realized – but in totally unintended ways.

Yet just as diverse social forces were uniting against one set of supra-local forces, nominal allies – namely ANC councilors and representatives of organized labor – were being pulled apart by disputes over 'local economic development' in ways that illuminate another dimension of intense contradictions inherent in the neoliberal post-apartheid order.

Accumulating Tensions: Contests over 'Local Economic Development'

Earlier in this chapter I alluded to a dramatic and potentially explosive moment in the open budget meeting in C Section of Ezakheni when a young man, quivering with anger, challenged the ANC mayor on his trip to China in late 1996. The mayor and councilors were visibly appalled, and an uneasy murmuring – even a *frisson* of fear – rippled through the crowd as an ANC councilor tried to take the microphone away from him and a group of his friends moved closer to help him resist. A number of earlier speakers had complained about wages and working conditions in Chinese factories; but this was the first time that local politicians were accused of identifying with capital.

This incident captures what is perhaps the most powerful of the multiple contradictory imperatives condensed in the local state: the conscription of newly elected township councilors into projects of 'Local Economic Development' (LED). In towns like Ladysmith and Newcastle, white local government officials have long been engaged in strategies to attract investment. What is new is that councilors representing township residents are now charged not only with securing the conditions of accumulation, but also with 'linking LED to poverty alleviation.' The contradictory imperatives inherent in this charge emerge with great clarity from a set of 10 case studies in different parts of South Africa commissioned by what was then the Department of Constitutional Development

(DCD 1998a, 1998b).[19] An unsurprising conclusion is that 'hardly any of the municipalities reviewed in this project have made any formal attempt to explicitly link economic development with poverty alleviation' (DCD 1998a: 5), and 'the essential policy direction appears to be a reliance upon market forces to allow the benefits of trickle-down to poor communities' (DCD 1998b: 31).[20] Efforts to draw more general lessons from the case studies politely avoid any reference to GEAR, although one interpreter notes that 'SA local governments on their own cannot solve the complex problems of poverty and erase the legacies of four decades of apartheid planning' (DCD 1998b: 32). Yet this point is flatly contradicted by another author in the same volume who blithely asserts that 'local initiative and *relative autonomy from national resources* are key elements to ensure robust local partnerships and collaborative strategies' (DCD 1998b: 52; emphasis added). The author goes on to claim that the key problem is one of ignorance: 'Municipalities generally do not know or understand how a structured inter-connection between economic promotion and poverty eradication could be conceptualised and implemented in concrete terms'; hence 'a major priority for DCD has to be a focused effort to build an understanding of the interrelationships between poverty alleviation and growth strategies' (DCD 1998a: 5). The DCD's emphatic assertion that 'we can re-define LED to ensure a deliberate link with anti-poverty objectives' (DCD 1998b: 41) stands in ironic contrast to the Centre for Development and Enterprisc's (1998) equally emphatic insistence that 'populist deviations' will undermine accumulation, and hence long-run poverty alleviation.

The ways in which active LED strategies have played out in practice in Ladysmith and Newcastle add extra ironic twists to these conflicting claims. In the late 1980s and early 1990s, Newcastle was probably one of the largest recipients of industrial foreign direct investment (FDI) relative to its size in South Africa; since the mid-1990s, Ladysmith may well have taken over that position. Both places are deeply connected with transnational centers of accumulation, and represent precisely the pattern of export-oriented FDI upon which GEAR is predicated. In both places these FDI-led local growth strategies have proven socially explosive, with intense workplace struggles carrying over into – and indeed reconfiguring – both the form of the local state and its relations with civil society. Yet as in other arenas, these struggles have assumed significantly different forms in the two places.

In Newcastle ANC councilors were largely sidelined from questions of local economic development. Eddie Liu appointed himself the key conduit through which transnational investment would pass and, despite their awkward relationships with him, the group of powerful white men who control the local state in Newcastle initially viewed him as a useful point of contact to continue to pull in Taiwanese investment. In practice, Eddie Liu's promises to attract large quantities of new Taiwanese investment failed to materialize. Ironically, his accession to power was followed a few months later by the South African government's severing diplomatic ties with Taiwan and recognizing Mainland China. One local government official described how he and Eddie Liu visited Taiwan in April 1997, but virtually no one attended the seminars they organized – whereas in the past there were always at least 200 people. They also went to China where there was what he described as 'massive interest' in investing in South Africa – but it was all being channeled through the KwaZulu Marketing Initiative (KMI) (an offshoot of the old KwaZulu Finance Corporation), and most of it was going to Ladysmith. The white power bloc in Newcastle rapidly distanced themselves from Eddie Liu, and built their industrial hope on the KMI (to which Eddie Liu was adamantly opposed). By 1998 they had managed to lure three Mainland Chinese firms into the KMI estate in Madadeni – significantly fewer than the 17 Mainland Chinese firms in the Ezakheni industrial estate.

Almost every edition of the *Ladysmith Gazette* trumpeted this reversal in industrial fortunes. 'Ladysmith leads the race for foreign investment' proclaimed one banner headline; 'R60m industrial boom' shouted another. In subsequent issues of the *Gazette,* the volume of prospective investment about to pour into Ladysmith from Mainland China escalated dramatically, and numerous articles pictured the town clerk and the mayor toasting visiting delegations from Mainland China. In fact, the Mainland Chinese connection predated the switch in diplomatic recognition – the initiative to attract Mainland Chinese investment came from the KMI in 1994. The location of the first round of industrialists in the Ezakheni rather than the Madadeni industrial estate reflected the historically close connection between provincial and local power blocs in Ladysmith – and their tense relationship with local power holders in Newcastle.

The newly elected ANC-dominated council in Ladysmith became associated with the Mainland Chinese initiative in a very public way in the latter part of 1996, when the mayor visited India and China as part of a delegation organized by the KMI that included businessmen (yes, men!), provincial members of parliament, and local government representatives. It was, in fact, during this trip that the South African government announced its diplomatic recognition of China. Soon after returning, the mayor held a report-back meeting to local representatives of capital and labor that came to represent an important symbolic turning point. For local white business-men, the meeting was a triumph and a vindication: 'The mayor got the unions together and then tore them off a strip,' declared an industrialist who had recently clashed with one of the industrial unions; 'he told them that they were driving business away with their unreasonable demands.' The article in the *Ladysmith Gazette* conveyed much the same message.

In fact, both the key industrial unions – NUMSA and SACTWU – boycotted the meeting. The union representatives who attended were from non-industrial unions with a history of direct support for the ANC; they were not directly affected by foreign investment, nor did they have any influence on it. NUMSA and SACTWU – both of which are relatively powerful in Ladysmith – have historically distanced themselves from Congress politics. During the 1980s, they provided logistic and other support for the UDF-linked youth movement in Ladysmith, while at the same time maintaining a formal distance. Ironically, the township councilors most closely associated with the foreign investment initiative were former members of the UDF youth movement who became teachers. It is also important to recall that the flurry of local activity around Mainland Chinese investment coincided with the announcement of GEAR at the national level. Within COSATU, NUMSA was at the forefront of the critique of GEAR, to which local NUMSA representatives in Ladysmith added their own criticisms. In short, patterns of attendance and non-attendance at the meeting reflected and reinforced important dimensions of local history and larger dynamics.

The mayor's trip to China and his alleged abandonment of the working class formed the central thrust of the anger that exploded at the C Section open budget meeting. This anger was probably fuelled by deeply problem-atic labor practices, culminating in a strike that had recently taken place at one of the Mainland Chinese factories. The strike in turn underscored an additional irony: the large Taiwanese yarn producer in the Ezakheni industrial estate had been unionized, whereas the newly established Mainland Chinese firms were opposing unionization.

In closing the meeting in C Section, the mayor departed from his usual statement to provide an impromptu reflection on the dilemmas of globaliza-tion that articulates these contradictions with great clarity:

This community is aware that I am the representative sent overseas to invite
industrialists to locate here. The issue of bringing industrialists is a real headache.
Industrialists are looking for a particular type of workforce. If we go overseas we
go kneeling to beg. It is difficult to beg a person and put conditions. Yes, we have
government by the people for the people. But the industrialists are not on our side.
What happened was that the only industrialists prepared to come are Chinese. The
Europeans are not interested. Once abroad, we asked why are you paying such low
wages? What they told us was that the products are cheap. When sold, they don't
bring much profits. These industries are just feelers. If conditions are good, they
say they will bring bigger industrialists. In this situation we are in difficulties. If we
demand more, they will go – we will send them away. We need to take this
seriously. When they say they will leave, they will do it. In Maritzburg, 600 workers
recently lost their jobs. I also give an example of an article I read. We have
countries around us that are poorer – like Zimbabwe. There was a government
employee there who worked for more than two months before he received his
salary. He was given two million in Zimbabwean money. But if we convert to
rands, he only got R48. As the situation is, when industrialists are threatening to
leave they really mean it. [In other places] they are paying less than in our
country. People should be able to differentiate these issues [i.e. those that we can
do something about from that which we cannot]. Roads, sewerage, and water –
these are issues for this municipality and we will see to it. I thank the community,
even if they are shouting at us. They are hard on us so we will be able to work
better in the future. (Closing speech by the Mayor of Ladysmith-Emnambithi at an
open budget meeting held in C Section of Ezakheni, July 6, 1997, translated from
isiZulu to English by one of the councilors)

This vivid statement of the vagaries of transnational capitalism, articulated
through official discourses of globalization, underscores the embattled
position in which ANC councilors found themselves.

The intensity of these contradictions became even more pronounced in
the second half of 1997, when provincial officials selected Ladysmith as the
site of a pilot project for the establishment of a LED forum. The forum is
basically a sort of local corporatism, structured around four key sets of
'stakeholders': capital, labor, the local state, and NGOs. From the perspective of provincial officials who led this initiative, the purpose of the pilot
project was to develop a province-wide framework for promoting local
economic development. The key question, a provincial official explained to
me, was 'whether to facilitate and manage local processes with local
participation, as opposed to quick expert identification of a few big projects
per area.'[21] In practice, the LED pilot project in Ladysmith exploded in a
battle over leadership, and very quickly spun out of the control of provincial
officials. Although unable to observe these struggles directly, I was regaled
with stories of monumental battles when I returned to Ladysmith at the end

of 1998. Not surprisingly, there are varying – and quite revealing – interpretations of how the battle lines were drawn.

Provincial officials saw the central conflict as a classic struggle between capital and labor – in particular between the members of the Ladysmith Chamber of Commerce and militant COSATU industrial unions who were fighting one another for the chair, and in the course of which local government had been sidelined: 'When we were formulating agreements, we wanted the TLC [local government] to liaise with other stakeholders,' one official explained; 'but in Ladysmith labor said they wanted a properly constituted forum – and this battle over the constitution has been running for 18 months.' He went on to note his concern that this struggle over the constitution had not only held up project formulation, but also that any future project would be bogged down by fights between capital and labor.

Local stakeholders' accounts diverge sharply from one another, but all accord central importance to an element notably missing from the provincial interpretation: the conflicts generated by Chinese industries. Together, these accounts underscore an intense irony – namely, that the very *success* of 'local economic development' strategies in attracting foreign direct investment was directly implicated in the failure of the LED forum to perform in accordance with official expectations.

Local representatives of organized labor prefaced their interpretation of the LED forum with a lengthy discussion of labor practices in Chinese factories:

> *People come to the office to complain about their treatment at a factory. We can tell by the name that it's Chinese. They say 'we are on strike'; then COSATU must come in and explain the proper procedures [under the Labor Relations Act]. Yes, they are on strike illegally. But it is the conditions that are making them strike. The wages are terrible, and they [Chinese employers] don't give a damn about hours and safety. Labor is chaotic, and we have to come in and sort it out. The Chinese factories are completely disruptive.*

They went on to explain that their primary motivation in becoming actively involved in the LED forum was to exercise control over local councilors who, in their pursuit of Chinese investment, had circumvented organized labor:

> *When they go to China, they don't tell about the LRA [Labor Relations Act]. Then when these guys come in, they think they can get away with paying R50 (US$8.33)*

per week . . . We want to tell local government 'If you go [to China], then you take
at least one labor person.' The councilors say they are creating jobs. They say we
are going to chase the Chinese away. Then when the factories open and conditions
are so terrible, they say they are shocked – but they didn't bother to tell us.

In short, representatives of the COSATU industrial unions made clear that
they saw the Ladysmith local government's foreign investment strategy as
the central problem, and the target of their engagement with the LED
forum. When I asked about their conflict with the Chamber of Commerce
(and South African industrialists more generally), they burst out laughing:
'Of course we are always in conflict with business,' explained one, 'but at
least local businesses abide by the LRA and we know how to deal with
them.' Besides, this particular speaker went on to note, 'local business
really dislikes the Chinese.' What we want, he declared, is a forum with
business that cuts out the local government.

Representatives of the Chamber of Commerce depicted COSATU as
engaging in power politics, and using the LED forum as a political weapon:
'Other people on the forum are not political; we're trying to bring industry
to Ladysmith and create employment,' noted one. Yet just as COSATU
representatives had predicted, this spokesman for business went on – in
overtly Orientalist language – to contend that Chinese industrialists were
not the answer:

> *They [the Chinese] are not big employers. They're basically trying to get a*
> *political foothold in Africa. Time means nothing to Orientals; if they have to wait a*
> *thousand years, they'll do it. However bad conditions are here, it's utopia*
> *compared to where they come from.*

Rather, he contended, bringing in 'good' investment required getting rid of
restrictive labor legislation. Even though ANC councilors were mistaken in
pursuing the Chinese strategy, he maintained, they were beginning to grasp
the evils of the Labor Relations Act.

Mention of the LED forum quickly brought forth an anguished
response from ANC councilors, similar in many ways to the mayor's speech
reported earlier: 'Our people desperately need jobs and money,' was a
typical response; 'how can we be seen to be chasing the Chinese away?' In
acknowledging the rift with organized labor, several made joking allusions
to themselves as having become 'managers' and 'petit bourgeois' – an
apparent reference to idioms in which the conflict with COSATU was
being conducted. These conflicts assume additional poignance when one

recalls that a number of ANC councilors are former youth activists, who received considerable support from militant industrial unionists in the 1980s. Others were former shop stewards. Accusations of having been co-opted by a combination of capital and the National Party were particularly painful, especially when coming from some of the very unionists who had supported the youth struggle. In addition, ANC councilors were torn between loyalty to the party on the one hand, and intense frustration with the way GEAR was handed down as a *fait accompli* on the other. Conversely, the capacity of organized labor to articulate a sharp critique of both local labor practices and macro-economic policy – and to link the two in ways that resonated with the lived experiences of their constituents – represented a profound threat to local politicians.

The question of NGO representation on the LED forum sparked yet another set of struggles between ANC councilors and organized labor. Councilors expressed deep resentment at NGOs being accorded a seat on the forum: 'We have been democratically elected,' was a typical comment, 'Who do they represent?' It turned out that the NGO that had garnered sufficient power to claim a seat on the forum was closely allied with COSATU, and part of a vision for the LED forum that included – but went beyond – insisting on rights under the Labour Relations Act, to include mobilizing support from people living in surrounding rural areas to put pressure on the local state. In laying out this strategy, the COSATU-NGO alliance made two central claims. First, they argued, COSATU had considerable support in surrounding rural areas:

> *COSATU members are coming from all over, not just from the townships but also from the rural areas. COSATU has everyone in it. If you are talking to COSATU you have eyes all over; COSATU has too much influence. As COSATU we are not only talking about jobs. We also say things like people are living in places without water.*

The second key claim was that, in the context of overall economic and industrial decline, there was a major exodus from townships to rural areas:

> *As jobs are being lost, people are moving to rural areas. There is a feeling that it is becoming too difficult to make a living through money – maybe it's better just to farm. Even the protected elite want to go to rural areas to live because they don't want to pay rates in the townships.*

These rural areas, they maintained, constitute the key terrain of a future – and much larger – struggle:

We feel that local development forums should look into these places and push the government very hard – that is what we plan to do. We also think that the TLC (Ladysmith local authority) is too narrow; we want to operate at the level of the Regional Council.

What these unionists were articulating, in short, was a strategy of mobilizing the countryside to surround the town, and forging direct connections between workplace struggles and the conditions of reproduction of labor.

In February 1999, just over a month after this conversation, the Department of Constitutional Development made a move that seemed destined to cede precisely this terrain to the Ladysmith COSATU-NGO alliance. The minister announced the appointment of a Demarcation Board with the task of reducing the number of local authorities as part of the final phase of local government restructuring. In a little over a year, the board slashed the number of local authorities countrywide from 843 to 284, vastly enlarging their size. In places like Ladysmith and Newcastle, the demarcation process has entailed stretching the boundaries of former white towns and black townships brought together under the interim phases of local government restructuring to encompass surrounding rural areas – precisely the amalgamation of town and countryside that industrial unions in Ladysmith were demanding.

The new system of demarcations not only remaps local state power, but has fundamentally reconfigured the terrain on which broader political struggles will play out in the future. Some broad contours of this new terrain started to emerge in the local government elections of December 2000. At the same time, election results in the expanded Ladysmith and Newcastle municipalities encapsulate dramatically divergent historical dynamics in the two places, and carry with them a series of far broader implications.

Remapping the Local State

The spatial and political reconfiguration of local state power set in train by the new system of demarcations was mandated in the post-apartheid constitution, and buttressed by legislation designed to rectify the compromises embedded in the first phases of local government restructuring.[22] Two are particularly significant. The new demarcations have swept away the disproportionate representation of former white areas that dogged the first phases of local government restructuring. In addition, the amalgamation of urban and rural areas redefines and effectively reduces the powers and

functions of traditional leaders, and replaces them with elected representatives – a fiercely contested process, discussed more fully below. In formal
terms, at least, the new system inaugurates a structure of local governance
in which, for the first time in the country's history, each vote counts
equally.

Alongside these liberal democratic impulses, government officials
proclaim that enlarged local authorities will enhance efficiency and fiscal
viability, and enable the 'developmental local state' in its enlarged form to
realize economies of scale in service delivery, and implement its dual
mandate of fostering economic growth and redistribution. By the end of
2000, they acknowledged, some 250 of the 843 municipalities were
effectively bankrupt, many others were under severe financial strain, and
most of the Regional (i.e. rural) Councils were 'financially nonviable.'[23] In
the 2000/01 budget, local government's 'equitable share' of national
revenue rose by 5.5 percent in real terms over the reduced allocation of the
preceding year but remained radically inadequate – particularly in light of
the enhanced powers and functions of local government. As the Provincial
and Local Government Portfolio Committee of the National Assembly
noted in its report on the budget vote, 'clearly if local government is going
to effectively fulfil the powers and functions allocated to it and the
increasing responsibilities heaped on it, and if it is to be the major site of
service delivery and development it is identified to be, it has to be allocated
more funding.'[24] By the end of 2000, the fiscal future of local government
remained unclear, despite the ANC's electoral promise to deliver free basic
services to all at an estimated capital cost of well over R30 billion (about
US\$4 billion) (*Sunday Independent* December 10, 2000: 4), roughly half of
the combined local government budget and some five times more than the
total transfer to local government in 2000/01. As the year drew to a close,
the only indication of increased financial support to local government was
an announcement that 'government is considering paying the salaries of
SA's 8951 local councillors directly from the national fiscus to ease the
pressure on cash-strapped municipalities' (*Business Day* December 12,
2000: 1).

While local government financial reform remained painfully slow and
halting, the Demarcation Board completed its gargantuan task of remapping
the boundaries of local state power with lightning speed. In little over a year
(mid-1999 to mid-2000), the board decreased the 843 transitional local
authorities to 284. These include six so-called 'unicities' or Category A

municipalities (basically the six metropolitan areas with expanded boundaries), and 232 Category B municipalities (encompassing towns or small cities and adjacent rural areas, as well as predominantly rural areas with no urban center). Each municipality, in turn, is divided into wards containing roughly equal numbers of voters. Groups of Category B municipalities form part of a set of 46 Category C municipalities or District Councils. KwaZulu-Natal, for example, contains the Durban Metro along with 50 new local (Category B) municipalities grouped into 10 District Councils. One of the unresolved issues in the 'powers and functions' debate that has accompanied the new system of demarcations is the division of responsibility and resources between local municipalities and the district councils, which remains open to negotiation.

To a remarkable degree, the Demarcation Board operated independently of other organs of the state. With clinical precision its chair, Michael Sutcliffe, reported to parliament on the procedures of consultation:

> The Board had scores of meetings of its own structures and with a wide variety of stakeholders, including the Minister [of Provincial and Local Government], MECs, parliamentary committees, political parties, government departments, SALGA (South African Local Government Association), and its affiliates, Houses of Traditional Leaders, private sector organisations, and NGOs. Following the publication of draft boundaries, the Board organised 148 public hearings, attended by 7286 people. The Board received 245 submissions following its Section 26 notice of intention to consider boundaries and 2353 submissions following its publication of the proposed boundaries. (Report of the Provincial and Local Government Portfolio Committee, June 6, 2000: 13).

In practice, the board deflected many of these disputes by invoking data from the 1996 Population Census to argue that boundary decisions reflected functional patterns of economic activity. To bolster its claims of transparency and technical objectivity, the board made extensive use of a colossal website (www.demarcations.org.za), containing detailed demographic and economic data for every ward in the country. In short, through an overtly depoliticized exercise in political cartography and data management, the Municipal Demarcation Board has quite literally redrawn the face of local power in South Africa, while at the same time adroitly sidestepping potentially explosive debate.

A closer look at the new boundaries around Ladysmith and Newcastle (KZ232 and KZ252) illustrates vividly the spatio-political extent of this exercise, and the conflicts it has provoked (Map 4). In the transitional phase, it will be recalled, the area covered by each local council included only the former white towns and black townships – roughly the shaded areas in Map 4. In redrawing boundaries, the Demarcation Board drew on the 1996 Population Census data, summarized in Table 7.2 for the newly demarcated Ladysmith and Newcastle municipalities. Local authorities in both Ladysmith and Newcastle insist that the 1996 Census vastly underestimates population. Those in Ladysmith claim that the number of people within their jurisdiction grew from 300,000 under the transitional boundaries to 400,000 under the new demarcations, while their Newcastle counterparts assert comparable discrepancies. These disputes over demographic data are, of course, struggles over access to resources, and are by no means limited to Ladysmith and Newcastle.

The new system of demarcations also brought about a major reconfiguration of electoral wards. Under the transitional system the former white towns, together with areas designated Indian and Coloured under the Group Areas Act, were guaranteed a third of the wards – considerably more than their share of the population. The new system of demarcations equalizes the number of voters in each ward, and eliminates the requirement that municipal budgets be passed with two-thirds majorities – thereby slashing the disproportionate influence of former white areas in local government. Across the country, the declining power of former white areas to control municipal budgets and resource allocation will almost certainly intensify redistributive pressures across spatial lines that are, to a large degree, still defined in racial and class terms. These prospects helped to accelerate a transformation of oppositional party politics. In anticipation of the local government elections the New National Party – direct descendant of the progenitors of apartheid – officially merged with the predominantly white (neo)liberal Democratic Party in June 2000 to form the Democratic Alliance (DA) in what became an extremely aggressive effort to counter the political dominance of the ANC, and lure African, Indian, and Coloured voters into their fold.

Perhaps the most significant feature of the new demarcations is the effective dissolution of rural-urban boundaries, and the incorporation of areas formerly under the control of customary authorities within the orbit of elected municipal government. Particularly in KwaZulu-Natal, the combined legislative, administrative, and judicial powers of the chieftancy remained more or less intact under the transitional system. Areas defined as 'rural' – many of them containing quite densely settled segments of the former bantustans – did not come under municipal government. Instead,

Table 7.2   Demographic data for 2000 demarcations.

	Emnambithi/Ladysmith Municipality (KZ232)		Newcastle Municipality (KZ252)	
	No.	*Percentage*	*No.*	*Percentage*
Population:				
African	154 085	86.3	249 479	86.9
Coloured	1 531	0.9	2 168	0.7
Indian	10 758	6.0	10 836	3.8
White	10 950	6.1	23 265	8.1
Other	1 227	0.7	1 512	0.5
Total	**178 551**	**100**	**287 260**	**100**
Household Classification:				
Urban:				
Formal	19 292	56.9	44 324	80.3
Informal	1 112	3.3	129	0.2
Other	23	–	327	0.6
Sub-total	20 427	60.2	44 780	81.1
Rural:				
Semi-formal	1 246	3.7	–	
'Tribal villages'	8 063	23.8	8 993	16.3
Farms	4 161	12.3	1 398	2.5
Sub-total	13 470	39.8	10 391	18.8
Total	**33 897**	**100**	**55 171**	**100**

Source: www.demarcation.org.za

they formed part of transitional Regional Councils in which traditional leaders (the *amakhosi*) exercised considerable power over resource alloca-tion. The new system not only institutes 'wall-to-wall' municipalities. [25] In its initial form, the Municipal Structures Act (1998) would have replaced the *amakhosi* with elected representatives and municipal bureaucracies.

Not surprisingly, these moves to strip the *amakhosi* of their powers provoked a head-on clash between the chiefs and government officials that delayed – and at points threatened to scuttle – the local government elec-

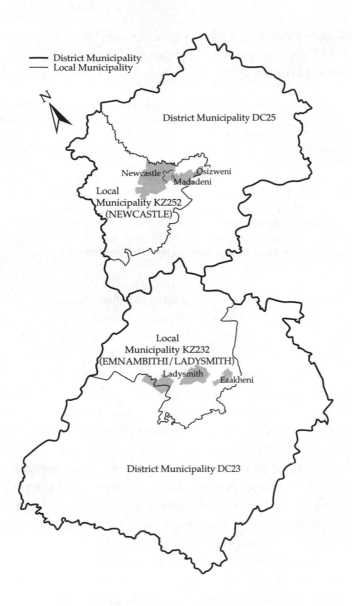

Map 4   New local government demarcations, 2000.

tions. A revealing statement by Nkosi Mpiyezintombi Mzimela, chair of the House of Traditional Leaders, staked out the position of the *amakhosi* in the following terms in August 2000:

> Rural people do not want democratically elected municipal structures. They prefer to keep the status quo of regional councils. The government is taking the amakhosi back to the heyday of apartheid, using the demarcation board. The constitution does not state that traditional leaders will be abolished, but the new demarcation act states clearly that there will be elected mayors and councillors, even in rural areas where chiefs still call the shots. The backbone of traditional leaders is communal land and if municipalities are introduced in the traditional authorities, that would be the end of the birthright of the amakhosi. Our people will have to prepare whatever means to defend the rights of the traditional leadership if the proposed demarcation areas are implemented in rural areas and the constitution is not amended. (Article entitled 'Chiefs threaten boycott of local polls,' www.star.co.za August 19, 2000)

A month later, the same spokesman demanded that 'the Constitution be amended to separate tribal authorities from urban municipalities and for them only to be linked through regional councils.'[26] On October 2, 2000 the government announced the appointment of a Joint Technical Committee to review the roles and functions of municipalities on the one hand, and traditional leaders on the other.[27] Shortly after that, President Mbeki assured traditional leaders that their concerns would be accommodated, and appealed to them 'to ensure that polling went ahead peacefully, and that people could exercise their right to vote freely.'[28] On November 17, the government set forth draft legislation amending the Municipal Structures Act to provide for the retention of a range of powers and functions by traditional leaders, but the parliamentary local government committee immediately withdrew it on grounds that it was unconstitutional – much to the outrage of traditional leaders.[29]

By late November, the threat by *amakhosi* to boycott local elections seemed likely to materialize. On December 1, a mere four days before the elections, Deputy President Jacob Zuma and Minister of Provincial and Local Government Sydney Mufamadi met with senior representatives of the *amakhosi* and came to an agreement over a statement of intent that made huge concessions to traditional leaders. These concessions were not made public, but they reputedly entailed significant representation and full voting powers for the *amakhosi* on District Councils – a move that flies in the face of the constitution and would require a constitutional amendment. Shortly after the elections, there were reports that President Mbeki and the cabinet had rejected the statement of intent (*Sunday Times* December 12, 2000), and as I write the question of the powers and functions of traditional authorities remains unresolved. What the statement of intent accomplished, however, was that the local government elections went forward with full participation of the *amakhosi* who, particularly in KwaZulu-Natal, instructed their subjects to go to the polls and vote for the IFP. The *amakhosi*, in turn, had been summonsed to an *imbiso* (gathering) in Durban the weekend before the elections by the IFP leadership.

At stake in the local elections was far more than the seemingly mundane matters of local government, or even the new structures of local democracy. First and foremost the elections represented a test of the Mbeki presidency, along with the broad policy thrust of the ANC government, as well as its performance in service delivery. Pervading and further enlarging these stakes was the question of race, driven in part by the formation of the Democratic Alliance (DA) from the National Party and the Democratic Party. Under the leadership of Tony Leon – whose earlier and deeply personalized clashes with Thabo Mbeki over issues of racism had become legendary – the DA embarked on a series of attacks on the ANC far more aggressive than anything seen before in post-apartheid politics. Holding the ANC directly responsible for job losses, crime, and poverty, the DA's campaign promised jobs for all, a tough clamp-down on crime and, quite significantly, free anti-retroviral drugs – a direct attack on Mbeki's deeply problematic stance on the HIV/AIDS epidemic. Signifying this broader struggle, the vast majority of the campaign posters bore images of either Thabo Mbeki or Tony Leon. Most political experts dismissed the IFP as a relic of an archaic rural past.

There is something profoundly moving about elections in post-apartheid South Africa. In April 1994 I reclaimed my South African identity and voted in the Oakland City Hall in California, but the 2000 local government election was the first I had experienced within the country. Each polling station was equipped with simple cardboard voting booths bearing the blue insignia of the Independent Electoral Commission (IEC), and each voter received a semi-indelible mark on his or her left thumbnail as a mark of participation in the exercise of citizenship before receiving a set of ballot papers and a pencil with which to make crosses.[30] Coming as it did in the vortex of dispute over the US presidential elections, the seeming simplicity of this electoral process was particularly compelling. That I was unable as a 'non-resident' to participate was dismaying, and I was painfully aware for days afterwards of my unblemished left thumbnail. I spent the morning of election day going to different polling stations in Ezakheni where lines of people waiting to cast their ballots in the blazing sun were typically very long. IEC officials invited me into the school and church rooms where the voting was taking place, and I was able to observe the calm determination with which large numbers of Ezakheni residents exercised their right to vote. As soon as IEC officials heard that I live in the US, we engaged in joking exchanges about how South Africans are far more skilled at running elections than Americans. In the afternoon I went to Watersmeet (Ward 15), a densely populated rural area to the west of Ladysmith, where ANC election monitors – some of them wearing their party T-shirts inside out – asked that I use my rental car to transport elderly and disabled people to the polling stations. Lines of voters were shorter there, but the officials with whom I met attributed this to the time of day.

When the national results were finally in, the ANC emerged with 59 percent of the vote – considerably less than the 66 percent it garnered in the 1999 national election, but only marginally below its 60.3 percent in the 1995/96 local government elections. The DA took 22 percent of the vote – notably more than the combined totals of the Democratic Party and the National Party in the 1999 national elections, but only slightly above the combined performance of the two parties in the 1995/96 local elections.[31] The IFP captured only 9 percent of the vote nationwide, but its gains in KwaZulu-Natal over the 1999 election results were substantial.

As significant as the vote itself was the pattern of turnout. In the country as a whole only 48 percent of registered voters went to the polls, compared with 84 percent in the 1999 national elections – although roughly similar to the 1995/96 local elections. Apparent gains by the DA relative to the ANC were primarily a reflection of racial differentials in turnout: only 42 percent of black voters went to the polls, while 57 percent of white voters cast ballots. What seemed to have happened, as a number of observers pointed out, was that relatively large numbers of voters felt let down by the ANC, but could not bring themselves to vote for the DA.

Prior to the elections, ANC activists in both Ladysmith and Newcastle were confident that they would sweep the polls. Their reactions, as the results emerged, were of profound shock. In the expanded Ladysmith municipality, the ANC failed to gain a majority – pulling in 46 percent of the total vote, not very far ahead of the IFP's 40 percent which, together with the DA's 12 percent resulted in an IFP-DA coalition that took power following the elections in the expanded Ladysmith municipality. Results in Newcastle were nothing short of a disaster for the ANC, which scraped a mere 33 percent of the total vote in the newly demarcated municipality, compared with 44 percent for the IFP and 18 percent for the DA. Minority parties in Newcastle earned over 4 percent of the vote, more than twice the proportion of those in Ladysmith. In aggregate terms, both Ladysmith and Newcastle appeared as intensified instances of the national shift away from the ANC as well as the resurgence of IFP support in KwaZulu-Natal.

A more finely grained and disaggregated examination of election results in the two places suggests a far more complex and interesting set of forces at play. Especially revealing are patterns of voting for ward candidates. Particularly in Ladysmith – and to a lesser degree in Newcastle – the gains of the IFP relative to the ANC took place in newly demarcated rural wards, where the turnout was also relatively low. Yet there is sufficient variation in the results among different rural wards to suggest that there is a lot more going on than just the overwhelming power of the *amakhosi* – a point to which we shall return later. What is clear, though, is that the new system of demarcations, and the ANC's limited capacity to reach into predominantly rural areas, played a major role in the party's inability to achieve a majority.

If one zooms in on the ward results in the urban townships in Ladysmith and Newcastle, a striking pattern jumps out: the ANC was, in fact, remarkably successful in Ezakheni, attracting nearly 70 percent of the vote with turnouts well above the national average. In Madadeni, the pattern was precisely the opposite.

For comparative purposes the results in Ezakheni and Madadeni are especially significant, both because the ward demarcations are similar to

Table 7.3   Voting patterns in Ezakheni and Madadeni wards.

	Ezakheni (Ladysmith)	Madadeni (Newcastle)
ANC	68.8	38.9
IFP	24.8	47.0
DA	1.8	9.6
Other parties	4.6	4.5
Total	100	100

Source: www.iec.org.za (Election Results 2000)

those in the 1995/96 elections discussed earlier in this chapter, and because the two townships were classified in the same category ('type a' townships) under apartheid. In Ezakheni, the ANC won all seven wards. Of the nine wards in Madadeni, the ANC took only three and the IFP the other six. IFP officials in Newcastle were reputedly stunned by their unexpected victory – although in many wards the results were quite close. Yet the IFP was not alone in gaining on the ANC in the Newcastle townships. In addition, the DA captured nearly 10 percent of the vote – a powerful indication of the disillusionment of township voters with the ANC.

To a degree that I found almost startling when they first appeared, results of the 2000 elections in Ladysmith and Newcastle encapsulate the dynamics traced throughout the book – both prior to the 1996 local elections, and what has unfolded during the interim phase of local government restructuring. In drawing this chapter to a close, I would like to reflect on their broader significance.

New Geographies of Power

> Boundaries are drawn by mapping practices; 'objects' do not pre-exist as such. Objects are boundary projects. But boundaries shift from within; boundaries are very tricky. What boundaries provisionally contain remains generative, productive of meanings and bodies. Siting (sighting) boundaries is a risky practice. (Haraway 1991: 201)

In a vivid and concrete way, the new demarcations and the elections that gave life to them exemplify Haraway's astute observations about boundary projects. The metaphor of a kaleidoscopic twist is perhaps too static to capture the generative processes and reconfigurations of power set in train by the formation of new municipalities, but it does convey the rapid emergence of new patterns. While the election results in Ladysmith and Newcastle reflect quite directly the processes traced throughout this book, they also provide new and unexpected twists. Three of these patterns of continuity and contingency are particularly important in illuminating possibilities as well as limits.

First, while the divergent ward-level results in Ezakheni and Madadeni provide powerful confirmation of the efficacy of participatory local democracy, they also warn against simplistic celebrations of 'social capital.' Seemingly mundane matters as local government finance are in fact deeply entwined with the exercise of power, the construction of political identities, and the forms and practices of local democracy. We saw, for example, how the Newcastle townships erupted in anger and resentment when newly elected councilors, under pressure from municipal bureaucrats, voted for large increases in service charges; and how the costly effort to break the boycott and 'win hearts and minds' through a local version of Masakhane was as singularly unsuccessful as its national counterpart. That a comparatively high proportion of residents of Ladysmith townships were willing to pay much lower service charges reflects different power dynamics through which civil society and the local state have constructed one another. These dynamics were palpably evident in the open budget meetings. From one perspective these encounters between township residents and local state officials could be seen as key sites for the production of consent. Yet the critical intensity with which participants in the meetings held local officials' feet to the fire suggests that such consent is conditional, precarious, and must be constantly renewed and recreated.

From these and other contrasts between the two places, it might be tempting to argue that levels of social capital are far higher in Ladysmith than in Newcastle. Drawing on his research in the Indian state of Kerala, Heller (1996) makes the important point that social capital is the *product* of political mobilization. I would go further to suggest that divergent dynamics in Ladysmith and Newcastle need to be understood relationally as ongoing *processes* – involving the constant making and remaking of what Roseberry (1996) calls common material and meaningful frameworks for living through, talking about, and acting upon social orders structured in dominance. What was happening in the Ladysmith open budget meetings, I suggest, was not just the production of trust or even consent, but intense plays of power in which the *terms* of consent were being renegotiated, along with a recreation of township dwellers' sense of themselves as political actors in relationship to elected officials as well as to local bureaucrats. Central to this process was the way words, images, and symbols were being deployed to define the terms and terrain of contestation.

The performatively brilliant power plays staged in the Ladysmith open budget meetings speak directly to broader debates, and perhaps have the potential to help reshape them. Of particular significance was the way township dwellers were pressing demands for urban services in the language of rural rights, and invoking histories of forced removals to drive home these claims. These histories went far beyond personal loss and hardship to address much broader issues of dispossession. A number of speakers drew attention to the much lower cost of living in surrounding rural areas that had managed to resist dispossession, contrasting how their own lives had become commodified, and stressing how any increase in service charges would be an impossible burden. They also made clear that the apartheid state had promised them basic amenities when they were moved into the township; how, they demanded, could the new government renege on those promises? That township residents articulated their concern over the prospect of rising service charges in terms of experiences of dispossession is undoubtedly a reflection in part of a specific regional history. Yet as a way of staking claims for economic and social justice, this theme of dispossession has the potential to resonate far more broadly. In the following chapter I suggest how East Asian trajectories could be deployed to support such claims, and call into question the 'natural' status of dispossession.

Yet there is also a twist. While the 2000 election results in the Ladysmith townships reflect empowered local democracy and accountability, they also reveal the dangers of parochialism. An instructive case is a settlement known as St Chads, located on land formerly owned by the Anglican church directly adjacent to Ezakheni, in which the IFP won – much to the dismay of ANC activists who had presumed that the majority of St Chads residents would vote their way. Under the interim demarcations, St Chads was excluded from the Ladysmith municipality, despite its location between Steadville and Ezakheni. In the second half of the 1990s, St Chads residents received little, if anything, in the way of material improvements other than a few boreholes and pumps. On many occasions, when driving into Ezakheni, I recall seeing women and children walking along the side of the road pushing wheelbarrows loaded with plastic water containers on their way to and from the boreholes. Yet all the houses in adjacent Ezakheni had running water. What made the lack of running water nearer people's homes in St Chads all the more inequitable and unjust is that the pipes bringing water to Ezakheni actually run through St Chads. During the transitional period, provincial and national representatives of the ANC in Ladysmith argued strongly that local resources should be deployed to improve access to water in St Chads. This initiative was, however, stymied by a block of ward councilors adamantly opposed to resources being channeled away from their constituents. In short, empowered local democracy coincided with parochialism – an example perhaps of what David Harvey (1996) would call 'militant particularism' – and cost the ANC dearly in the 2000 local elections.

The second more broadly significant aspect of the election results turns around the politically charged character of struggles over LED. We have seen how both places are deeply connected with transnational centers of accumulation, and represent precisely the pattern of export-oriented FDI upon which GEAR is predicated. In both places these FDI-led local growth strategies have proven socially explosive, with intense workplace struggles carrying over into – and indeed reconfiguring – both the form of the local state and its relations with civil society. The intensity of struggles on the factory floor derives not only from relatively low wages and poor working conditions, but also the way racial, ethnic, and gendered forms of difference are produced along with material commodities. In their convoluted passages from the workplace to pressures on the local state, these struggles sparked by LED have transmuted into much broader demands for social security.

Yet these links have been forged in quite different ways in Newcastle and Ladysmith. Chaotic political dynamics in Newcastle include the historical weakness of industrial unions; Eddie Liu's efforts to take over the local state to secure the conditions of accumulation; how this in turn contributed to the unexpected victory of the ANC in the 1996 local government elections; the way white local bureaucrats were able to overpower township councilors and push through huge increases in service charges in the townships; and the almost total boycott of payments that ensued.

In Ladysmith the sequencing of linkages between LED strategies and redistributive demands has been quite different, as has their political character. They include the long-standing alliance between highly organized labor and youth movements that helped ensure a large ANC victory in the 1996 local government elections; the engagement of ANC councilors with promoting Mainland Chinese investment; the ensuing tensions with key industrial unions as well as with working-class constituencies in the townships; the way tensions between organized labor and ANC councilors crystallized around GEAR and reverberated in the Local Economic Forum; and how, by the late 1990s, key industrial unions were planning to embark on a strategy of constituting a broad new political base around the social wage, building in part on township residents' fears of increasing rates and service charges in the townships, and forging connections between townships and surrounding rural regions.

These struggles intensified in the period leading up to the 2000 elections, and helped to propel the results in both places – but again with some significant twists. Most spectacularly, Eddie Liu abandoned the IFP in Newcastle and was welcomed into the ANC, on the expectation that he would at last become mayor! Invoking Taiwanese experience and expertise, he promised to help solve unemployment and fight crime by fostering rural development. A key question is how this mutually opportunistic move shaped the elections results. Following the 1996 local elections, as we saw earlier, interviews that Phelele Tengeni and I conducted with township residents suggested strongly that the IFP's embrace of Eddie Liu had helped win the election for the ANC. Although I do not have any direct evidence of how township residents interpreted his shift to the ANC in 2000, it seems very likely that the electoral price tag for the party was quite high.

Connections between LED and political dynamics in Ladysmith took a different, but equally interesting twist in the period leading up to the elections. When I returned to South Africa in May 2000, the industrial unions had abandoned their plans to launch an oppositional agrarian strategy and had thrown in their lot with the ANC. 'We are, after all, part of the alliance,' one union official explained to me, going on to speak with great enthusiasm about how the new demarcations would enable rural residents to lay claim to resources concentrated in urban centers like Ladysmith where rural-based workers earned and spent their money. 'It's their money,' he claimed, 'and now they will be able to get some real development.' For Ladysmith-based ANC activists, the industrial unions' rural connections appeared as a particularly valuable resource.

Yet the unions were unable to deliver a sufficiently large chunk of the rural vote to win a majority of wards in the newly demarcated Ladysmith municipality. In the post-election stock-taking, a senior unionist living in one of these rural communities called attention to how broader political-economic forces, along with ongoing job losses in the local economy, undermined the campaign for the ANC. He described how, in August 2000, union representatives and shop stewards had returned from their national conference angry and frustrated with the ANC government over what he revealingly and repeatedly called 'this GEAR thing' – 'this thing' being the euphemism widely used to refer to HIV/AIDS. Not only were they – and he – fed up; they also felt 'empty' towards the ANC, making it difficult to mobilize enthusiasm. At the same time, rurally-based workers were apprehensive about their jobs, angry about ongoing retrenchments, and had not experienced any of the improvements to which township residents had enjoyed access. In addition, he claimed, there were large numbers of retrenched workers living in surrounding rural communities who placed direct blame on the ANC for job losses, and steadfastly refused to vote for the party.[32]

This brings us to the third issue – namely the broader implications of new local government demarcations that effectively dissolve rural-urban boundaries. In general terms, the election results in KwaZulu-Natal made clear the ANC's limited reach into these more rural regions. It may be tempting here to invoke Mamdani's (1996) notion of decentralized despotism, and view these divisions in terms of a battle between 'the rural' and 'the urban' over the existence and future of the bifurcated state. Yet decentralized despotism is too blunt and static an instrument to come to grips with the diverse and changing configurations of social forces in predominantly rural regions. There was, for example, sufficient variation in election results in predominantly rural wards surrounding Ladysmith and Newcastle to suggest that there is more going on in these places than just the overwhelming power of the *amakhosi*.[33] Whether and how the national-level dispute over the role and functions of traditional leaders is resolved will obviously be important in shaping how local processes unfold in future. Even so, there remain endemic tensions, contradictions, and instabilities within the local state, such that struggles over tradition and custom will almost certainly overlap and intertwine with struggles over extremely scarce material resources, no doubt in locally specific ways.

As the rural-based unionist cited above pointed out with great clarity, new demarcations open up significant new possibilities for rural residents to stake claims on urban resources. Unless the volume of resources allocated by the central government to local authorities expands rapidly and substantially, the probabilities are extremely high that tensions between township and rural residents will escalate.[34] In short, there may well be an impending battle between 'the rural' and 'the urban,' but it extends well beyond decentralized despotism to encompass the contradictory imperatives of the local state in this era of neoliberal globalization.

CHAPTER 8

Enabling Alternatives
Re-Envisioning the Future

> The study of how 'situations' should be analyzed, in other words how to establish the various levels of the relations of force, offers an opportunity for an elementary exposition of the science and art of politics – understood as a body of practical rules for research and of detailed observations useful for awakening an interest in effective reality and for stimulating more rigorous and more vigorous political insights. (Gramsci 1971: 175–176)

LETTING GO OF this study has been difficult. Each time I returned to Ladysmith and Newcastle in the second half of the 1990s, I was confronted with new twists and turns in local political dynamics. Some were quite predictable – at least in retrospect – but many were not, propelling me into new arenas of complexity and a growing appreciation of local contingency, but also impelling confrontation with additional layers of historical determination and connections with wider arenas. What made completion of this study possible was the new system of municipal demarcations, and the local elections in December 2000. By then it was clear that this remapping of the local state represented a crucial turning point in the processes I had been following since 1994, defining at least a temporary point of closure for what remains a work in progress – as well as a vantage point from which to reflect on the wider significance of this work, and how it might be helpful in thinking about the future.

In this final chapter I re-engage with the idea of multiple trajectories of socio-spatial change, drawing attention both to how I have made use of this concept throughout the book, and to the political stakes. The chapter unfolds in three parts. First I return to the broader argument about why popular and academic discourses of globalization are so disabling, and how the concept of multiple trajectories of socio-spatial change reconfigures underlying assumptions so as to enable fresh understandings and encourage practical action. I also spell out more fully how intensive historical and ethnographic studies grounded in particular places can do broader critical work. The political stakes in these understandings are twofold, each closely linked with the other. They represent an effort to transcend the antinomy between economism and voluntarism – between, as Michael Burawoy (1985) put it, the economism that only one thing is possible, and the voluntarism that anything is possible. The concept of multiple trajectories of socio-spatial change offers a way of grappling with the question of limits and possibilities: of recognizing that room to maneuver is always present, but never unconstrained. It is also, very importantly, a way of thinking about the politics of alliance: of the possibilities for defining broad constellations of shared or compatible interests, and mobilizing social forces across a wide spectrum while also recognizing irreducible differences.

The second part of the chapter draws out the larger implications of the specific connections between East Asia and South Africa traced in this book. In the vast oceans of global capital, flows of industrial investment from East Asia to South Africa amount to no more than a few droplets. Yet the diverse *forms* in which they have taken hold, and the power-laden practices that have shaped them, contribute directly to dissolving economistic models of globalization and to disrupting neoliberal orthodoxy. They also thrust land and agrarian questions to the forefront of attention, along with the relationships between production and the conditions of reproduction of labor. This move, in turn, underscores the need to go beyond an exclusive focus on 'global cities' as the privileged site for discerning the contradictory dynamics of global capitalism, and to attend to the contemporary salience of histories of agrarian transformation.

In the third and final section of this chapter I put these arguments to work in engaging with debates about the possibilities for redistributive social justice in South Africa, and the formation of new alliances to press for social change. These debates assume particular urgency and salience in the context of intensifying poverty and inequality that are undermining the promises of democratic citizenship, while also provoking growing discontent. In his pessimistic assessment entitled 'Cry for the Beloved Country,' John Saul – a long-time and astute observer of conditions in South Africa – speaks of the sad dénouement of South Africa's mass democratic movement, 'a movement that in its march to victory promised so much more in terms of sustaining positive social purpose and releasing social possibility' (Saul 2001: 33). Yet, as Hein Marais (1998) has pointed out, this 'victory' was far from unalloyed. In addition, while it is difficult to disagree with Saul's claim that the ANC is constructing its hegemonic project on the altar of the marketplace, the altar itself is shot through with cracks and fissures that call for close attention. Without question, though, a yawning chasm has opened up between the promise of liberation from the malignant apartheid state and the harsh reality of the neoliberal post-apartheid order – a chasm that heightens the stakes in grasping the slippages, openings and contradictions in neoliberal capitalism, and in defining alternatives.

The analysis in this book makes several related contributions to how we think about a project of enabling alternatives, in South Africa as well as more generally. First, I have called attention to the importance of the local state as a key terrain on which some of the most intense contradictions of the neoliberal post-apartheid order are taking shape. At the same time, the sharply divergent trajectories of socio-spatial change in Ladysmith and Newcastle in the first phases of local government restructuring highlighted both the possibilities opened up by a highly organized and mobilized civil society, as well as the limits imposed by multi-layered forces that have come into conjuncture in these places. Second, the East Asian connections not only underscore the ongoing significance of histories of racialized dispossession in shaping the conditions of reproduction of labor. They also suggest how the land questions might be disarticulated from agriculture and individual restitution claims, and re-articulated in terms of the moral and material imperative for a social wage.

More generally, a focus on multiple, interconnected trajectories of socio-spatial change encourages attention to how emancipatory alternatives might be prefigured within already existing capitalisms. At the same time, this sort of approach sounds strong warnings against any sort of abstract, idealized definition of alternatives. It also points to the limits of conceiving alternatives simply or primarily in terms of institutional design or legal forms. Insistent attention to situated practice and the exercise of power means that *any* alternative must be firmly grounded within existing material and cultural conditions. It must, in other words, work with the ruins of the past, recognizing particular historical geographies not just as the site of causal explanation, but also as Mariane Ferme (2001: 227) puts it, 'as a source of particular forms – symbolic, linguistic, practical – that social actors deploy to rework anew the social fabric in response to contingent events.' The challenge then is how to forge connections and alliances across arenas of social practice and spatial scales – a challenge that compels attention to multi-layered and interconnected articulations and trajectories that have gone into the making of what has come to be termed 'globalization.'

Disabling Neoliberal 'Globalization'

A central premise of this book is the importance of understanding 'globalization' *both* in terms of intensified processes of spatial interconnection associated with capitalist restructuring, *and* as a set of discourses through which knowledge is produced. Discourses and processes of globalization are inextricably – indeed dialectically – connected with one another, and deeply infused with the exercise of power. Precisely because the categories and discursive strategies that we use to describe processes have real effects – defining and delimiting terrains of practical action and the formation of political identities – discourses of globalization actively shape the very processes they purport to describe. The discursive power of globalization is most clearly evident in practices of meaning-making that portray neoliberal forms of capitalism as natural, inevitable, and beyond question.

Neoliberal discourses of globalization operate through the dualistic logic of what I call the 'impact model,' typically framed in terms of the impact of 'the global' on 'the local.' A series of other dualisms then map onto the global/local dichotomy, resonating with and reinforcing one another. Running through the dichotomous logic of the impact model are three closely related elements that render it so disabling. First is an abstract economism that conjures up disembodied technology and markets as the key driving forces. Second are understandings of time as an active force and space as a passive container. Third, and encompassing both of these, is a core-centric 'global-centrism' that accords active primacy to 'the global.' Like all dualistic constructions, the impact model is deeply gendered. Thus 'the global' becomes equated with an active, inexorable set of technological and market forces restlessly roving the globe, while 'the local' appears as the passive feminine recipient of these forces that must make itself as attractive and glamorous as possible to lure capital and technology. Within overtly prescriptive neoliberal discourses these gendered images are often accompanied by a sort of economic Darwinism, in which export-oriented, low-wage production forms the lowest set of rungs on a predetermined evolutionary ladder that 'backward' societies – or elements within them – must ascend in an orderly fashion, or risk sinking into the abyss of what Castells (1996) calls a 'fourth world' of racialized marginalization.

There are, of course, a plethora of critiques of neoliberal globalization, as well as a variety of efforts to develop alternative understandings. Yet as we saw in Chapter 1, a number of these critical formulations of globalization – both economic and cultural – concede either explicitly or implicitly to disabling elements of the neoliberal impact model. Thus, for example, understandings of economic globalization cast in terms of time-space compression or a space of flows eclipsing a space of places effectively endorse 'the global' as the site of active primacy. Even more ironically, conceptions of cultural globalization often rest implicitly on an a-spatial economism in which deterritorialized technological and market forces are taken as given.

In short, my argument about the 'impact model' is *not* simply that it is 'false,' but rather that it is a thin, one-sided abstraction that is deeply disabling. The central concern of the book turns around the question of what is entailed in more politically enabling understandings? The answer I suggest is an analytical framework centered on the idea of multiple trajectories, understood *not* just as capitalism taking different or path-dependent forms in different places, but as spatially interconnected sets of situated practices – with their associated discourses and power relations – that actively *produce* the processes we call 'globalization.'

What is so crucial and potentially enabling about the conception of spatiality (or space-time) derived from Lefebvre is that it forces attention to power-laden practices in the multiple arenas of everyday life. It enables us to move beyond defining globalization in disembodied terms such as speed up, time-space compression, spaces of flows and the like. Instead, the focus shifts to situated everyday practices, their spatial interconnec-tions, and the changing forms of spatial organization of social relations, where those social relations are full of power and meaning, and where social groups are very differently placed in relation to this reorganization (Massey 1994: 156). It also directs our attention to the multiplicity of historical geographies, not simply as the *effects* of global flows but rather as *constitutive* of them.

Lefebvrian ideas of the production of space form the foundation of politically enabling conceptions of globalization. Yet it is also important to recall the point made in Chapter 1 about how these basic concepts of spatiality can – and have – been taken in significantly different directions. At the risk of oversimplifying a complex and diverse body of theorizing one can, I think, identify a central tension between those who insist on radical contingency and openness, and those who focus far more explicitly on the spatial contradictions of capitalism. This tension between contingency and structure is most clearly evident in sharply divergent conceptions of the meaning and significance of geographical difference. The former tendency represents an effort to introduce explicitly spatialized understandings into post-Marxist conceptions of radical democracy derived from Laclau and Mouffe (1985). A central concern among those who adhere to this view is that 'recognizing a true spatiality necessitates recognizing a greater degree of difference and a different kind of difference' (Massey 1999b: 32) – thus holding open the possibility of alternatives, and precluding the violence of closure. The opposing position – broadly framed in terms of uneven capitalist development – views geographical difference as produced through the differentiating powers of capital accumulation and market structures. From this perspective, the political imperative is to 'go beyond particularities to emphasize the pattern and the systemic qualities of the damage being wrought across geographical scales and differences' (Harvey 2000: 81).

The concept of multiple trajectories of socio-spatial change represents an effort to steer a course between these two positions, while recognizing both of their insights and contributions. It does so by combining Lefebvrian conceptions of the production of space with understandings of praxis that trace their descent from Marx via Gramsci, and attending as well to elements of feminist and post-colonial thinking. From the Gramscian lineage I have taken a rejection of economism, while holding on to the materialist premise that historically and geographically specific configurations of economic forces and relations set the conditions of existence for other practices. I have also taken a conception of politics and power as operating in multiple, interconnected arenas; the idea that hegemonic articulations are crucial in the production of political subjects; but at the same time an insistence on understanding hegemony as an ongoing process that must be constantly renovated and renewed, and that always contains slippages, contradictions, and openings. From Lefebvre I have taken a relational conception of space (or space-time) as actively produced through everyday, situated practices that are simultaneously material and symbolic; how spatiality is central to the exercise of power; and an understanding of capitalist dynamics as encompassing not only the capital-labor relation, but also land and nature. I use the term *trajectory* as a sort of mid-level concept designed to capture quite concretely the idea of ongoing processes of socio-spatial change, produced through situated, spatialized practices in the multiple arenas of everyday life at different spatial scales.[1]

What is vitally important about geographical difference from this perspective is its potential capacity to illuminate *both* structure and contingency. It is perhaps useful here to recall Gramsci's eloquent warning about the twin dangers of economism and voluntarism:

> A common error in historico-political analysis consists in an inability to find the correct relation between what is organic and what is conjunctural. This leads to presenting causes as immediately operative which in fact only operate indirectly, or to asserting that the immediate causes are the only effective ones. In the first case there is an excess of 'economism' or doctrinaire pedantry; in the second, an excess of 'ideologism.' In the first case there is an overestimation of mechanical causes, in the second an exaggeration of the voluntarist and individual element ... The dialectical nexus between the two categories of movement, and therefore of research, is hard to establish precisely. Moreover if error is serious in historiography, it becomes still more serious in the art of politics, when it is not the reconstruction of past history but the construction of present and future history which is at stake. (Gramsci 1971: 178)

Profoundly mindful of the difficulties and dangers of such an exercise, I have tried to put the idea of multiple trajectories of socio-spatial change to work in tracing some of the contours of what Gramsci termed 'the terrain of the conjunctural.' While focusing on a specific set of processes in post-apartheid South Africa and following connections to East Asia, I have also sought to contribute to broader critiques of neoliberal 'globalization' and to discussions about the possibilities for alternatives.

In coming to grips more concretely with questions of structural constraints and conjunctural possibilities, I have deployed a methodological strategy of what I call relational comparison to distinguish it from positivist models as well as Weberian ideal-types. Instead of starting with a presumption of pre-existing bounded entities – whether spatial, social, or individual – a relational approach attends explicitly to ongoing *processes* of constitution. This processual understanding, in turn, is grounded in a theory of praxis that asserts the inseparability of situated practices and their associated meanings and power relations. Drawing on Massey's (1994) useful reinterpretation of Lefebvre, a relational strategy of socio-spatial comparison entails a concept of spatiality that views place not as a bounded unit, but as dense bundles of social relations and power-infused interactions that are always formed out of entanglements and connections with dynamics at work in other places, and in wider regional, national, and transnational arenas. It is also attentive to structure in the sense of historically and spatially sedimented processes of what Williams (1977) called the setting of limits and the exertion of pressures. The concept of multiple trajectories and the strategy of relational comparison entail insistent attention to economic forces, relations, and the dynamics of accumulation at different levels or scales. Yet this approach refuses to read political interests and identities off economic structures, or to reduce race, gender, ethnicity and other dimensions of difference to class processes. Instead it demands relentless attention to how material economic practices, power relations, and the production of meaning and difference constantly play upon one another.

In addressing questions of difference, I have drawn on the concept of articulation – understood in an extended sense as joining together of diverse elements and the production of meaning through language – while also attending to the material and cultural conditions that shape articulatory practices, and are in turn reconfigured by them. The comparative histories of Ladysmith and Newcastle show how racial, ethnic, and gendered forms of difference are produced in relation to one another in locally specific ways, and how the politics of production and processes of class formation more generally are deeply intertwined with the production of difference. We also saw how political interests and identities were forged through power plays and struggles in interconnected local arenas, as well as through very different forms of connection to other places and to dynamics originating at other spatial scales, and how they assumed significantly different forms in seemingly similar places. In short, larger political-economic forces and discourses did not simply descend upon passive places. Rather they were actively reworked and reconfigured in ways that would have been difficult – if not impossible – to predict or read off structural conditions.

That class processes operate *through* race, ethnicity, and gender emerged with even greater clarity in Chapters 5 and 6, which traced how Taiwanese forms of production diverge in different contexts. These relational comparisons showed clearly how racial, ethnic, and gendered forms of difference are inextricably linked with practices and processes of class formation; and how these articulations both express and reconfigure multi-layered, historically specific and spatially sedimented forms of power. Rather than just the *products* of uneven capitalist development, locally specific articulations of race, ethnicity, gender, and other dimensions of difference with class are more usefully understood as *constitutive processes* through which political subjects are made, and that actively shape and inflect diverse trajectories of socio-spatial change and forms of accumulation.

The relational comparisons of decentralized industrialization in East Asia and South Africa also disclose how diverse practices and processes of accumulation have their own at least partial autonomy that cannot be read directly off either the logic of capital or the differentiating powers of market structures, and that refuse to be aligned in a linear, Eurocentric story of capitalist modernity (cf. Massey 1999b: 32). These processes provide partial yet powerful illustrations of the distinctively 'non-Western' capitalist and post-socialist modernities that have gone into the making of 'globalization.' They also radically undermine the evolutionary logic of the impact model and, as we shall see later, are deeply disruptive of neoliberal orthodoxy.

While vividly illustrating the co-existence and constitutive character of difference, these divergent trajectories warn strongly against claims of radical contingency. Far from endless openness and diversity, they compel attention to locally and regionally specific forms of struggle, *and* to the multi-layered structural limits and constraints within which they operate, and of which they are a part. What emerges, in other words, are structured contingencies – sets of situated practices that are contingent on what is already there, which is itself the outcome of previous processes.

Yet they also make clear the inadequacies of understandings that insist we transcend such 'particularities' to emphasize the overarching logic of capital, and interpret geographical difference in terms of the uneven consequences of neoliberal globalization. The rationale behind this insistence is the imperative to recognize the powers of capital to 'fragment, divide, differentiate, absorb, transform, and exacerbate ancient cultural divisions' (Harvey 2000: 40). Thus, Harvey goes on to argue, 'it is precisely in such localized contexts that a million and one oppositions to capitalist globalization also form, crying out for some way to be articulated as a general oppositional interest' (Harvey 2000: 81). The key to constituting such a movement, in this view, lies in exposing the systemic qualities and commonalities of the depredations wrought by global capital accumulation.

Clearly the question of how dispersed oppositional practices can cohere more broadly is crucial. Yet there are vitally important practical as well as analytical reasons why this emphasis on transcending the fragmenting powers of capital is important but insufficient, and why attention to both structure and contingency, and to the constitutive character of difference is essential. They have to do with both the formation of alliances and with defining alternatives.

If one refuses to allow that gender, race, ethnicity, and other dimensions of difference can simply be stripped away to reveal the gleaming bare bones and commonalities of class interests, the challenge becomes how to form political alliances that recognize multiple forms of difference, while also emphasizing the need for solidarities. Whether and how alliances can be forged depends crucially on how particular articulations have taken shape historically in particular socio-spatial contexts, and on how they are understood. As Stuart Hall has pointed out, 'We can think of political situations in which alliances could be drawn in very different ways, depending on which of the different articulations in play become the dominant ones' (Hall 1985: 111). A recognition of the complexity and spatial diversity of articulations of difference warns strongly against any simple presumption of alliance. Yet it also opens up the possibility of re-articulations of interests, political subjectivities, and social relations that are grounded in existing conditions and understandings, but take them in new directions. Recognition of difference as constitutive also bears directly on the possibilities for linking struggles in different arenas, places, and across spatial scales.[2]

The possibilities I suggest in this book entail focusing on historically specific forms of so-called 'primitive accumulation' as *ongoing processes* (as opposed to distant events), intimately linked with the material and political conditions of reproduction of labor. In the South African and East Asian contexts with which I am concerned, sharply divergent trajectories of agrarian transformation bring out very clearly the inextricable connections between capitalist (and post-socialist) forms of industrial production and the reproduction of labor, as well as the centrality of gender and other dimensions of difference in shaping these trajectories. Far from just 'particularities,' the insights yielded by these relational comparisons and connections are simultaneously analytical and political. In addition to foregrounding histories of redistribution and dispossession, they disrupt and denaturalize neoliberal orthodoxy in ways that extend beyond claims about East Asian 'developmental states.' In the context of post-apartheid South Africa, they open up possibilities not only for redistributive claims, but also for re-articulations of interests and the formation of broader alliances to press for these claims.

South African/East Asian Refractions

> **Refract** . . . deflect (a ray of light etc.) at a certain angle when it enters obliquely from another medium . . . (*The Oxford Encyclopedic English Dictionary*)

A central concern of this book has been to engage key post-apartheid debates through the prism of post-war East Asian historical geographies, but in ways distinctively different from models, miracles, or well-worn debates over the market versus the state. Instead, I have taken as one starting point the question of how highly competitive East Asian capitalists – who have driven one of the most spectacular episodes of industrial accumulation in modern history – inserted themselves into the racial geographies of peripheral regions of South Africa. I have followed a group of Taiwanese industrialists along transnational circuits, focusing on how they refashioned their strategies and everyday practices of accumulation as they relocated to northwestern KwaZulu-Natal and then, with the help of Hsing (1998), tracing other Taiwanese industrialists to small towns in southern China. Drawing mainly on the work of others, I have also made brief excursions to towns and villages in other regions of China where collectively owned industries have mushroomed from the soil of the socialist past.

Dramatic differences in the forms and dynamics of Taiwanese and Chinese industries in semi-rural regions of East Asia and South Africa disclose the multiplicity of meanings, practices, subjectivities, plays of power, and historically specific structures and articulations that go into the making of material commodities. These forms and practices of accumulation are not only diverse. Their very diversity is also richly and mutually revealing of the circumstances from which Taiwanese industrialists emerged; of the already existing conditions they encountered in different places in South Africa; and of how their presence played into profound, often unintended, transformations of these places – yet in ways that retain the powerful imprint of multiple and multi-layered historical geographies.

From one perspective, the dispersal of labor-intensive industries to predominantly rural regions of Taiwan, China, and South Africa – and indeed many other parts of the world – since the mid- to late 1970s can be seen as a manifestation of overaccumulation of capital, intensified competition, and falling profit rates in established urban industrial centers. Essentially this is a story of uneven capitalist development, emphasizing capital's inexorable and unending search for a spatial fix. On a very general and abstract level, as I have argued in earlier chapters, it carries greater analytical bite than alternative interpretations. What is crucially missing from this story, though, are precisely the diverse forms, dynamics, and distributional outcomes that have emerged so clearly from this study. These are not simply a reflection of passive variations in local conditions on to which mobile capital has latched. Instead, they have been forged through active, ongoing, and changing processes of class and non-class struggles in multiple, intersecting arenas within and beyond industrial workplaces.

Accounts from South Africa and East Asia have also brought into sharp focus the centrality and contemporary salience of historically specific paths of agrarian transformation; their sharply divergent trajectories; and the multi-layered forms of power through which they have taken shape – including, very importantly, how ongoing productions of racial, ethnic, and gendered forms of difference are inseparably linked with class processes.

Part of what is so significant about the East Asian histories of agrarian transformation and rural industrialization outlined in Chapter 6 is that they represent rapid industrial accumulation *without* dispossession. These histories not only disrupt teleological narratives of a linear, universal trajectory of capitalist development. They also compel attention to the intense power struggles through which these trajectories of agrarian transformation have taken shape. The neglect of agrarian questions in narratives of post-Second World War developments in East Asian political economies really is quite remarkable. While land reforms in Japan, South Korea, and Taiwan in the late 1940s do on occasion appear in these narratives – usually in order to explain relatively egalitarian paths and/or the elimination of the landlord class – these land reforms are typically presented as yet another exemplar of the omniscient, relatively autonomous developmental state. Notably missing is the link to peasant mobilization in Mainland China in the 1930s and 1940s, and official fears of peasant uprisings elsewhere in East Asia as major forces behind land reforms.

When the history of peasant struggle and mobilization in China and its regional reverberations are accorded a more central role, narratives about East Asian development/s acquire new meaning and political significance in relation to South Africa. Re-envisioning East Asian trajectories in terms of the forces that drove land reform and other redistributive measures throughout the region provides a stark and dramatic contrast with histories of dispossession in South Africa. This shift in emphasis not only propels apartheid-era dispossession and its historical antecedents to the forefront of attention. In addition, as we saw in Chapter 6, East Asian trajectories of agrarian transformation speak directly to South African versions of market/ state debates that have increasingly tended to define dispossession as a natural concomitant of capital accumulation. In other words, by calling into question Eurocentric and unilinear understandings of capitalist develop-ment, East Asian trajectories not only turn the spotlight on South African histories of dispossession, but also render them peculiar and contestable.

These sharply divergent histories of redistribution and dispossession illuminate another dimension that is typically missing from both East Asian and South African debates, as well as narratives of 'economic globaliza-tion': the crucial importance of historically specific configurations of agrarian social property relations and forms of collective consumption in shaping contemporary conditions of global competition. While some observers have called attention to state-sponsored housing in Singapore and Hong Kong in subsidizing industrial wages, there is remarkably little recognition of the role of land in supporting the social wage, and underwriting the massive mobilization of industrial labor elsewhere in East Asia. This point emerged with great clarity from the contrasting conditions in which Taiwanese industrialists found themselves when they moved to South Africa. What renders this contrast particularly ironic is that Taiwan-ese were drawn to South Africa in part by cheap luxury housing, good public schools and medical facilities, and other appurtenances and infra-structures of racialized class privilege that they are using to educate their children as English-speaking global citizens capable of forging yet further transnational connections. Yet on arriving in South Africa, Taiwanese industrialists confronted a workforce stripped of subsistence guarantees, and heavily reliant on commodified forms of livelihood. In a further ironic triangulating twist, we saw in Chapter 6 how Taiwanese industrialists who moved to China have been able to take advantage of – while also running down – the massive social investments set in place under communist rule.

Connections between relations of production and the conditions of reproduction of labor can, however, assume entirely different forms. In certain
localities in China where collectively owned township and village enterprises have taken hold, some of the profits have been plowed back into
schools, hospitals, and other forms of collective consumption. Whether and
how this happens, though, depends crucially on local political dynamics.

In short, broadly based structures of agrarian property relations and
forms of collective consumption – themselves the embodiment of locally
specific past and ongoing struggles – define the social wage, and have been
crucial in shaping forms and processes of decentralized industrial accumulation in key regions of East Asia *and* South Africa. That relatively
labor-intensive Taiwanese – and more recently mainland Chinese – forms
of production explode when grafted onto South African conditions derives
at least in part, I suggest, from the troubled histories of dispossession that
have produced severely eroded social wages for the large majority of South
Africans on the one hand and, on the other, highly concentrated forms of
property, wealth, and privilege.

Before we move on to explore how these insights might contribute to
struggles for social change in South Africa, let me clinch my earlier claim
about their capacity to disrupt neoliberal nostrums. During the 1990s,
forces emanating from East Asia punctured two large holes in the edifice of
the neoliberal Washington Consensus: irrefutable evidence of the substantial involvement of East Asian states in the economy, and recognition of the
damage wrought by unfettered capital markets following the Asian 'crisis'
that erupted in 1997 (Hart 2001). In this study I have challenged another
key tenet of neoliberal orthodoxy – one which holds that low-wage export
production forms the lowest set of rungs on an evolutionary ladder that
'economically backward' societies must ascend in an orderly fashion,
biting the bullet of low wages and oppressive labor conditions. The ladder
itself is constituted through foreign direct investment, supposedly lured in
by restraints on government spending, high interest rates, and favorable
exchange rates.

In practice, as a number of critics have pointed out, foreign capital
drawn in by these measures is far more likely to be volatile portfolio
investment than directly productive investment. The relational comparisons
of rural industrialization in South Africa and East Asia carry this critique a
step further. By illuminating the connections between production and the
conditions of reproduction of labor, they call attention to the historically

specific – and deeply gendered as well as racialized – processes and practices that have shaped what are, in effect, sharply divergent trajectories of labor-intensive forms of industrialization. They also underscore how the East Asian 'cases' that neoliberal proponents invoke in support of their evolutionary claims are sharply at odds with the evolutionary model. Instead, they represent distinctively non-Western forms of accumulation, effectively underwritten by massive redistributive reforms driven originally by Mao's mobilization of the Chinese peasantry in the first part of the twentieth century.

Historically constituted connections between production and the conditions of reproduction of labor also have a direct bearing on contemporary questions of redistribution and social protection more generally, along with the political impulses that underpin them. It is important to recall here Karl Polanyi's (1944) exposition of what he called capitalism's 'double movement.' The unleashing of markets for labor, land, and money, Polanyi maintained, wreaks profound havoc and generates counter-tendencies and demands for intervention and social protection. Far from the counter-movement representing some sort of external intervention in an inexorably unfolding teleology, these opposing tendencies are contained *within* capitalism. By the same token, the conditions for global capital accumulation must be actively created and constantly reworked. Key questions (on which Polanyi was somewhat agnostic) concern the social and political forces through which the counter-movement is constituted in any particular historical-spatial conjuncture, and how these opposing tendencies play out – or are fought out – within and across multiple, interconnected social and spatial arenas.

The most spectacular contemporary manifestations of the double movement are, of course, the anti-globalization protests that sprang to life in Seattle at the end of 1999 to oppose the depredations of global capitalism.[3] Yet even before Seattle, we saw the emergence of conservative redistributive impulses aimed at enabling the neoliberal project to move forward. An influential statement of this position was Dani Rodrik's book *Has Globalization Gone too Far?* (1997) in which, in true Polanyian fashion, he points to social pressures unleashed by global economic integration. Noting that social spending has in the past had the important function of buying social peace, Rodrik calls for state intervention 'to provide social insurance and thereby foster stability in the new global economy' (Rodrik 1997: 67). Precisely this sort of revisionist neoliberalism is now ascendant in the World Bank in the guise of 'social development' and 'social capital' (Hart 2001). There are close affinities between this sort of revisionist neoliberalism and 'third way' social democracy that is currently quite influential at high levels within the ANC.

The arguments I am making about the connections between production and the conditions of reproduction of labor could, of course, be accommodated quite easily within this sort of technocratic and institutionally conservative social democracy to argue for wage subsidies and other forms of redistribution aimed at containing dissent. Yet, as I will now try to show, they can also be deployed in support of a more radically transformative vision of social change.

Re-Articulating the Future? Post-Apartheid Possibilities

> A crisis occurs, sometimes lasting for decades. This exceptional duration means that incurable structural contradictions have revealed themselves, and that, despite this, the political forces which are struggling to conserve and defend the existing structure itself are making every effort to overcome them. These incessant and persistent efforts ... form the 'terrain of the conjunctural', and it is upon this terrain that the forces of the opposition organise. (Gramsci 1971: 178)

Part of what is so difficult about writing a book like this is that events overtake one's own analytical efforts. As I was drawing the manuscript to a close in July 2001, a deeply significant land dispute erupted at Kempton Park on the East Rand between Johannesburg and Pretoria when the Pan African Congress (PAC) 'sold' plots of land on Bredell farm, a dusty 32,000 ha stretch of land jointly owned by Transnet, Eskom, and two individuals described as farmers, for R25 (just over $3).[4] According to press reports some 7,000 claimants put down their money, and within hours thousands of rudimentary shelters started springing up at Bredell. The day before I had driven through this area *en route* from Pretoria to Johannesburg airport, and was struck – as I had been many times before – by the huge swaths of empty land.

The event provoked a national uproar, in which the specter of Zimbabwean land invasions was widely invoked, along with intense critique of the opportunism of the PAC by ANC government officials, the opposition Democratic Alliance, and the popular press. ANC officials moved swiftly to arrest some 300 of the 'squatters' and those collecting money, and calm the fears of prospective international investors. Television broadcasts carried images, eerily reminiscent of the apartheid era, showing heavily armed police pushing people into armored vehicles, while others who had evaded arrest declared their defiance of the state. Other vivid images include Housing Minister Sankie Mthembi-Mahanyele beating a hasty retreat as angry settlers shouted '*hamba! hamba!*' (go away), and Land Affairs Minister Thoko Didiza declaring on television that 'when foreign investors see a decisive government acting in the way we are acting, it sends the message that the government won't tolerate such acts from whomever.'

In a dramatic way, the land struggles at Bredell and their wider reverberations exemplify a central theme running through this book: the moral and material imperative for redistributive social justice, and the centrality to this imperative of histories and memories of racialized dispossession from the land. The book began by sketching out key dimensions of a regional colonial history of dispossession, and then traced how locally specific and divergent forms of acquiescence and opposition to apartheid-era dispossession played a formative role in shaping political dynamics in relocation townships. From here we followed the sharply different character of both the youth movement and the labor movement in the two places, and the relationships between them. We saw as well how these locally specific configurations of social forces and dynamics carried over into – and indeed defined the character of – the post-apartheid local state, and how histories and memories of dispossession are directly and indirectly implicated in key arenas of struggle that are likely to intensify with the new system of local government demarcations. The links with East Asia, and contrasting trajectories of dispersed industrialization, also brought the land question to the fore. In short, land and dispossession form major threads that wind their way through each of the chapters and tie them all together. When the land dispute erupted at Bredell, the arguments I had been piecing together over the years sprang suddenly to life.

Immersed at the time in the hard labor process of bringing closure to this book, I was moved by these events to set the manuscript aside and produce an article on the larger significance of the land occupation for the national *Sunday Independent*.[5] What follows, then, is the product not only of seven years of research, but also a sense that events at Bredell represented a crucial conjunctural moment – a moral crisis of the state, one that laid bare the systemic tensions and contradictions of efforts to construct a hegemonic project on the basis of neoliberal capitalism in conditions of profound inequality.[6] It embodies as well a sense that this episode marked a key turning point in the trajectory of post-apartheid society. As Patrick Bulger put it in his far more poetic companion piece to my own in the same issue of the *Sunday Independent*, 'These badlands – with giant concrete water coolers on the horizons, rusting fence posts standing without purpose, a lone horse here and there, troupes of ragged scavengers picking what nutrition they can from last season's mealie [maize] fields – are an unlikely setting for a battle over land that, in its own small way, could yet have a bearing on South Africa's future political direction out of all proportion to its size.'[7]

Most immediately, this battle exposed land issues as a vulnerable flank in the ANC's armory of state – a reflection, in part, of the historic neglect of agrarian questions more generally by the liberation movement. Part of the problem, as we saw in Chapter 6, lies in the disjuncture between how dispossession has been romanticized in terms of individual restitution claims, while in practice land policy has been extremely technocratic (Walker 2000). It has also been narrowly focused in terms of agriculture, with a miniscule budget. These problems intensified in 1999, when the minimally redistributive Settlement and Land Acquisition Grant gave way to a scheme to develop a black commercial farming class that had not even started in July 2001. Essentially this scheme represents the agrarian counterpart of black empowerment – but in conditions in which agriculture has become increasingly competitive.

Bredell also dramatized the lack of organized social forces on the left around the land question. Discontent over land issues had been simmering for some time prior to the Bredell occupation of July 2001, punctuated by episodes of violence. Yet apart from NGOs with an explicitly rural orientation, organized political movements around the land question were conspicuously absent at the time of the Bredell episode. COSATU policy documents made mention of the land question, but neither organized labor nor a range of other movements had engaged substantively with land issues or sought to link them more broadly.

One of the main thrusts of my *Sunday Independent* article was that Bredell exemplified not just the shortcomings of land reform or even housing provision, but the systemic crisis of livelihood associated with the collapse of formal employment, and the palpable failure of neoliberal macro-economic policies on their own terms. As the Brazilian activist and intellectual Roberto Unger has observed, the neoliberal project is inherently unsustainable, particularly in the context of profound inequalities:

Carried to the hilt, it produces massive unemployment . . . and accelerates internal dualism: the division of the country between a minority of beneficiaries and a majority of victims. More generally, it leaves government without the resources and capabilities with which to invest in either people or infrastructure. As social needs go unattended, bottlenecks in the production system begin to build up. Moreover, the draconian policy may prove self-defeating by sapping the very confidence it was designed to inspire, as domestic and foreign investors begin to expect future political trouble from present social unrest. (Unger 1998: 57)

Yet the character and substance of such 'social unrest' is crucial to any project to define alternatives to neoliberalism.

What catapulted the Bredell incident into national prominence was not only the invocation of Zimbabwe, but also the involvement of the PAC, a party with a minimal political base whose role in the post-apartheid era had, until this point, been extremely marginal. The PAC's involvement in the land occupation probably was indeed highly opportunistic, as a number of critics pointed out, and far more a reflection of its own disorganization than any coordinated political strategy. Yet in flouting property rights and encouraging takeovers of apparently unused land, the PAC was simultaneously tapping into deep veins of morality, history, memory, and meaning, as well as the depth and intensity of poverty and inequality. In the process, it not only exposed deep and growing discontent. It also dramatized land issues as a key potential site of counter-hegemonic struggle singularly lacking organized social forces, yet widely available as the basis for mobilization that could move in significantly different directions.

Within existing structures and conditions, several possibilities present themselves. One is ongoing land occupations driven not only by the PAC, but also by various forms of authoritarian patronage. As in Bredell, such moves are almost certain to elicit hard line reaction from the state. Second, coming out of Bredell, it seems possible that a coalition within the state will step up some sort of land and perhaps other forms of redistribution through technocratic measures, but seek to depoliticize rumblings from below.

Realistically the chances appear slim for a broadly based democratic movement that could move society in new directions.[8] Yet the stakes are sufficiently high, and the contradictions of the neoliberal post-apartheid order sufficiently intense, that this question assumes a particular urgency. As Hein Marais has argued, the formation of this sort of coalition is not just a matter of reviving the national democratic movement that fought for the end of apartheid, but of reconfiguring a new set of social forces with an explicitly transformative perspective. It also entails forging connections and alliances across multiple arenas of struggle in different socio-spatial contexts.

In drawing to a close, I would like to make some concrete suggestions about how the analysis contained in this book might contribute to the formation of a broad alliance along these lines. First is the need to delink the land question from agriculture and individual restitution claims, and re-articulate it in terms of the moral and material imperatives for redistributive social change and livelihood guarantees. Second, I want to underscore the importance of the local state as a key terrain for political action on which concrete alliances must be forged and extended. The two sets of arguments are closely related to each other, and to the larger critique of neoliberal globalization.

First let me spell out more fully the proposal to delink land issues from agriculture and individual claims, and connect them to broader national discourses of citizenship rights and redistributive imperatives. Precisely because it is so deeply imbued with history and meaning, both moral and material, the land question in South Africa has the potential to become a key articulatory principle capable of both joining together and giving expression to a series of linked claims and demands around redistributive social change. The East Asian connections traced in this book provide a means not only for denaturalizing racialized dispossession, but also framing it in broader and more collective terms than just the restitution of property to former landowners – a process that excludes the millions evicted from white-owned farms, as well as former tenants of African landowners. In addition, by dramatizing the historically constituted and varied connections between production and the conditions of reproduction of labor, the East Asian connections are powerfully suggestive of how histories of dispossession might be transmuted into claims not only for land, but also for a social wage and livelihood guarantees.

This reformulation, in turn, holds open the possibility for a wide array of social forces to unite behind redistributive demands. Whether and how organized labor might participate in such a movement is crucial. In response to the ongoing implosion of formal sector jobs, COSATU has waged a series of campaigns predicated on a critique of GEAR. Yet organized labor's position has been severely compromised by a series of constraints, including its rearguard defense of shrinking employment, as well as its inclusion within corporatist arrangements and the ANC Alliance. A number of rank-and-file unionists have, however, been active in a second key set of struggles over rising service charges, electricity and water cutoffs, and the privatization of municipal services. In different localities these oppositional movements are assuming increasingly organized forms.[9] As Ferial Haffajee noted in an article in the business-oriented *Financial Mail* in mid-2001, 'The protests are small, but what they signify is that ANC supporters can't be taken for granted and that hardship will push poor people into protest.'[10] The Treatment Action Campaign formed to confront the state's deeply problematic position on the HIV/AIDS pandemic constitutes another significant arena of political action, as does the small but active anti-globalization movement. A fourth key set of struggles focuses on the imperative for a minimum income. Indeed, the day before the Bredell episode, a coalition consisting of COSATU, church groups, and the South African National NGO Coalition or Sangoco presented proposals for a basic income grant of R100 ($12.50) per person per month.

My *Sunday Independent* article of July 8, 2001, immediately following the Bredell land occupation, was partly an effort to suggest how those engaged in a range of struggles in different arenas could possibly use the wider resonances of the land question as an articulatory principle to connect more closely with one another (Appendix). In the following issue of the *Sunday Independent* (July 15, 2001), Ari Sitas and I proposed what we called our 'eleven theses on what can be done,' published under the less flamboyant title 'Decisive Redistribution Urgently Needed' (Appendix). We intended this article as a provocation, aimed at dislodging national debate from land questions narrowly defined. Instead, we insisted that the debate be extended to encompass a broader critique of claims that 'there is no alternative' to neoliberalism. While acknowledging fiscal and other constraints, we sought to offer a series of concrete suggestions about how resources could be re-allocated in more progressive ways. Our purpose in focusing on the imperatives of livelihood was to extend redistribution debates beyond welfarist definitions to address the conditions of access to productive resources.[11]

Land issues and disputes not only offer a key point of leverage into national debates over neoliberal globalization, and a potential principle of articulation through which a series of movements opposed to neoliberalism might connect with one another. They also resonate powerfully with another major theme of this study: the vital significance of the local state as a terrain of practical action. I am emphatically *not* invoking 'the local' as the pre-eminent site of social capital or of grassroots mobilization and resistance against 'the global.' On the contrary, *both* versions of the 'new localism' derive from deeply problematic conceptions of power and spatiality, as well as misbegotten notions of civil society. In place of these romanticized readings of local democracy, I am asserting the importance of the local state in terms of what Gramsci called 'the terrain of the conjunctural' – namely, as a particularly significant site on which the contradictory imperatives of the neoliberal post-apartheid order are being constituted and fought out in everyday practice.

We have seen how, in conditions of fiscal austerity and within the racialized spaces inherited from the past, the ruling bloc at the center has assigned to the 'developmental local state' major responsibility for securing the conditions of both accumulation and the reproduction of labor. At the same time, the local state is officially invoked as the originary site of participatory democracy. Yet these structural contradictions have been constituted and inflected very differently, even in seemingly similar places, through overlapping struggles in multiple arenas, both local and translocal. The relational comparisons between Ladysmith and Newcastle and their adjacent townships brought out very clearly how the gendered and racialized politics of production in industrial workplaces both reflects and reconfigures struggles in other arenas. They also illuminated the locally and regionally specific articulations and translocal connections through which local political dynamics in the two places have moved in different directions, as well as the limits and constraints that they share. The local state, in short, is not only the site of key contradictory forces; it is also deeply revealing of both structural constraints and conjunctural possibilities.

Primary among these possibilities are deep connections between the crisis of the local state and histories of racialized dispossession. Memories and meanings of dispossession sharpen and intensify the tensions between neoliberal austerity and managerialism on the one hand, and democratic impulses on the other. A vivid illustration of these tensions – as well as their political possibilities – came from the Ladysmith participatory budget meetings, in which township residents insistently staked their claims for urban resources in the language of rural rights. Similar sentiments of (in)justice fed into the fury with which residents of Newcastle townships reacted to the sharp increase in service charges. Locally specific but related demands and reactions are suggestive of how a broader strategy to re-frame the land question and histories of dispossession in terms of a social wage and livelihood guarantees might resonate across struggles in different places, and help them to connect with one another and cohere more broadly.

The analysis in Chapter 7 also sounds strong warnings about the complexity of such a politics of alliance – particularly in the context of the new system of municipal demarcations that has effectively dissolved rural-urban boundaries. While expanding opportunities for residents of impoverished rural regions to lay claim to material rights, the new demarcations also increase the likelihood of intensified struggles over scarce resources. New demarcations, in short, intensify the contradictions inherent in the local state, and carry with them the danger of new sources of division along rural-urban lines. At the same time it is vitally important to recognize that they also hold open the possibility of new alliances, and of forging connections across arenas of struggle and registers of difference to constitute new social forces to press for redistributive social justice and alternatives to neoliberal capitalism.

This combination of possibilities and dangers defines an important dimension of the challenge confronting the left in South Africa today. On a more general level, it also speaks to the possibilities and limits of the anti-capitalism movement. The enormous breadth of the movement, as Sam Gindin (2000) has pointed out, is both its strength and its weakness. He goes on to observe that, in order to sustain its momentum and move beyond largely symbolic attacks on global capitalism towards implementing an alternative vision, the new politics will have to develop its oppositional foundation locally without narrowing its goals.

Although strongly endorsing this position, I also want to reiterate the dangers of uncritical invocations of 'the local' together with related presumptions that the nation state is on its last legs. One of the central arguments of this book – namely the importance of understanding the local state as a key conjunctural site – applies, I suggest, not only in South Africa but also more generally. Inherent within many forms of neoliberal capitalism is the devolution to the local state of responsibility not only for securing the conditions of accumulation and reproduction of labor, but also for shouldering an important part of the burden of manufacturing consent. Yet the relative power, mobility, and lack of accountability of capital renders this hegemonic project increasingly difficult. There is, in short, a profound spatio-structural instability at the heart of neoliberal capitalism, which is part of what defines the local state as a key conjunctural terrain, shot through with slippages, openings, and possibilities.

While these structural contradictions broadly define the importance of the local state in this era of neoliberalism, they do not in any way determine the character and forms of struggle, or the formation of political subjectivities – which, as we have seen, are in practice enormously variable. It is for precisely this reason that any strategy to mobilize broadly based support must be firmly grounded in particular configurations of material and cultural conditions, and engage directly with specific local histories and translocal connections, as well as with meanings, memories, and the making and re-making of political subjects.

Postscript and Acknowledgements

> Going 'out' to the field now sometimes means going 'back,' the ethnography becoming a 'notebook of return to a native land.' In the case of the diasporic scholar, the 'return' may be to a place never known personally but to which she or he ambivalently, powerfully 'belongs.' (Clifford 1997: 208)

This book represents a much larger political and personal re-engagement with a society to which, as Clifford puts it, I ambivalently yet powerfully belong. In 1971 I left my native South Africa, convinced – like many other white South African students of my generation at that bleak moment – that apartheid and capitalism were mutually reinforcing and that, as we would go around muttering, 'if you can't be part of the solution, don't be part of the problem.' I moved to the United States where I did a PhD, became involved in research in Southeast Asia, and taught at Boston University, the Massachusetts Institute of Technology, and the University of California at Berkeley.

On the morning of February 2, 1990, when I awoke to the news that the South African government had unbanned the ANC and other political parties, my life changed decisively. Through much of the 1970s and 1980s, at least in principle, I had bracketed off my research in Asia from my US-based political activism around South Africa. In practice, I was increasingly aware that these spheres of my life were deeply entangled in ways that seemed largely irreconcilable. During the magical days of early February 1990, when Nelson Mandela and other political prisoners were released and fundamental social change in South Africa suddenly seemed possible, I envisaged bringing these disparate pieces of my life together, combining research, political commitments, and activism in a seamless whole. Things have, of course, turned out to be far more complicated – both in terms of social change

314

in South Africa, and my own understandings of the relationships between research and political commitments.

My initial return to South Africa at the end of 1990 made powerfully concrete the limits on social change; the ambiguities of research in the post-apartheid context where politics no longer revolved around the anti-apartheid struggle; and the tensions in my own position as a product of class and race privilege whose birth more or less coincided with that of apartheid. Immediately upon arrival in Johannesburg, I boarded a bus and literally went home to the site of my upbringing in the northern suburbs. In place of the bougainvillea hedge stood a 10-foot concrete wall topped with broken glass. The house that had figured so prominently in my memory was being rebuilt as a windowless fortress. A guard allowed me to go in, and I went from room to room trying in vain to locate familiar spaces. All that was recognizable was the squeak of an old closet door that had not yet been ripped out. The rage I experienced at the time encompassed both the larger system that had produced this hideous transformation, and a deep sense of personal loss. In retrospect, the irony of this multi-layered reaction has become painfully clear. If, as Visweswaran (1994) suggests, ethnographic work should be combined with 'homework' – defined as critical confrontation with the often invisible processes of learning that shape us as subjects, and questioning of unexamined points of privilege and blindness – my own confrontation with 'home' was particularly dramatic, concrete, and intense. It decisively shattered any vestigial nostalgia acquired during my years in self-imposed exile. It also reshaped in profound ways my sense of self, and underscored the ambiguities of re-engaging with the land of my birth – and of doing so through research.

Just over a month later I attended a Conference on Women and Gender in Southern Africa that took place at the University of Natal, Durban. As the first large-scale conference on gender to be held in the region, the organizers saw it as a forum for consolidating feminism as a political force in the new dispensation, and for forging creative new connections between theory and practice. In fact, the conference exploded in a series of bitter conflicts along every imaginable axis of difference. As a simultaneous insider and outsider, I became increasingly aware of the historical depth and extent of the multiple overlapping conflicts being played out in the Durban conference and, at the same time, of how an absence of nearly 20 years placed limits on my capacity to grasp the sub-texts of these debates. Like many other white academics, I came away from the conference disabused of romantic notions of action research in the new South Africa. Suddenly uncertain about whether or how I might engage in research, I clearly needed to reflect and regroup.

Fortunately, two institutional connections helped me work through these processes. First, I was invited to help establish an exchange program between the University of Durban-Westville (UDW) and the University of California (UC) Berkeley, and to teach in a newly established masters degree program at UDW. The early 1990s was a particularly difficult and confusing period in South Africa, punctuated by episodes of state-sponsored violence, crises in the negotiation process, and intense jostling for position. My own oblique transnational position with academic bases both in Berkeley and Durban gave me vantage points from which to work out how to relate to this rapid reconfiguration of social forces. It also helped me rethink my insider-outsider status and, if not to come to terms with being stretched across the world, at least to become more practiced in the negotiations entailed in living and working transnationally. In retrospect, it is hardly surprising that I chose a research topic concerned with questions of transnationalism.

My other key relocation was into the Geography Department at UC Berkeley, where I became more closely associated with exciting new thinking and research in critical human geography that spoke vividly to the questions and experiences with which I was grappling. Some of the key ideas, discussed in greater detail in Chapter 1, derive from Henri Lefebvre's *The Production of Space* (1991), originally published in 1974 in the wake of the student-worker uprising in Paris. They include the inseparability of space and time; a conceptualization of space not as a passive backdrop but as actively produced through everyday practices and struggles that are simultaneously material and symbolic; and a concept of place not as bounded enclosure, but as constituted through multiple relations and connections. These seemingly abstract claims in practice offer considerable analytical and political purchase into the questions of socio-spatial change that animated this study.

I started this research in June 1994, in the afterglow of the extraordinary national election that brought the ANC to power. There was, of course, plenty of reason for pessimism. Most obviously, the negotiated settlement had left intact many of the older configurations of power. It was also evident that the forces of national and global capitalism would press heavily against the goals of redistributive justice. Even so, in those heady post-election days it was difficult not to get caught up in an optimistic excitement about the transformations underway in South Africa. Once again, things have turned out more complicated and constrained – and the stakes in how we understand and grapple with these constraints are extraordinarily high.

My research spanned the first six years of the post-apartheid era, culminating with the second local government election in December 2000, and extending into 2001. For reasons explained in the Introduction, I decided to work in Ladysmith-Ezakheni and Newcastle-Madadeni, two former white towns and adjacent black townships in northwestern KwaZulu-Natal, about halfway between Durban and Johannesburg. Between 1994 and 2000 I spent part of every year in these seemingly out-of-the-way places. As I hope to have conveyed in the book, they provided extremely valuable vantage points from which to engage with the reworking of South African society from the ruins of the apartheid past, as well as key points of connection into wider regional, national, and transnational sites and processes.

Indeed, this book is the product of transformations and reworkings at every possible level, a necessarily partial effort to illuminate one of the great social experiments of our time.

* * *

In the pivotal meeting described in the Introduction, Ezakheni councilors and activists posed the crucial question of who was funding and sponsoring my research. In the initial phases, I enjoyed generous financial support from three sources: a research and writing fellowship from the MacArthur Foundation; a research grant from the Geography and Regional Science Program at National Science Foundation; and the Jill Nattrass Memorial Fellowship at the Centre for Social and Development Studies (CSDS) at the University of Natal, Durban. CSDS also provided me with valuable logistic support, access to an excellent library, and a stimulating environment. Over the years I received additional funding from the Committee on Research at UC Berkeley, including the Chancellor's Opportunity Fellowship.

While based at CSDS I was fortunate to make contact with Alison Todes, and we quickly discovered our closely overlapping interests and concerns. During the first two years of this project (1994–95) we worked collaboratively in Newcastle, sharing the pleasures and vicissitudes of fieldwork. In addition to companionship I benefited tremendously from her insights and knowledge, and many of the arguments in this book owe a great deal to Alison's powerful grasp of the relationships between production and the conditions of reproduction of labor.

My other key collaborative relationship has been with Phelele Tengeni, a political scientist at the University of Zululand, to whom I also owe enormous gratitude. We worked very closely together in 1996 in Newcastle and Ladysmith in the period immediately following the first local government election. At this crucial moment in post-apartheid history, Phelele taught me a great deal about local political dynamics, as well as the history of forced removals. She and her mother Christine Mabaso welcomed me into their home in Madadeni, and Phelele inserted me into networks of relationships that profoundly shaped the subsequent course of my research.

Hundreds of men and women in the towns and townships contributed their time and insights over the course of this project, and it is impossible to express my thanks to them all individually. Clearly this book could not have been written without their generosity, and I am deeply grateful. There are, however, several people whose role has been so central in shaping my understandings that I must pay explicit tribute to them – while of course taking full responsibility for the interpretations (and misinterpretations) I have placed on their contributions. With infinite wisdom, patience and modesty, Alfred Duma helped me to appreciate the larger significance of his participation over many decades in the struggle for liberation, and the meaning of local democracy in practice. He also comforted me through the death of both my parents in 1998. In addition to friendship, feedback, and support, Lizzie Shabalala and Mbuso Khubeka gave unstintingly of their extensive experience, and pushed me to confront the complex interplay of local, provincial, and national political dynamics. My profound thanks to all of them.

Government officials in a wide array of departments at municipal, provincial, and national levels have been unfailingly helpful and courteous over the years, as have members of parliament and those running independent commissions. Yunus Carrim and Mike Sutcliffe warrant special mention for their ongoing willingness to accommodate my needs and engage in stimulating discussions despite extremely busy schedules. At crucial points along the way, they guided me through the intricacies of local government restructuring, and allowed me to accompany them to key functions and take advantage of their expertise – although, as with those in Ladysmith and Newcastle whose help was so essential, they bear no responsibility for the uses I have made of it. A number of NGOs and research organizations – including AFRA, the Institute for Democracy in South Africa (Idasa), the National Land Committee, the National Institute for Economic Policy, and the South African National NGO Coalition (Sangoco) – have also provided me with tremendous assistance.

At UC Berkeley I have been blessed with superb research assistants. In the early phases of the project Ananya Roy reviewed and organized huge amounts of bibliographic material, constructed tables, and provided critical feedback. Over the past several years Aaron de Grassi, Sasha Lilley, and Jessica Rhodes carried on this work under the auspices of the Undergraduate Research Assistance Program. This book would not have been possible without their participation. Darin Jensen drew the maps, and I am deeply grateful for his cartographic skill, patience, and good humor. The Institute for Urban and Regional Development managed my grants in the first two years of the project, and since then Natalia Vonnegut helped me keep the financial part of my professional life in order with characteristic competence.

Joint publication of this book by the University of Natal Press and the University of California Press entailed complex negotiations that have been handled with smooth professionalism by publishers, editors and editorial staff at both ends. For this I am indebted to Glenn Cowley and Monica McCormick, as well as Veronica Klipp and Randy Heyman. Sally Hines carried out the substantive editorial work, and I deeply appreciate her intelligent judgement, efficiency, and sensitivity to my concerns. My thanks also to Trevor Makhoba for allowing his powerful painting to appear on the cover.

I wrote and rewrote large chunks of the manuscript at 8a Musgrave Avenue, Durban, a wonderful space created by Costas and Jenny Criticos for migrant academics. Their warmth, wisdom, and hospitality have been invaluable.

The circuits of friendship, intellectual and political engagement from which this book has emerged traverse three continents. Among the many friends and colleagues in South Africa who helped shape my ideas, challenged me, and contributed both directly and indirectly are Ahmed and Rookeya Bawa, Jo Beall, Patrick Bond, Debby Bonnin, Lisa Bornstein, Shirley Brooks, Ben Cashdan, Ben Cousins, Ashwin Desai, Mark Gevisser, Jeff Guy, Adam Habib, Karen Harrison, Phil Harrison, Rob Haswell, Patrick Heller, Dave Hemson, Doug Hindson, Firoz Khan, Meshack Khosa,

Merle and Michael Lipton, Alan Mabin, Xolela Mangcu, Hein Marais, Bobby Mare, Monique Marks, Julian May, I.M. Meer, Shamim Meer, Darlene Miller, Mike Morris, James Murombedzi, Niccoli Nattrass, Lungisile Ntsebeza, Devan Pillay, Laurine Platzky, Greg Ruiters, Abdi Samatar, Jeremy Seekings, Mala Singh, Pauline Stanford, Ann Vaughan, Imraan Valodia, Sheila Weinberg, and Thokozani Xaba. David Moore read the manuscript for the University of Natal Press, and provided incisive and constructive comments for which I am deeply grateful.

Extended discussions of macro-economic issues with Trevor Bell, Bill Freund, and Vishnu Padayachee were indispensable, as was their feedback on key chapters. Vishnu and I have shared many projects and concerns over the years, and his friendship has been extremely important to me. Cherryl Walker gave generously of her extensive knowledge of land issues, and helped me work through central arguments. Jabulani Sithole's innovative historical research on locally specific forms of violence has been formative in my own understandings. Both he and Zanele have been the best of comrades, sharing with me their warm hospitality and powerful insights. I owe a special debt of intellectual gratitude to Astrid von Kotze, who pushed me to convey complex concepts in plain English and make clear the political stakes. Ari Sitas was the first person to read a full first draft, offering much-needed encouragement along with valuable critique informed by his own creative research on closely related topics. Astrid and Ari became in effect my family in Durban, drawing me into their circle of conviviality and suffering through my endless nattering about Newcastle and Ladysmith with good humor. In the course of two very detailed readings, Francie Lund also went far beyond the call of friendship. Combining warm supportiveness with intellectual rigor, she insisted that I strip away jargon and sharpen arguments. I have followed her suggestions as closely as I could, and take full responsibility for the infelicities and lack of clarity that remain.

Colleagues at Berkeley have endured years of my immersion in 'the book,' offering unstinting camaraderie, intellectual stimulus, and emotional support. The long list includes Carol Clover, Elizabeth Colson, Meg Conkey, Kurt Cuffey, Louise Fortmann, Ruthie Gilmore, Michael Johns, Caren Kaplan, Kristin Luker, Aihwa Ong, Nancy Peluso, Isha and Raka Ray, Barrie Thorne, and Dick Walker. Michael Burawoy, You-tien Hsing, Allan Pred, Candace Slater, and Michael Watts read all or parts of the manuscript, providing powerful and constructive comments. Donald Moore has played a central role in this project from its inception, with wonderfully stimulating conversations and close readings of different versions of the text. In an extraordinary exercise of intellectual generosity, Donald, Lisa Rofel, and Sylvia Yanagisako offered collective feedback on the entire manuscript in the final stages that prompted me to restructure key chapters. The book also owes a great deal to many brisk walks up and down Spruce Street with Carol Stack that soothed my soul, lifted my spirits, and sparked my ideas. Sometime in the late 1990s, Jean Lave and I discovered that we were working on convergent projects. Through her own collaborative practices, Jean helped me understand the importance of everyday life and learning. Our friendship has been a pure delight, and her imprint is everywhere in the text. Working with generations of remarkable graduate students has vastly enhanced my own everyday life, and I have learned more from them than they can ever know.

Important contributions to the book have also come from colleagues located beyond my bases in South Africa and Northern California. Prominent among the South Africanists from whom I have gained a great deal during this project are Henry Bernstein, Heinz Klug, Shula Marks, Jenny Robinson, Gay Seidman, and Gavin Williams. While many geographers have shaped my thinking, those whose direct input has been particularly significant include Kevin Cox, Derek Gregory, Linda McDowell, Doreen Massey, Katharyne Mitchell, Gerry Pratt, and Neil Smith. At crucial points along the way, Cindi Katz sustained me with intellectual and moral support along with large doses of humor that helped put things in perspective. Sara Berry's influence was formative in an earlier phase of my work, and it has endured along with her encouragement and insightful comments. I would also like to thank Shahra Razavi and Ruth Pearson for thoughtful feedback on a paper I wrote for the United Nations Research Institute for Social Development. In a detailed critical reading of the manuscript for the University of California Press, Jim Ferguson posed challenges that I found tremendously energizing and productive.

A powerful influence throughout this book is Govan Mbeki, one of the great leaders and intellectuals of the liberation movement, who insisted on the necessity of linking rural and urban struggles. Alfred Duma first told me of his central role in Ladysmith in the early 1950s. Mark Gevisser subsequently explained the importance of this transitional phase in his life, bridging his rural organizing in the Transkei and his urban activism in Port Elizabeth, and coincident with his active participation in the formulation of the Freedom Charter. Colin Bundy's work has also been central to my understandings of the contributions of Oom Gov, as he was affectionately known. Early in 1999 Yunus Carrim helped arrange a meeting with Oom Gov, the details of which remain deeply imprinted in my memory. I subsequently had the privilege of extended discussions with him in Port Elizabeth on each of my visits to South Africa until his death in August 2001. These discussions were central to crystallizing my arguments, and it is with deep respect and affection that I dedicate the book to him.

Hope Hale Davis has played a special role, exhorting me to write concretely, correcting my grammar, and enlivening my life with her encouragement, humor, and sharp political insights. The book will appear as she approaches her 100th year.

The book was made possible by my comrade-in-arms, David Szanton. Apart from emotional support, his intellectual involvement in this book is so deep and extensive that the boundaries of our joint production of it are heavily blurred. David accompanied me on my initial return to South Africa in 1990, and through all the subsequent pleasures and traumas of re-engaging with the land of my birth and living a transnational existence. It seems wonderfully appropriate that, as the book finally draws to a close, we prepare to move into our own home in Durban.

Appendix

The Struggle for Land and Citizenship Rights
By Gillian Hart

(Published in the *Sunday Independent* July 8, 2001 under the title 'Desperate Need for Land Requires a Rethink of Policy')

LAND DISPUTES ON the East Rand this past week are the tip of an iceberg of popular discontent that should send a powerful message to the ANC government, and to South African society generally. Demands for land are not simply about housing, and still less about agriculture. Rather they mark deep frustration at both the nature and slow progress of government policies and programmes. They also convey urgent moral, material, and political imperatives for redistributive social change to secure livelihoods and expand life chances for the majority of South Africans.

While it is easy to invoke the spectre of Zimbabwean land invasions and condemn the illegality of what has happened, we cannot ignore the political and symbolic significance of the events at Kempton Park. For the majority of people in this country, the land question resonates profoundly with histories and memories of racialised dispossession and the meaning of citizenship rights, as well as with the basic material conditions of life. The thousands of people who 'bought' plots for R25 were enacting precisely these understandings.

The moral and material significance of land in South African society underscores the ANC's inadequate approach to land issues since 1994. The problem lies not only with the low priority accorded to land reform as evidenced by the miniscule budget and the snail's pace of settlement of restitution claims. More fundamentally problematic is the narrowly technocratic framing of land reform largely in terms of agriculture. With agriculture becoming increasingly competitive as markets are deregulated, it becomes easy for the ANC to dismiss the land question as a relatively minor matter. Thus, for example, the minimally redistributive Settlement and Land Acquisition Grant was replaced in 1999 by a scheme to develop a black commercial farming class that has yet to get off the ground.

Efforts to claim a plot of land in Kempton Park cannot simply be blamed on the delinquency of the PAC. Nor is it sufficient to invoke the million or so houses that the ANC government has built over the past six years. There remain massive unmet needs, and millions of people cannot cover the ongoing costs of formal housing despite the housing subsidy. The so-called 'land invasion' reflects the systemic crisis associated with the collapse of formal employment and rising service charges that millions of people are simply unable to pay.

In the face of shrinking job opportunities and minimal redistribution, increasing numbers of desperately poor people are cobbling together livelihoods from a multiplicity of sources. These multiple livelihood strategies hinge crucially on a secure home base, and on access to urban areas. That the recent land claims took place in the region between Johannesburg and Pretoria is not surprising. What *is* surprising is that more actions like this one have not happened sooner.

In the absence of other organised social forces coming to grips with the land question, there is a distinct possibility that more such actions will take place in future, and that warlords and other forms of authoritarian patronage will move in to drive these efforts.

The time has come to rethink land questions, delinking them from agriculture, and connecting them to broader demands for livelihood, secure housing, and a social wage. Such livelihood strategies might well include some form of agriculture, but would extend well beyond it. The key question is whether and how a broadly based democratic movement to support expanded livelihoods and citizenship rights could be constituted and forge connections with elements of the ANC/SACP/COSATU Alliance.

There are two key reasons why land should figure prominently in such a movement. First, the history of racialised dispossession forms a moral cornerstone in demands for redistributive social justice. Second, the issue of land compels attention to regionally and locally specific conditions of livelihood and access to resources that are, in practice, extremely varied.

In addition to land claims, we have witnessed intensified struggles on a number of related fronts over the past year. These include opposition to GEAR spearheaded mainly by COSATU, but increasingly taken up by anti-globalisation forces linked to the transnational movement that sprang up in Seattle; escalating protests in many parts of the country over the rising costs of basic services; the emergence of the Treatment Action Campaign to confront the terrible suffering wrought by the HIV/AIDS pandemic; and recent proposals for a Basic Income Grant.

All these movements reflect different dimensions of the same issue: the difficulty of addressing massive poverty within the framework of neoliberal capitalism combined with minimal redistribution. Yet they remain at best only loosely connected. At this point there is a pressing need for these different social forces to link more closely with one another and with receptive elements within the state.

The challenge is particularly profound for organised labour. A full-scale commitment to broader livelihood issues would mean moving away from a rearguard defence of rapidly diminishing formal sector jobs, and incorporation within corporatist arrangements. It would also entail engaging with other social forces on terms very different from those of the largely urban social movement unionism of the 1980s. At the same time, a movement to secure livelihoods is unlikely to succeed without the active contribution of organised labour, and a revival of the democratic practices forged in the labour struggles of the 1970s and 1980s.

The obvious objection to a broadly based livelihood strategy is that 'populist' moves to redistribute income and opportunities will scare away global capital. This narrowly economistic position ignores much useful experience from other parts of the world. Important examples come from different parts of Asia, where a variety of measures to redistribute land and other resources have guaranteed social security, enhanced productive capacity, and directly challenged Thatcherite claims that there is no alternative to orthodox neoliberalism.

South Africa recently passed Brazil as the most unequal society on earth. A successful livelihoods strategy will require a new social pact with privileged elements of South Africa society, predominantly white but increasingly deracialised. Those who command a huge proportion of the wealth of this country need to comprehend that their interests and security would be better served by effective measures to create a more equitable distribution of welfare and well-being, and realise the promises of democratic citizenship.

We cannot of course simply emulate Asian 'models.' A concerted effort to move South African society in new directions will have to build on conditions given by our own past, both positive and negative. Obviously, too, there are constraints imposed by global political economy. Yet the room to manoeuvre is considerably larger than neoliberals would have us believe.

Eleven Theses on What Can Be Done
By Gillian Hart and Ari Sitas
(Published in the *Sunday Independent* July 15, 2001 under the title 'Decisive Action on Redistribution Urgently Needed')

THE VISION OF a new democratic society is under threat. Citizenship alone does not guarantee living rights, and without basic livelihood guarantees the promise of citizenship remains hollow. It should not take an occupation of land by several thousand desperately poor people to bring home to SA society that something is seriously wrong, and that there is an urgent responsibility for serious and decisive action.

We strongly disagree with the claim that, because of globalisation, there are no alternatives to present policies. Clearly there is a pressing need to reconfigure global political economy that requires transnational action, and no single country can find respite in old protectionist measures. Yet even within existing fiscal constraints, we believe that a great deal more could be done to enhance the living rights and life chances of the majority of South Africans.

In the spirit of encouraging national debate and action to achieve the vision of a democratic society, we propose the following eleven theses that seek to address the crisis of livelihoods, ongoing job losses, increasing service charges, and demands for security and a place to call home. Theses 1–4 suggest a set of basic principles, while theses 5–11 make a set of specific suggestions for redirecting resources.

1. Escalating poverty and inequality pose a threat to all. It is in the interests of all South Africans to create new arrangements for decisive redistribution of resources that will both secure basic livelihoods and enhance productive capacity.

2. South Africa has moved faster and further than the highly industrialised countries in acceding to the WTO rules. We need more regulated and responsible forms of engagement with the global economy. In particular, tariffs in key labour intensive sectors must be reintroduced, and only phased out gradually after these sectors have recovered some of the massive job losses of the past few years.

3. The present emphasis on high-tech, high value-added forms of production are at best very partial, and fail to address pressing needs for jobs and other economic opportunities. More attention must be paid to sectors that produce the basic necessities of life, even if their contribution to value added is relatively low. We also need to focus on creative new ways to produce and deliver basic goods and services.

4. The terms and pace of privatisation need to be rethought. Markets in and by themselves provide no automatic guarantee of efficiency and service delivery. By definition, market arrangements are not geared to the needs of the poor. Accordingly, short-term profitability can undermine long-term social viability because the poor are not 'consumers'. In addition, short-term financial gains from the sale of parastatals can impose high social costs.

5. The logic of debt reduction is that the country avoids dependence on international financial institutions. While we support this logic, it is imperative that reductions in the debt be directly linked to productive forms of redistribution. Priority must be given to recent proposals for a basic income grant. In addition we propose that the basic income grant should increase concommitantly with debt reduction to provide people with a basic security net to participate more directly in the economic life of the country.

6. The military budget should be reduced by 5% per annum for the next 10 years, and the reduction should be directed to a comprehensive public works scheme that not only provides jobs but also improves infrastructure.

7. Luxury goods and items of conspicuous consumption should be taxed at much higher rates than at present, and the revenues channelled into supporting and encouraging indigenous creativity and innovation.

8. The provincial tier of parliamentary government presently costs the country some R75 billion per annum. This tier should be drastically reduced, and the savings directed to newly formed and expanded local governments, many of which are starved of resources. Increased revenues to local government would both increase capacity, and enable creative new programmes. One example is a multiple livelihoods land reform that would make available land and basic services close to towns and cities.

9. There needs to be a decisive rationalisation of the tertiary education sector to create one locally relevant and world-class university and technikon system

in each major region of the country, and minimise duplication and wastage. Savings should be directed towards enhancing access to higher education.

10. We should extend significantly the state's rights to expropriate criminal assets from anyone found guilty of serious crime, and release these funds directly to improving the prevention and treatment of HIV/AIDS and poverty-related diseases.

11. Massive state expenditures on private consultants must be slashed. Instead there should be concerted support for non-profit NGOs engaged in service delivery, along with tight measures to ensure performance and accountability.

Notes

Notes to Chapter 1

1. The following quotations capture the language of these warnings: 'The democratic movement and the state must never entertain the notion of voluntarism with regard to economic questions, according to which the concept takes hold that the subjective can assume ascendancy and preponderance over the objective, in violation of the laws of motion governing the objective sphere' (African National Congress 1997: 56); and 'If the democratic movement allowed that the subjective approach to socio-economic development represented by "economism" should overwhelm the scientific approach of the democratic movement towards such development, it could easily create the conditions for the possible counter-revolutionary defeat of the democratic revolution' (African National Congress 1997: 52).

2. See for example Habib and Padayachee (2000) and Fine and Padayachee (2000).

3. Habib and Padayachee (2000) tend at certain points toward this position, although Fine and Padayachee (2000) approximate far more closely to the fourth argument outlined below.

4. For an incisive outline and critique of this position, see Marais (1998).

5. See Bundy (1989) for a succinct review and critique of 'colonialism of a special type.'

6. For a discussion of the history of MERG, see Padayachee (1998).

7. The phenomenon of 'comrades in business'(Adam et al. 1997) is closely linked to white corporate unbundling in the 1990s, along with the privatization and commercialization of state assets. There are also significant historical precedents. Large (English) conglomerates such as the Anglo-American Corporation transferred subsidiary companies to Afrikaners in much the same way soon after the National Party came to power in 1948 (Freund and Padayachee 1998). In addition, as we shall see in Chapter 2, the African bourgeoisie and its close association with the ANC – as well as with the Zulu nationalist Inkatha Freedom Party – has roots in a landowning class that emerged in the nineteenth century.

8. One indication is the remarkable degree to which UK consulting firms are playing a key role in a number of key government departments. Largely undocumented, these ANC links into transnational sites of knowledge and power would undoubtedly make a fascinating research project.

9. For a fascinating account, see Davis-Floyd (1998).

10. While deeply cynical about Asian models, a group of intellectuals in the labor movement quickly embraced a far more glamorous set of models emanating from Europe and the US – namely the so-called Third Italy, and Silicon Valley. For a critique of these models and their theoretical underpinnings in regulation theory and notions of flexible specialization, see Hart (1998a).

11. The most widely available text is the set of *Selections from the Prison Notebooks of Antonio Gramsci* edited by Quintin Hoare and Geoffrey Nowell Smith (1971). See also the recent Gramsci reader edited by David Forgacs (2000).

12. As discussed more fully later, in using a concept of historical determination I specifically reject historicism, or what Dipesh Chakrabarty (2000) calls the 'waiting room' version of history: 'Historicism is what made modernity or capitalism look not simply global but rather as something that became global over time, by originating in one place (Europe) and then spreading outside it' (Chakrabarty 2000: 7).

13. See Li (2000) and Moore (2000) for illuminating deployments of this extended concept of articulation.

14. For a useful exposition of the Althusserian foundations of the concept of articulation of modes of production, see Foster-Carter (1978). Two aspects are particularly important. Articulation always entails relations of dominance and subordination – articulated modes of production are 'structured in dominance.' At the same time, the dominated structure (or mode of production) does not simply collapse into capitalist form, but retains some of its own specificity. The concept of overdetermination is crucial in this respect.

15. The volume edited by William Beinart and Saul Dubow (1995) reprints key elements of this literature with useful commentary; in addition to Wolpe's original article, see in particular the pieces by Beinart, Bozzoli, Dubow, Marks, and Posel which are, directly or indirectly, in conversation with Wolpe in particular and the race-class debate more generally. Indeed, in *Race, Class, and the Apartheid State* (1988), Wolpe himself was deeply critical of reductionist tendencies in some of the radical contributions to the race-class debate.

16. Hall's piece attracted remarkably little attention in specifically South African debates; indeed, it was primarily Wolpe (1988) who seems to have picked up on it in his own later critique of economism.

17. This neglect of gender persists in Hall's later piece entitled 'Gramsci's Relevance for the Study of Race and Ethnicity' (reprinted in Morley and Chen 1996). For an incisive discussion of how deeply influential work emanating from the Centre for Contemporary Cultural Studies at Birmingham where Hall was based – including for example Willis (1977) – failed to encompass gender adequately, see Lave et al. (1992). Ironically, just as Hall was developing his analysis of articulation in relation to race and class, feminists at the same institution – the Birmingham Centre for Contemporary Cultural Studies – launched a powerful critique of Western feminisms, calling attention to their neglect of race and insisting that gender is inseparably connected with race and class (Carby 1982; Parmar 1982). In the US, a related and extremely important black feminist statement by the Combahee River Collective in 1977 is reprinted in Nicholson (1997). These charges of racism and ethnocentrism formed by far the most important challenges to Euro-American feminist theory and practice at the time.

18. Some of the most influential subsequent expositions of 'race,' culture, nationality, and ethnicity build on Hall's insights – including for example Gilroy (1987, 1993).

19. More recent interventions by the two authors include Laclau (1990, 1994, 1996), Mouffe (1992, 1995), and Butler et al. (2000).

20. See for example Norval (1996) and Howarth and Norval (1998). See also Laclau (1990).

21. I am indebted for this point to conversations with Donald Moore. Judith Butler (in Butler et al. 2000: 165) recently made a similar point: 'As Laclau begins to specify this problem of representation ... he makes a turn away from Marxian analysis towards phenomenology, structuralism and post-structuralism as they in consonant fashion, distinguish between signifier and signified ... The intellectual effort to bring this contingency into view, to expose what is necessary as contingent and to mobilize an insight into the political uses of this contingency assumes the form of a structural analysis of language itself.' Some time ago, Stuart Hall made much the same point in an interview with Lawrence Grossberg, noting that, in *Hegemony and Socialist Strategy*, 'there is no reason why anything is or isn't potentially articulable with anything else. The critique of reductionism has apparently resulted in the notion of society as a totally open discursive field' (Hall [1986] 1996a: 146), and goes on to observe that this 'fully discursive position' results in a reductionism upward rather than a reductionism downwards, as economism was.

22. In an incisive critique of radical democracy, Wendy Brown makes a related point: 'It is interesting ... that the optimism of radical (social) democratic vision is fueled by that dimension of liberalism which presumes social and political forms to have relative autonomy from economic ones to be that which can be tinkered with independently of developments in the forces of capitalism. Indeed, it is here that the radical democrats become vulnerable to the charge of "idealism," where idealism marks the promulgation of select political ideals de-linked from historical configurations of social powers and institutions ... ' (Brown 1995: 12).

23. He notes, for example, that 'Foucault never explains what space it is that he is referring to, nor how it bridges the gap between the theoretical (epistemological) realm and the practical one, between mental and social, between the space of the philosophers and the space of people who deal with material things' (Lefebvre 1991: 4), and goes on to charge that 'most if not all authors ensconce themselves comfortably enough within the terms of mental (and therefore neo-Kantian or neo-Cartesian) space, thereby demonstrating that "theoretical practice" is already nothing more than the egocentric thinking of specialized Western intellectuals – and indeed may soon be nothing more than an entirely separate schizoid consciousness' (Lefebvre 1991: 24).

24. Smith and Katz (1993: 75) usefully elucidate this point as follows: 'The emergence of capitalist social relations in Europe brought a very specific set of social and political practices. The inauguration of private property as the general basis of the social economy, and the division of the land into privately held and precisely demarcated plots; the juridical assumption of the individual body as the basic social unit; the progressive outward expansion of European hegemony through the conquest, colonization and defence of new territories; the division of global space into mutually exclusive nation-states on the basis of some presumed internal homogeneity of culture (albeit a division brought about with economic motivation and through military force): these and other shifts marked the emerging space-economy of capitalism from the sixteenth century onwards and

represented a powerful enactment of absolute space as the geographical basis for social intercourse.'

25. As Allan Pred (2000: 23) puts it, 'Even under the most isolated of circumstances, "local" social forms have always to some extent been synonymous with a hub of material and relational flows, with a more or less developed mesh of interactions and interrelations across multiple geographical scales, with comings and goings that have made a virtual impossibility of the unselfconsciously "local".'

26. Critical geographers who have drawn in some quite different ways on Lefebvre include Pred (1990); Harvey (1989, 1996); Massey (1992, 1994); Pred and Watts (1992); Smith (1991, 1997); Sparke (1994); Mitchell (1997); and a number of the authors in the collection edited by Keith and Pile (1993). See also Brenner (1997), Brenner and Elden (2001), Merrifield (2000), and Shields (1999). Anthropologists whose work engages questions of spatiality quite directly – although with differing relationships to Lefebvre – include Gupta and Ferguson (1992, 1997), Coronil (1997), and Moore (1998).

27. For a brilliant analysis of Harvey's ambiguous relationship to Lefebvre in *The Condition of Postmodernity* (1989), see Gregory (1994).

28. Originally published in the *New Left Review* (1992), Massey's critique of Laclau is reprinted in her 1994 collection, *Space, Place, and Gender*. For a more recent statement that is far closer to the radical democratic position see Massey (1999a).

29. In this text, Scott is calling into question much feminist theorizing in the 1960s and 1970s which, in an effort to challenge biological determinism, subscribed to an idea of gender as the social construction of biological/sexual difference. Within what Donna Haraway (1991) calls this sex/gender binary, categories of biological sex and nature remained as passive givens, with 'biology' denoting the body itself rather than a social discourse open to different interpretations. The sex/gender binary also left untouched notions of an essential gendered identity as a woman or a man, and was incapable of coming to grips with other dimensions of difference. In short, the foundational concept that sex is to nature what gender is to culture meant that much feminist theory not only reinscribed the dualisms that it set out to transcend; it was also vulnerable to precisely the charges of racism and ethnocentrism that Hazel Carby (1982) and others laid – see note 17.

30. For an incisive critique of Lefebvre on precisely these grounds, see Blum and Nast (1996).

31. See for example McClintock (1995) and Stoler (1995).

32. Lefebvre points out that the binary model that opposes capital to labor makes it possible to grasp their conflictual development in a formal manner, but it presumes the disappearance from the picture of land, the landowning class, ground rent, and agriculture. Marx engaged only fleetingly with these issues at the end of Volume III of *Capital*. He did so through the profoundly gendered 'trinity formula,' in which not only land/agriculture but the Earth (in the character of Madame la Terre) enters into relationships with Monsieur le Capital and the Workers. In speaking of the earth, Lefebvre reminds us, Marx did not simply mean agriculture. Nor was he only concerned with natural resources, but also with 'the nation state confined within a specific territory, and hence, ultimately, in the most absolute sense [with] politics and political strategy' (Lefebvre 1991: 325).

33. For a critique of these institutionalist formulations, which rest on a static concept of 'embeddedness' and the structure of social relations, see Hart (1998a) and Burawoy (2001).

34. The classical debates include Kautsky ([1899] 1988), Lenin ([1899] 1964), Chayanov ([1923] 1966), and more recent contributions by, among others, Brenner (1976), Byres (1996), and Bernstein (1996a, 1996b). Particularly important contributions to bringing together political economy and cultural politics have come from the Africanist literature – including, for example, Guyer and Peters (1987), Berry (1989, 1993), and Moore (1993). Carney and Watts (1990) and Hart (1991) focus on gender as a constitutive force.

35. Debates surrounding industrial dispersal are discussed more fully in Chapter 4.

36. A key argument in the race-class debate that raged during the 1970s was the reserve subsidy thesis, which posited that, at least until the first half of the twentieth century, capital latched onto women's labor in subsistence agriculture in the former reserves to subsidize low wages of male migrant workers. The functionalist tendencies in this argument came under attack from those who pointed out that the deeply gendered migrant labor system, at least in part, reflected a degree of agency by patriarchal societies resisting full proletarianization (see Beinart and Dubow 1995, as well as Freund 1989). Despite this and other critiques, there is no question that mining capital, in particular, derived huge benefits from workers' access to land in the reserves, particularly in the earlier phases of capitalist expansion (Freund 1989).

37. See Bundy (1987), Drew (1996), and Levin and Weiner (1996) for important discussions of this point.

38. Later in the book, Mamdani makes clear that the conception of political economy he regards as partial is actually an early version of the 'cheap labor power thesis' by Wolpe (1972): 'In South African studies, the finest fruit of the political economy perspective was the cheap labor power thesis: it argued that apartheid was functional to capitalism, critical to ensuring a regular supply of cheap labor power' (Mamdani 1996: 294). In fact, in *Race, Class and the Apartheid State* (1988), Wolpe himself offered a far more sophisticated analysis.

39. In debates around globalization, a chief point of contention has been whether or not the growing role of local and regional governance signifies the demise of the nation state. Recently, attention has shifted to the far more interesting question of how state power is being re-articulated at different spatial scales. Those who have addressed this question include Swyngedouw (1997), Jessop (1997), and Brenner (1997, 1998). Neil Brenner, for example, argues that neoliberalism as an accumulation strategy entails a profound tension between deregulation (which favors capital's geographical mobility) and reregulation (related to its geographical fixity): 'In the current context of neoliberal globalization, therefore, configurations of state territorial organization – if now significantly rescaled – continue to play a constitutive role in circumscribing the spatial orbit of capital, in constructing its territorial preconditions, and in mediating its uneven geographical development'(Brenner 1998: 477).

40. For a useful summary of these initiatives, see Mohan and Stokke (2000).

41. I have developed this argument more fully elsewhere (Hart 2001), drawing a distinction between 'big D' Development as a post-war international project that emerged in the context of decolonization, and 'little d' development as the

development of capitalism. See also Fred Block's introduction to the new edition of Polanyi (2001).

42. For a review of literature on social capital see Woolcock (1998), and for a critique see Fine (2001).

43. See for example Escobar (1995, 2001), and Esteva and Prakash (1998).

44. See Watts (1995), and Mohan and Stokke (2000).

45. See Welsh (1971) and Mamdani (1996), both of which are discussed more fully in Chapter 2.

46. As explained more fully in Chapter 7, there have been several phases of local government restructuring.

47. Although Harvey's earlier book *Limits to Capital* (1982) is not framed in these terms, it speaks in far more useful ways to questions of globalization, yet it is significantly less influential than *The Condition of Postmodernity*.

48. Two trenchant observations by Derek Gregory about the top-down narratives entailed in exclusive foregrounding of time-space compression are particularly relevant. First, Gregory (1994: 413) notes, in analyzing postmodern ways of thinking, feeling, and doing in terms of the intensity of experiences of time-space compression, Harvey 'glides from society to the individual through a series of downward moves.' In addition, while Harvey seeks to illuminate the social relations implicated in the production of (postmodern) space, 'the multiple and compound geographies of these processes seem to disappear' (Gregory 1994: 413).

49. See for example the issue of the journal *Development* edited by Escobar and Harcourt (1998), and Escobar (2001).

Notes to Chapter 2

1. The summary report for South Africa as a whole was edited by Laurine Platzky and Cherryl Walker, and published in 1985 under the title *The Surplus People: Forced Removals in South Africa* by Ravan Press in Johannesburg.

2. For a history of Waaihoek produced by the Association for Rural Advancement, see Henderson (1986).

3. Until the mid-1990s, Blaaubosch received virtually no government spending, despite its rapidly growing population.

4. Cited by Pickles and Weiner (1991): 18.

5. The earliest white permanent settlement in southeast Africa was in the 1820s, when a group of British traders set up in Port Natal (Durban) under the protection of the Zulu king, Shaka. In 1837 Dutch-speaking trekkers arrived, demanding territorial concessions from Shaka's successor, Dingane. After defeating Zulu forces at Ncome (Blood) River in 1838, the trekkers established an alliance with Mpande who wrested control of the throne from Dingane. The trekkers then divided the territory with Mpande who retreated to the core of the Zulu kingdom north of the Thukela, while the trekkers gained control of areas to the south of the Thukela that became known as the Republic of Natalia. In 1844 Britain annexed Natalia: 'The annexation was reluctantly ratified by the Imperial Government, which was swayed by the argument that continued instability in the region would destabilize the Cape Colony's eastern frontier, while it was imperative for strategic reasons to contain the Trekker population in the interior of the subcontinent. Apart from these strategic considerations, the new colony was of

little economic value' (Ballard 1989: 125); see also Wright and Hamilton (1989) and Colenbrander (1989).

6. Stiff opposition to the reserves also came from the large missionary community, which argued that 'so long as Kafirs live in large communities, where their own customs and usages operate with the greatest vigour, and where the power and influences of chiefs are felt with the greatest intensity, so long will missionary exertion be comparatively ineffectual . . . ' (cited in Welsh 1971: 45).

7. 'On deposit of the survey fees, grants were to be made of five hundred acres – henceforth called 'glebes' – for each of the twelve stations; and at each station a further area of from six to eight thousand acres (supposing that quantity to be available) was to be marked out as a reserve for the use of Zulus and held in trust for them by a Board consisting of the Secretary of Native Affairs and the Chairman, Secretary, and Treasurer of the Mission; the land not be alienable except with the concurrence of the Lieutenant-Governor. Within each of these areas allotments were to be made from time to time to Zulus who might wish to have individual titles . . .' (cited by Welsh 1971: 47)

8. These data exclude Zululand which was conquered by Britain in 1879 and subsequently incorporated into the reserves. The definitive study is *The Destruction of the Zulu Kingdom* by Jeff Guy (1994).

9. See Marks (1970), Lambert (1995), and a revisionist study by Carton (2000) who argues that the tax revolt was the product not only of colonial demands for land, labor, and taxes, but also generational conflicts in which young African men challenged the authority of household heads and chiefs.

10. See for example Beinart and Bundy 1987; Beinart et al. (1986), Keegan (1986), and Van Onselen's (1996) magisterial account of the sharecropper Kas Maine. For a broad overview of this literature, see Bozzoli and Delius (1990).

11. Indeed, Bundy concedes many of these points in the Preface to the 2nd edition of *The Rise and Fall of the South African Peasantry* (1988).

12. See Fair (1955) for comparative data on soil and rainfall conditions in this region of Natal.

13. See McClendon (1995) for a fascinating account of this process in the Natal Midlands that draws on court records and illustrates the intense controversy surrounding 'customary law.'

14. See 'On the South African Theses: to the South African Section,' in *Writings of Leon Trotsky: 1934–35.*

15. Mbeki was arrested at Lilliesleaf Farm in Rivonia, and incarcerated on Robben Island from 1964–88.

16. Govan Mbeki wrote much of *The Peasants' Revolt* on rolls of toilet paper while in solitary confinement awaiting trial. He described to me how he obtained those toilet rolls. At the time of his arrest in 1962 he had in his pocket a florin [a two shilling piece], with which he managed to buy a packet of tobacco. Using one of the eight sheets of toilet paper allotted each day, he rolled a cigarette which he gave to the African prisoner who delivered his food in exchange for additional toilet paper. In this way, he managed to ensure a supply of toilet paper sufficient to complete his manuscript, which he was able to smuggle out of prison. 'They [the prison authorities] thought they had deprived us of all contact, but they didn't think about exchange,' he noted with a twinkling smile.

17. The classic text is *Native Life in South Africa* by Sol Plaatje ([1917] 1987), a major figure in the formation of the ANC.

18. In the late 1970s, the large block of Driefontein farms was excised from KwaZulu, and therefore also became a 'black spot' and subject to removal.

19. For insights into ongoing relations of patronage in Madadeni, I am indebted to Phelele Tengeni.

Notes to Chapter 3

1. AFRA had its roots in the Northern Natal Landowners Association (NNLA), an organization formed in the 1950s to oppose removals with backing of the ANC and the Liberal Party. After the banning of the ANC in the early 1960s, the NNLA collapsed. At least in its initial phases, AFRA came into conflict with Inkatha on numerous occasions. AFRA coordinated the Natal segment of the Surplus People's Project which, along with films like *Last Grave at Dimbaza* and in combination with the broader anti-apartheid movement, was important in mobilizing support for opposition to removals in Europe and the United States.

2. See for example Beinart (1994: 212–235).

3. Desmond goes on to note that by the late 1960s 'most have built very good houses and it appears to be a well-settled community. In fact it is one of the more prosperous places in the area' (Desmond 1970: 79). In the 1970s, however, the Vulandondo community was moved into Ezakheni to make way for a dam.

4. Technically, only landowners with more than 20 morgen qualified for access to agricultural land as compensation (a morgen is just over a hectare). In practice a number of landowners refused the land on offer, because it was in distant, isolated places. Instead they received cash compensation which many described as 'peanuts' and way below the value of their losses.

5. Desmond (1970: 77) reported that 65 percent of the African children in the Newcastle hospital were suffering from malnutrition, and that of these 60 percent were from Osizweni.

6. For a discussion of *inboekselings* and *oorlams*, see Delius and Trapido (1983).

7. Mmutlana (1993: 60) reports a small but telling indication of the contradictions inherent in Inkatha's efforts to oppose forced removals: in 1986 Steven Sithebe, the leading Inkatha figure in the district, deployed the language of the liberation movement to claim that 'Inkatha can make this area ungovernable.'

8. 'The Origins and the Decline of Roosboom,' AFRA File 11.2.iii.

9. The battle waged by the three families is recounted by Mmutlana (1993).

10. Maré and Hamilton (1987: 111–116) describe operations of the BIC, and how in KwaZulu it evolved into the KwaZulu Finance Corporation (KFC) discussed more fully in Chapter 4.

11. Tripcos were also a means by which particular retail chains sought monopoly privileges. Maré and Hamilton (1987: 110) cite the following revealing comment by the financial editor of the *Sunday Tribune* on August 3, 1975: 'Homeland trading is the obvious plum for the large chains, particularly Checkers which is having to seek new trading areas in the face of the Pick 'n Pay and OK hypermarket developments. Checkers submitted a series of proposals to KwaZulu ... [including that] no similar venture unless wholly owned by Africans, be allowed to operate near Checkers' KwaZulu outlets for 10 years.'

12. Mdladlose subsequently became Minister of the Interior in the KLA, and was the first premier of KwaZulu-Natal after the 1994 election.

13. Bonnin et al. (1996: 155) provide the following useful sketch: 'Harry Gwala (1920–1995) was born in New Hanover and became a teacher in Pietermaritz-

burg. He joined the SACP in 1942 and the ANC in 1944. He was banned in 1951. He was detained on numerous occasions (the first time in 1960) and served an eight year sentence for sabotage (1964–1972). He was given a life sentence in 1976 but was released on medical grounds in 1988. He had a reputation as a hardline communist and opposed Inkatha until his death.'

14. Bonnin et al. (1998: 12) note: 'It was the youth who defended the townships from the South African Defence Force, and who, in KwaZulu-Natal, challenged the political leadership of Inkatha, taking over the role of "useless" adults as they did so. In instances of radical social change it can happen that gender relations alter. In this case, however, the rights of male elders were arrogated by the youth: women were not allowed to fight or to express opinions, and were not elected onto civic and other organizations.' See also Seekings (1991).

15. For discussions of the Inkatha Women's Brigade, see Maré and Hamilton (1987), and Hassim (1993).

16. See Swilling and Phillips (1989) for an excellent discussion of the National Security Management System and its *modus operandi.*

Notes to Chapter 4

1. I am indebted to Rob Haswell for his insights into Ghandi's links with Ladysmith and its contemporary significance.

2. In a piece entitled 'The Uses of Complicity in the Changing Mise-en-Scene of Anthropological Fieldwork,' George Marcus (1998) makes the interesting point that the ethical ambiguities arise not just from the 'necessarily open and cordial demeanor of the fieldworker wanting access' but from how the ethnographer and his/her subjects are 'broadly engaged in a pursuit of knowledge with resemblances in form and context that they can recognize' (Marcus 1998: 125).

3. The quotations are from Clark (1994): 131.

4. For a fascinating account of the formation of Zwelitsha township, see Mager (1999).

5. For a discussion of the early history of the textile industry, see Hirsch (1979).

6. As in Consolidated Cotton, the immediate issues were low wages and poor working conditions. The 'model township' that the Native Trust had built at no cost to the IDC to house workers in regulated conditions near the factory was not free to workers; extremely low wages were inadequate to cover rents. After a series of strikes in 1950–51, they went on a prolonged strike in 1952 in conjunction with the ANC's Defiance Campaign in which more than 200 were jailed (Clark 1994: 142; see also Hirsch 1979). Recognizing at last that 'the average native could barely afford to live in the township,' the IDC was forced to abandon its plan for a 'model settlement' for black industrial workers and their families, and instead constructed 'huts' for single males on company property: 'Acknowledging failure in its attempts to create an ideal labor force at King William's Town, the IDC turned to traditional methods of containing production costs by seeking total control over its workers' (Clark 1994: 142). Although the IDC's experiment in 'border industrialization' was not exactly a model of 'industrial and technical efficiency,' it established important principles that were incorporated in apartheid regional planning, including exemption from minimum wages under the industrial council system.

7. The other clothing factory that moved from Charlestown had (and still has) the reputation of exercising much tighter labor discipline.

8. For a critical account of regional planning in the 1960s and 1970s, see Gore (1984).

9. Under the terms of the Industrial Conciliation Act, employers are required to meet jointly with industry-wide unions to determine common, equitable standards for work in all factories.

10. See, for example, Maree (1987).

11. The *South African Labour Bulletin* (Vol. 6, No. 5, December 1980) contains a number of articles describing the early Frame strike in detail, and working conditions in the Frame industrial empire more generally. See also Berger (1992).

12. See Cobbett et al. (1987: 14–15) for a discussion of the Buthelezi Commission in KwaZulu-Natal and its relationship to federalism.

13. In practice, these 'deconcentration points' were all in designated bantustan areas.

14. See for example Webster (1988) and Seidman (1994).

15. The 1991 RIDP offered a tax-free start-up cash grant payable over two years based on investment up to R15 million and equal to 10.5 percent of investment each year; a tax-exempt profit/output incentive payable in cash over three years; and a relocation grant of up to R1 million for foreign investment projects.

16. The reduced incentives were made available throughout the country, with the exception of the Pretoria-Witwatersrand-Vereeniging area and the central area of Durban; the remainder of the Durban Functional Region, Cape Town, and the deconcentration areas in what is now Gauteng received 60 percent of the establishment grant and the full profit/output incentive.

17. The reports produced by both institutions (DBSA 1989; Urban Foundation 1990) contain a great deal of critical rhetoric on the evils of regional planning and the distortionary effects of the 1982 RIDP, but remarkably little evidence. In addition to calling attention to the casual empiricism of both reports, Platzky's (1995) far more detailed study of forces at work in three industrial estates in the late 1980s challenges a number of the conclusions of the Urban Foundation and the DBSA.

18. The data that Wilsenach and Lichthelm (1993) used were ostensibly for projects approved in South Africa as a whole, but they excluded data for the so-called 'independent' bantustans – Transkei, Ciskei, Venda, and Bophuthatswana.

19. The results of Reid's survey are contained in Harrison and Todes (1996).

20. A number of those that closed or moved were footwear producers who were forced to pay Industrial Council wages, and who were faced with intensified competition from cheap imports.

21. In addition to this small-scale, largely endogenous growth, two large Asian multinationals received incentives under the 1991 RIDP for export production. One of the main incentives for these companies was that, at the time, clothing produced in South Africa was not subject to quotas under the Multi-Fiber Agreement. Since the late 1990s, the US Africa Growth and Opportunity Act has opened up possibilities for exports.

Notes to Chapter 5

1. See for example Cheng and Gereffi (1994); Hamilton (1998); Chan and Clark (1994); and Shieh (1992).

2. See for example Berger and Hsiao (1988); Redding (1990); and Rozman (1991).

3. See for example Hamilton and Biggart (1988); Hamilton and Kao (1990); Biggart (1991); Numakazi (1991); Castells (1996); and Hamilton (1998).
4. See also Hamilton and Biggart (1988), and Biggart (1991).
5. The concept of 'embeddedness' derives from Polanyi (1944) who deployed it in a considerably more nuanced and dynamic way than does Granovetter (1985).
6. The other main locus of Taiwanese settlement is Bloemfontein, which is estimated to have a population of 1,500–2,000. Many own factories in the former bantustan areas of Botshabelo and Selosesho, roughly 50 km from Bloemfontein. As we saw in the Introduction, in the early 1990s the town council of Bronkhorstspruit was also in the process of trying to establish the town as a center of Taiwanese settlement.
7. When one drew attention to particularly egregious contradictions in these neoliberal narratives – most notably the huge subsidies that Taiwanese industrialists had enjoyed through precisely the sort of state interference that they were railing against – Taiwanese industrialists responded in two sorts of ways. One argument was that subsidies represented just compensation for the higher cost of doing business in South Africa. The other was that Taiwanese industry had continued to expand despite the cut in subsidies in 1991, thus attesting to the superior efficiency of Taiwanese forms of production.
8. At that time industrialists in places like Dimbaza were receiving subsidies under the RIDP that essentially provided them with free labor – see Chapter 4.
9. For an account of the Japanese occupation of Taiwan, see Gold (1986).
10. In December 1949 the KMT moved its capital to Taipei, and the Communist Party seemed set to take over the island. According to Gold (1986), the US government ceased additional assistance to the KMT, and 'decided to stand back until the dust had settled' (1986: 53). There was a sharp reversal of policy following the invasion of South Korea by North Korea in June 1950; at this point, Truman reversed the hands-off policy towards the KMT, sent the Seventh Fleet into the Taiwan Straits to protect the Nationalists from Communist invasion, and poured large amounts of aid into Taiwan.
11. Under KMT rule, martial law was in effect until 1987. The main opposition to the KMT is the Democratic Progressive Party (DPP) which 'has consolidated its political power by drawing a distinction between oppressed *Benshengren* (Taiwanese and Hakka) and the oppressor *Waishengren* (mainlanders). Even though its political doctrine mainly represents the interests of middle-class entrepreneurs, the DPP appeals to various classes of *Benshengren*, all of whom have been excluded from political power under the KMT' (Hsiung 1996: 25–26).
12. Unfortunately I did not have the opportunity to observe these relationships in action; but it would be surprising if some form of mutual masculinity did not feature in these relationships.
13. Although much of the production was for retail chain stores, the most rapidly-growing segment of the market seemed to be a more informal one. A number of factories had shops adjoining them, and on several occasions interviews with Taiwanese industrialists were interrupted by the arrival of a busload of hawkers. By the mid-1990s Newcastle had become established as a center of knitwear production, and its location on a major transport route halfway between Durban and Johannesburg makes it easily accessible to hawkers.
14. See, for example, Cho (1987); Fernandes (1997); Lee (1993, 1995); Ong (1987, 1991); Rofel (1992, 1999); Salzinger (1997); and Wolf (1992).

15. This comment displays a profound misunderstanding of African kinship terms and relations.
16. Ideally, of course, one would compare the cost structure in the two locations. This simply is not possible. Even in Newcastle, it was extremely difficult to gain anything other than a very general sense of production costs: yarn was the largest component (probably about 50 percent of direct production costs), and subject to what industrialists claimed were extremely high import duties. Labor represented somewhere between 25–35 percent of direct costs.

Notes to Chapter 6

1. See Hart (1998a) and Burawoy (2001) for a fuller critique of notions of path dependency.
2. The delegation was sponsored by the National Committee on US-China Relations, and the report is entitled 'Economic Development and Human Rights in China's Interior,' (National Committee China Policy Series, No. 7, September 1993). Our itinerary included the cities of Chengdu, Chongqing, Yichang, and Wuhan, as well as trips to the surrounding towns and villages.
3. Following the collectivization of agriculture in 1955, the Chinese state implemented a nationwide system of population registration (*hukou*) through which all Chinese were defined as either (rural) peasants or (urban) workers. Particularly after 1960 the state moved decisively to enforce these distinctions, and effectively barred 'peasants' from migrating to the cities (or, indeed, from poorer to more prosperous rural regions). Those with urban residence permits were (and to some degree still are) defined as members of work units (*danwei*) that govern access not only to housing but an entire panoply of services and social security.
4. While these connections are particularly dramatic in China and Taiwan, they have also been important in Japan and South Korea.
5. Hsing (1998) points out that official figures are severe underestimates because a huge proportion of Taiwanese companies are registered in Hong Kong.
6. The fiscal reforms that underwrote local state corporatism in China after 1984 are discussed in the following section. For an explanation of different arrangements across provinces – and the particularly favorable status of the southern coastal provinces – see Wong (1992).
7. Yang (1994: 172) argues that 'throughout the 1950s and early 1960s, as China was experiencing a fundamental social, structural and ideological transformation, the personalistic "nepotism" or kinship orientation of prerevolutionary social life all but disappeared. Then in the years 1966–69, the society underwent another major political reconstitution, only this time the methods and effects were much more drastic and, for many traumatic and devastating. The political mobilization of the masses in the Cultural Revolution meant that state ethics penetrated into the very fabric of the social-cultural make-up, deeply affecting personal relationships. The ascendancy of "political relationships" left very little room for the sphere of private/personal relationships and sentiments. What resulted was a social body that had become so politicized that it could not be differentiated from the state. In the period between 1969 and 1972, signs of social resistance against the total state saturation began to appear. What emerged were personalistic ethics in everyday life, often in form of guanxixue or renqing ethics very much at odds with the dominant state system of universalistic ethics. Then in the 1980s, during

the economic reform period, guanxixue took on a new life and in many respects experienced a transformation as it intersected with a growing commodity economy with its attendant social mobility and consumer desires.' Yang also takes issue with those that maintain guanxi in China operates to extend official or bureaucratic power, whether as official corruption or as patron-client ties wielded by government officials to control their dependents (see for example Walder 1986). Instead, Yang argues, guanxi in all its multiple forms has re-emerged as a set of practices and forms of subjectivity oppositional to larger strategies of power exercised through the central party-state: 'Guanxi subjectivity . . . does not oppose the state directly, but forges a multiplicity of links through and across state segments. Where the state creates atomized individuals through mutual surveillance, guanxi joins these individuals together in relationships of exchange. Where the state binds persons together into collective state segments, guanxi subjects form networks that cut across these divisions' (Yang 1994: 286).

8. This in turn, Yang argues, hinges on a construction of personhood that is very different from the construction of the autonomous individual dominant in the West: 'Rather than creating discrete and unified ontological categories of person each having the same equality of rights, it appears that the Chinese subscribe to a relational construction of persons . . . Chinese personhood and personal identity are not given in the abstract as something intrinsic to and fixed in human nature, but are constantly being created, altered, and dismantled in particular social relationships' (Yang 1989: 39).

9. Yet several of the white local government officials with whom I met during visits to Bronkhorstspruit in 1994 were quite unequivocal in their invocation of discourses of *guanxi*.

10. 'Almost all the Taiwanese managers I interviewed stressed the importance of "military-like" management. The obligatory two-year service in Taiwan had well prepared these Taiwanese male managers with military-style training techniques [which] they adopted to discipline their workers in China. Workers had to line up when walking from the factories to the dining halls; no chatting was allowed in the dining hall. Each time workers left the factory building they were subjected to a body check to see if they had stolen anything from the factory' (Hsing 1998: 103).

11. 'It is not very clear if workers in the factory were convinced by the analogy of the family in their relationship with management. But young women workers did adopt the idea of family themselves and developed a sisterhood for mutual support. Worker organization was forbidden in the factory . . . but there was informal mutual help among workers. A group of six or seven women, usually from the same province, would establish a ranking system based on their ages and call each other "sister"' (Hsing 1998: 100).

12. As explained in Chapter 5, industrial enterprises in Taiwan seldom employ more than 30 workers. In Newcastle, the average size of Taiwanese firms was around 100 workers, although the 'good bosses' described in Chapter 5 seldom employed more than 30 workers. Average firm size of Taiwanese industries in China in the mid-1990s was around 260 (Hsing 1995: 9).

13. 'During the overtime hours at night, when most Taiwanese managers were in the dorm watching TV, playing games, gambling or relaxing in a nearby karaoke bar, the Chinese managers were running around the assembly lines to see if the

specifications of the orders were followed correctly and helping with the final quality inspection before the finished products were packaged and loaded on the trucks' (Hsing 1998: 97).

14. Weitzman and Xu (1994) estimated that total factor productivity in TVEs grew at an annual rate of 12 percent between 1979 and 1991: 'It would not be an exaggeration to identify the TVE sector as a major engine, perhaps the major engine, of recent Chinese economic growth' (Weitzman and Xu 1994: 130). While China's industry grew at an annual rate of 13 percent between the mid-1980s and the early 1990s, TVEs expanded far more rapidly (Jefferson and Rawski 1994).

15. Odgaard (1990/01) provides a useful discussion of the problems inherent in classifying enterprises.

16. These include Chang and Wang (1994); Christiansen (1992); Huang (1990); Ody (1992); Oi (1992, 1999); Putterman (1989); Judd (1994); Yang (1994); Rozelle (1994); Wong (1992); Lin (1995); Smart (1998). For an overview of TVEs until the late 1990s, see Perotti et al. (1999). Zhang (1999) explains how TVEs emerged from a series of rural industrialization thrusts in the Maoist era.

17. See for example Wong (1988, 1992) and Oi (1992, 1999).

18. In addition, there are wide variations in the forms and intensity of industrialization not only across regions, but also in closely adjacent communities. In visits to townships and villages in Sichuan province in December 1992, for example, I was struck by quite dramatic differences in levels and patterns of economic activity in communities located within a few kilometers of one another with quite similar endowments of land and population.

19. Those who emphasize fiscal incentives include Byrd and Gelb (1990); Oi (1992, 1999); and Wong (1988, 1992).

20. 'The collective is strongest precisely in those areas where the economy is diversified, where agriculture is performed by specialized households, where the contract responsibility system is flourishing, and most important, where industry is booming. In such environments, the power of the local government has grown along with the provision of collective welfare. It is common for highly industrialized villages to build schools, housing, movie theaters, and community centers for their members. In the mid-1980s, some provided the community with free water, electricity, and liquid fuel, as well as subsidies for education ...' (Oi 1999: 79–80).

21. See for example Peng (1992); Nee (1992); and Sachs and Woo (1994).

22. See for example Riskin (1971), and Perkins et al. (1977).

23. At the same time, there has been a dramatic reduction in the proportion of the working population covered by the state welfare system (Vohra 1994). Smart (1998: 437) cites data indicating that those who received housing, health care and pensions from the state dropped from 19 percent of the workforce in 1980 to 9 percent in 1990, and the figures have undoubtedly declined further since then.

24. 'State-owned enterprises struck deals with villagers' committees or township governments, providing funds, blueprints, raw materials, market outlets, and technical training: in return, they received land, buildings, and rural workers ... Apart from providing cheap labor, this form of cooperation has the advantage of simplifying the procedure for making land available ... By involving rural communities in the investment and diverting existing equipment to collective enterprises, state-owned enterprises can keep costs low and simplify procedures.

In some cases, existing rural collective enterprises have been expanded and include production lines that service the urban "mother company."

'The effect on the local communities is great: (a) they can use their labor resources in a way which generates higher income than can be derived from agriculture, (b) they need only put up a limited initial investment; and (c) they benefit from technological knowledge which is transferred from the urban "mother" enterprise . . . (From the viewpoint of the urban enterprise) the internal structure is unaffected. It is able to maintain its basic structure at the same level of cost while radically expanding its production capacity. It is not forced to provide housing, medical care, social facilities or pension schemes for the workers in the subsidiary enterprise. Second, it can reduce the size of initial investment in new production lines. Third, it can use the increasing output derived from the subsidiary to negotiate better allocation conditions for raw materials within the state plan, and it can use this avenue for a fully legal form of excess sale . . . Fourth it can keep operational expenses and taxation low by using the advantages of the collective economic sector, for example, by making use of cheaper labor, lower administrative costs, partial access to the free market (for excess production), initial tax exemption for rural collective enterprises, lower operational taxes, etc. The structure of subcontracting, therefore, could and ought to be seen as basically a protective measure, one which reinforces the internal structure of state-owned enterprises and enables them to proceed with a form of production which is based on comparatively low productivity' (Christiansen 1992: 83–84).

25. In the Guangdong township adjacent to Hong Kong where he did research, for example, local residents receive revenue streams primarily composed of rent: 'The locals are becoming an elite rentier class benefiting from the export-generated profits resulting from foreign investment and the poorly remunerated efforts of migrant workers' (Smart 1998: 442). At the other extreme, Judd (1994) describes a situation in which villagers assigned to work in rural factories receive work points rather than cash wages, and profits are redistributed throughout the community. More generally Smart argues that, while instances of local corporatism or local market socialism are common in China and have produced remarkable rates of growth, such forms only exist 'where the majority of productive property is held by a local governmental agency or agencies, where all local citizens (which usually excludes migrants who might outnumber citizens) have rights to some revenues or benefits from collective property, and where few significant alternative channels to prosperity exist' (Smart 1998: 441).

26. See Kitching (1982) for a discussion of the Narodniks and Russian populism.

27. For a discussion of the role of how both the KMT leadership and their US advisors conceived of land reform as a counter-revolutionary strategy, see McCoy (1971).

28. Taiwanese land reform proceeded in three stages. In 1949 the KMT implemented a rent reduction program that limited farm rents to a maximum of 37.5 percent of the main crop. In the second stage, which began in 1951, land confiscated from the Japanese government and individuals was leased or sold to tenants. The landlord system was finally dismantled in 1953–54 through a land to the tiller program which placed a ceiling on land ownership above a certain minimum size (3 ha of medium quality wet rice land per worker). The state purchased excess land for resale to farmers at the same price, 2.5 times the purchase price of the

annual yield of the land – a price far below land values in the pre-war period. Owner-cultivated land rose from 56 percent in 1948 to 86 percent in 1959. By the 1960s, 80 percent of farm households were owner-cultivators, and 90 percent of farms were less than 2 ha (Amsden 1979: 352–353).

29. See for example Anderson and Leiserson (1980); Ho (1978, 1982); Ranis and Stewart (1987, 1993); Park and Johnston (1995); Ranis (1995); and Tomich et al. (1995). Proponents of this interpretation place primary emphasis on redistributive land reforms in the late 1940s and early 1950s, combined with measures to increase agricultural productivity. There are, according to this view, two key mechanisms through which agricultural growth propelled rural industrialization. First, farmers generated demand for agricultural inputs, such as simple manufactured implements; at the same time, increasing agricultural output stimulated processing industries. Rising demand for consumer goods and services – or the expansion of the home market – constituted the second key set of mechanisms. When agricultural incomes rose as a consequence of increasing agricultural productivity, farm households spent a relatively large proportion of incremental income on non-agricultural goods and services. The presumption is that these commodities were produced in small-scale, labor-intensive enterprises located in rural areas, thereby generating expanding demand for labor and growth of non-agricultural jobs. Agriculture thus played a historical role in Taiwan's agrarian transformation not only as a source of labor, foreign exchange, and savings, but also through demand linkages in generating 'a dynamic nonagricultural sector in rural areas' (Ranis 1995: 512).

   For a fuller discussion and critique of the growth linkage hypothesis, see Hart (1998b).

30. Lee is widely regarded as the most authoritative source. He trained as an agricultural economist at Cornell, and the book is based on his PhD dissertation. In the late 1980s he became the first native Taiwanese president of Taiwan.

31. Lee's data indicate that between 1950 and 1960 real per capita income rose by 9 percent (from T$87 to T$95), consumption declined by 4 percent (from $75 to $72), and savings rose by 84 percent (from T$12.5 to T$23) (Lee 1971: Table 1). Over the same period, population was growing rapidly due to a decline in the crude death rate.

32. Ethnographic studies that trace changes over time in different villages include Gallin and Gallin (1982); Harrell (1981, 1985); Hu (1983); Stites (1982); Niehoff (1987).

33. See Gold (1986) and Haggard (1990) for discussions of how import substitution operated in Taiwan, and the forces that led to a growing emphasis on manufactured exports in the 1960s.

34. See also Park and Johnston (1995: 188).

35. After 1968, according to Tsai (1984), tight state control over land use and zoning, combined with heavy investment in infrastructure, resulted in most officially recorded industrial development taking place outside the main metropolitan areas in export-processing zones and industrial parks located in rural and suburban counties rather than in the five largest cities. According to Ranis (1995), however, export-processing zones accounted for no more than 1 percent of total employment and 3 percent of total investment, although they contributed 6 percent of exports. Foreign investors in Taiwan were subject to strict local

content requirements; Schive and Majumdar (1990) document how numerous small Taiwanese producers became component suppliers to multinationals, and also began establishing subcontracting links with export firms.

36. 'As Taiwan felt the effects of the worldwide oil crisis in 1974, and later faced increasing competition from other third world countries, hundreds of small urban factories closed. Many laid-off workers returned to their native villages. Taking advantage of manufacturing techniques learned in city factories, these returnees set up factories which tended to be very small in scale, family-owned, and labor-intensive. These factories tended to require very little capital, minimizing start-up costs and operating expenses in many ways. For example, since most families had at least a small plot of land due to land reform, the factories could be set up on family land adjacent to, or even inside, the family house for extremely little cost. They could rely upon unpaid family labor and the much lower rural labor rates of part-time farmers. In addition, as many as 65 percent of these factories remained unregistered, thus escaping taxation and regulation. Finally, being less subject to regulation they could manufacture with even less regard for the natural environment than their urban counterparts. These small manufacturing concerns were an integral part of the larger industrialized economy, tied by personal and informal relationships to larger factories through subcontracting work, or to urban buyers' (Buck 1995: 24). See also Buck (2000).

37. The subjects of Greenhalgh's study were all urban-based industrialists, some of them former landlords.

38. See Amsden (1985). Writing in the 1980s, Niehoff noted that 'households owning rice land, including many that were losing money by continuing to farm, can only stop producing two crops per year at the risk of having their land expropriated and transferred to households that would continue farming' (1987: 304).

39. See for example Hu (1983); Niehoff (1987); Gallin and Gallin (1982).

40. For a general description of the distribution of land rights in the context of decollectivization, see McKinley and Griffin (1993). Claims about egalitarian distribution of land among households need to be modified by recognition of significant gender inequalities within households.

41. See for example Siu (1989); Huang (1990); Chan et al. (1992); and Ruf (1998).

42. For an interesting comparative study of rural industrialization in Taiwan and South Korea, see Ho (1982).

43. In the context of the economic crisis of the early 1970s, the central government was cutting back on heavy farm subsidies and enforcing rice acreage reductions. At the same time, however, there was large-scale public spending on infrastructure in rural regions. McDonald notes that while public spending policies for rural infrastructure have been seen as compensation to the regions to secure their electoral allegiance to the conservative regime, these public works also transformed rural regions to suit the interests of industry. The farm crisis also propelled local governments into aggressive local development strategies, while at the same time 'town halls were coached by the national government into the business of brokering land to industry': 'Tax breaks, low land prices, low labor costs, and ready labor availability were the attractions offered to national firms by these farm town industrial site promotions. Although in 1971 neither local nor national planners could be sure that private firms would be willing to expand into the farm towns, when factory expansion did begin again, it headed for the

"regions." Thus began in the early 1970s a new wage of industrial location at the rural periphery ... Businesses and jobs grew in the regions, while older manufacturing prefectures lost manufacturing jobs. A new wave of rural industrial expansion rolled outward to the farming periphery, to engage more and more of the labor residing in farm households. This process has extended to almost every margin of the country' (McDonald 1996: 62).

44. See Chapter 1.

45. I am indebted to Cherryl Walker for calling attention to this meeting and quotation by Heinz Klug in her extremely useful unpublished paper entitled 'Evolving Government Policies 1991–2001' (July 2001).

46. A draft World Bank document entitled 'Options for Land Reform and Rural Restructuring in South Africa' was initially distributed in a series of workshops around the country in May and June 1993. This initiative in turn was the product of competing elements within the Bank between those promoting an agrarian vision, and those who insisted on an urban future for South Africa. For a fuller exposition of the pro-peasant arguments, see Binswanger and Deiniger (1993), and Lipton and Lipton (1993). For a critique, see Williams (1996). Cherryl Walker (2001b) points to important continuities between the Bank recommendations and the apartheid government's land reform policy between 1990 and 1993.

47. The basic government document is the *White Paper on South African Land Policy* (Department of Land Affairs 1997). Detailed descriptions and critiques include Cousins (2000); Turner and Ibsen (2000); Lahiff (2001); and Walker (2001a, 2001b). For recent documents from the Programme on Land and Agrarian Studies at the University of the Western Cape, see www.uwc.ac.za/plaas.

48. Walker (2001b: 11–12) cites data from the Department of Land Affairs indicating that by December 1999 78,758 beneficiaries (47 percent of them listed as women) had bought 667,825 hectares of land.

49. By the middle of 2001, 17.9 percent of the 68,878 restitution claims had been settled, the majority urban claims settled in cash. Lahiff (2001: 4) estimates that at current budgetary levels it will require 150 years to complete the restitution process.

50. See for example Ben Cousins 'Didiza's New Land Law: Forward to the Past?' *Mail and Guardian* November 23, 2001, and Ntsebeza 2000.

51. The key NGO involved in land issues is the National Land Committee, an umbrella organization comprised of regional organizations, most of which were active in opposing forced removals during the apartheid era.

52. See for example the book edited by Lipton, et al. (1996), which brings together papers from a wide-ranging project on 'Land, Labour and Livelihoods in Rural South Africa' underway at the time.

53. See for example Kaplinsky (1994), and Joffe et al. (1995).

54. See Chapter 1.

Notes to Chapter 7

1. Municipal privatization began in 1996, when the Department of Constitutional Development and the Development Bank of Southern Africa worked with the local authority in the town of Nelspruit to set up a pilot 'public-private partnership' for water delivery and sanitation (Maralack 1998). The contract was

awarded to a consortium of Biwater, a British multinational, and a company established by black business leaders and former community activists. By the following year, powerful opposition to the privatization scheme took shape through an alliance of the South African Municipal Workers Union (SAMWU), the ANC Youth League, the South African Communist Party. SAMWU and COSATU more generally used the pilot status of the Nelspruit project to pilot their own national anti-privatization strategy, and to develop an alternative approach to the provision of water and sanitation. The fight over water and sanitation in Nelspruit very quickly became a fight over GEAR. The Nelspruit battle has carried over to privatization struggles in a number of other areas, including some of the main metropolitan centers.

2. For the critique from the right, see Centre for Development and Enterprise (1998), summarized by Bernstein (1998). For a critical left perspective, see Bond (2000b).

3. For a useful discussion of this process, see Robinson (1996): 209–219.

4. For documentation of some of these protests, see Barchiesi (1998), and Phadu (1998).

5. Cited in *Business Day*, July 21, 1999 (Internet version).

6. For a description of this system, see Chapter 4.

7. These estimates are contained in a report entitled 'Economic and Financial Analysis for the Ladysmith Integrated Development Framework,' prepared in 1997 by Philip Harrison and Karen Harrison-Migochi, and supplied to me by the town clerk of Ladysmith.

8. These data are from the Department of Finance *Budget Review* (1999/2000), and are cited in UNDP 2000 (Table 3.1: 90).

9. Seethal (1992) provides a vivid description of the formation of a civic organization in Pietermaritzburg that used the property taxation issue to press for the elimination of racially based Local Affairs Councils and the Group Areas Act.

10. For a discussion of Indian and Colored Local Affairs Councils, see Cameron (1991).

11. According to the *Klipriver Mirror* of December 14, 1996, 137 of these signatures were duplicates: 'Petitioners represent 22% of ratepayers in town. Of the total ratepayers, 5476 are from "disadvantaged areas" [i.e. former Indian and Colored areas] and 3430 from the other areas.'

12. A survey of township residents revealed that large numbers of people did not receive their accounts, and that the logistics of payment were extremely difficult since there was only one pay point in Ezakheni. The strategy to increase payment included such simple measures as hiring a township company to distribute accounts, and increasing the number of pay points.

13. There were a total of nine open budget meetings. In addition to the failed meeting for residents of the formerly white areas of the town, there were four in Ezakheni, two in Steadville, and one each in the former Colored and Indian sections of town.

14. See Chapter 4 for a description of Joint Services Boards.

15. Because of the ongoing dispute between the ANC and IFP over the location of the capital of KwaZulu-Natal, provincial government is split between Pietermaritzburg and Ulundi; Newcastle comes under the authority of Ulundi, Ladysmith under Pietermaritzburg.

16. ExpertPlanners' somewhat turgid description of their sampling technique runs as follows: 'At face value, the suggested sample size [440 households] may appear to be too small to warrant the extrapolation of the results to the 44,000 households which form the population of the study. This, however, is only true if one considers the proportional value of the sample (i.e. one percent of the population). Our initial understanding of the study objective gave the impression that it is not the absolute value but the probabilistic validity of the sample that matters. In other words, the study will have to estimate certain ranges within which the true mean of the population will lie and, if our understanding is correct, there is no apriori sample size of population that could be regarded as rule of thumb. In fact, under cases of uniformity or homogeneity in the population to be studied, the 440 households would be too excessive. However, this scenario of uniformity has not been assumed in our study proposal, hence the suggestion of a stratified random sample as opposed to a completely random sample.' The basis for stratification was settlement type – i.e. Newcastle, Madadeni, Osizweni, and the 'informal settlement' of Blaaubosch; no mention is made of wide variations *within* settlement types. In fact, it seems very likely that middle class households were overrepresented.

17. His main interest, not surprisingly, seemed to be in divisions within the local ANC.

18. The 'roleplayers' identified in the meeting were development committees in Steadville, Ezakheni, Shayamoya (an informal settlement), Acaciaville (a working class Indian suburb), the Chamber of Commerce, different ratepayers groups, and COSATU.

19. After the 1999 elections, the Department of Provincial and Local Government took over local government affairs.

20. The key exception is the wealthy suburb of Midrand, and a relatively small adjacent township.

21. The Provincial Department of Economic Affairs (controlled at the time by the ANC) envisaged some combination of government and private financing for these projects.

22. The key pieces of legislation include the Municipal Structures Act (1998), the Municipal Demarcation Act (1998), the Municipal Electoral Act (2000), and amendments to the Structures Act in 2000.

23. The crisis in local government finance is made clear in the Report of the Workshop on Local Government Finance held on November 12, 1999 in Cape Town. The meeting was convened by the parliamentary Portfolio Committee on Provincial and Local Government and the Select Committee on Local Government and Administration.

24. 'Report of the Provincial and Local Government Portfolio Committee on Budget Vote 22: Provincial and Local Government,' June 6, 2000, p. 4.

25. In place of the Regional Councils comprised of non-municipal areas, the new District Councils incorporate groups of these new municipalities. Thus, for example, the expanded Ladysmith and Newcastle municipalities (KZ232 and KZ252) in turn form part of much larger – and more rural – District Councils (KZ23 and KZ25 in Map 4).

26. Article entitled 'Traditional leaders warned against hostility,' www.iol.co.za, September 18, 2000.

27. The committee included Provincial and Local Government Director Zam Titus,

Head of the House of Traditional Leaders Inkosi Mzimela, ANC MP Inkosi Patekile Holomisa, Home Affairs Minister Mangosuthu Buthelezi and the IFP leader's special advisor Dr Mario Ambrosini (article entitled 'Traditional leaders' role in the spotlight,' www.iol.co.za, October 3, 2000).

28. Article entitled 'Mbeki: Laws may change to accommodate chiefs,' www. iol.co.za, October 12, 2000.

29. The constitutional basis for the withdrawal was that the version that came before parliament would have required all nine provinces to reconvene to approve the measure. (Article entitled 'Outrage greets the withdrawal of municipal bill,' www.iol.co.za, November 17, 2000.)

30. In Category B municipalities, there were three ballots: one for a municipal ward candidate, one for the proportional representation (PR) list for a party in the municipality, and one for the PR list in the District Council. The allocation of seats in the municipal council was determined by the sum of ward and PR votes.

31. Nationwide, a variety of smaller parties (the United Democratic Front, the Pan African Congress, the United Christian Democratic Party, and the African Christian Democratic Party) emerged with 1–2 percent each.

32. Along with many ANC activists, he claimed that most of the rural residents who did go to the polls were elderly people who had been told by the *amakhosi* that they would lose their pensions if they did not vote for the IFP.

33. In at least two such instances (Ward 25 in Ladysmith and Ward 1 in Newcastle), there had been successful restitution claims by landowners dispossessed during the apartheid era. In a third (Ward 15 in Ladysmith), a former unionist whom ANC activists described as a 'social giant' was able to swing the election in his favor.

34. I caught a glimpse of this impending battle during a brief trip to Ladysmith in June 2001, when I was invited to attend a meeting about the division of powers and responsibilities between the new district council and the expanded Ladysmith municipality. It became clear that not only was there a huge fight developing between these two tiers of local government over who would control water distribution. In addition, it appeared that the 'equitable share' resources – i.e. the funds disbursed by central government to cover basic needs of poor residents – had actually *fallen* from R14 million in 2000 to R11 million in 2001, despite the enlarged size of the Ladysmith municipality.

Notes to Chapter 8

1. I am using the term 'mid-level' not in relation to 'micro' and 'macro,' but rather to refer to levels of abstractness and concreteness.

2. The potential emancipatory possibilities of what Smith (1992) calls a politics of scale figure prominently in a number of recent discussions of globalization; see, for example, Brenner (1997), Cox (1997), Smith (1997), Swyngedouw (1997), and Harvey (2000). These discussions have increasingly recognized the limits of narrowly economistic understandings, and the need to attend more closely to questions of power. Thus, for example, Swyngedouw (1997: 169) insists that interconnected scales become produced as temporary stand-offs 'in a perpetual transformative and on occasion transgressive, social-spatial power struggle' that alter and express changes in the geometry of social power by strengthening some

and disempowering others. Yet as Marston (2000) points out, much of the scholarship on the production and politics of scale focuses on capitalist production while at best only tacitly acknowledging – and frequently ignoring – social reproduction and consumption. See also Katz (2001).

3. They have also underscored the contradictions inherent in these movements, such as the xenophobia that surfaced in efforts to keep China out of the World Trade Organization. See for example a particularly insightful article by Jim Smith entitled 'The China Syndrome – or, How to Hijack a Movement,' to be found on the web at www.Lalabor.org.

4. Eskom (Electricity Supply Commission) and Transnet are parastatals, slated at the time for partial privatization. According to press reports, some PAC officials claimed that they had not orchestrated the occupation, but had merely been invited to help by the African Renaissance Civic Movement after it had been turned down by the ANC (*Natal Mercury* July 6, 2001: 3). Others made clear that this move was part of a larger strategy that the party intended pursuing in other parts of the country.

5. Article entitled 'Desperate Need for Land Requires Rethink of Policy,' *Sunday Independent* July 8, 2001: 9, reproduced in the Appendix.

6. Not inconsequentially, the Bredell incident coincided with a national furore over a R43 billion ($5.4 million) arms deal, in which a number of senior government officials were accused of having accepted cut-rate Mercedes Benzes from a European arms manufacturer.

7. Article entitled 'Battle Lines Drawn in the Dust of Bredell,' *Sunday Independent* July 8, 2001: 1.

8. The emergence of the Landless People's Movement in the second half of 2001 represents a significant development, although it remains to be seen whether the movement will be able to forge broader connections.

9. These include the Soweto Electricity Crisis Committee led by Trevor Ngwane, a former ANC councilor for Pimville who left the ANC in 2000 in protest over Egoli 2002, the highly corporatized 'vision plan' for Johannesburg, and the Concerned Citizens' Group led by Fatima Meer that has helped mobilize citizens against cutoffs and evictions in parts of the Durban metropolitan area. The COSATU-aligned South African Municipal Workers Union is a driving force behind anti-eviction committees working in different parts of Cape Town.

10. Article entitled 'Many Rivers to Cross,' *Financial Mail* June 22, 2001: 26–27.

11. Neither article engages directly with the deeply contentious debate over whether the SACP and COSATU should split from the Alliance to form a working class party. My appeal in the first article to 'receptive elements within the state' reflects my own perception at the time of deep divisions within the coalition in control of the state, along with a sense that the Bredell episode was likely to have sharpened those divisions. It also embodies the presumption that a strategy of connecting struggles in multiple arenas is not simply a matter of pitting 'civil society' against 'the state,' but of recognizing how they define one another through constantly shifting engagements.

Select Bibliography

Adam, H., F. v. Z. Slabbert, and K. Moodley. 1997. *Comrades in Business: Post-Liberation Politics in South Africa*. Cape Town: Tafelberg.

Adelzadeh, A., and V. Padayachee. 1994. 'The RDP White Paper: Reconstruction of a Development Vision.' *Transformation* 25: 1–18.

AFRA. 1976. *The Origins and the Decline of the Roosboom Village and the Struggle of its Community for Survival*. Association for Rural Advancement 11.2.iii.

African National Congress. 1994. *The Reconstruction and Development Programme: A Policy Framework*. Johannesburg: Published by Umanyano Publications for the ANC.

——. 1997. 'The State and Social Transformation.' *The African Communist* 146: 37–61.

Amin, S. 1983. *The Future of Maoism*. New York: Monthly Review Press.

Amsden, A. 1979. 'Taiwan's Economic History: A Case of Etatisme and a Challenge to Dependency Theory.' *Modern China* 5: 341–380.

——. 1985. 'The State and Taiwan's Economic Development,' in *Bringing the State Back In*. Edited by P. Evans, D. Rueschemeyer, and T. Skocpol, pp. 78–106. Cambridge: Cambridge University Press.

Anderson, D., and M. Leiserson. 1980. 'Rural Nonfarm Employment in Developing Countries.' *Economic Development and Cultural Change* 28: 227–249.

Anon. 1979. 'Bus Boycotts.' *Work in Progress* 10: 65–72.

——. 1980. 'Bus Boycotts.' *Work in Progress* 13: 51–62.

Appadurai, A. 1996. *Modernity at Large: Cultural Dimensions of Globalization*. Minneapolis: University of Minnesota Press.

Balassa, B.A. 1981. *The Newly Industrializing Countries in the World Economy*. New York: Pergamon Press.

Ballard, C. 1989. 'Traders, Trekkers and Colonists,' in *Natal and Zululand from Earliest Times to 1910*. Edited by A. Duminy and B. Guest, pp. 116–145. Pietermaritzburg: University of Natal Press.

Barchiesi, F. 1998. 'Delivery from Below, Resistance from Above.' *Debate* 4: 12–27.

Beinart, W. 1994. *Twentieth-Century South Africa*. Oxford and New York: Oxford University Press.

Beinart, W., and C. Bundy. 1987. *Hidden Struggles in Rural South Africa: Politics & Popular Movements in the Transkei & Eastern Cape, 1890–1930*. Berkeley: University of California Press.

350

Beinart, W., and S. Dubow. 1995. *Segregation and Apartheid in Twentieth-century South Africa*. London and New York: Routledge.

Beinart, W., P. Delius, and S. Trapido. 1986. *Putting a Plough to the Ground: Accumulation and Dispossession in Rural South Africa, 1850–1930*. New History of Southern Africa Series. Johannesburg: Ravan Press.

Bekker, S. 1991. 'Cities Straddling Homeland Boundaries,' in *Apartheid City in Transition*. Edited by M. Swilling, R. Humphries, and K. Shubane, pp. 108–118. Oxford: Oxford University Press.

Bell, T. 1983. 'The Growth and Structure of Manufacturing Employment in Natal.' Occasional Paper No. 7. University of Durban-Westville: Institute for Social and Economic Research.

———. 1986. 'The Role of Regional Policy in South Africa.' *Journal of Southern African Studies* 12: 276–292.

Benjamin, W. 1969. *Illuminations*. New York: Schocken Books.

Berger, I. 1992. *Threads of Solidarity: Women in South African Industry, 1900–1980*. Bloomington and London: Indiana University Press and James Currey.

Berger, P.L., and H. Hsiao. 1988. *In Search of an East Asian Development Model*. New Brunswick, N.J.: Transaction Books.

Bernstein, A. 1998. 'Response to the White Paper by the Centre for Development and Enterprise.' *Development Southern Africa* 15: 297–306.

Bernstein, H. 1996a. 'Agrarian Questions Then and Now.' *Journal of Peasant Studies* 24: 22–59.

———. 1996b. 'South Africa's Agrarian Question: Extreme and Exceptional?' *Journal of Peasant Studies* 23: 1–52.

Berry, S. 1989. 'Social Institutions and Access to Resources.' *Africa* 59: 41–55.

———. 1993. *No Condition is Permanent: The Social Dynamics of Agrarian Change in Sub-Saharan Africa*. Madison, Wis.: University of Wisconsin Press.

Bertelsen, E. 1998. 'Ads and Amnesia: Black Advertising in the New South Africa,' in *Negotiating the Past: The Making of Memory in South Africa*. Edited by S. Nuttall and C. Coetzee, pp. 221–241. Cape Town: Oxford University Press.

Biggart, N. 1991. 'Explaining Asian Economic Organization: Toward a Weberian Institutional Perspective.' *Theory and Society* 20: 199–232.

Binswanger, H., and K. Deininger. 1993. 'South African Land Policy: The Legacy of History and Current Options.' *World Development* 21: 1451–1485.

Blum, V., and H. Nast. 1996. 'Where's the Difference: The Heterosexualization of Alterity in Lefebvre and Lacan.' *Environment and Planning D* 14: 559–580.

Bond, P. 2000a. *Elite Transition: From Apartheid to Neoliberalism in South Africa*. London and Pietermaritzburg: Pluto Press and University of Natal Press.

———. 2000b. *Cities of Gold, Townships of Coal: Essays on South Africa's New Urban Crisis*. Trenton, N.J.: Africa World Press.

Bonnin, D., R. Deacon, R. Morrell, and J. Robinson. 1998. 'Identity and the Changing Politics of Gender in South Africa,' in *South Africa in Transition:*

New Theoretical Perspectives. Edited by D.R. Howarth and A.J. Norval, pp. 111–131. New York: St Martin's Press.

Bonnin, D., G. Hamilton, R. Morrell, and A. Sitas. 1996. 'The Struggle for Natal and KwaZulu: Workers, Township Dwellers and Inkatha, 1972–1985,' in *Political Economy and Identities in KwaZulu-Natal: Historical and Social Perspectives.* Edited by R. Morrell, pp. 141–178. Durban: Indicator Press.

Bowles, P., and X.Y. Dong. 1994. 'Current Successes and Future Challenges in China's Economic Reform.' *New Left Review* 208: 49–76.

Bozzoli, B., and P. Delius. 1990. 'Radical History and South African Society.' *Radical History Review* 46: 13–45.

Bradford, H. 1987. *A Taste of Freedom: The ICU in Rural South Africa, 1924– 1930.* New Haven: Yale University Press.

——. 1990. 'Highways, Byways and Culs-de-sacs: The Transition to Agrarian Capitalism in Revisionist South African History.' *Radical History Review* 46: 59–88.

Brenner, N. 1997. 'Global, Fragmented, Hierarchical: Henri Lefebvre's Geographies of Globalization.' *Public Culture* 10: 135–167.

——. 1998. 'Between Fixity and Motion: Accumulation, Territorial Organization and the Historical Geography of Spatial Scales.' *Environment and Planning D* 16: 459–481.

Brenner, N., and S. Elden. 2001. 'Henri Lefebvre in Contexts: An Introduction.' *Antipode* 33: 763–768.

Brenner, R. 1976. 'Agrarian Class Structure and Economic Development in Preindustrial Europe.' *Past and Present* 70: 30–70.

Brookes, E.H., and N. Hurwitz. 1957. *The Native Reserves of Natal.* Natal Regional Survey Volume 7. Cape Town: Published by Oxford University Press for the University of Natal.

Brown, W. 1995. *States of Injury: Power and Freedom in Late Modernity.* Princeton: Princeton University Press.

Buck, D. 1995. 'Geographical Industrialization: Factors Causing Overseas Dispersal of Taiwanese Industry.' *Berkeley Journal of Asian Studies* 6: 19–33.

——. 2000. 'Growth, Disintegration, and Decentralization: The Construction of Taiwan's Industrial Networks.' *Environment and Planning A* 32: 245–262.

Bundy, C. 1979. *The Rise and Fall of the South African Peasantry.* Perspectives on Southern Africa 28. Berkeley: University of California Press.

——. 1987. 'Land and Liberation: Popular Rural Protest and the National Liberation Movements in South Africa, 1920–1960,' in *The Politics of Race, Class and Nationalism in Twentieth Century South Africa.* Edited by S. Marks and S. Trapido, pp. 254–285. London: Longman.

——. 1988. *The Rise and Fall of the South African Peasantry,* 2nd edition. Cape Town and London: David Philip and James Currey.

——. 1989. 'Around which Corner? Revolutionary Theory and Contemporary South Africa.' *Transformation* 8: 1–23.

Burawoy, M. 1979. *Manufacturing Consent: Changes in the Labor Process under Monopoly Capitalism*. Chicago: University of Chicago Press.

——. 1985. *The Politics of Production: Factory Regimes under Capitalism and Socialism*. London: Verso.

——. 2001. 'Neoclassical Sociology: From the End of Communism to the End of Classes.' *American Journal of Sociology* 106: 1099–1120.

Burawoy, M., and K. Verdery. 1999. *Uncertain Transition: Ethnographies of Change in the Postsocialist World*. Lanham: Rowman & Littlefield.

Butler, J., E. Laclau, and S. Zizek. 2000. *Contingency, Hegemony, Universality: Contemporary Dialogues on the Left*. London: Verso.

Byrd, W.A., and A.H. Gelb. 1990. 'Township, Village, and Private Industry in China's Economic Reform.' Policy, Research, and External Affairs Working Papers. Washington, DC: Country Economics Dept., World Bank.

Byrd, W.A., and C. Lin. 1990. *China's Rural Industry: Structure, Development, and Reform*. A World Bank Research Publication. Oxford: Oxford University Press.

Byres, T.J. 1996. *Capitalism from Above and Capitalism from Below: An Essay in Comparative Political Economy*. Houndmills, Basingstoke and New York: Macmillan Press and St Martin's Press.

Cameron, R. 1991. 'Managing the Coloured and Indian Areas,' in *Apartheid City in Transition*. Edited by M. Swilling, R. Humphries, and K. Shubane, pp. 48–63. Oxford: Oxford University Press.

Carby, H. 1982. 'White Women Listen! Black Feminism and the Boundaries of Womanhood,' in *The Empire Strikes Back: Race and Racism in 70s Britain*. Edited by the Centre for Contemporary Cultural Studies, Birmingham, pp. 212–235. London: Hutchinson.

——. 1987. *Reconstructing Womanhood: The Emergence of the Afro-American Woman Novelist*. New York: Oxford University Press.

Carney, J., and M. Watts. 1990. 'Manufacturing Dissent: Work, Gender and the Politics of Meaning in a Peasant Society.' *Africa* 60: 207–241.

Carton, B. 2000. *Blood from Your Children: The Colonial Origins of Generational Conflict in South Africa*. Pietermaritzburg: University of Natal Press.

Castells, M. 1996. *The Rise of the Network Society*. Oxford: Blackwell.

Castells, M., L. Goh, and R. Kwok. 1990. *The Shek Kip Mei Syndrome: Economic Development and Public Housing in Hong Kong and Singapore*. London: Pion.

Centre for Development and Enterprise. 1998. *Response to The White Paper on Local Government*. Johannesburg: Centre for Development and Enterprise.

Chakrabarty, D. 2000. *Provincializing Europe: Postcolonial Thought and Historical Difference*. Princeton: Princeton University Press.

Chan, A., R. Madsen, and J. Unger. 1992. *Chen Village under Mao and Deng*. Berkeley: University of California Press.

Chan, S., and C. Clark. 1994. 'Economic Development in Taiwan: Escaping the State-Market Dichotomy.' *Environment and Planning C* 12: 127–143.

Chang, C., and Y. Wang. 1994. 'The Nature of the Township-Village Enterprises.' *Journal of Comparative Economics* 19: 434–452.

Chari, S. 1997. 'Agrarian Questions in the Making of the Knitwear Industry in Tiruppur, India: A Historical Geography of the Industrial Present,' in *Globalising Food: Agrarian Questions and Global Restructuring*. Edited by M. Watts and D. Goodman, pp. 79–105. London: Routledge.

Chayanov, A.V. [1923] 1966. *The Theory of Peasant Economy*. Homewood, Ill.: Published for the American Economic Association by Irwin.

Cheng, L., and G. Gereffi. 1994. 'The Informal Economy in East Asian Development.' *International Journal of Urban and Regional Research* 18: 194–219.

Cho, S. 1987. 'How Cheap is Cheap Labor?: The Dilemmas of Export-Led Industrialization.' PhD thesis, University of California, Berkeley.

Christiansen, F. 1992. 'Market Transition in China: The Case of the Jiangsu Labor Market, 1978–1990.' *Modern China* 18: 72–93.

Christopher, A. 1969. 'Natal: A Study in Colonial Land Settlement.' PhD thesis, University of Natal.

Clark, N.L. 1994. *Manufacturing Apartheid: State Corporations in South Africa*. New Haven: Yale University Press.

Clifford, J. 1997. 'Spatial Practices: Fieldwork, Travel, and the Disciplining of Anthropology,' in *Anthropological Locations: Boundaries and Grounds of a Field Science*. Edited by A. Gupta and J. Ferguson, pp. 185–222. Berkeley, Los Angeles and London: University of California Press.

Clinton, C. 1982. *The Plantation Mistress: Women's World in the Old South*, 1st edition. New York: Pantheon Books.

Cobbett, W., D. Glaser, D. Hindson, and M. Swilling. 1987. 'South Africa's Regional Political Economy: A Critical Analysis of Reform Strategy in the 1980s,' in *Regional Restructuring under Apartheid: Urban and Regional Policies in Contemporary South Africa*. Edited by R. Tomlinson and M. Addleson, pp. 1–27. Johannesburg: Ravan Press.

Colenbrander, P. 1989. 'The Zulu Kingdom, 1828–79,' in *Natal and Zululand from Earliest Times to 1910*. Edited by A. Duminy and B. Guest, pp. 83–115. Pietermarizburg: University of Natal Press.

Cope, N. 1990. 'The Zulu Petit Bourgeoisie and Zulu Nationalism in the 1920s: The Origins of Inkatha.' *Journal of Southern African Studies* 16: 431–451.

——. 1993. *To Bind the Nation: Solomon kaDinuzulu and Zulu Nationalism 1913–1933*. Pietermaritzburg: University of Natal Press.

Coronil, F. 1997. *The Magical State: Nature, Money, and Modernity in Venezuela*. Chicago: University of Chicago Press.

Cousins, B. (Ed.). 2000. *At the Crossroads: Land and Agrarian Reform in South Africa into the 21st Century*. Cape Town: Programme on Land and Agrarian Studies, University of the Western Cape.

——. 2001. 'Uncertainty and Institutional Design: Proposals for Tenure Reform in South Africa.' *Ids Bulletin-Institute of Development Studies* 32: 54–63.

Cox, K.R. 1997. 'Introduction: Globalization and its Politics in Question,' in *Spaces of Globalization: Reasserting the Power of the Local*. Edited by K.R. Cox, pp. 1–18. New York: Guilford Press.

Davis-Floyd, R. 1998. 'Storying Corporate Futures: The Shell Scenarios,' in *Corporate Futures: The Diffusion of the Culturally Sensitive Form*. Edited by G. Marcus, pp. 141–176. Chicago: University of Chicago Press.

DBSA. 1989. 'Report of the Panel of Experts on the Evaluation of the Regional Industrial Development Programme as an Element of the Regional Industrial Development Policy in Southern Africa.' Midrand: DBSA.

DCD. 1998a. *Case Studies on LED and Poverty*. Cape Town: Published by The Isandla Institute for the Department of Constitutional Development.

——. 1998b. *Linking Local Economic Development to Poverty Alleviation*. Cape Town: Published by The Isandla Institute for the Department of Constitutional Development.

Delius, P., and S. Trapido. 1983. 'Inboekselings and Oorlams: The Creation and Transformation of a Servile Class,' in *Town and Countryside in the Transvaal: Capitalist Penetration and Popular Response*. Edited by B. Bozzoli, pp. 53–88. Johannesburg: Ravan Press.

Desai, A. n.d. *The Poors of Chatsworth: Race, Class and Social Movements in Post-Apartheid South Africa*. Durban: Institute for Black Research/Madiba Publishers.

Desmond, C. 1970. *The Discarded People: An Account of African Resettlement*. Braamfontein: The Christian Institute of South Africa.

Deutscher, I. 1984. *Marxism, Wars, and Revolutions: Essays from Four Decades*. London: Verso.

Diamond, N. 1979. 'Women and Industry in Taiwan.' *Modern China* 5: 317–340.

Donald, I. 1984. 'Removals of a Quiet Kind: Evictions from Indian, Coloured and White-owned Land in Natal.' Carnegie Conference Paper 75.

Drew, A. 1996. 'The Theory and Practice of the Agrarian Question in South African Socialism, 1928–1960.' *Journal of Peasant Studies* 23: 53–92.

Dubow, S. 1989. *Racial Segregation and the Origins of Apartheid in South Africa, 1919–36*. Houndmills, Basingstoke, Hampshire: Macmillan in association with St Antony's College, Oxford.

Escobar, A. 1995. *Encountering Development: The Making and Unmaking of the Third World*. Princeton: Princeton University Press.

——. 2001. 'Culture Sits in Places: Reflection on Globalism and Subaltern Strategies of Localization.' *Political Geography* 20: 139–174.

Escobar, A., and W. Harcourt. 1998. 'Creating Glocality.' *Development* 41: 3–5.

Esteva, G., and M.S. Prakash. 1998. *Grassroots Post-Modernism: Remaking the Soil of Cultures*. London: Zed Books.

Etherington, N. 1978. *Preachers, Peasants, and Politics in Southeast Africa, 1835–1880: African Christian Communities in Natal, Pondoland, and Zululand*. London: Royal Historical Society.

——. 1989. 'The "Shepstone System" in the Colony of Natal and Beyond the Borders,' in *Natal and Zululand from Earliest Times to 1910*. Edited by A. Duminy and B. Guest, pp. 170–192. Pietermaritzburg: University of Natal Press.

Evans, P.B. 1995. *Embedded Autonomy: States and Industrial Transformation*. Princeton: Princeton University Press.

Fair, T.J.D. 1955. *The Distribution of Population in Natal*. Cape Town and New York: Published by Oxford University Press for the University of Natal.

Ferme, M.C. 2001. *The Underneath of Things: Violence, History, and the Everyday in Sierra Leone*. Berkeley: University of California Press.

Fernandes, L. 1997. *Producing Workers: The Politics of Gender, Class and Culture in the Calcutta Jute Mills*. Philadelphia: University of Pennsylvania Press.

Fine, B. 2001. *Social Capital versus Social Theory: Political Economy and Social Science at the Turn of the Millennium*. London and New York: Routledge.

Fine, B., and V. Padayachee. 2000. 'A Sustainable Growth Path,' in *Development: Theory, Policy, and Practice*. Edited by J. Coetzee, J. Graaff, F. Hendricks, and G. Wood, pp. 269–281. Cape Town: Oxford University Press.

Fine, B., and Z. Rustomjee. 1996. *The Political Economy of South Africa: From Minerals-Energy Complex to Industrialisation*. London: Hurst.

Foster-Carter, A. 1978. 'The Modes of Production Debate.' *New Left Review* 107: 47–77.

Foucault, M. 1977. *Discipline and Punish: The Birth of the Prison*. New York: Vintage Books.

Fraser, N. 1989. *Unruly Practices: Power, Discourse, and Gender in Contemporary Social Theory*. Minneapolis: University of Minnesota Press.

Freund, B. 1989. 'The Social Character of Secondary Industry in South Africa: 1915–1945,' in *Organisation and Economic Change*. Edited by A. Mabin, pp. 78–119. Johannesburg: Ravan Press.

Freund, B., and V. Padayachee. 1998. 'Post-Apartheid South Africa: The Key Patterns Emerge.' *Economic and Political Weekly* 33: 1173–1180.

Galenson, W. 1979. *Economic Growth and Structural Change in Taiwan: The Postwar Experience of the Republic of China*. Ithaca, N.Y.: Cornell University Press.

Gallin, B., and R.S. Gallin. 1982. 'Socioeconomic Life in Rural Taiwan: Twenty Years of Development and Change.' *Modern China* 8: 205–246.

Gallin, R. 1984. 'Women, Family and the Political Economy of Taiwan.' *Journal of Peasant Studies* 12: 76–92.

Gaonkar, D. 2001. 'On Alternative Modernities,' in *Alternative Modernities*. Edited by D. Gaonkar, pp. 1–18. Durham, N.C.: Duke University Press.

Gates, H. 1979. 'Dependency and the Part-Time Proletariat in Taiwan.' *Modern China* 5: 381–408.

——. 1981. 'Social Class and Ethnicity,' in *The Anthropology of Taiwanese Society*. Edited by H. Gates and E. Martin, pp. 241–281. Stanford: Stanford University Press.

Gibson-Graham, J.K. 1994. 'Stuffed if I Know! Reflections on Post-modern Feminist Social Research.' *Gender, Place and Culture* 1: 205–224.

Gilroy, P. 1987. *'There Ain't No Black in the Union Jack': The Cultural Politics of Race and Nation*. London: Hutchinson.

——. 1993. *The Black Atlantic: Modernity and Double Consciousness*. London and New York: Verso.

Gindin, S. 2000. 'Turning Points and Starting Points: Brenner, Left Turbulence, and Class Politics,' in *Working Classes, Global Realities: Socialist Register 2001*. Edited by L. Panitch and C. Leys, pp. 343–366. London: The Merlin Press.

Glaser, D. 1987. 'A Periodisation of South Africa's Industrial Dispersal Policies,' in *Regional Restructuring under Apartheid: Urban and Regional Policies in Contemporary South Africa*. Edited by R. Tomlinson and M. Addleson, pp. 28–54. Johannesburg: Ravan Press.

Gold, T. 1986. *State and Society in the Taiwan Miracle*. Armonk: M.E. Sharpe.

Gore, C.G. 1984. *Regions in Question: Space, Development Theory, and Regional Policy*. London: Methuen.

Gramsci, A. 1971. *Selections from the Prison Notebooks*. Edited by Q. Hoare and G.N. Smith. London: Lawrence and Wishart.

——. 2000. *The Gramsci Reader: Selected Writings, 1916–1935*. Edited by D. Forgacs. New York: New York University Press.

Granovetter, M. 1985. 'Economic Action and Social Structure: The Problem of Embeddedness.' *American Journal of Sociology* 91: 481–510.

Greenhalgh, S. 1994. 'De-Orientalizing the Chinese Family Firm.' *American Ethnologist* 21: 746–775.

Gregory, D. 1994. *Geographical Imaginations*. Cambridge, Mass.: Blackwell.

Guest, B. 1989. 'The New Economy,' in *Natal and Zululand from Earliest Times to 1910*. Edited by A. Duminy and B. Guest, pp. 302–323. Pietermaritzburg: University of Natal Press.

Gupta, A., and J. Ferguson. 1992. 'Beyond "Culture": Space, Identity, and the Politics of Difference.' *Cultural Anthropology* 7: 6–23.

——. 1997. 'Culture, Power, Place: Ethnography at the End of an Era,' in *Culture, Power, Place: Explorations in Critical Anthropology*. Edited by A. Gupta and J. Ferguson, pp. 1–29. Durham, N.C.: Duke University Press.

Guy, J. 1994. *The Destruction of the Zulu Kingdom: The Civil War in Zululand, 1879–1884*. Pietermaritzburg: University of Natal Press.

Guyer, J., and P. Peters. 1987. 'Conceptualizing the Household: Issues of Theory and Policy in Africa.' *Development and Change* 18: 197–214.

Habib, A., and V. Padayachee. 2000. 'Economic Policy and Power Relations in South Africa's Transition to Democracy.' *World Development* 28: 245–263.

Haggard, S. 1990. *Pathways from the Periphery: The Politics of Growth in the Newly Industrializing Countries*. Ithaca, N.Y.: Cornell University Press.

Hall, S. 1980. 'Race, Articulation and Societies Structured in Dominance,' in *Sociological Theories: Race and Colonialism*, pp. 305–345. Paris: UNESCO.

——. 1985. 'Signification, Representation, Ideology: Althusser and the Post-Structuralist Debates.' *Critical Studies in Mass Communication* 2: 91–114.

——. 1988. *The Hard Road to Renewal: Thatcherism and the Crisis of the Left*. London: Verso.

———. 1990. 'Cultural Identity and the Diaspora,' in *Identity, Community, Cultural Difference*. Edited by J. Rutherford, pp. 222–237. London: Lawrence and Wishart.

———. 1996a. 'On Postmodernism and Articulation: An Interview with Stuart Hall edited by Lawrence Grossberg,' in *Stuart Hall: Critical Dialogues in Cultural Studies*. Edited by D. Morley and K.-H. Chen, pp. 131–150. London and New York: Routledge.

———. 1996b. 'When was "The Post-Colonial"? Thinking at the Limit,' in *The Post-Colonial Question*. Edited by I. Chambers and L. Curti, pp. 242–260. London and New York: Routledge.

———. 1996c. 'Gramsci's Relevance for the Study of Race and Ethnicity,' in *Stuart Hall: Critical Dialogues in Cultural Studies*. Edited by D. Morley and K.-H. Chen, pp. 411–440. London and New York: Routledge.

Hamilton, C. 1998. *Terrific Majesty: The Powers of Shaka Zulu and the Limits of Historical Invention*. Cambridge, Mass.: Harvard University Press.

Hamilton, G. 1998. 'Culture and Organization in Taiwan's Market Economy,' in *Market Cultures: Society and Morality in the New Asian Capitalisms*. Edited by R. Hefner, pp. 41–77. Boulder: Westview Press.

Hamilton, G., and N. Biggart. 1988. 'Market, Culture, and Authority: A Comparative Analysis of Management and Organization in the Far East.' *American Journal of Sociology* 94: S52–S94.

Hamilton, G., and C. Kao. 1990. The Institutional Foundations of Chinese Business: The Family Firm in Taiwan. *Comparative Social Researach* 12: 95–112.

Haraway, D.J. 1991. *Simians, Cyborgs, and Women: The Reinvention of Nature*. New York: Routledge.

Harrell, S. 1981. 'Effects of Economic Change on Two Taiwanese Villages.' *Modern China* 7: 31–54.

———. 1985. 'Why Do the Chinese Work So Hard? Reflections on an Entrepreneurial Ethic.' *Modern China* 11: 203–226.

Harris, V. 1994. 'Changing Forms of Agricultural Labour on White-owned Farms in Northern Natal, 1910–1936,' in *Receded Tides of Empire*. Edited by B. Guest and J. Sellers, pp. 241–261. Pietermaritzburg: University of Natal Press.

Harrison, P. 1990. 'The Economic Development of North-Western Natal.' Physical Planning Directorate, Natal Provincial Administration Report No. 1.

Harrison, P., and K. Harrison-Migochi. 1997. 'Economic and Financial Analysis for the Ladysmith Integrated Development Framework.'

Harrison, P., and A. Todes. 1996. 'Evaluation of the Regional Industrial Development Programme in KwaZulu-Natal: Report to the Board for Regional Industrial Development.' University of Natal.

Hart, G. 1991. 'Engendering Everyday Resistance: Gender, Patronage and Production Politics in Rural Malaysia.' *Journal of Peasant Studies* 19: 93–121.

———. 1995. '"Clothes for Next to Nothing": Rethinking Global Competition.' *South African Labour Bulletin* 19: 41–47.

——. 1996a. 'The Agrarian Question and Industrial Dispersal in South Africa: Agro-Industrial Linkages Through Asian Lenses.' *Journal of Peasant Studies* 23: 243–277.

——. 1996b. *Global Connections: The Rise and Fall of a Taiwanese Production Network on the South African Periphery*. Institute for International Studies Working Paper 6. University of California, Berkeley.

——. 1998a. 'Multiple Trajectories: A Critique of Industrial Restructuring and the New Institutionalism.' *Antipode* 30: 333–356.

——. 1998b. 'Regional Growth Linkages in the Era of Liberalization: A Critique of the New Agrarian Optimism.' *Development and Change* 29: 27–54.

——. 2001. 'Development Critiques in the 1990s: Culs de sac and Promising Paths.' *Progress in Human Geography* 25: 649–658.

Harvey, D. 1982. *The Limits to Capital*. Chicago: University of Chicago Press.

——. 1989. *The Condition of Postmodernity: An Enquiry into the Origins of Cultural Change*. Oxford: Blackwell.

——. 1996. *Justice, Nature, and the Geography of Difference*. Cambridge, Mass.: Blackwell.

——. 2000. *Spaces of Hope*. Berkeley: University of California Press.

Hassim, S. 1993. 'Family, Motherhood, and Zulu Nationalism: The Politics of the Inkatha Brigade.' *Feminist Review* 43: 1–25.

Heller, P. 1996. 'Social Capital as a Product of Class Mobilization and State Intervention: Industrial Workers in Kerala, India.' *World Development* 24: 1055–1071.

Henderson, P. 1986. *Waaihoek*. Pietermaritzburg: Association for Rural Advancement.

Hindson, D. 1987. 'Alternative Urbanisation Strategies in South Africa: A Critical Evaluation.' *Third World Quarterly* 9: 583–600.

Hirsch, A. 1979. 'An Introduction to Textile Worker Organisation in Natal.' *South African Labour Bulletin* 4: 3–42.

Ho, S. 1978. *Economic Development of Taiwan, 1860–1970*. New Haven: Yale University Press.

——. 1982. 'Economic Development and Rural Industry in South Korea and Taiwan.' *World Development* 10: 973–990.

hooks, b. 1990. *Yearning: Race, Gender, and Cultural Politics*. Boston, MA.: Southend Press.

Howarth, D.R., and A.J. Norval. (Eds). 1998. *South Africa in Transition: New Theoretical Perspectives*. New York: St Martin's Press.

Hsing, Y.-T. 1995. 'Cheap Hands and Cheap Brains: Chinese Workers in Taiwanese Factories.' Institute of International Studies. Unpublished.

——. 1996. 'Blood, Thicker than Water: Interpersonal Relations and Taiwanese Investment in Southern China.' *Environment and Planning A* 28: 2241–2261.

——. 1998. *Making Capitalism in China: The Taiwan Connection*. New York: Oxford University Press.

Hsiung, P.-C. 1991. 'Class, Gender, and the Satellite Factory System in Taiwan.' Doctoral Dissertation, University of California, Los Angeles.

——. 1996. *Living Rooms as Factories: Class, Gender, and the Satellite Factory System in Taiwan*. Philadelphia: Temple University Press.

Hu, T. 1983. *The Emergence of Small-Scale Industry in a Taiwanese Rural Community: Women, Men, and the International Division of Labor*. Albany: State University of New York Press.

Huang, P. 1990. *The Peasant Family and Rural Development in the Yangzi Delta, 1350–1988*. Stanford: Stanford University Press.

Ishikawa, S. 1967. *Economic Development in Asian Perspective*. Tokyo: Kinokuniya Bookstore Co.

——. 1988. 'Technology Import and Indigenous Technology Capacity in China.' World Employment Programme Research Working Paper. Geneva: International Labour Office.

Jameson, F. 1991. *Postmodernism, or, the Cultural Logic of Late Capitalism: Post-Contemporary Interventions*. Durham, N.C.: Duke University Press.

——. 1998. 'Preface,' in *The Cultures of Globalization: Post-Contemporary Interventions*. Edited by F. Jameson and M. Miyoshi, pp. xi–xvii. Durham, N.C.: Duke University Press.

Jefferson, G.H., and T.G. Rawski. 1994. 'Enterprise Reform in Chinese Industry.' *Journal of Economic Perspectives* 8: 47–71.

Jessop, B. 1982. *The Capitalist State: Marxist Theories and Methods*. Oxford: M. Robertson.

——. 1997. 'Capitalism and its Future.' *Review of International Political Economy* 4: 561–581.

Joffe, A., D. Kaplan, R. Kaplinsky, and D. Lewis. 1995. *Improving Manufacturing Performance in South Africa: Report of the Industrial Strategy Project*. Cape Town: University of Cape Town Press.

Johnston, A.M., and R.W. Johnston. 1997. 'The Local Elections in KwaZulu-Natal: 26 June 1996.' *African Affairs* 96: 377–398.

Judd, E.R. 1994. *Gender and Power in Rural North China*. Stanford: Stanford University Press.

Kaplinsky, R. 1994. 'Economic Restructuring in South Africa: The Debate Continues. A Response.' *Journal of Southern African Studies* 20: 533–538.

Kapur, G. 1998. 'Globalization and Culture: Navigating the Void,' in *The Cultures of Globalization*. Edited by F. Jameson and M. Miyoshi, pp. 191–217. Durham, N.C.: Duke University Press.

Karshenas, M. 1995. *Industrialization and Agricultural Surplus: A Comparative Study of Economic Development in Asia*. Oxford: Oxford University Press.

Katz, C. 2001. 'Vagabond Capitalism and the Necessity of Social Reproduction.' *Antipode* 33: 709–728.

Kautsky, K. [1899] 1988. *The Agrarian Question*. London: Zwan Publications.

Keegan, T.J. 1986. *Rural Transformations in Industrializing South Africa: The*

Southern Highveld to 1914. New History of Southern Africa Series. Johannesburg: Ravan Press.

Keith, M., and S. Pile. 1993. 'Introduction: The Place of Politics,' in *Place and the Politics of Identity*. Edited by M. Keith and S. Pile, pp. 22–40. London: Routledge.

Kentridge, M. 1993. *Turning the Tanker: The Economic Debate in South Africa*. Johannesburg: Centre for Policy Studies.

Kitching, G. 1982. *Development and Underdevelopment in Historical Perspective: Populism, Nationalism and Industrialization*. London and New York: Metheun.

Klug, H. 2000. *Constituting Democracy: Law, Globalism, and South Africa's Political Reconstruction*. Cambridge: Cambridge University Press.

Krueger, A.O. 1981. *Trade and Employment in Developing Countries*. Chicago: University of Chicago Press.

Kung, L. 1976. 'Factory Work and Women in Taiwan: Changes in Self-Image and Status.' *Signs* 2: 35–58.

Laclau, E. 1977. *Politics and Ideology in Marxist Theory: Capitalism, Fascism, Populism*. London: New Left Books.

——. 1990. *New Reflections on the Revolution of Our Time*. London: Verso.

——. 1994. *The Making of Political Identities*. London: Verso.

——. 1996. *Emancipation(s)*. London: Verso.

Laclau, E., and C. Mouffe. 1985. *Hegemony and Socialist Strategy: Towards a Radical Democratic Politics*. London: Verso.

Lahiff, E. 2001. *Land Reform in South Africa: Is it Meeting the Challenge?* Cape Town: Programme on Land and Agrarian Studies, University of the Western Cape.

Lam. 1989. 'Guerrilla Capitalism: Export Oriented Firms and the Economic Miracle in Taiwan.' *Journal of Sinology* 4.

Lambert, J. 1989. 'From Independence to Rebellion: African Society in Crisis, 1880–1910,' in *Natal and Zululand from Earliest Times to 1910*. Edited by A. Duminy and B. Guest, pp. 373–401. Pietermaritzburg: University of Natal Press.

——. 1995. *Betrayed Trust: Africans and the State in Colonial Natal*. Pietermaritzburg: University of Natal Press.

Lambert, J., and R. Morrell. 1996. 'Domination and Subordination in Natal 1890–1920,' in *Political Economy and Identities in KwaZulu-Natal*. Edited by R. Morrell, pp. 63–95. Durban: Indicator Press.

Lardy, N.R. 1983. *Agriculture in China's Modern Economic Development*. Cambridge: Cambridge University Press.

Lave, J., P. Duguid, N. Fernandez, and E. Axel. 1992. 'Coming of Age in Birmingham: Cultural Studies and Conceptions of Subjectivity.' *Annual Review of Anthropology* 21: 257–282.

Lazar, J. 1993. 'Verwoerd versus the "Visionaries": The South African Bureau of Racial Affairs (Sabra) and Apartheid, 1948–1961,' in *Apartheid's Genesis, 1935–1962*. Edited by P. Bonner, P. Delius, and D. Posel, pp. 362–392. Johannesburg: Ravan Press.

Lee, C.K. 1993. 'Familial Hegemony: Gender and Production Politics on Hong-Kongs Electronics Shopfloor.' *Gender & Society* 7: 529–547.

———. 1995. 'Engendering the Worlds of Labor: Women Workers, Labor Markets, and Production Politics in the South China Economic Miracle.' *American Sociological Review* 60: 378–397.

Lee, T.-H. 1971. *Intersectoral Capital Flows in the Economic Development of Taiwan, 1895–1960*. Ithaca, N.Y.: Cornell University Press.

Lefebvre, H. [1974] 1991. *The Production of Space*. Oxford: Blackwell.

Lenin, V.I. [1899] 1964. *The Development of Capitalism in Russia*, 2nd rev. edition. Moscow: Progress Publishers.

Levin, R., and D. Weiner. 1996. 'The Politics of Land Reform in South Africa after Apartheid: Perspectives, Problems, Prospects.' *Journal of Peasant Studies* 23: 93–119.

Li, T. 2000. 'Articulating Indigenous Identity in Indonesia: Resource Politics and the Tribal Slot.' *Comparative Studies in Society and History* 42: 149–179.

Lin, N. 1995. 'Local Market Socialism: Local Corporatism in Action in Rural China.' *Theory and Society* 24: 301–354.

Lipton, M., F. Ellis, and M. Lipton. (Eds). 1996. *Land, Labour and Livelihoods in Rural South Africa*. Durban: Indicator Press.

Lipton, M., and M. Lipton. 1993. 'Creating Rural Livelihoods: Some Lessons for South Africa From Experience Elsewhere.' *World Development* 21: 1515–1548.

Lu, X. 1997. 'The Politics of Peasant Burden in Reform China.' *Journal of Peasant Studies* 25: 113–138.

Mabin, A. 1989. 'Struggle for the City: Urbanisation and Political Strategies of the South African State.' *Social Dynamics* 15: 1–28.

Mager, A.K. 1999. *Gender and the Making of a South African Bantustan: A Social History of the Ciskei, 1945–1959*. Portsmouth, N.H.: Heinemann.

Mamdani, M. 1996. *Citizen and Subject: Contemporary Africa and the Legacy of Late Colonialism*. Princeton: Princeton University Press.

MaoTse-tung. [1927] 1967. 'Report on an Investigation of the Peasant Movement in Hunan,' in *Selected Works of Mao Tse-tung*, Vol. 1, pp. 25–59. Peking: Foreign Languages Press.

Marais, H. 1998. *South Africa: Limits to Change: The Political Economy of Transition*. London and Cape Town: Zed Books and University of Cape Town Press.

Maralack, D. 1998. 'The Provision of Water and Sanitation Services in Nelspruit,' in *Case Studies on LED and Poverty*. Edited by Department of Constitutional Development, pp. 303–319. Cape Town: The Isandla Institute.

Marcus, G.E. 1998. *Ethnography through Thick and Thin*. Princeton: Princeton University Press.

Maré, G., and G. Hamilton. 1987. *An Appetite for Power: Buthelezi's Inkatha and South Africa*. Johannesburg and Bloomington: Ravan Press and Indiana University Press.

Maree, J. 1987. *The Independent Trade Unions, 1974–1984: Ten Years of the South African Labour Bulletin.* Ravan Labour Studies 2. Johannesburg: Ravan Press.

Marks, S. 1970. *Reluctant Rebellion: The 1906–8 Disturbances in Natal.* Oxford Studies in African Affairs. Oxford: Clarendon Press.

——. 1978. 'Natal, the Zulu Royal Family, and the Ideology of Segregation.' *Journal of South African Studies* 4: 172–194.

——. 1986. *The Ambiguities of Dependence in South Africa: Class, Nationalism, and the State in Twentieth-Century Natal.* Johannesburg: Ravan Press.

——. 1989. 'Patriotism, Patriarchy and Purity: Natal and the Politics of Zulu Ethnic Consciousness,' in *The Creation of Tribalism in Southern Africa.* Edited by L. Vail, pp. 215–240. London and Berkeley: James Currey and University of California Press.

Marston, S.A. 2000. 'The Social Construction of Scale.' *Progress in Human Geography* 24: 219–242.

Marx, K. [1887] 1954. *Capital,* Volume I. Moscow: Progress Publishers.

Massey, D. 1992. 'Politics and Space Time.' *New Left Review* 196: 65–84.

——. 1994. *Space, Place, and Gender.* Minneapolis: University of Minnesota Press.

——. 1999a. 'Spaces of Politics,' in *Human Geography Today.* Edited by D.B. Massey, J. Allen, and P. Sarre, pp. 279–294. Cambridge: Polity Press in association with Blackwell.

——. 1999b. 'Imagining Globalization: Power-Geometries of Space-Time,' in *Global Futures: Migration, Environment and Globalization.* Edited by A. Brah, pp. 27–44. Houndmills, Basingstoke and New York: Macmillan Press and St Martin's Press.

Mbeki, G. 1964. *South Africa: The Peasants' Revolt.* Baltimore: Penguin Books.

McClendon, T.V. 1995. 'Tradition and Domestic Struggle in the Courtroom: Customary Law and the Control of Women in Segregation-Era Natal.' *International Journal of African Historical Studies* 28: 527–562.

McClintock, A. 1995. *Imperial Leather: Race, Gender, and Sexuality in the Colonial Contest.* New York: Routledge.

McCoy, A. 1971. 'Land Reform as Counter-Revolution.' *Bulletin of Concerned Asian Scholars* 3: 14–49.

McDonald, M. 1996. 'Farmers as Workers in Japan's Regional Economic Restructuring, 1965–1985.' *Economic Geography* 72: 49–73.

McKinley, T., and K. Griffin. 1993. 'The Distribution of Land in Rural China.' *Journal of Peasant Studies* 21: 71–84.

Meer, S. 1988. 'Community Unions in Natal.' *South African Labour Bulletin* 13: 74–84.

Meissner, M. 1982. *Marxism, Maoism, and Utopianism: Eight Essays.* Madison, Wis.: University of Wisconsin Press.

MERG. 1993. *Making Democracy Work: A Framework for Macroeconomic Policy in South Africa.* Cape Town: Oxford University Press.

Merrifield, A. 2000. 'Henri Lefebvre: A Socialist in Space,' in *Thinking Space*. Edited by M. Crang and N. Thrift, pp. 167–182. New York: Routledge.

Mitchell, K. 1997. 'Different Diasporas and the Hype of Hybridity.' *Environment and Planning D-Society & Space* 15: 533–553.

Mmutlana, R. 1993. 'Forced Removals in Northern Natal: A Comparative Study of the Steincoalspruit and Roosboom Communities in Historical Perspective.' MA thesis, University of Natal.

Mohan, G., and K. Stokke. 2000. 'Participatory Development and Empowerment: The Dangers of Localism.' *Third World Quarterly* 20: 247–268.

Moore, D.S. 1993. 'Contesting Terrain in Zimbabwe's Eastern Highlands: Political Ecology, Ethnography, and Peasant Resource Struggles.' *Economic Geography* 69: 380–401.

——. 1998. 'Subaltern Struggles and the Politics of Place: Remapping Resistance in Zimbabwe's Eastern Highlands.' *Cultural Anthropology* 13: 344–381.

——. 2000. 'The Crucible of Cultural Politics: Reworking "Development" in Zimbabwe's Eastern Highlands.' *American Ethnologist* 26: 654–689.

Morley, D., and K.-H. Chen. (Eds). 1996. *Stuart Hall: Critical Dialogues in Cultural Studies*. London and New York: Routledge.

Morrell, R., J. Wright, and S. Meintjies. 1996. 'Colonialism and the Establishment of White Domination 1840–1890,' in *Political Economy and Identities in KwaZulu-Natal: Historical and Social Perspectives*. Edited by R. Morrell, pp. 33–62. Durban: Indicator Press.

Morris, M. 1976. 'The Development of Capitalism in South African Agriculture: Class Struggle in the Countryside.' *Economy and Society* 5: 292–343.

——. 1991. 'State, Capital and Growth: The Political Economy of the National Question,' in *South Africa's Economic Crisis*. Edited by S. Gelb, pp. 33–58. Cape Town: David Philip.

Morris, M., and V. Padayachee. 1989. 'Hegemonic Projects, Accumulation Strategies and State Reform Policy in South Africa.' *Labour, Capital and Society* 22: 65–109.

Mouffe, C. 1992. *Dimensions of Radical Democracy: Pluralism, Citizenship, Community*. London: Verso.

——. 1995. 'Post-Marxism: Democracy and Identity.' *Environment and Planning D* 13: 259–265.

Murray, C. 1988. 'Displaced Urbanization,' in *South Africa in Question*. Edited by J. Londsdale. London: James Currey.

Mzala. 1988. *Gatsha Buthelezi: Chief with a Double Agenda*. London: Zed Books.

Nee, V. 1992. 'Organizational Dynamics of Market Transition: Hybrid Forms, Property Rights, and Mixed Economy in China.' *Administrative Science Quarterly*: 1–27.

Nicholson, L. (Ed.). 1997. *The Second Wave: A Reader in Feminist Theory*. London and New York: Routledge.

Niehoff, J.D. 1987. 'The Villager as Industrialist: Ideologies of Household Manufacturing in Rural Taiwan.' *Modern China* 13: 278–309.

Nonini, D. and A. Ong. 1997. 'Chinese Transnationalism as an Alternative Modernity,' in *Ungrounded Empires: The Cultural Politics of Modern Chinese Transnationalism.* Edited by A. Ong and D. Nonini, pp. 3–33. New York: Routledge.

Norval, A.J. 1996. *Deconstructing Apartheid Discourse.* New York: Verso.

Ntsebeza, L. 2000. 'Traditional Authorities, Local Government and Land Rights,' in *At the Crossroads: Land and Agrarian Reform in South Africa into the 21st Century.* Edited by B. Cousins, pp. 280–305. Cape Town: Programme on Land and Agrarian Studies.

Numazaki, I. 1991. 'State and Business in Postwar Taiwan: Comment on Hamilton and Biggart.' *American Journal of Sociology* 96: 993–1000.

Nzimande, B., and J. Cronin. 1997. 'We Need Transformation not a Balancing Act: Looking Critically at the ANC Discussion Document.' *The African Communist* 146: 62–70.

Odgaard, O. 1990/1. 'Inadequate and Inaccurate Chinese Statistics: The Case of Private Rural Enterprises.' *China Information* 5: 29–38.

Ody, A.J. 1992. *Rural Enterprise Development in China, 1986–90.* Washington, DC: World Bank.

Ohmae, K. 1995. *The End of the Nation State: The Rise of Regional Economies.* New York: The Free Press.

Oi, J.C. 1992. 'Fiscal Reform and the Economic Foundations of Local State Corporatism in China.' *World Politics* 45: 99–126.

——. 1999. *Rural China Takes Off: Institutional Foundations of Economic Reform.* Berkeley: University of California Press.

Olver, C. 1998. 'Metropolitan Government for the 21st Century.' *Development Southern Africa* 15: 289–291.

O'Meara, D. 1983. *Volkskapitalisme: Class, Capital, and Ideology in the Development of Afrikaner Nationalism, 1934–1948.* African Studies Series 34. Cambridge, Cambridgeshire and New York: Cambridge University Press.

Ong, A. 1987. *Spirits of Resistance and Capitalist Discipline: Factory Women in Malaysia.* SUNY Series in the Anthropology of Work. Albany: State University of New York Press.

——. 1991. 'The Gender and Labor Politics of Postmodernity.' *Annual Review of Anthropology*: 279–309.

——. 1997. '"A Momentary Glow of Fraternity": Narratives of Chinese Nationalism and Capitalism.' *Identities-Global Studies in Culture and Power* 3: 331–366.

——. 1999. *Flexible Citizenship: The Cultural Logics of Transnationality.* Durham, N.C.: Duke University Press.

Orru, M. 1991. 'The Institutional Logic of Small-Firm Economics in Italy and Taiwan.' *Studies in Comparative International Development* 26: 3–28.

Padayachee, V. 1998. 'Progressive Academic Economists and the Challenge of Development in South Africa's Decade of Liberation.' *Review of African Political Economy* 25: 431–450.

Pang, C. 1992. *The State and Economic Transformation: The Taiwan Case*. New York: Garland Publishers.

Park, A., and B. Johnston. 1995. 'Rural Development and Dynamic Externalities in Taiwan's Structural Transformation.' *Economic Development and Cultural Change* 44: 181–209.

Parmar, P. 1982. 'Gender, Race, and Class: Asian Women in Resistance,' in *The Empire Strikes Back: Race and Racism in 70s Britain*. Edited by the Centre for Contemporary Cultural Studies, Birmingham, pp. 236–275. London: Hutchinson.

Peng, Y.S. 1992. 'Wage Determination in Rural and Urban China: A Comparison of Public and Private Industrial Sectors.' *American Sociological Review* 57: 198–213.

Perelman, M. 2000. *The Invention of Capitalism: Classical Political Economy and the Secret History of Accumulation*. Durham, N.C.: Duke University Press.

Perkins, D. 1977. *Rural Small-Scale Industry in the People's Republic of China*. Berkeley: University of California Press.

Perotti, E., L. Sun, and L. Zou. 1999. 'State-owned versus Township and Village Enterprises in China.' *Comparative Economic Studies* 41: 151–179.

Phadu, T. 1998. 'An Inside View of the Tembisa Struggles.' *Debate* 4: 28–30.

Pickles, J., and D. Weiner. 1991. 'Rural and Regional Restructuring of Apartheid: Ideology, Development Policy and the Competition for Space.' *Antipode* 23: 2–32.

Pickles, J., and J. Woods. 1989. 'Taiwanese Investment in South Africa.' *African Affairs* 88: 507–528.

Piore, M., and C. Sabel. 1984. *The Second Industrial Divide*. New York: Basic Books.

Plaatje, S.T. [1917] 1987. *Native Life in South Africa*. Edited and introduced by B. Willan. Burnt Mill: Longman.

Platzky, L. 1995. 'The Development Impact of South Africa's Industrial Location Policies: An Unforeseen Legacy.' PhD thesis, Institute of Social Studies, The Hague.

Platzky, L., and C. Walker. 1985. *The Surplus People: Forced Removals in South Africa*. Johannesburg: Ravan Press.

Polanyi, K. 1944. *The Great Transformation*. New York: Farrar & Rinehart.

———. 2001. *The Great Transformation: The Political and Economic Origins of Our Time*. Introduced by F. Block. Boston: Beacon Press.

Pred, A. 1990. *Making Histories and Constructing Human Geographies: The Local Transformation of Practice, Power Relations, and Consciousness*. Boulder: Westview Press.

———. 1995. 'Out of Bounds and Undisciplined: Social Inquiry and the Current Moment of Danger.' *Social Research: An International Quarterly of the Social Sciences* Winter: 1065–1091.

———. 2000. *Even in Sweden: Racisms, Racialized Spaces, and the Popular Geographical Imagination*. Berkeley: University of California Press.

Pred, A., and M. Watts. 1992. *Reworking Modernity*. Brunswick, N.J.: Rutgers University Press.

Putterman, L. 1989. 'Entering the Post-Collective Era in North China: Dahe Township.' *Modern China* 15: 275–320.

 Pycroft, C. 1998. 'Integrated Development Planning or Strategic Paralysis? Municipal Development During the Local Government Transition and Beyond.' *Development Southern Africa* 15: 151–163.

Ranis, G. 1995. 'Another Look at the East Asian Miracle.' *World Bank Economic Review* 9: 509–534.

Ranis, G., and F. Stewart. 1987. *Rural Linkages in the Philippines and Taiwan: Macro-Policies for Appropriate Technology in Developing Countries.* Boulder: Westview Press.

——. 1993. 'Rural Nonagricultural Activities in Development: Theory and Application.' *Journal of Development Economics* 40: 75–101.

Redding, S.G. 1990. *The Spirit of Chinese Capitalism.* Berlin: W. de Gruyter.

Richardson, P. 1986. 'The Natal Sugar Industry in the Nineteenth Century,' in *Putting a Plough to the Ground: Accumulation and Dispossession in Rural South Africa, 1850–1930.* Edited by W. Beinart, P. Delius, and S. Trapido, pp. 129–175. Johannesburg: Ravan Press.

Riskin, C. 1971. 'Small Industry and the Chinese Model of Development.' *China Quarterly* 46: 245–273.

——. 1987. *China's Political Economy: The Quest for Development since 1949.* Oxford: Oxford University Press.

Robinson, J. 1996. *The Power of Apartheid.* Oxford: Butterworth-Heinemann Ltd.

Rodrik, D. 1997. *Has Globalization Gone too Far?* Washington, DC: Institute for International Economics.

Rofel, L. 1992. 'Rethinking Modernity: Space and Factory Discipline in China.' *Cultural Anthropology* 7: 93–114.

——. 1999. *Other Modernities: Gendered Yearnings in China after Socialism.* Berkeley: University of California Press.

Roseberry, W. 1996. 'Hegemony and the Language of Contention,' in *Everyday Forms of State Formation.* Edited by G. Joseph and D. Nugent, pp. 355–366. Durham, N.C. and London: Duke University Press.

Rozelle, S. 1994. 'Rural Industrialization and Increasing Inequality: Emerging Patterns in China's Reforming Economy.' *Journal of Comparative Economics* 19: 362–391.

Rozman, G. 1991. *The East Asian Region: Confucian Heritage and its Modern Adaptation.* Princeton: Princeton University Press.

Ruf, G.A. 1998. *Cadres and Kin: Making a Socialist Village in West China, 1921–1991.* Stanford: Stanford University Press.

Sachs, J.D., and W.T. Woo. 1994. 'Experiences in the Transition to a Market Economy.' *Journal of Comparative Economics* 18: 271–275.

Salzinger, L. 1997. 'From High Heels to Swathed Bodies: Gendered Meanings under Production in Mexico's Export-processing Industry.' *Feminist Studies* 23: 549–574.

Saul, J.S. 2001. 'Cry for the Beloved Country: The Post-Apartheid Dénouement.' *Monthly Review* 52: 1–51.

Sayer, A. 1991. 'Behind the Locality Debate: Deconstructing Geography's Dualisms.' *Environment & Planning A* 23: 283–308.

Schive, C., and B.A. Majumdar. 1990. 'Direct Foreign Investment and Linkage Effects: The Experience of Taiwan.' *Revue Canadienne D Etudes Du Developpement – Canadian Journal of Development Studies* 11: 325–342.

Scott, J.C. 1985. *Weapons of the Weak: Everyday Forms of Peasant Resistance.* New Haven: Yale University Press.

Scott, J.W. 1988. *Gender and the Politics of History.* New York: Columbia University Press.

Seekings, J. 1991. 'Township Resistance in the 1980s,' in *Apartheid City in Transition.* Edited by M. Swilling, R. Humphries, and K. Shubane, pp. 290–308. Cape Town: Oxford University Press.

Seethal, C. 1992. 'The Transformation of the Local State in South Africa (1979–1991): Group Areas, Property "Super-Taxation," and Civic Organizations.' *Urban Geography* 13: 534–556.

Seidman, G. 1994. *Manufacturing Militance: Workers' Movements in Brazil and South Africa, 1970–1985.* Berkeley: University of California Press.

Selden, M., and C. Ka. 1993. 'Original Accumulation, Equity, and Late Industrialization: The Case of Socialist China and Capitalist Taiwan,' in *The Political Economy of Chinese Development.* Edited by M. Selden. Armonk: M.E. Sharpe.

Shieh, G.S. 1992. *'Boss' Island: The Subcontracting Network and Micro-Entrepreneurship in Taiwan's Development.* New York: Peter Land.

Shields, R. 1999. *Lefebvre, Love, and Struggle: Spatial Dialectics.* London and New York: Routledge.

Shih, J.T. 1983. 'Decentralized Industrialization and Rural Nonfarm Employment in Taiwan.' *Industry of Free China* August: 1–20.

Simkins, C.E.W. 1983. *Four Essays on the Past, Present & Possible Future of the Distribution of the Black Population of South Africa.* Rondebosch: Southern Africa Labour and Development Research Unit, University of Cape Town.

Sitas, A. 1984. 'The Dunlop's Strike: A Trial of Strength.' *South African Labour Bulletin* 10: 62–84.

———. 1990. 'Ethnicity, Nationalism and Culture in Natal's Labour Movement,' in *The Societies of Southern Africa.* Edited by S. Marks, pp. 267–278. London: Institute of Commonwealth Studies.

———. 1998. 'South Africa of the 1990s: The Logic of Fragmentation and Reconstruction.' *Transformation* 36: 37–51.

Sithole, J. 1997. 'Land Disputes and Izimpi Zemibango in the Umlazi Location of the Pinetown District, 1920–1936.' *South African Historical Journal* 37: 78–106.

Siu, H. 1989. *Agents and Victims in South China: Accomplices in Rural Revolution.* New Haven: Yale University Press.

Slater, H. 1975. 'Land, Labour and Capital in Natal: The Natal Land and Colonisation Company, 1860–1948.' *Journal of African History* XVI: 257–283.

———. 1980. 'The Changing Pattern of Economic Relationships in Rural Natal, 1938–1914,' in *Economy and Society in Pre-Industrial South Africa.* Edited by S. Marks and A. Atmore, pp. 148–170. Hong Kong: Longman.

Smart, A. 1998. 'Economic Transformation in China: Property Regimes and Social Relations,' in *Theorizing Transition: The Political Economy of Post-Socialist Transformations*. Edited by J. Pickles and A. Smith, pp. 428–449. London and New York: Routledge.

Smart, J., and A. Smart. 1993. 'Obligation and Control: Employment of Kin in Capitalist Labor Management in China.' *Critique of Anthropology* 13: 7–31.

Smith, A. [1776] 1986. *The Wealth of Nations, Books I–III*. London: Penguin Classics.

Smith, N. 1991. *Uneven Development: Nature, Capital, and the Production of Space*. Oxford: Blackwell.

——. 1992. 'Geography, Difference and the Politics of Scale,' in *Postmodernism and the Social Sciences*. Edited by J. Doherty, E. Graham, and M. Malek, pp. 57–79. New York: St Martin's Press.

——. 1997. 'The Satanic Geographies of Globalization: Uneven Development in the 1990s.' *Public Culture* 10: 169–189.

Smith, N., and C. Katz. 1993. 'Grounding Metaphor: Towards a Spatialized Politics,' in *Place and the Politics of Identity*. Edited by M. Keith and S. Pile, pp. 67–83. London: Routledge.

Soni, D., and B. Maharaj. 1991. 'Emerging Urban Forms in Rural South Africa.' *Antipode* 23: 47–67.

Sparke, M. 1994. 'White Mythologies and Anemic Geographies: A Review.' *Environment and Planning D* 12: 105–123.

SPP. 1983. *Forced Removals in South Africa*. Volume 4 of the Surplus People Project Report. Pietermaritzburg: Association for Rural Advancement.

Stites, R. 1982. 'Small-scale industry in Yingge, Taiwan.' *Modern China* 8: 247–279.

——. 1985. 'Industrial Work as an Entrepreneurial Strategy.' *Modern China* 11: 227–246.

Stoler, A.L. 1995. *Race and the Education of Desire: Foucault's History of Sexuality and the Colonial Order of Things*. Durham, N.C.: Duke University Press.

Sun, L. 2000. 'Anticipatory Ownership Reform Driven by Competition: China's Township-Village and Private Enterprises in the 1990s.' *Comparative Economic Studies* 42: 49–75.

Swilling, M., W. Cobbett, and R. Hunter. 1991. 'Finance, Electricity Costs, and the Rent Boycott,' in *Apartheid City in Transition*. Edited by M. Swilling, R. Humphries, and K. Shubane, pp. 174–196. Oxford: Oxford University Press.

Swilling, M., and M. Phillips. 1989. 'The Emergency State: Its Structure, Power, and Limits,' in *South African Review 5*. Edited by G. Moss and I. Obery, pp. 68–90. Johannesburg: Ravan Press.

Swyngedouw, E. 1997. 'Neither Global nor Local: "Glocalization" and the Politics of Scale,' in *Spaces of Globalization: Reasserting the Power of the Local*. Edited by K.R. Cox, pp. 137–166. New York: The Guilford Press.

Taylor, C. 2001. 'Two Theories of Modernity,' in *Alternative Modernities*. Edited by D. Gaonkar, pp. 153–174. Durham, N.C.: Duke University Press.

Thornton, R. 1995. 'The Colonial, the Imperial, and the Creation of the "European" in Southern Africa,' in *Occidentalism: Images of the West*. Edited by J. Carrier, pp. 192–217. Oxford: The Clarendon Press.

——. 1996. 'The Potentials of Boundaries in South Africa: Steps Towards a Theory of the Social Edge,' in *Postcolonial Identities in Africa*. Edited by R. Werbner and T. Ranger, pp. 136–161. London: Zed Books.

Todes, A. 1997. 'Restructuring, Migration and Regional Policy in South Africa: The Case of Newcastle.' PhD, University of Natal.

——. 1999. 'Industrial Restructuring in South Africa: The Case of Newcastle.' *Tijdschrift Voor Economische En Sociale Geografie* 90: 379–390.

Tomich, T.P., P. Kilby, and B.F. Johnston. 1995. *Transforming Agrarian Economies: Opportunities Seized, Opportunities Missed*. Ithaca, N.Y.: Cornell University Press.

Trotsky, L. 1973. 'On the South African Theses: To the South African Section,' in *Writings of Leon Trotsky, 1934–35*. Edited by G. Breitman, pp. 245–255. New York: Pathfinder Press.

Tsai, H.C. 1984. 'Rural Industrialization in Taiwan.' *Industry of Free China* May, June, July.

Turner, S., and H. Ibsen. 2000. *Land and Agrarian Reform in South Africa*. Cape Town: Programme on Land and Agrarian Studies, University of the Western Cape.

UNDP. 2000. *South Africa: Transformation for Human Develpoment*. Pretoria: United Nations Development Programme.

Unger, R.M. 1998. *Democracy Realized: The Progressive Alternative*. London: Verso.

Urban Foundation. 1990. *Regional Development Reconsidered*. Urban Foundation Policies for a New Urban Future Series No. 1.

Van Onselen, C. 1996. *The Seed is Mine: The Life of Kas Maine, a South African Sharecropper, 1894–1985*, 1st edition. New York: Hill and Wang.

Visweswaran, K. 1994. *Fictions of Feminist Ethnography*. Minneapolis: University of Minnesota Press.

Vohra, R. 1994. 'Deng Xiaping's Modernization: Capitalism with Chinese Characteristics.' *Developing Societies* 10: 46–58.

Wade, R. 1990. *Governing the Market: Economic Theory and the Role of Government in East Asian Industrialization*. Princeton: Princeton University Press.

Walder, A. 1986. *Communist Neo-Traditionalism: Work and Authority in Chinese Industry*. Berkeley: University of California Press.

——. 1994. 'The Varieties of Public Enterprise in China: An Institutional Analysis.' Unpublished paper written for the project on The Changing Role of the State: Strategies for Reforming Public Enterprise. Washington, DC: The World Bank.

——. 1995. 'Local Governments as Industrial Firms: An Organizational Analysis of China's Transitional Economy.' *American Journal of Sociology* 101: 263–301.

Walker, C. 2000. 'Relocating Restitution.' *Transformation* 44: 1–16.

——. 2001a. 'Evolving Government Policies, 1991–2001.' United Nations Research Institute for Social Development, Geneva.

——. 2001b. 'Piety in the Sky? Gender Policy and Land Reform in South Africa.' United Nations Research Institute for Social Development, Geneva.

Wang, X. 1997. 'Mutual Empowerment of State and Peasantry: Grassroots Democracy in Rural China.' *World Development* 25: 1431–1442.

Ware, V. 1996. 'Defining Forces: "Race", Gender and Memories of Empire,' in *The Post-Colonial Question: Common Skies, Divided Horizons.* Edited by I. Chambers and L. Curti, pp. 142–156. London: Routledge.

Watts, M. 1995. 'A New Deal in Emotions,' in *Power of Development.* Edited by J. Crush, pp. 44–62. London and New York: Routledge.

——. 1996. 'Development III: The Global Agrofood System and Late 20th Century Development (or Kautsky Redux).' *Progress in Human Geography* 20: 230–245.

Watts, M., and D. Goodman. 1997. 'Agrarian Questions,' in *Globalising Food: Agrarian Questions and Global Restructuring.* Edited by M. Watts and D. Goodman, pp. 1–32. London and New York: Routledge.

Webster, E. 1988. 'The Rise of Social Movement Unionism: The Two Faces of the Black Trade Union Movement in South Africa,' in *State, Resistance and Change in South Africa.* Edited by P. Frankel, N. Pines, and M. Swilling, pp. 174–196. London: Croom Helm.

Weitzman, M.L., and C. Xu. 1994. 'Chinese Township-Village Enterprises as Vaguely Defined Cooperatives.' *Journal of Comparative Economics*: 121–145.

Welsh, D.J. 1971. *The Roots of Segregation: Native Policy in Colonial Natal, 1845–1910.* Cape Town and New York: Oxford University Press.

Whiteford, A., and D. van Seventer. 1999. *Winners and Losers: South Africa's Changing Income Distribution in the 1990s.* Menlo Park: WEFA Southern Africa.

Williams, G. 1996. 'Setting the Agenda: A Critique of the World Bank's Rural Restructuring Programme for South Africa.' *Journal of Southern African Studies* 22: 139–166.

Williams, R. 1977. *Marxism and Literature: Marxist Introductions.* Oxford: Oxford University Press.

Willis, P.E. 1977. *Learning to Labour: How Working Class Kids get Working Class Jobs.* Farnborough: Saxon House.

Wilsenach, A., and A. Lichtelm. 1993. 'A Preliminary Evaluation of the New RIDP and its Impact on Regional Development in South Africa.' *Development Southern Africa* 10: 361–381.

Wolf, D. 1992. *Factory Daughters: Gender, Household Dynamics, and Rural Industrialization in Java.* Berkeley: University of California Press.

Wolpe, H. 1972. 'Capitalism and Cheap Labor in South Africa: From Segregation to Apartheid.' *Economy and Society* 1: 425–456.

———. 1975. 'The Theory of Internal Colonialism: The South African Case,' in *Beyond the Sociology of Development*. Edited by I. Oxaal, T. Barnett, and D. Booth, pp. 229–252. Boston: Routledge Kegan Paul.

———. 1988. *Race, Class and the Apartheid State*. London: James Currey.

———. 1995. 'The Uneven Transition from Apartheid in South Africa.' *Transformation* 27: 88–101.

Wong, C.P.W. 1988. 'Interpreting Rural Industrial Growth in the Post-Mao Period.' *Modern China* 14: 3–30.

———. 1992. 'Fiscal Reform and Local Industrialization: The Problematic Sequencing of Reform in Post-Mao China.' *Modern China* 18: 197–227.

Woolcock, M. 1998. 'Social Capital and Economic Development: Toward a Theoretical Synthesis and Policy Framework.' *Theory and Society* 27: 151–208.

Wright, J., and C. Hamilton. 1989. 'Traditions and Transformations: The Phongolo-Mzimkulu Region in the Late Eighteenth and Early Nineteenth Centuries,' in *Natal and Zululand from Earliest Times to 1910*. Edited by A. Duminy and B. Guest, pp. 49–82. Pietermaritzburg: University of Natal Press.

Yang, M. 1989. The Gift Economy and State Power in China. *Comparative Studies in Society and History* 31: 25–55.

———. 1994. *Gifts, Favors, and Banquets: The Art of Social Relationships in China*. Ithaca, N.Y.: Cornell University Press.

Zhang, Z. 1999. 'Rural Industrialization in China: From Backyard Furnaces to Township and Village Enterprises.' *East Asia: An International Quarterly* 17: 61–88.

Index

AAC *see* All-Africa Convention
Adelzadeh, A. 18
AFRA *see* Association for Rural
Advancement
African National Congress (ANC) 1,
7–9, 17–24, 32, 42, 64, 82–85,
97–100, 104, 106, 109, 111,
115–124, 142, 154–155, 158,
166, 195–196, 226–227, 229,
239–245, 249–253, 255–263,
265–266, 270, 272–277, 281–
284, 288, 305
Afrikaners 29, 100, 137, 139, 245, 255
agrarian
questions, politics of 5, 11, 38–44,
70, 215–217, 301–302, 307
reform 10–12, 38–43, 55, 143, 155,
198, 200–201, 212–230, 221–
224, 291, 299, 301–302,
307–310
transformations 10–11, 17, 38–40,
78, 218–224, 300–304
agriculture 5, 11–12, 29, 38–39, 41–
43, 64, 74–80, 104, 146, 200,
217–218, 222–224, 225, 309
Alcockspruit 102
All-Africa Convention (AAC) 84
alliance, politics of 11–12, 41, 55, 231,
291, 293, 299–300
amakhosi 278–283, 289, *see also* tribal
authority
Amin, S. 217
Amsden, A. 173
ANC *see* African National Congress
Anderson, Benedict 59
Anglo-Boer (South African) War 255
apartheid 1, 4, 22, 24–26, 29–30, 46,
66, 68, 89–95, 144, 155, 236–
237, 246, 267, 280

Appadurai, Arjun 51
articulation 25–32, 41, 88–89, 125,
191, 231, 293, 295, 297–299,
309–310
Association for Rural Advancement
(AFRA) 97, 99, 103–104,
106, 109

Balassa, B.A. 173
Bantu Affairs Department 66, 68
Bantu Authorities Act, 1951 69
Bantu Investment Corporation (BIC)
114–116
Bantu Laws Amendment Act, 1952 69
bantustans 2–3, 6, 11, 42, 46, 67–69,
91, 111, 113, 114, 139, 144,
156
Beaumont Commission, 1916 91
Bekker, S. 247
Bell, Trevor 131, 137, 156
Bernstein, A. 236
Bernstein, H. 38
Bertelsen, Eve 25
Besters 99–100, 105
Bhambatha rebellion 77
BIC *see* Bantu Investment Corporation
Biggart, N. 169
Blaaubosch 67, 146
black empowerment 307
Black Local Authorities 46, *see also*
local government
Black Sash 97
Boers 78, 255–256, *see also*
Afrikaners
Bond, Patrick 23–24
Bonnin, D. 111, 125–126
border industries 4, 66, 136–139
Botha, P.W. 46, 120, 144

373

bourgeoisie
    black   20, 23, 74–75, 85, 86, 88,
        111–115, 121, 229
    Taiwan   220
Bowden, A. Cornish   134
Bowles, P.   207
boycotts
    bus   115–116, 138, 147
    rates   246, 249–253
    rent   247, 253
    school   117
    service charges   245–246, 287
Bradford, Helen   68, 78, 81–82
Bredell Farm   305–308, 310
Bretton Woods   22
British   255–256
Bronkhorstspruit   4, 156
Brookes, E.H.   72–73, 78, 91
Brown, Peter   100
Buddhists   156
buffer zones   230
Bulger, Patrick   307
Bundy, Colin   42, 73–76, 78, 82, 84
Burawoy, Michael   187, 199, 291
bureaucrats, retrenchment   261
Buthelezi Commission   145
Buthelezi, Gatsha   89, 103, 114–115,
        124
Byrd, W.A.   208
Byres, T.J.   219

capitalism   10–12, 14, 21–22, 29–40,
        165, 173, 215, 235, 292–295,
        304
    Confucian   168–171
    free market   26
    racial   2, 22, 127
    Taiwan   173, 298
Carby, Hazel   37, 191
Castells, Manuel   50, 168, 169, 200,
        294
CDE   *see* Centre for Development and
        Enterprise
Centre for Development and Enterprise
        (CDE)   236, 267
Chari, Sharad   39
Charlestown   128, 137–138
Chengdu   213

China   10, 40, 157, 171, 195, 196, 198,
        268
    industry   198–213
    output   207
Chinese
    culture   168, 171
    sign   179–180, 196–197
Christianity   74, 123
Christiansen, F.   211
Christopher, A.   76
citizenship   12, 18
civil society   12, 21, 26, 33, 45, 111,
        126, 254, 285–287, 292, 311
Clarence, Lester   135
Clark, N.L.   141
class   10, 16, 29–32, 297–298, 301
Clinton, Catherine   191
coal   67, 79, 93, 100–103, 112, 146
Cobbett, W.   144, 145
collective ownership   *see* ownership,
        collective
colonialism   69–73, 129
Coloureds   277
communism
    China   212–217, 222, 302
comparative method   6, 13–14, 16, 40–
        43, 48, 55, 296, 299
Concerned Residents Association   252,
        253
conflict, political   154, 166, 239, 243
Congress of South African Trade Unions
        (COSATU)   7, 17, 19, 155,
        243, 269, 271–274, 307, 309,
        310
Conservative Party   141, 240–242, 244,
        252
Consolidated Lancaster Cotton Company
        135
Constitution   280
Constitutional Development, Department
        of (DCD)   246, 260, 266–267,
        274
conjuncture   15, 27, 47, 237, 296
contingency   9, 15, 47, 295, 298–299
Co-operation and Development,
        Department of   107
Cope, N.   86–88
Coronil, Fernando   38

COSATU   *see* Congress of South African
    Trade Unions
Cousins, B.   229
crime   257, 281, 288
Cronin, Jeremy   19
Crown land   76, 77
culture   26–29, 168–170, 188, 215
custom   86–88

DAB   *see* Drakensburg Administration
    Board
Dannhauser   95, 100
Danskraal   139–140, 149
DBSA   *see* Development Bank of South
    Africa
DCD   *see* Constitutional Development,
    Department of
DDA   *see* Development Administration,
    Department of
decentralization   2, 44, 131, 260
    China   210, 223–224, 298
    industrial   67, 127, 131, 134, 137–
        145, 155–156, 178
    Japan   224
    Taiwan   178, 220–221
Defiance Campaign   83
De Klerk, Jan   137–138
demarcation   *see* Municipal Demarcation
    Board
democracy   17, 25, 46–47, 132, 212,
    266, 275, 280, 285
    radical   15, 31–32, 36, 45, 295
Democratic Alliance   281–284, 305
Democratic Party   277, 281–282
Desmond, Cosmas   97–99, 101, 102,
    112, 113
determinism   27–28, 31, 36, 51
deterritorialization   *see* space, spatial
    metaphors
Deutscher, I.   216
development
    consultants   261–262
    expert discourses   3–4
    planning   261–266
    post-development   31, 45–46
Development Administration, Depart-
    ment of (DDA)   247, 262
Development Bank of South Africa
    (DBSA)   155

Development Facilitation Act, 1995
    260–261
Diamond, N.   188–189
dichotomies   13, 25, 43, 49, 126, 190,
    293
Didiza, Thoko   228, 306
difference   5, 10, 16, 37, 298, 301
Dimbaza   173, 180
dispossession   10–11, 39, 41–44, 89–
    110, 201, 231, 235, 286, 292,
    299, 303
DLA   *see* Land Affairs, Department of
Dlamini, Stephen   98
Donald, I.   92–93
Dong, X.Y.   207
Drakensburg Administration Board
    (DAB)   107
Drew, Alison   82
Driefontein   74–75, 91, 98, 112, 153
drought   77, 146
dualisms   *see* dichotomies
Dube, John   85, 87
Dubow, S.   86
Dundee   80, 82, 95
Dunlop Tyre Company   140, 143, 152,
    158
Durban   137, 139, 152
Durban Metro   276
Durban Navigation Colliery   100

Economic Development Corporation
    (EDC)   150
economism   15, 27, 31, 49, 51–52, 291,
    293, 295–296
Edendale Wesleyan Mission   74
education   64, 67, 94, 104, 113, 117,
    225, 302
Ekuvukeni   65–67, 103, 153
Elandslaagte   92, 103
Emnambithi, population   63
employment figures   147, 156–157, 159
    China   207
Esididini   101
Etherington, N.   70, 72, 74, 75
ethnicity   10, 16, 88, 196, 297–298, 301
ethnography   17, 291
Eurocentrism   45, 37–38, 51, *see also*
    West, non-Western

Evans, P.B. 173
exchange controls 18
Ezakheni 1–3, 6–8, 12, 16, 112, 156–157
  elections 282–284
  industry 40, 67, 127–128, 146–149, 268–269
  local government 40, 47, 235, 254, 257–259, 266
  services 235, 247, 254, 286
  township 66, 70, 89, 97–98, 105, 110–112, 119–125, 130, 152–154
  violence 67, 106, 239, 243

Fairleigh 98, 114
farmers, black 74–75, 228
farming, stock 72, 79, 100–101, *see also* agriculture
FCI *see* Federated Chamber of Industries
FDI *see* Foreign Direct Investment
Federated Chamber of Industries (FCI) 136
Federation of South African Trade Unions (FOSATU) 142, 143
feminism 33, 36–37, 133, 174, 187–191, 215, 295
Ferme, Mariane 292–293
finance, municipal 246–248, 260, 275
Fine, Ben 23, 44
Foreign Direct Investment (FDI) 267, 287
FOSATU *see* Federation of South African Trade Unions
Foucault, M. 34, 166
Frame, Philip 135
Frame Company 135, 138, 143, 152, 158
Fraser, Nancy 257
free trade 241
Freedom Charter, 1955 85, 124, 226
Fujian 202

Galenson, W. 173
Gallin, B. 174
Gandhi, Mahatma 84, 85, 129
Gaonkar, D. 14

Garment Workers' Union 137
Gates, H. 176, 219–220
GEAR *see* Growth, Employment and Redistribution
Gelb, A.H. 208
gender 10, 13, 16, 30, 36–37, 119, 174, 182–192, 220–221
Gibson-Graham, J.K. 133
Gindin, Sam 312
Glaser, D. 136, 145, 146
globalization 12–14, 19, 21, 32, 37, 40–44, 48–52, 129, 269–270, 293–299, 304
Gold, T. 173, 177, 217
Good Hope plan 144
Good Hope Textiles 134, 136
Goodman, D. 38
Gramsci, Antonio 16, 26–28, 31, 33, 42, 237, 290, 295, 296, 305, 311
Granovetter, M. 169
graves 94
Greenhalgh, S. 167, 174, 177, 178, 185, 186, 221
Group Areas Act 46, 235–236, 247–250, 277
Growth, Employment and Redistribution (GEAR) 7, 18–21, 24, 160, 236, 267, 269, 273, 287–288, 309
Guangdong 202
guanxi 171–175, 202–203
Guest, B. 77, 79
Gumede, Zacheus Mack 114
Gwala, Harry 117

Haffajee, Ferial 310
Hall, Stuart 27–32, 41, 51, 299
Hamilton, Carolyn 71, 88
Hamilton, Gary 111, 114, 167, 173, 184
Hanekom, Derek 228
Hani, Chris 117
Haraway, Donna 190–191, 284
Harris, V. 79, 80, 81
Harrison, P. 140, 146, 156
Hart, Gillian 38, 224, 230, 303, 305
Harvey, David 35, 41, 50, 287, 295, 298

hegemony 26, 29, 31, 89, 111, 114,
    295, 306
Heller, P. 285
Hindson, D. 68
HIV/AIDS 281, 288, 310
Hlatswayo, Nokhutula 160
Hobsland 98, 99
Hong Kong 171, 188, 200
hooks, bell 259
hospitals 113
housing 101, 105, 107, 112–113, 151,
    179, 201, 206, 225, 255, 260,
    302
Hsing, You-Tien 198–199, 201–206,
    300
Hsiung, P.-C. 174, 176–177, 185, 189
Huang, P. 223
Hunan 199
Hunan Report 216
Hurwitz, N. 72, 78, 91

ICU *see* Industrial and Commercial
    Workers Union
IDP *see* Industrial Development Points
IEC *see* Independent Electoral
    Commission
IFP *see* Inkatha Freedom Party
IMF *see* International Monetary Fund
incentives
    investors 150–151, 179, 202–203,
        225
    workers 193
identity, political 12–14, 28, 33, 88,
    231, 285, *see also* subjectivity
Independent Electoral Commission (IEC)
    281–282
Indians in South Africa 74, 240, 243–
    244, 248–250, 277
Industrial Development Points (IDPs)
    145
Industrial and Commercial Workers'
    Union (ICU) 81–83, 226
industrialization 10, 25, 38–40, 44,
    111, 127–161, 165–195, 304
    rural 40–44, 218–224, 301, 303
industry 2–5
    clothing and textiles 127–128, 138,
        140, 148, 152, 154

decentralization 127, 131, 134, 138,
    139, 144–145, 298
    footwear 148
    heavy 128, 159
influx control 155, 201, 204
Ingonyama Trust 251
institutionalism 169
Inkatha 86–89, 97, 103–104, 106,
    108–109, 111, 114, 119–124,
    142, 151–154, 243, 258–259
Inkatha Freedom Party (IFP) 8, 64,
    103, 109, 158, 165, 166, 173,
    195, 238–244, 281–284, 288
    Womens' Brigade 119
Integrated Development Framework 261
International Monetary Fund (IMF) 23
investment 18, 44
    foreign 149–150, 156–157, 160,
        167, 204, 266, 270, 287, 303
Iron and Steel Corporation (ISCOR)
    113, 128–130, 140–142, 146,
    149, 150, 153, 159, 242
Isandlwana 196
ISCOR *see* Iron and Steel Corporation
Isethebe 146, 150, 156
Ishikawa, S. 222

Jabavu, D.D.T. 84
Jameson, F. 48, 52
Japan and Japanese 177–178, 191, 217
JCRR *see* Joint Commission on Rural
    Reconstruction
Jenvey, Nicola 160
Jessop, B. 15
Jiangsu Province 208, 211
JMC *see* Joint Management Centre
job reservation 137
Johnston, A.M. 240
Johnston, B. 219
Joint Commission on Rural Reconstruction
    (JCRR) 217
Joint Management Centre (JMC) 120,
    125, 153
Joint Services Board 262
Joint Technical Committee 280
Jonono's Kop 65, 110

Ka, C. 217–219, 221–222

Kapur, G. 51
Karbochem 150
Karshenas, M. 218–219, 222
Katz, C. 34, 52
Kautsky, K. 38
Keith, M. 36
Kempton Park 305
Kentridge, M. 23
Kershoff, P.C. 105
KFC *see* KwaZulu, Finance Corporation
kholwa 74–75, 80, 85, 87, 113
Khuleka Development Consultants 264
Khumalosville 98–100, 106
King Williams Town 134
Kingsley 105
KLA *see* KwaZulu, Legislative Assembly
Kleu Report, 1983 145
Klip River 76, 80–81, 94–95, 97, 102–105, 121, 130
Klug, Heinz 226–227
KMI *see* KwaZulu, Marketing Initiative (KMI)
KMT *see* Kuomintang
knitwear 148, 151, 157, 160, 167–168, 182–183, 186, 194
imports 183, 195, 198, 224
Koornhof, Piet 107–108
Kreuger, A.O. 173
Kung, L. 188
Kuomintang (KMT) 175–177, 216–219
KwaZulu 91, 107
Finance Corporation (KFC) 127–129, 132, 146–150, 157, 178, 268
government 93, 103, 109, 110
Legislative Assembly 111, 114, 121
Marketing Initiative (KMI) 268

labor
agricultural 91–93
cheap 4, 77, 135, 180
costs 211
discipline 187–188, 194–195
disputes 166, 181, 189, 224, 287, *see also* strikes
industrial 109, 136, 141, 156
laws 160, 204
migrant 94, 204, 206, 211, 225

relations 39, 132, 166–169, 180, 187–195, 204, 296, *see also* trade unions
reproduction of 10, 42, 47, 215, 218–225, 299, 302–305
Labour, Department of 160
Labour Relations Act 271–273
Ladysmith 2, 6, 8, 9, 66–70, 129, 297
black farmers 74–75, 80, 84, 91–95, 108
budget meetings 256–258, 285, 311
Chamber of Commerce 239, 271–272
demarcation 274–289
development planning 262–265, 268
finance, municipal 247–248
industry 11, 109–110, 123–126, 134–144, 147–149, 152, 154–158, 167, *see also* Ezakheni
investment, foreign 267–269, 271–272
Joint Bodies Association 65
local government 12, 40, 47, 130
elections 239–245, 274, 281–284, 288
restructuring 235–289
map 61, 62, 279
officials 255–257
politics 98, 129–131, *see also* ANC; IFP
Ratepayers' Association 239
rates 248–250, 254, 287
service charges 254
squatters 104
town/township amalgamation 254
townships 46, 53, 97, *see also* Ezakheni, etc.
Transitional Local Council 274
workforce 120–121
Lahiff, E. 228, 229
laissez-faire 26, *see also* neoliberalism
Lam, D.K. 178
Lambert, J. 74, 76, 77, 79, 80
Land Affairs, Department of (DLA) 229, 260
Land Commission, 1990 226
land, Crown *see* Crown land
Land Development Objectives (LDOs) 260–261

land redistribution finance 229
land reform *see* agrarian, reform
Land Reform for Agricultural Development (LRAD) 228–229
land reservation 70
land tenure 76–81, 85, 136, 200–201, 213, 226–227, 229, 231, 296
  China 217, 223
  Taiwan 217
land use 260, 308
language 190, 194, 203, 256, 297
Lardy, N.R. 222
Lasher Tools 140
Lazar, J. 136, 137, 138
LDOs *see* Land Development Objectives
LED *see* Local Economic Development
Lee, C.K. 188, 192
Lee, Teng Hui 218–219
Lefebvre, Henri 33–36, 38–39, 49, 294–297
Lennoxton 98, 114
Leon, Tony 281
Liberal Party 100
liberation movement 21, 111, 117–120, 154, 201, 226–227, 307
libraries 258
Lichthelm, A. 155–156
Limehill 65–66
Liu, C. 208
Liu, Eddie 165–166, 173, 179–180, 182, 195, 198, 241–242, 245, 268, 287–288
Local Economic Development (LED) 266–273, 287–288
Local Economic Forum 287
local government 6–8, 47, 132, 154, 274
  China 209–212
  elections 1, 7, 124, 239, 280–284
  representation 248
  restructuring 235–289
local state
  and civil society 12, 285–287
  contradictions of 7–10, 42–48, 235–237, 265–266, 292, 311–312
Local Government Transition Act, 1996 260–261

Local Government White Paper, 1998 236–237, 259–261
Lu, X. 212
Luthuli, Albert 85, 98, 99

Mabin, Alan 68, 93
Macro-Economic Research Group (MERG) 22, 23
Madadeni
  education 117–118
  elections 241–242, 283–284
  industry 111, 141–142, 146–153, 156, 159, 268
  local government 8, 12, 40, 47, 235, 238, 251
  politics 111, 116, 117, 121, 142, 153, 242, 283–284
  population 63, 67
  services 245
  township 67, 69–70, 89, 93–97, 102, 113–118, 130, 136
  violence 106, 118, 123, 243
Madonsela, H.T. 114
Madonsela, Richard 121
Maharaj, B. 68
maize 75, 146
malnutrition 112
Mamdani, Mahmood 43, 46, 68–69, 88, 110, 289
management 181, 189–192
  China 204–205
Mandela, Nelson 32, 105, 241
Manuel, Trevor 18
Mao Tse-Tung 10, 200, 214, 216–217, 304
Maoism 209, 216
Marais, Hein 17, 21–22, 33, 230, 292, 308
Marais, Peet 148
Maré, G. 111, 114
Maree, Willie 130, 140
markets, free 172, 173
Marks, Shula 70–72, 74, 80, 81, 85–86
Marx, Karl 214–215
Marxism 16, 27–29, 31, 38, 39, 216, 295
  post-Marxism 15, 31–32, 36, 295
Masakhane 246, 285

Massey, Doreen   34–36, 294–296, 298
Matiwane's Kop   59–65, 106–110, 112,
          120, 143
     population   63
MAWU   see Metal and Allied Workers
          Union
Mbeki, Govan   42, 83–85, 97–98, 136,
          226, 230, 243
Mbeki, Thabo   32, 228, 280–281
McClintock, Anne   72
McDonald, Mary   223–224
Mdlalose, Frank   115–116, 121, 196,
          241
mealies   see maize
mechanisation   91
Meer, S.   142
Meissner, M.   216
memory   9, 11, 44, 235
MERG   see Macro-Economic Research
          Group
Metal and Allied Workers Union (MAWU)
          109, 123, 141, 143, 152
mining   81
Minority Front   240
missions   73–75, 90, 104
MK   see Umkhonto we Sizwe
Mmutlana, R.   102–104, 106
Mngadi, Elliot   99, 104–106, 121
Mohan, G.   44, 45
Morrell, R.   79, 80
Morris, Mike   19–20, 78, 230
Mouffe, C.   31, 36, 45, 295
Msimang, H.S.   85
Msinga   121
Mthembi-Mahanyele, Sankie   306
Mufamadi, Sydney   280
Municipal Demarcation Board   237,
          274–280, 283–284, 289–290,
          306, 312
municipal services   145, 251
     charges   245–246, 251
Municipal Structures Act, 1998   278,
          280
Murray, C.   68
Mzala   111
Mzimela, Nkosi Mpiyezintombi   280

Natal, climate   79
Natal Code of Native Law, 1891   70, 86

Natal colony   46, 76–77
Natal Indian Congress   84, 85, 129, 243
Natal Land and Colonization Company
          73, 108
Natal Native Congress (NNC)   85, 87,
          129
Natal Native Landowners Association
          104
Natal Steam and Coal Company   103
National Land Committee   97
National Party   68, 91, 98, 130, 139,
          140, 239–242, 244, 249, 257,
          273, 281–282
National Union of Metal Workers of
          South Africa (NUMSA)   141–
          142, 152–154, 243, 269
National Union of Textile Workers
          (NUTW)   123–124, 143
Native Affairs Act, 1920   86, 87
Native Affairs Commission, 1939   103
Native Affairs Department (NAD)   68–
          69, 88, 138
Natives Land Act, 1913   77–78, 80, 85,
          89–91
Natives Trust and Land Act, 1936   91,
          104
Nee, V.   209
neo-apartheid   246, 249–250
neoliberalism   3, 7, 9–13, 17, 18, 21–
          27, 40, 42, 44, 46–47, 144,
          154–155, 172–173, 235, 261,
          292–293, 298, 308, 312–313
network production   167–169
New National Party   277
Newcastle   6, 129, 297
     demarcation   274–289
     development planning   262, 268
     finance, municipal   245–254
     industry   11, 40, 111, 128–132, 136,
          138, 140–144, 148, 150–161,
          165–197
     investment, foreign   148–151, 156,
          158, 165–199, 235–289
     landowners, black   74–77, 80–81
     local government   132
          elections   239–243, 274, 283–284,
          288
          officials   147, 181–182, 199, 244

restructuring 235–289
map 61, 62, 279
politics 8–9, 12, 98, 116–118, 153, 239
rates 248, 250–253
relocation 96–102
reserves (land) 91
Residents and Ratepayers Association 251–252
security 120
service charges 311
Tenants Association 256
town/township amalgamation 251–254
townships 46–47, 53, 67–70, 96–102, 111–120, *see also* Madadeni, etc.
unions 123–125, 153, 159, 166
wages 224–225
NGOs *see* non-governmental organizations
Nguni 77
NIC *see* Natal Indian Congress
Nicholls, George N. Heaton 86
Niehoff, J.D. 178, 220
Nkosi Sikelele i'Africa 257
NNC *see* Natal Native Congress
non-governmental organizations (NGOs) 11, 33, 270, 273, 274, 307
Nonini, D. 171, 174–175
Northern Natal African Landowners Association 99
NUMSA *see* National Union of Metal Workers of South Africa
NUTW *see* National Union of Textile Workers
Nyanda, Siphiwe 117
Nyembe, J. 98, 99
Nzimande, Blade 19

Ohmae, Kenichi 49, 51
Oi, Jean 209
oil crisis 146
Olver, C. 246
O'Meara, D. 137, 139
Ong, A. 169, 171, 174–175, 188, 191
Orientalism 168, 172, 272
Orru, M. 167

Osizweni 67, 96, 100–102, 110–116, 120, 128, 130, 138, 141–142, 150, 153, 238, 243, 245, 251
ownership, collective 199, 208–210, 213

PAC *see* Pan African Congress
Padayachee, V. 18, 19, 23
Pan African Congress (PAC) 97, 305, 308
Pan-Africanism 88
Pang, C. 173
Park, A. 219
Parmar, Pratibha 37
paternalism 153, 175, 185, 189, 192–195, 220
path dependency 14
peasants 10, 42, 74–75, 78, 81, 83, 85, 226
Chinese 200, 212–214, 216–218, 222, 301–302
Taiwanese 218–220
Perelman, M. 214–215
Perotti, E. 207, 211–213
Phillips, M. 120
Physical Planning and Utilisation of Resources Act, 1967 139
Pickles, J. 3
Pile, S. 36
Pine, Lieutenant Governor 71–72
Piore, M. 167
Platzky, L. 89, 91
place *see* space
Polanyi, Karl 45, 304
police 119, 122, 124, 135, 143, 243, 257
polygyny 72
Pondo Revolt 83
population 60, 63, 67–68, 73, 75, 80, 104, 112, 140, 147
census, 1996 276–278
populism 32–33
post-Marxism *see* Marxism, post-Marxism
poverty 11, 20, 32, 166–167, 281
power
and practice 10, 12–15, 28, 33–40, 52, 170, 285–286, 295–296

Pred, A. 165
primitive accumulation 39, 214–216,
    299, *see also* dispossession
privatization, municipal services 235–
    236, 310
Programme for Land and Agrarian Studies
    229
Progressive Party 106
Promotion of the Economic Develop-
    ment of Bantu Homelands Act,
    1968 139
protest 151–152, 204, 310, *see also*
    strikes
provinces 145
purchasing power 225
Pycroft, C. 260

race 10, 16, 29–32, 190–192, 196,
    245, 299, 301–302
  race-class debates 29–30, 225
  racism 30, 32, 37, 191–192, 235,
    249, 254, 281, 299
radical democracy *see* democracy,
    radical
railways 79–80, 105
Rainbow Nation 5, 257
rates, municipal 246–254, 273, 287,
    see also under individual towns
RDAC *see* Regional Development
    Advisory Committee
RDP *see* Reconstruction and Develop-
    ment Programme
Reconstruction and Development Office
    260
Reconstruction and Development
    Programme (RDP) 17–19, 22,
    227, 254, 255, 260–261
Redding, S.G. 168
redistribution 7, 10, 22–23, 309–310,
    see also land reform
Regional Development Advisory
    Committee (RDAC) 145
Regional Industrial Development
    Programme (RIDP) 146–148,
    150–152, 154–160, 182
Regional Service Councils (RSC) 145,
    247
Reid, Kabelo 158

relational comparison *see* comparative
    method
relocation *see* removals, forced
removals, forced 60–66, 69, 89–95,
    97–110, 120, 121, 125–126,
    130, 133, 143, 215, 242, 259,
    285
Renaissance, African 32
reproduction of labor *see* labor,
    reproduction of
Reserves (Reservations) 71–74, 77–78,
    83, 89–92, 136
  Mission 73, 77
rice 219
Richards Bay 146
Richardson, P. 74
RIDP *see* Regional Industrial Develop-
    ment Programme
Riskin, C. 222
Robben Island 1, 255
Rodrik, Dani 304
Rofel, Lisa 166
Roosboom 99, 103–106, 121
Rorke's Drift 196
Roseberry, W. 285
rural/urban 5–6, 12, 42–44, 110, 240,
    277–289, 312
Rustomjee, Zav 44

Sabel, C. 167
Sachs, J.D. 209
SACP *see* South African Communist
    Party
SACTU *see* South African Congress of
    Trade Unions
SACTWU *see* South African Clothing
    and Textile Workers Union
Sader, Achmad 84, 98, 243
SADT *see* South African Development
    Trust
SANNC *see* South African Native
    National Congress
Saul, John 291–292
Scheepers, Anna 137
Scobie, J. 75
Scott, Joan 36–37, 93
Seattle 304
Seidman, G. 46

Selden, M. 217–219, 221–222
Seme, Pixley 85
services, municipal 236–238, 245–247, 253–254, 257–259, 285
 charges 251, 254, 285–287, 310–311
Settlement and Land Acquisition Grant (SLAG) 227–230, 307
Shabalala tribe 108
Shanghai 208, 216
Sharpeville 97
Shenzhen 188, 202
Shepstone, Theophilus 70–72, 74
Shieh, G.S. 185
Shih, J.T. 220
Sibankulu, Hlalanati 118, 120
Sichuan 199
Simkins, C.E.W. 67–68
Sitas, Ari 143, 310
Sithebe, Steven 106, 109, 121–123, 125
SLAG see Settlement and Land Acquisition Grant
Slater, H. 73, 77, 78
slavery 191
Smart, Alan 92, 211–212
Smart, J. 192
Smith, Adam 214–215
Smith, Neil 34, 35, 52
social capital 45, 112, 285, 305
social change 31, 36, 45, 69, 291, 298, 305
social movement unionism 110
social reproduction see labor, reproduction of
social services 210
social wage see wages
social welfare 200, 206
 China 210–211
 Taiwan 220
socialism 209
SOEs see state-owned enterprises
Soni, D. 68
South African Clothing and Textile Workers Union (SACTWU) 124, 152–153, 158, 160–161, 165–166, 242, 243, 269
South African Communist Party (SACP) 7, 19, 42, 82, 111, 117, 226, 243

South African Congress of Trade Unions (SACTU) 136, 142
South African Development Trust (SADT) 65, 91, 92, 96, 101
South African Institute of Race Relations 105–106
South African Native National Congress (SANNC) 85
South African Native Trust 91
South African National NGO Coalition (Sangoco) 310
Soweto 117, 124, 151
space, production of 14, 16, 33–37, 49–52, 296–299
 and place 14, 35, 51
 space-time 34–35, 49–50, 52, 294–295
 spatial metaphors 34, 51–52, 198
Spies, Marius 148
SPP see Surplus People's Project
squatters 80–81, 92, 104–107, 112, 305
SST see State and Social Transformation
St Chads 286
Stalinism 216, 217
state 18, 26, 51, see also local state
State and Social Transformation (SST) 19
state-owned enterprises (SOEs) 209, 211
Steadville 66, 85, 98, 106–107, 125, 247, 254–258
Steincoalspruit 103–106
Stites, R. 185
Stokke, R. 44, 45
strikes 81, 125, 135, 136, 139, 140, 143, 269, 271
subjectivity
 formation of political subjects 9–10, 45, 47, 166, 295, 299, see also identity, political
subsidies 144, 145, 151, 154, 179, 181, 182, 187
sugar 74, 79
Sun, L. 207, 213
Surplus People's Project 60–66, 69, 89–90, 92, 93, 99–100, 104, 105, 107–110, 146–147

Sutcliffe, Michael 276
Suzman, Helen 106
Swilling, M. 120, 247
Szanton, David 129

Tabata, I.B. 84
Taiwan
  history 172, 176–178
  industry in China 10, 40, 54, 198–206, 300–302
  industry in South Africa 2–6, 10–11, 40, 53–55, 128–132, 148, 151, 156–161, 165–197, 225, 242, 300–302
  industry in Taiwan 2, 10, 40, 53, 182, 184–186
  labor practice 165–166, 168, 180, 188–189, 241–242
  land 217, 301
  languages 176
  living conditions 178–179
  trade delegations, South African 150, 171, 268
taxation 72, 74, 77, 178
  China 222
  local (SA) 237
  Taiwan 218–219
Tengeni, Phelele 241, 288
textiles 53, 127, 134, 152, 174
Thatcherism 27, 29
'there is no alternative' (TINA) 7, 21
Thornton, R. 59, 71
Tiananmen Square 201
TINA see 'there is no alternative'
TLCs see Transitional Local Councils
Todes, Alison 112–114, 119, 132–133, 140, 154, 157, 159, 172, 179, 181, 192, 195, 241
Tomlinson Commission, 1955 136
tourism 60
Township and Village Enterprises (TVEs) 199–200, 206–213, 303
townships 66–70, 192, 193
  establishment 96–126, 136, 306
  local government 46, 235, 240, 247, 254–255, 287
  rates 248, 250–252
  services 257–258

  charges 247, 251
  upgrading 145
  violence 46, 121–123, 151, 153, 239
trade unions 118–119, 123, 125, 132, 144, 151–154, 157–158, 170, 172, 181, 194, 236, 269, 287–289, see also individual trade unions, e.g. South African Clothing and Textile Workers Union
  trajectories 13–14, 16, 33, 36, 39, 48, 291–300
Trans Tugela Transport (TTT) 115–116
transformation, agrarian 40–44, 59–95, see also agrarian, reform
Transitional Local Councils (TLCs) 237–239, 271
Transkei Organised Bodies (TOB) 84
transport 115
Treatment Action Campaign 310
tribal (traditional) authority 68–69, 151, 229, 275, 277–281
Trotsky, L. 82
Truth and Reconciliation Commission (TRC) 117
TTT see Trans Tugela Transport
TVEs see Township and Village Enterprises

UDF see United Democratic Front
Ulundi 108
Umbulwane 66, 106–107
Umhlumayo 121
Umkhonto we Sizwe (MK) 116–118, 142
Umviko Party 100
Umvoti 81
unemployment 20, 138, 258, 262, 281, 288–289, 308
Unger, Roberto 307–308
unicities 275–276
unionism 151
United Democratic Front (UDF) 111, 118, 124–125, 144, 151–153, 255, 269
United States Eastern Advisors 217
Urban Foundation 5, 155, 236
urban see rural/urban

urbanization   136, 139

Van der Walt, P.J.   137
Van Seventer, D.   20
Veka   128, 137–139
Verdery, K.   199
Verwoerd, Hendrik   46, 68, 104, 136–137
Viljoen, Marais   137
violence   67, 106, 121–123, 154, 166, 246, 254
Vryheid   87, 99
Vulandodo   99, 100
Vumela Facilitation Services   253, 254, 262

Waaihoek   66, 67, 92
Wade, R.   173, 177
wages   18, 41–42, 77, 79–82, 101–102, 115, 135, 137–138, 141–143, 160, 167, 173, 187, 190, 193, 200, 204, 211–212, 224–225, 242, 270, 271, 287, 303
  minimum   166, 194
  social   10, 12, 231, 287, 292, 302–303, 311
  women   220
Walder, A.   209, 211
Walker, Cherryl   42, 89, 91, 227–229, 307
Ware, Vron   37
Wasbank   66
Washington Consensus   23, 24, 303
water   101, 135, 273, 286
Watts, Michael   38
Weenen   66, 92–93
Weitzman, M.L.   207
Welsh, David   70, 71
West, non-West   49, 171, *see also* Eurocentrism

Whiteford, A.   20
Williams, Raymond   26–28, 297
Wilsenach, A.   155–156
Wolpe, Harold   18, 19, 29–30, 41, 225
Women
  and politics 119, 124, 133, 185–186, 191, 215
  workforce   148, 151, 152, 159, 166, 170, 173, 184, 187–189, 203
  see also gender
Woo, W.T.   209
Woods, J.   3
working class
  China   217, 272
  Taiwan   217, 220
  see also labor
working conditions   160, 167, 190, 272, 287
  China   204
  Taiwan   171, 178
World Bank   5, 23, 42, 155, 173, 208, 211, 227, 230

Xu, C.   207
Xuma, A.B.   84

Yang, Mayfair   171, 203
Yangzi delta   208, 223
youth movements   123–125, 143, 144, 153, 243, *see also* Umkhonto we Sizwe

Zhang, Z.   207
Zimbabwe   270
  land invasions   305, 308
Zulu/s   71, 72, 255–256
  nationalism   65, 70, 85–89, 111, 114, 125, 141, 142, 172
  royalty   87–88, 115, 141, 244
Zuma, Jacob   280

+ lives

My Positive bias from the start given Hart's constancy
with a Gramscian perspective.
The rise + fall of indignation in this
impassioned but sober analysis.
The sheer depth + breadth — breadth
from 'relational comparison' + v'multiple
trajectories!
depth from
The 1st obvious SA/ Taiwan in context of
(globalisation
The 2nd less obvious but worth mining the
text for — from the inner self + the personal
up to global forces (not impact).